Ontological Arguments

Ontological arguments are one of the main classes of arguments for the existence of God, and have been influential from the Middle Ages right up until our own time. This accessible volume offers a comprehensive survey and assessment of them starting with a sequence of chapters charting their history – from Anselm and Aquinas, via Descartes, Leibniz, Kant and Hegel, to Gödel, Plantinga, Lewis and Tichý. This is followed by chapters on the most important topics to have emerged in the discussion of ontological arguments: the relationship between conceivability and possibility, the charge that ontological arguments beg the question, and the nature of existence. The volume as a whole shows clearly how these arguments emerged and developed, how we should think about them, and why they remain important today.

Graham Oppy is Professor of Philosophy at Monash University and is a Fellow of the Australian Academy of Humanities. He has published a number of books, most recently *Reinventing Philosophy of Religion* (2014), *Describing Gods* (2014), *Naturalism and Religion* (2018) and, co-authored with Nick Trakakis, *Interreligious Philosophical Dialogues* (2018).

Classic Philosophical Arguments

Over the centuries, a number of individual arguments have formed a crucial part of philosophical enquiry. The volumes in this series examine these arguments, looking at the ramifications and applications which they have come to have, the challenges which they have encountered and the ways in which they have stood the test of time.

Titles in the Series

The Prisoner's Dilemma
Edited by Martin Peterson
The Original Position
Edited by Timothy Hinton
The Brain in a Vat
Edited by Sanford C. Goldberg
Pascal's Wager
Edited by Paul Bartha and Lawrence Pasternack
Ontological Arguments
Edited by Graham Oppy
Newcomb's Problem
Edited by Arif Ahmed

Ontological Arguments

Edited by

Graham Oppy
Monash University

CAMBRIDGE
UNIVERSITY PRESS

University Printing House, Cambridge CB2 8BS, United Kingdom

One Liberty Plaza, 20th Floor, New York, NY 10006, USA

477 Williamstown Road, Port Melbourne, VIC 3207, Australia

314–321, 3rd Floor, Plot 3, Splendor Forum, Jasola District Centre, New Delhi – 110025, India

79 Anson Road, #06–04/06, Singapore 079906

Cambridge University Press is part of the University of Cambridge.

It furthers the University's mission by disseminating knowledge in the pursuit of education, learning, and research at the highest international levels of excellence.

www.cambridge.org
Information on this title: www.cambridge.org/9781107123632
DOI: 10.1017/9781316402443

First published 2018

Printed and bound in Great Britain by Clays Ltd, Elcograf S.p.A.

A catalogue record for this publication is available from the British Library.

Library of Congress Cataloging-in-Publication Data
Names: Oppy, Graham, 1960- editor.
Title: Ontological arguments / edited by Graham Oppy, Monash University.
Description: 1 [edition]. | New York : Cambridge University Press, 2018. |
Series: Classic philosophical arguments | Includes bibliographical references and index.
Identifiers: LCCN 2018030094| ISBN 9781107123632 (hardback : alk. paper) |
ISBN 9781107559127 (pbk. : alk. paper)
Subjects: LCSH: God–Proof, Ontological.
Classification: LCC BT103 .O58 2018 | DDC 212/.1–dc23
LC record available at https://lccn.loc.gov/2018030094

ISBN 978-1-107-12363-2 Hardback
ISBN 978-1-107-55912-7 Paperback

Contents

Contributors

Michael J. Almeida is Professor of Philosophy in the Department of Philosophy and Classics in the University of Texas at San Antonio. He is the author of *The Metaphysics of Perfect Beings* (2008), *Freedom, God, and Worlds* (2012) and *Cosmological Arguments*.

Maria Rosa Antognazza is Professor of Philosophy at King's College London. She is the author of *Leibniz on the Trinity and the Incarnation: Reason and Revelation in the Seventeenth Century* (2007), *Leibniz: An Intellectual Biography* (2009) and *Leibniz: A Very Short Introduction* (2016).

Michael Inwood is Emeritus Fellow of Trinity College at the University of Oxford. His books include *A Hegel Dictionary* (1992), *A Heidegger Dictionary* (1999), *Hegel: Arguments of the Philosophers* (2002), *Heidegger: A Very Short Introduction* (2002), *A Commentary on Hegel's Philosophy of Mind* (2010) and *Heidegger* (2011).

Brian Leftow is William P. Alston Professor of the Philosophy of Religion at Rutgers University. He is the author of: *Time and Eternity* (1991), *God and Necessity* (2012), and *Anselm's Proofs* (2019).

Peter Millican is Gilbert Ryle Fellow and Professor of Philosophy at Hertford College in the University of Oxford. He is the author of *Reading Hume on Human Understanding: Essays on the First Enquiry*, and co-editor, with Andy Clark, of *The Legacy of Alan Turing*, two volumes (1996).

Lawrence Nolan is Professor of Philosophy at California State University at Long Beach. He is the editor of *Primary and Secondary Qualities: The Historical and Ongoing Debate* (2011) and the *Cambridge Descartes Lexicon* (2016).

Graham Oddie is Professor of Philosophy at the University of Colorado at Boulder. His books include *Likeness to Truth* (1986) and *Value, Reality, and Desire* (2005); he is also co-editor, with Roy Perret, of *Justice, Ethics and New Zealand Society* (1993) and, with David Boonin, of *What's Wrong? Applied Ethicists and their Critics* (2004).

Lawrence Pasternack is Professor of Philosophy at Oklahoma State University. He is the author of *Immanuel Kant's Groundwork for the Metaphysics of Morals in Focus* (2002) and *Kant's Religion with the Boundaries of Mere Reason: An*

Interpretation and Defence (2014). He is also co-editor, with Pablo Muchnik, of *Immanuel Kant's Sources in Translation, Volumes I–IV* (2016–).

Graham Priest is Distinguished Professor of Philosophy at the CUNY Graduate Center, City University of New York. His books include *In Contradiction: A Study of the Transconsistent* (1987), *Beyond the Limits of Thought* (1995), *Logic: A Very Short Introduction* (2000), *An Introduction to Non-Classical Logic* (2001), *Towards Non-Being: The Logic and Metaphysics of Intentionality* (2005) and *Doubt Truth to be a Liar* (2006).

Alexander Pruss is Professor of Philosophy at Baylor University in Waco, Texas. His books include *The Principle of Sufficient Reason: A Reassessment* (2010), *Actuality, Possibility, and Worlds* (2011), *One Body: An Essay in Christian Sexual Ethics* (2012) and, with Joshua Rasmussen, *Necessary Existence* (2018).

Joshua Rasmussen is Associate Professor of Philosophy at Azura Pacific University. His books include *Defending the Correspondence Theory of Truth* (2014) and, with Alexander Pruss, *Necessary Existence* (2018).

Joshua Spencer is Associate Professor of Philosophy in the University of Wisconsin at Milwaukee. His dissertation was on material objects in tile space–time. He has published on various metaphysical topics in *The Monist, Philosophical Studies, Analysis, Erkenntnis, Philosophy Compass* and *Oxford Studies in Metaphysics*.

Peter van Inwagen is John Cardinal O'Hare Professor of Philosophy at the University of Notre Dame. His books include *An Essay on Free Will* (1983), *Material Beings* (1990), *Metaphysics* (1993), *God, Knowledge, and Mystery* (1995), *Ontology, Identity, and Modality* (2002), *The Problem of Evil* (2006), *Existence: Essays in Ontology* (2014) and *Thinking about Free Will* (2017).

Acknowledgements

This volume would not exist but for those wonderfully talented and generous philosophers who wrote the chapters that it comprises. The volume also would not exist but for the initiative and expert guidance of Hilary Gaskin and other members of the team at Cambridge University Press, including Marianne Nield and Ian McIver. Given that work on this book began in March 2014, there are many other people who made less direct contributions to it, including my friends and colleagues at Monash University – in the Department of Philosophy, the School of Philosophical Historical and International Studies, the Faculty of Arts and the University at large – and my wider circle of friends and colleagues within and beyond the Australasian academy. Special thanks to my immediate family – Camille, Gil, Cal and Alf – who are the ground for all of my possibilities.

Introduction: Ontological Arguments in Focus

Graham Oppy

Ontological arguments are arguments for the existence of God. The label 'ontological argument' was introduced by Immanuel Kant, who identified three major proofs of the existence of God: 'the ontological argument', 'the cosmological argument' and 'the teleological argument'. While cosmological arguments and teleological arguments were developed in the earliest stages of the history of philosophy – for example, in the West, there are cosmological arguments in Plato's *Laws* and Aristotle's *Physics* and *Metaphysics*, and there are teleological arguments in Plato's *Timaeus* and *Phaedo* – ontological arguments did not appear on the scene until the eleventh century CE. Moreover, while there have been periods of widespread endorsement of cosmological arguments and teleological arguments, there has never been a time at which there has been widespread endorsement of ontological arguments. However, some of the greatest figures in Western philosophy – including Descartes, Leibniz, Spinoza, Hegel and (for a brief period) Bertrand Russell – have been proponents of ontological arguments, and there has been significant support for ontological arguments in some quarters of the Western academy since the middle of the twentieth century CE.

Much about ontological arguments is highly controversial. In this Introduction, we begin with two relatively uncontroversial matters: the broad contours of the history of discussion of ontological arguments, and the major topics that require discussion in connection with ontological arguments. We then move on to consideration of the much more difficult task of the characterization of ontological arguments – i.e., the task of saying exactly what ontological arguments are and explaining how they differ from, say, cosmological, teleological and moral arguments for the existence of God – and then the equally contested question of the provision of general objections to ontological arguments, including, in particular, attempts to show that there could not possibly be a successful ontological argument. Finally, we consider some often-neglected questions about how to assess the merits of arguments, with a particular eye on the assessment of the merits of ontological arguments.

1 History

The pivotal text on ontological arguments, the work on which all subsequent literature depends, is Anselm's *Proslogion*. The text of *Proslogion II* – the centrepiece of the work, discussed in the present volume by Peter Millican – has puzzled and inspired generations of philosophers; its interpretation and assessment remains deeply controversial. The text of *Proslogion III* – while not, I think, intended as an argument for the existence of God – has also puzzled and inspired generations of philosophers, leading eventually, in the work of Charles Hartshorne and Alvin Plantinga, to the development of a new family of (modal) ontological arguments.

The argument of *Proslogion II* was met with immediate criticism. In 1079 – the year after the publication of the *Proslogion* – Gaunilo of Marmoutiers attempted to show that the argument of *Proslogion II* did not succeed in proving that God exists. While Gaunilo's critique, and Anselm's reply to that critique, seem not to be always on target, Gaunilo did establish one enduring kind of response to ontological arguments: many have since followed him in supposing that ontological arguments can be parodied in ways which conclusively show that there are not successful proofs of the existence of God. Famously, Gaunilo provided a parody of Anselm's *Proslogion II* argument which purported to establish the existence of the 'Lost Island': an island superior everywhere in abundance of riches to all those lands that actually exist.

Despite Gaunilo's immediate response, Anselm's argument passed into a lengthy period of obscurity, from which it emerged not long before Aquinas subjected it to criticism which is discussed in the present volume by Brian Leftow. *Proslogion II* and *Proslogion III* are both objects of Aquinas' attention, e.g., in his commentary on Lombard's *Sentences*, in the *Summa Contra Gentiles* and in the *Summa Theologiae*. Roughly speaking, Aquinas thinks that, while there is a sense in which God's existence is self-evident, and while it is also true that God's existence can be demonstrated to us, Anselm's argument fails to be a demonstration of God's existence. Given only the considerations to which the *Proslogion II* argument appeals, there is no inconsistency in the Fool's claim that there is no being than which none greater can be conceived.

At least from the time of Aquinas' criticism, Anselm's *Proslogion II* argument was a staple of discussion for medieval philosophers. However, the next major event in the history of ontological arguments was Descartes's various attempts, discussed in the present volume by Lawrence Nolan, to argue that the existence of God – a supremely perfect being – is given in intuition and so is ultimately self-evident. The various works in which Descartes broaches this topic – *The Discourse on Method* (1637), *The Meditations* (1641), The First, Second and Fifth *Replies* to the *Objections* in the *Meditations*, and *The Principles* (1644) – have puzzled and inspired philosophers in much the same way as Anselm's *Proslogion II*; the interpretation and assessment of these texts remains deeply controversial. The First Objector, Caterus, supposes that Descartes's argumentative moves can be parodied in ways that utterly discredit them. The Second Objector, Mersenne, raises legitimate concerns about whether we can have the kinds of intuitions that Descartes supposes make it evident to us that God exists. The Fifth Objector, Gassendi, provides criticisms that anticipate Kant's famous attempt to defeat what are now typically called 'Cartesian ontological arguments'.

Descartes's views on the demonstration of the existence of God were much discussed by his successors, including More, Malebranche, Cudworth, Spinoza and Clarke. However, the next major episode in the history of ontological arguments was Leibniz's attempt, discussed in the present volume by Maria Rosa Antognazza, to fill what Leibniz – following in the footsteps of Mersenne – took to be a hole in Cartesian ontological arguments. Given the way that Leibniz proposed to construct his ontological argument, he needed a proof that the perfections are possibly jointly instantiated. The line of inquiry that Leibniz pursued eventually paved the way to Gödel's development of his higher-order modal ontological argument.

Descartes's views on the demonstration of the existence of God continued to be discussed after Leibniz: Wolff and Baumgarten both defended 'Cartesian ontological arguments', and Crusius provided them with criticism, which, to some extent, anticipated the next major step in the history of ontological arguments, taken by Kant, and discussed in the present volume by Lawrence Pasternack. As part of his systematic attack on the arguments of natural theology, Kant eventually – in *The Critique of Pure Reason* – provided a multi-pronged attack on what he there was the first to call 'the ontological argument'. Kant's most famous objection – that 'existence is not a real predicate' – initially advanced in *The Only Possible Argument in Support of a Demonstration of the Existence of God*, immediately became *the* standard criticism of ontological arguments, or, at any rate, of ontological arguments that were known to Kant.

Hegel refused to accept Kant's criticism of 'the ontological argument'. Moreover, Hegel provided his own defence of 'the ontological argument', discussed in the present volume by Michael Inwood. Hegel's claim that there is a successful ontological argument was accepted by many for at least one hundred years after his initial staking out of the claim. However, as has been widely recognized, Hegel has a rather idiosyncratic conception of proof, and, perhaps, an even more idiosyncratic conception of God. Nonetheless, Hegel's courses of lectures on 'the ontological argument' have provided a very rich resource for subsequent students of ontological arguments.

After Hegel, there was a long period in which there were few innovations in discussion of ontological arguments. That is not to say that the arguments were ignored: Bertrand Russell reported that, for a brief period, he was converted to theism by a Hegelian ontological argument; and, throughout the Idealist age, there were many affirmations of the value of ontological arguments. But the next significant episode in the history of ontological arguments, discussed in the present volume by Alexander Pruss, was Kurt Gödel's 'systematization' of the argument that was developed by Leibniz, which – eventually – launched investigation of a new family of (higher-order (modal)) ontological arguments. Gödel's work – which took advantage of developments in logic for which he was, himself, partly responsible – introduced a new level of sophistication to the formulation of ontological arguments.

Before Gödel's work became publicly available – i.e., while it was simply sitting in his notebooks – there were two other significant advances in understanding of ontological arguments. The first of these advances, discussed in the present volume by Michael Almeida, was made by David Lewis, as an application of his theory of metaphysical modality. Lewis considered the representation of Anselm's *Proslogion II* argument in a language in which there is direct quantification over possible worlds, and arrived at the interesting conclusion that the argument admits of two quite distinct readings, one of which is invalid, and the other of which contains a premise that is evidently question-begging. This idea proved very influential in the subsequent literature. (Interestingly, in his analysis of the *Proslogion II* argument in this volume, Peter Millican finds that there are three quite distinct readings of the argument: one that is invalid, one that is evidently question-begging, and one that fails to establish the existence of anything divine.)

The other advance in understanding of ontological arguments that occurred prior to the publication of Gödel's notebooks was the development, by Charles Hartshorne and Norman Malcolm, of (modal) ontological arguments that they 'found' in *Proslogion III*. The kind of argument that they developed found its most impressive presentation, discussed in the present volume by Josh Rasmussen, in the work of Alvin Plantinga, primarily in his

1974 book, *The Nature of Necessity*. Plantinga, while accepting that his modal ontological argument is not a proof of the existence of God, nonetheless maintains that it is a 'victorious' argument: it shows that it is rational to accept the claim that God exists.

The final chapter in our history of ontological arguments requires some further scene-setting. In the last part of the nineteenth century, in Austria, work began on what we might call 'theories of non-existent objects'. On its face, Anselm's *Proslogion II* requires a background theory of non-existent objects. Those – such as Alexius Meinong, John Findlay, Richard Sylvan (né Routley), Terence Parsons, Graham Priest and Ed Zalta – who have participated in the development of theories of non-existent objects have *all* argued that successful ontological arguments cannot be developed in the context of those theories. Pavel Tichý provided an interesting alternative to theories of non-existent objects – through a comprehensive metaphysics of *roles* or *offices* – laid out in the present volume by Graham Oddie. Unlike almost all other authors Tichý takes Anselm's argument in *Proslogion III* as the more promising starting-point, and argues that it is not vulnerable to the well-known objections levelled by Kant and Frege against Descartes's argument, or that can be laid against Anselm's argument in *Proslogion II*. Tichý argues that while Anselm's argument in *Proslogion III* is logically valid, a key axiological premise – that necessary existence is a good property – is deeply implausible. Oddie digs deeper into the assumptions that Anselm could appeal to, and concludes that there is no plausible way of repairing them to yield a logically and axiologically sound ontological argument.

2 Topics

One part of the perennial fascination of ontological arguments is that adequate discussion of ontological arguments requires taking up a number of intrinsically interesting philosophical topics. This volume is rounded out by discussion of three of these intrinsically interesting topics.

The first topic, discussed in the present volume by Joshua Spencer, and of particular interest both in the context of assessment of the claim that it is possible that God exists and in the context of the interpretation of Anselm's *Proslogion II*, concerns the connections between conceivability and possibility. Many philosophers have been tempted by some version of the thought that what they can conceive provides them with some evidence about what is possible. Given some version of that thought, we might then be tempted to suppose that conceiving of God's existence provides some evidence that it is possible that God exists; and we might also be tempted to suppose that we can reinterpret Anselm's 'conceiving'-talk as 'possibility'-talk.

The second topic, discussed in the present volume by Peter van Inwagen, and raised in connection with every ontological argument, concerns the nature of the alleged fallacy of begging the question. It is very common to hear people say that a particular ontological argument begs the question; it is not so uncommon to hear people say that 'the ontological argument' begs the question. But what, exactly, is it for an argument to be question-begging? This is a surprisingly difficult, and, I think, not very well understood, question. It is not hard to see, for example, that an argument that has its conclusion as one of its premises is not a successful argument. However, no interesting ontological arguments suffer from that defect. It is also not hard to see, for example, that we should not want to say that every valid argument is circular. Yet is surprisingly tricky to find a criterion for argumentative question-begging that neither entails that all valid arguments beg the question nor entails that the only arguments that beg the question are those that are transparently and obviously deficient in the way of arguments that have their conclusion as one of their premises.

The third topic was introduced above, in the examination of the last chapter in the history of ontological arguments, and is discussed in the present volume by Graham Priest. The conclusion of ontological arguments is an existence claim: either it is the claim that God exists, or it is a conclusion that is taken to evidently and immediately entail that God exists. Moreover, it is very often the case that premises in ontological arguments are also 'existence' claims, i.e., claims in which the concept of existence – or a cognate concept of, say, being – is deployed. But the interpretation and analysis of the concept of existence – and cognate concepts such as being – is a fascinating and intimidating topic in its own right. Any theorizing about existence and non-existence takes us into very deep water in both philosophy of language and metaphysics.

Of course, there are other topics that are important for the examination of ontological arguments. In particular, given that ontological arguments are arguments, the full investigation of ontological arguments requires some theory of argumentation, and some account of what it is for an argument to be successful. It is important to see, for example, that we cannot just be interested in determining, to our own satisfaction, which arguments are sound. Consider, for example, the following pair of arguments:

1. Necessarily, if God exists, then, necessarily, God exists. (Premise)
2. Possibly God exists. (Premise)
3. (Therefore) God exists. (From 1 and 2, by S5.)

1. Necessarily, if God exists, then, necessarily, God exists. (Premise)
2. Possibly God does not exist. (Premise)
3. (Therefore) God does not exist. (From 1 and 2, by S5.)

One of these arguments is valid just in case the other is valid. (If, for example, we suppose that S5 is the modal logic in employment, then both are valid.) Moreover, these arguments share the same first premise. So, if we are to suppose that only one of them is sound, it will be because we accept the second premise in one, and deny the second premise in the other. So – holding fixed the various things that we've supposed to this point – we can see that theists will suppose that the first argument is sound, and atheists will suppose that the second argument is sound, and agnostics will be undecided about which of the two arguments is sound. Given that we already knew that theists, atheists and agnostics divide in their attitudes towards the proposition that God exists, these arguments have done nothing to advance the state of anyone's knowledge. Moreover, insofar as theists, atheists and agnostics are rational, these arguments can do nothing to advance the state of anyone's knowledge. That we have satisfied ourselves that an argument is sound is not enough to allow us to conclude that it is a successful argument.

Another topic that is important in the examination of ontological arguments is the significance of ontological parodies. We noted earlier that several critics of ontological arguments have attempted to discredit ontological arguments by parodying them to their discredit. To illustrate the issues, consider the following – toy – ontological argument.

1. God is, by definition, a supremely perfect being.
2. Existence is a perfection.
3. (Therefore) God exists.

A critic of this argument might think that the following argument presents a challenge to the proponent of that first argument:

1. Rod is, by definition, a supremely perfect Martian.
2. Existence is a perfection.
3. (Therefore) Rod exists.

Why might this parody be a challenge to the first argument? Well, the only difference between the arguments lies in the first premise. And the first premise is a definition. If the proponent of the first argument is free to define 'God' using the expression 'a supremely perfect being', then surely the critic is free to define 'Rod' using the expression 'a supremely perfect

Martian'. Given that there are no other differences between the arguments, the second argument goes through if the first argument goes through. But we all know that the second argument does not go through: there are no Martians, so, in particular, there is no Martian that is supremely perfect *qua* Martian. So there must be something wrong with *both* arguments. While the production of a successful parody does not identify the flaw in the argument that is parodied, it is clear that a successful parody can suffice to discredit an argument.

There are many hard questions that come up in connection with particular ontological arguments. For example, Gödel's ontological argument is formulated in a classical third-order quantified modal logic with lambda-abstraction. There have been vigorous philosophical debates about: (a) whether we should embrace classical logic; (b) whether we should embrace modal logic; (c) whether we should embrace quantified modal logic; (d) whether we should embrace higher-order logic; and (e) whether we should embrace lambda-abstraction. Moreover, if we do decide to embrace classical third-order quantified modal logic with lambda-abstraction, there remains the very thorny question of *which* classical third-order quantified modal logic with lambda-abstraction to embrace. (Perhaps you will be relieved to learn that, in this volume, Alex Pruss evades most of these issues by considering stripped-back versions of Gödel's argument that do not require all of the machinery that Gödel himself introduces.)

Consider Anselm's *Proslogion II* argument. That argument, as it is formulated by Anselm, takes for granted that some things exist only in the understanding, some things exist only in reality, and some things exist both in the understanding and in reality. But what is taken for granted here requires a great deal of explanation if it is also to be taken at face value. One option is to assess Anselm's *Proslogion II* argument against the background of the kinds of theories of non-existent objects developed by Meinong, Findlay, Sylvan, Parsons, Priest, Zalta et al. (Graham Priest gives this kind of assessment of Anselm's argument in the present volume.) Another option is to recast Anselm's *Proslogion II* argument in ways that replace reference to existence in the understanding with talk about concept possession (see Peter Millican's contribution to this volume) or with talk about offices (see Graham Oddie's contribution to this volume). Yet another option is to recast Anselm's *Proslogion II* argument by reinterpreting Anselm's talk about conceivability as talk about possibility, following the lead of David Lewis and Robert Adams (see Mike Almeida's contribution to this volume).

3 Taxonomy

It is not straightforward to provide an accurate characterization of ontological arguments. When Kant introduced the term 'ontological argument' he said that ontological arguments 'abstract from all experience and argue, completely *a priori*, from mere concepts'. But it is not clear that any of the well-known arguments 'proceed completely *a priori*, from mere concepts'. Here are formulations of four of the best-known ontological arguments (due ultimately, respectively, to Anselm, Descartes, Plantinga and Gödel):

1. Whatever is understood exists in the understanding. (Premise)
2. The words that-than-which-no-greater-can-be-conceived are understood. (Premise)
3. (Therefore) That-than-which-no-greater-can-be-conceived exists in the understanding. (From 1 and 2.)
4. If that-than-which-no-greater-can-be-conceived exists only in the understanding, then that-than-which-no-greater-can-be-conceived-and-that-exists-in-reality is greater than that-than-which-no-greater-can-be-conceived. (Premise)
5. It is impossible for anything to be greater than that-than-which-no-greater-can-be-conceived. (Premise)
6. (Therefore) That-than-which-no-greater-can-be-conceived does not exist only in the understanding. (From 4 and 5.)
7. (Therefore) That-than-which-no-greater-can-be-conceived exists in reality. (From 3 and 6.)

1. The idea of a supremely perfect being includes the idea of existence. (Premise)
2. The idea of a supremely perfect being is the idea of a being with a true and immutable nature. (Premise)
3. Whatever belongs to the true and immutable nature of a being may be truly affirmed of it. (Premise)
4. (Therefore) A supremely perfect being exists. (From 1, 2 and 3.)

1. A being is maximally excellent iff it is omnipotent, omniscient and morally perfect. (Definition)
2. A being is maximally great iff it is necessarily maximally excellent and necessarily existent. (Definition)
3. It is possible that there is a maximally great being. (Premise)
4. (Therefore) There is a maximally great being. (From 1, 2 and 3.)

1. A is an essence of x iff for every property B, x has B necessarily iff A entails B. (Definition)
2. x necessarily exists iff every essence of x is necessarily exemplified. (Definition)

3. x is God-like iff x has as essential properties those and only those properties that are positive. (Premise)
4. If a property is positive, then its negation is not positive. (Premise)
5. Any property entailed by a positive property is positive. (Premise)
6. The property of being God-like is positive. (Premise)
7. If a property is positive, then it is necessarily positive. (Premise)
8. Necessary existence is positive.
9. (Therefore) Necessarily, the property of being God-like is exemplified. From 1–8.)

I think that it is pretty clear that not all of the premises in any of these arguments can plausibly be claimed to be true in virtue of conceptual containment; that is, I think that it is pretty clear that not all of the premises in any of these arguments can plausibly be taken to be conceptual truths. Moreover – though this is not immediately relevant to Kant's taxonomy – it is pretty clear that not all of the premises in any of these arguments can plausibly be claimed to be analytic. Certainly, no *objectors* to these arguments are going to suppose any of these things.

Perhaps it might be said: what matters is whether those who constructed the arguments suppose that they are abstracting from all experience, and arguing completely *a priori* from mere concepts. But I think that it is no less clear that Anselm, Descartes, Plantinga and Gödel do not take themselves to be arguing completely *a priori* from mere concepts. Indeed, it is not at all clear that either Plantinga or Gödel really is mounting any kind of argument for the given conclusion. Gödel claims that his interest is just in showing that, using the materials that Leibniz took to be available to him, you can reach the conclusion that Leibniz wanted; and Plantinga claims that the argument actually establishes only the conclusion that it is rational to believe that there is a maximally great being.

Perhaps it might be said: what matters is whether those who endorse the arguments suppose that they are abstracting from all experience, and arguing completely *a priori* from mere concepts. But I think that it is pretty clear that many of those who now endorse these arguments do not suppose that they are abstracting from all experience and arguing completely *a priori* from mere concepts. In my experience, when people endorse the arguments, they simply rely upon all-things-considered judgments about the various premises; and those all-things-considered judgments are not themselves arrived at by abstracting from all experience and arguing completely *a priori* from mere concepts.

Suppose we abandon the Kantian characterization. What should we put in its place? Perhaps we might say that what is distinctive of ontological arguments is that they have no premises whose justification relies upon perceptual experience. To bolster this suggestion, we might observe that there is no premise in any of these arguments that might be taken for a report based upon perceptual experience.

But if we think about the way in which people now try to justify their acceptance of premises in these arguments, it really isn't clear that reliance upon perceptual experience plays no role in that justification. Consider Plantinga's claim that it is possible that there is a maximally great being. How does Plantinga justify that claim? Certainly not by appealing to the conceivability of there being a maximally great being. For, plausibly, on any standards of conceivability, it is no less conceivable that there is no maximally great being. If all we have to go on is considerations about conceivability, then it seems that we should accept neither the claim that it is conceivable that there is a maximally great being, nor the claim that it is conceivable that there is no maximally great being. So how does Plantinga justify the claim? By appealing to what seems all-things-considered plausible to him. When he considers the matter carefully, he judges that it is possible that there is a maximally great being (and he judges that it is not possible that there is no maximally great being). Is that judgment in no way reliant upon perceptual experience? I don't suppose that Plantinga thinks so. On his own account, he believes that it is possible that there is a maximally great being because he believes that there is a maximally great being, and he believes that there is a maximally great being because he makes certain kinds of judgments when he has certain kinds of perceptual experiences (e.g., he judges 'a maximally great being made all this' when he looks at the starry heavens).

Does this mean that we should abandon any attempt to characterize ontological arguments? No. What it does mean, I think, is that we should think about them in a very different way. I have come to think that ontological arguments are arguments with a particular *genealogy*: what is distinctive of ontological arguments is that their formulation has the right kind of connection to Anselm's argument. The brief history that I gave above sets out the line of descent that runs from Anselm's *Proslogion II* argument through the works of Aquinas, Descartes, Leibniz, Kant, Hegel, Gödel, Lewis, Plantinga and Tichý. Of course, it is conceivable that someone could produce an argument that is very similar to the arguments in the actual line of descent but that is entirely independent of them – and, in that case, we might wish to expand our characterization of ontological arguments so that that argument is included. But, as things stand, there is no reason for us to contemplate any such expansion.

4 Objections

There are many people who have taken themselves to be in possession of a decisive general objection to ontological arguments. We have already noted that Aquinas took himself to have compelling general reason for thinking that there could be no *a priori* argument for the existence of God that is successful for us; and that Kant took himself to have compelling general reason for thinking that 'the ontological argument' is a spectacular failure. Others have given quite different general objections to ontological arguments.

Johnston (1992) claims to be able to show that, if it is accepted that it is possible that God's knowledge of the free actions of human beings is based upon those free actions, then there can be no *a priori* grounds for believing that any ontological argument is sound. Johnston assumes that we know *a priori* that, if God exists, God is omnipotent, omniscient, perfectly good, and so forth. He then notes, if we suppose that there is a sound ontological argument, then we are committed to the following pair of claims:

(1) It is *a priori* that, for any proposition that p, God judges that p iff it is that p.
(2) It is possible that, for some proposition that p, God judges that p because it is the case that p.

But, according to Johnston, given (1) and (2), it plausibly follows – by employing a principle of substitution that is licensed by (1) to make a substitution in (2) – that:

(3) It is possible that, for some proposition that p, God judges that p because God judges that p.

But there is no proposition that p for which it is possible that God judges that p because God judges that p: the claim that God judges that p because God judges that p is always an explanatory solecism. So (3) is false. But, if there were a sound ontological argument, then (1) would be true. So, unless we deny that it is possible that God's knowledge of the free actions of human beings is based upon those free actions, we must accept that there are no sound ontological arguments, i.e., no sound *a priori* arguments for the existence of God. While some fans of ontological arguments may respond to this argument by rejecting (2), there is another option: reject the principle of substitution on which the argument relies. (See Oppy (1995: 120–2) for details.)

Barnes (1972) claims that ontological arguments fail because of the use that they make of singular terms, e.g., the proper name 'God' and the definite descriptions 'the being than which none greater can be conceived' and 'the supremely perfect being'. In his view: arguments that make primary use of definite descriptions are question-begging because primary use of a definite description requires that there is exactly one thing that satisfies that definite description; and arguments that make primary use of names are question-begging because primary use of names must be underwritten by primary use of definite descriptions. While the details of Barnes' analysis are open to challenge – particularly his claim that primary use of names must be underwritten by primary use of definite descriptions – and while it seems implausible to suppose that Barnes' analysis defeats any of the four arguments given in the previous section of this Introduction, there are many who have followed him in thinking that there are considerations drawn from the theory of reference that suffice to establish that, quite generally, ontological arguments are question-begging. I think that this view is implausible; it is, for example, very hard to see how any considerations drawn from a plausible theory of reference could suffice to defeat any of the four arguments given in the previous section.

Some people have thought that, while Barnes' focus on the use of singular terms is mistaken, he is nonetheless right to think that all ontological arguments are question-begging. As we have already noted, it is not altogether easy to say exactly what it is for an argument to be question-begging. But, in any case, this general objection to ontological arguments seems needlessly overstated: some of the historically well-known ontological arguments are plausibly either invalid or else possessed of not uncharitable readings on which they are invalid. For these arguments, we do not need to decide whether we can stretch an account of begging-the-question to allow them to fall within its scope. (In the present volume, Peter van Inwagen argues that all, or, at any rate, almost all, modal ontological arguments are question-begging, while other ontological arguments – e.g., Meinongian ontological arguments and conceptual ontological arguments – are, for quite different reasons, irremediably flawed.)

There are various 'general objections' that we might now think to try. Perhaps all ontological arguments are invalid or question-begging. Perhaps all ontological arguments are invalid or question-begging or uncontroversially unsound. Perhaps all ontological arguments are invalid or question-begging or uncontroversially unsound or possessed of a conclusion that uncontroversially has no religious significance. Et cetera. Whether there is much interest that attaches to these 'general objections' turns upon the details. It is one thing to argue by cases; perhaps, for example, a consideration of cases shows that, hitherto, all of the ontological arguments that have ever been formulated are invalid or question-begging or uncontroversially unsound or possessed of a conclusion that uncontroversially has no religious significance. It is quite another thing to argue in principle that it never will be, because it never could be, that there is a non-question-begging ontological argument that is both sound and possessed of a conclusion that has religious significance.

What should be the target of opponents of ontological arguments? Is it enough for opponents of ontological arguments to give detailed accounts of the failing of extant ontological arguments? Or is it incumbent upon opponents of ontological arguments to try to argue that it is impossible for there to be a successful ontological argument?

I doubt that there is any good all-things-considered reason for opponents of ontological arguments to look for successful arguments for the conclusion that it is impossible for there to be successful ontological arguments. It is obvious that, if God does not exist, then there are no successful arguments for the existence of God. It is also obvious that, if the key premise in modal ontological arguments,

(*) Necessarily, if God exists, then, necessarily, God exists

is accepted, then, if God does not exist, it is impossible that there are successful arguments for the existence of God. If you have good all-things-considered reason to suppose that God does not exist, then you have all the reason you need to suppose that there are no successful ontological arguments. Perhaps your having good all-things-considered reason to suppose that God does not exist requires you to have – though perhaps it also supplies you with – good all-things-considered reason for thinking that no extant ontological arguments are sound; but, if, for each extant ontological argument, you have good all-things-considered reason for saying that it is not a sound argument for the existence of God, then there is nothing more – and can be nothing more – that is required of you, in connection with ontological arguments, to make it the case that you have good all-things-considered reason to believe that there is no God.

5 Standards

In order to think well about the assessment of ontological arguments, we need to have some general theory for the evaluation of arguments. Quite generally, what does it take for an argument to be successful? Since successful ontological arguments would be successful deductive arguments, we can make our question more specific: what does it take for a deductive argument to be successful?

Suppose that we have an argument $P_1, \ldots, P_n$ *therefore* Q with premises $P_1, \ldots, P_n$ and conclusion Q. In order for $P_1, \ldots, P_n$ *therefore* Q to be a successful deductive argument, one necessary condition is that Q is a logical consequence of $P_1, \ldots, P_n$, i.e., $P_1, \ldots, P_n \vdash Q$. If we suppose that the logical consequence relation is classical, then, given $P_1, \ldots, P_n \vdash Q$, we also have that $\{P_1, \ldots, P_n, {\sim}Q\}$ is a logically inconsistent set, and we have that the negation of any of the P_i is a logical consequence of the rest of the P_i together with the negation of Q: $\{P_i\}/P_k, {\sim}Q \vdash {\sim}P_k$. Given that the logical consequence relation is classical, we can establish that $P_1, \ldots, P_n$ *therefore* Q is valid by establishing that $\{P_1, \ldots, P_n, {\sim}Q\}$ is logically inconsistent, or by establishing that $\{P_i\}/P_k, {\sim}Q \vdash {\sim}P_k$ for some k.

Suppose that Q is a philosophical contested claim, and that our interest in arguments for Q is philosophical: we are interested in whether there is good reason for philosophers to believe that Q. In particular, suppose that we are interested in whether there are successful deductive arguments for Q. What further properties should we require of our successful argument for Q, beyond the validity of that argument?

Suppose that A and B are philosophers who disagree about Q: A believes that Q and B believes that ~Q. Suppose, further, that A and B agree about $S_1, \ldots, S_i$, and disagree about $T_1, \ldots, T_j$, with A believing $T_{1A}, \ldots, T_{jA}$ and B believing $T_{1B}, \ldots, T_{jB}$, where, for each of the T_{iA} and T_{iB}, $T_{iA} \vdash {\sim}T_{iB}$ and $T_{iB} \vdash {\sim}T_{iA}$. Given that A believes that Q, what premises can there be in an argument that A presents to B that is a plausible candidate to be a successful argument for Q?

Clearly, it is fine for A to take any of the S_i as premises. But, if A takes any of the T_k as premises, then it must be the T_{kB} that A takes as premises. For, if A takes any of the T_{kA} as premises, B can immediately reply that, because he does not believe any of the T_{kA}, the argument gives B no reason to accept Q. But, if A takes only the S_i and T_{kB} as premises, and gets Q as a logical consequence, then A has shown that B's beliefs are logically inconsistent: the S_i, T_{kB} and ~Q form a logically inconsistent set. In response, B needs to set about changing something: but, obviously, it need not be that B changes from ~Q to Q; B might change to one (or more) of the T_{kA}, or B might change one (or more) of the S_i to ${\sim}S_i$.

The lesson here is that, if A and B have well-developed philosophical views, and if A and B have mapped out the extent of their disagreement, then the only role left for deductive argument in the direct prosecution of their dispute is to provide *reductio*s, in those cases where the views of one or the other are logically inconsistent. While it may be disappointing, this is all that we can expect from deductive arguments with perennially contested conclusions in areas where disagreement has already been thoroughly mapped.

Note that nothing substantive changes in the above discussion if we consider, instead, C, who withholds judgment about Q, and about propositions $R_1, \ldots, R_k$ that A believes, agrees with A on propositions $S_1, \ldots, S_i$, and disagrees with A on propositions $T_1, \ldots, T_j$. In order to give C a reason to reconsider C's beliefs, by presenting C with a deductive argument, A needs to show that there is an inconsistency in C's beliefs. If the S_i entail Q, or one or more of the R_j, or one or more of the T_i, then A can show to C that C should make some change in belief, by presenting C with a deductive argument. Otherwise, A cannot give C a good reason to make some change in belief simply by presenting C with a deductive argument, if the goodness of the reason is to flow from the goodness of the deductive argument.

It is, of course, true that, by A's lights, there are lots of other inconsistent sets of sentences that are linked to valid arguments with Q as conclusion. Moreover, there are lots of such arguments that, by A's lights, are sound. Whether these arguments are '*a priori* arguments' for Q depends upon whether the premises are knowable *a priori*. Consider, as a toy example:

1. Either $2 + 2 = 5$, or Q
2. $2 + 2 \neq 5$
3. (Therefore) Q.

2 is paradigmatically knowable *a priori*; whether 1 is knowable *a priori* depends upon whether Q is knowable *a priori*. If it is, then our toy example is an *a priori* argument for Q. Wherever A thinks that a proposition Q is knowable *a priori*, A will have an endless supply of what A judges to be sound *a priori* arguments for Q. (And if B thinks that it is knowable a priori that ~Q, then B will have an endless supply of what B judges to be sound *a priori* arguments for ~Q.) Make sure that you are not misled by the simplicity of our toy argument: anyone with a little logical facility can generate complicated many-premise arguments of this kind for which it is a major undertaking to determine whether or not they are valid. But, of course, it really does not profit those with genuine philosophical interests to be in the business of generating these kinds of arguments.

Despite the limitations on the utility of arguments, with perennially contested conclusions, in areas where disagreement has already been thoroughly mapped, for those engaged in dispute about those perennially contested claims, there are clearly other uses for derivations for those engaged in such dispute. Anyone can learn about their own present commitments by making derivations from what they believe, so long as the conclusions of those derivations are not things that they already believe. (Of course, the result of such derivation might be to revise what they already believe, rather than to continue with the commitment once they recognize that they have it: there is no guarantee in advance that this will not be the case.) Anyone can help others to learn about their present commitments, by making derivations from what they believe. And so forth.

Perhaps, though, we should not be concentrating on what derivations can do for individuals or for the parties to particular disputes. The ontological arguments set out in Section 3 above are not just any old derivations: some are derivations that have been scrutinized for centuries. Is there some other purpose that these ontological arguments might be intended to serve, and that might justify the attention that has been paid to them?

One thought is that we might idealize. Suppose, for example, that an ideal – best possible – theist and an ideal – best possible – naturalist are locking horns. The theist is maximally rational, maximally reflective, maximally well-informed, and so forth, among theists; the naturalist is maximally rational, maximally reflective, maximally well-informed, and so forth, among naturalists. Is there any mileage that our ideal theist can gain by presenting one of our ontological arguments to an ideal naturalist? It is hard to see how that could be the case. Current rational, reflective, well-informed naturalists do not think that any extant ontological arguments are sound; why would we think that things would be different for maximally rational, maximally reflective, maximally well-informed naturalists? At the very least, it seems pretty clear that thinking about this kind of idealization is not going to help to narrow any gap in judgment of the merits of ontological arguments between current theists and current naturalists.

A different thought is that there is an alternative philosophical role that arguments can play that has nothing to do with persuasion of those who do not initially accept the conclusions of these arguments. Perhaps, for example, there is a role that arguments can play in *justifying* beliefs. Some philosophers have thought that a person is only justified in believing a proposition if it is appropriately related to an argument that has that proposition as its conclusion. If that is right, then perhaps ontological arguments can play that role for some people for the propositions that are the conclusions of those ontological arguments. But what would the mooted 'appropriate relation' be? Not that there *are* valid arguments with premises that are entailed by what one believes and the proposition in question as conclusion: we have already seen that this condition is satisfied for everything that you believe, no matter how well-justified or ill-justified your beliefs are. Not that you *have framed* valid arguments with premises that are entailed by what one believes and the proposition in question as conclusion: it is obvious that you have countless justified beliefs – e.g., beliefs concerning your current environment – for which you have framed no such arguments. Not that you *could frame* valid arguments with premises that are entailed by what one believes and the proposition in question as conclusion: after all, as we have already noted, it is obvious that, for any of your beliefs, no matter how well-justified or ill-justified, you could frame an argument that meets this condition.

Perhaps, instead, we should be focusing on *inferential* beliefs; perhaps there is a role for arguments to play in justifying those among your beliefs that you adopted by inferring them from other beliefs that you held at the time that you made the inference. Or perhaps we should be focusing on those among your inferential beliefs that have not subsequently received justification from sources other than inference: perhaps arguments have a role in the justification of your *purely inferential* beliefs? But suggestions along these lines seem to conflate implication and inference (and perhaps also to conflate context of discovery with context of justification). At the time that inferential beliefs are adopted, what matters, from the standpoint of justification, is simply whether you do a good enough job of updating your beliefs; whether you have constructed – or can construct – arguments that have the newly adopted beliefs as conclusions seems to be completely beside the point.

One final thought – at least for this occasion – is that we should now idealize: ideal epistemic agents who adopt purely inferential beliefs acquire (extra?) justification for those beliefs if they (can?) construct arguments, with premises all entailed by their other beliefs, that have those inferential beliefs as conclusions. But, in this case, too, the arguments are surely just fifth wheels to the justificatory coach. Consider ideal Bayesian agents who update by conditionalization: in this case, there is nothing for arguments to do. Of course, it is a substantive claim that ideal epistemic agents are ideal Bayesian agents; nonetheless, the case seems highly suggestive.

One gap in our understanding of ontological arguments – and arguments more generally – that might be filled in the next fifty years concerns the standards of assessment that successful arguments must meet. This gap gives us much to ponder.

1 Anselm

Peter Millican*

Anselm's *Proslogion* II presents the original and classic version of the Ontological Argument, which has inspired many others yet still remains the most intriguing and ingenious. It forms the first part of an extended meditation based on Anselm's understanding of God as 'that than which nothing greater can be thought', and the role of this first part is to prove that God – so understood – truly exists. *Proslogion* III then builds on this by arguing that God – again as understood by Anselm's formula – cannot even be thought not to exist, and this has been taken by some philosophers (starting with Charles Hartshorne and Norman Malcolm) as inspiration for modal forms of Ontological Argument whose logic is quite different.[1] Here, however, I shall focus only on the argument of *Proslogion* II, though what I say about Anselm's formula and its troublesome ambiguities would potentially have negative implications for his later arguments also. Space precludes discussion of all the relevant interpretative issues even in respect of this initial argument, and my emphasis will be primarily philosophical: exploring how far it can provide a basis for a *successful* Ontological Argument, whether or not the version that results is entirely faithful to Anselm's own thought.[2]

Anselm's reasoning takes the form of a *reductio ad absurdum*, in which 'the Fool' of Psalms 14 and 53 – who 'says in his heart "there is no god"' – is shown to contradict himself. Addressing God, Anselm expresses his belief 'that You are something than which nothing greater can be thought', but then immediately

* I am very grateful to Robin Le Poidevin and Dave Leal for helpful comments on this paper, to Ian Logan for discussion of Anselm's text, and to Stephen Boulter for drawing my attention to the Scotus and Ockham texts of which I was previously unaware.

[1] For a detailed analysis concluding that *Proslogion* III does not itself aim to present an independent argument for the existence of that-than-which-nothing-greater-can-be-thought, see Smith (2014: ch. 4).

[2] Again for reasons of space, I shall not here give many references to older secondary sources, except where these are likely to be of continuing relevance. In an earlier paper (Millican 2004: 442–5), I gave a catalogue of nine standard objections to Anselm's argument, noting influential presentations of these in the literature.

raises the question prompted by the Fool's denial: 'can it be that a thing of such a nature does not exist?' The subsequent *reductio* proceeds as follows:[3]

> (A) But surely, when this same Fool hears what I am speaking about, namely, 'something-than-which-nothing-greater-can-be-thought', he understands what he hears, and what he understands is in his mind, even if he does not understand that it actually exists . . . Even the Fool, then, is forced to agree that something-than-which-nothing-greater-can-be-thought exists in the mind, since he understands this when he hears it, and whatever is understood is in the mind. And surely that-than-which-a-greater-cannot-be-thought cannot exist in the mind alone. For if it exists solely in the mind, it can be thought to exist in reality also, which is greater. If then that-than-which-a-greater-cannot-be-thought exists in the mind alone, this same that-than-which-a-greater-*cannot*-be-thought is that-than-which-a-greater-*can*-be-thought. But this is obviously impossible. Therefore there is absolutely no doubt that something-than-which-a-greater-cannot-be-thought exists both in the mind and in reality.

Let us now go through this argument stage by stage, interpreting Anselm's words as clearly and charitably as we can in contemporary terms, and identifying relevant problems and issues. For convenience, I shall abbreviate 'than-which-nothing-greater-can-be-thought' (and also the harmless variant 'than-which-a-greater-cannot-be-thought') as 'TWNG'.[4]

1 'Something-than-which-nothing-greater-can-be-thought exists in the mind'

The first two sentences in passage (A) are clearly aimed at demonstrating that something-TWNG 'exists in the mind', on the basis that the Fool

[3] This text is taken from the translation of Charlesworth (Anselm 1077/8: 87–8), differing from Charlesworth (1965) only in dropping the word 'even' after 'solely in the mind'. In Millican (2004: 439), I emended the fourth sentence in a way that Anscombe (1993) advocates and the Latin permits, to read 'For if it exists solely in the mind, something that is greater can be thought to exist in reality also.' (Duns Scotus also apparently preferred this interpretation; see the quotation in note 29 below.) But I have dropped the emendation here in recognition of the fact that a sentence in Anselm's *Reply to Gaunilo* II – 'For if it exists even in the mind alone, cannot it be thought to exist also in reality?' (p. 114) – can only properly be interpreted as involving *the same thing* existing also in reality. For more on this issue, see note 30 below.

[4] Here I have deliberately avoided subsuming the initial 'something-' or 'that-' within the abbreviation, since the variation between these two options may have logical significance (see Section 2.3 below). Keeping the acronym to four letters also makes it easy to pronounce, either to oneself or others, as 'twing'.

understands the formula and 'whatever is understood is in the mind'. Questions have been raised here both about the meaning of the formula itself, and about this potentially problematic notion of *existence in the mind.*

1.1 What Is 'Greatness'?

Anselm does not explicitly define what 'greater' means, though he goes on to argue that supreme greatness involves both *real existence* and possession of an impressive catalogue of divine qualities – 'whatever it is better to be than not to be' – which we can here simplify to *omnipotence, omniscience* and *perfect goodness* (henceforth '*omniperfection*').[5] Thus it seems to follow that, in general, *x* can be greater than *y* by having more impressive *power, knowledge* and *goodness*, and/or by having a higher degree of existence (e.g., in reality as opposed to the mind alone). For now, let us put aside the tricky question of how *x* and *y* are to be compared if these criteria pull in different directions (for example, if *x* is more powerful than *y* but less knowledgeable; or if *x* is omniperfect but in the mind only, while *y* is imperfect but exists in reality also). Perhaps Anselm might reasonably consider that such details can be ignored, for however they work out, it seems already to be clear that the ultimate limit of greatness – than which nothing greater can be thought – will be reached only by a really existing omniperfect being, i.e., God.[6]

1.2 What Is 'Existence in the Mind'?

The interpretation of existence 'in the mind' is constrained by Anselm's clear statement that 'whatever is understood is in the mind'. The level of 'understanding' required here indeed seems to be fairly minimal, since it is achieved by the Fool in so far as he merely 'understands what he hears'. Moreover in the text which has been elided from passage (A) above, Anselm tells us that a painter who 'plans beforehand what he is going to execute' has the envisaged picture 'in his mind'. So this form of 'existence' clearly

[5] The formula 'whatever it is better to be than not to be' is at *Proslogion* V and the relevant qualities include 'just, truthful, happy' (V), 'perceptive, omnipotent, merciful, impassible' (VI), 'living, wise, good, blessed' (XI), 'limitless and eternal' (XIII), existing 'everywhere and always' (XIV), without parts (XVIII) and 'outside all time' (XIX).

[6] Anselm's later argument in *Proslogion* III purports to show that even this level of greatness can be exceeded where the omniperfect being also has the property of *necessarily existing*, but we can ignore this here.

cannot require either deep understanding or full determinacy: it seems to be enough to be thinking of the relevant thing in the sense of having in mind an identifying concept of it.

We must avoid some well-known mistakes if this way of speaking is to escape absurdity or devastating parody (in the tradition of Gaunilo and Gassendi). First, if I think of a winged zebra, and thus a winged zebra 'exists in my mind', this cannot be taken to imply that a winged zebra *really is* somewhere – namely, in my mind – and that therefore a winged zebra *really exists*. If this were all that real existence required, then the real existence of God would be far too insubstantial to give any religious reassurance: Zeus, Vishnu, Thor, the Flying Spaghetti Monster – and even the immortal invisible rabbit that I have just invented on the spur of the moment – would all have real existence too. Secondly, if a winged zebra 'exists in my mind', this cannot be taken to imply that there is some specific winged zebra there, a zebra that has, for example, a particular number of stripes or a particular weight. For mere understanding of the phrase 'winged zebra' – which on Anselm's account suffices for mental existence – clearly implies no such detailed particularity.[7]

These points strongly suggest that talk of 'existence in the mind' is at best misleading in apparently conflating *my thinking of an X* with *there being an X of which I am thinking*. Obviously I can think of a unicorn without there being any *real* unicorn of which I am thinking; but this need not mean that instead there must be some *unicorn-in-my-mind* to which I bear that relation. The fallacy here becomes more obvious with other intentional attitudes: when I go searching for *a picture that will look good above my fireplace*, this does not mean that there must be (either in reality or my mind) some *specific* picture that I am looking for. Thinking relationally about some individual – whether real or mental – should not be taken as a model for all of our thinking, and if there is a risk of confusion or fallacy from talk reflecting that model, then we would be well advised to find some other way of expressing our reasonings about the Anselmian formula. We shall be returning to this issue very shortly (in Section 2.1 below).

[7] Moreover we are clearly unable to imagine any concrete entity (such as an animal) in all its detail. A real zebra must have a host of specific properties (including a particular weight, height, number of stripes, ancestry, genetic make-up, behavioural history, etc.). A merely imagined zebra can have at most a small proportion of these specific properties.

2 'That-than-which-a-greater-cannot-be-thought cannot exist in the mind alone'

The third sentence of passage (A) brings two new features into the argument. First, Anselm's terminology changes from *something*-TWNG to *that*-TWNG. Secondly, he now speaks of this as existing *beyond* 'the mind alone', which the following sentence then clarifies as meaning that it also exists 'in reality'. Let us deal first with the latter, since it relates closely to points just made.

2.1 Existence in the Mind and in Reality

Much of Anselm's argument seems to hinge on the idea that the same thing can potentially exist both in the mind and in reality, which – in the light of Section 1.2 above – is looking somewhat problematic. Quite apart from the issues specific to existence in the mind that we have already discussed, there are also potentially serious problems involving *identity* and *inconsistent predication.* To illustrate the former, and elaborating on Anselm's own example, suppose that a painter plans a painting of Canterbury Cathedral, perhaps with a view to presenting this to the Archbishop, and first executes his plan by producing the mediocre *PaintingA*, but then has another go and does better with *PaintingB*. Both of the real paintings match the initial plan, and on completing each of them, the painter could truthfully reply 'Yes' when asked 'Is that the painting you were planning to paint for the Archbishop?'. But they are clearly distinct from each other, so we cannot without contradiction say that they are both *one and the same thing* as the painting that was originally 'in the mind' of the painter (since identity is transitive: if x is identical with y, and y with z, then it follows that x is identical with z). Any would-be vindication of Anselm's argument that depends on a claim of literal identity between *that-TWNG* as it 'exists in the mind' and God as existing in reality must first do serious work to explain how such a theoretical framework can avoid absurdity. This sort of point is particularly significant given that Anselm's argument proceeds indirectly, by *reductio ad absurdum.* For if the argument is situated within a theoretical framework that is itself inconsistent, then the derivation of a contradiction from the Fool's initial atheist assumption cannot legitimately be presumed to refute that assumption: responsibility for the contradiction might lie within the framework itself.

Turning next to problems of predication (and leaving aside for the moment some further issues to be discussed in Section 3.1 below), suppose I return home to find my house burgled, having just seen a dark-haired man drive away. Is the *dark-haired burglar* in my mind identical to the light-haired man who actually burgled me? If so, then that individual combines being *really* light-haired with being *thought* dark-haired, so we must distinguish between real- and thought-predicates to avoid immediate contradiction. If, on the other hand, the men are not identical, then suppose I later think simply about *the burglar* (e.g., when reflecting on the theft rather than the car driver): that description *does* match to reality – i.e., to the light-haired man who actually committed the crime – so apparently there must now be two distinct burglars in my mind, one of whom is also real. If we then imagine a more complex scenario, with many predicates in play, it looks as though we could have an indefinite number of burglars in mind, some matching reality and some not. Making good sense of this might perhaps be possible, but it is far from obvious that contradiction is avoidable, and the onus is clearly on the proponent of such a theory to demonstrate its plausibility, before attempting to persuade us that a successful Ontological Argument can be built on it.

None of this is intended to cast doubt on the natural idea that our thought often concerns real, objective things; nor on the appropriateness of describing such things as being 'in our mind' in a non-literal sense, most obviously when our thoughts are caused by conscious *perceptions* of them. In such cases, indeed, it is tempting to say that those perceptions are *essentially* of the objects concerned (so that perceptions caused by different objects, even if qualitatively similar, would count as numerically different perceptions).[8] Even then, however, it is highly problematic to *identify* external and internal 'objects' (because, for example, we can have multiple distinct perceptions of a single external object, without realizing that we are doing so). And anyway this sort of option is available only if we are prepared to presuppose that *there is some corresponding object*, which in the case of the Ontological Argument would obviously beg the question. Some commentators, encouraged by the prayer-like language with which *Proslogion* II begins, have suggested that it

[8] This point about individuation does not imply that we grasp some essence of the object in perceiving it; nor does it require any commitment to such essences. Anselm himself seems to believe in individual essences that exist prior to God actualizing them (e.g., *Monologion* IX–X), but his Ontological Argument is unlikely now to gain plausibility from being tied to such a framework, which raises plenty of problems of its own. One obvious issue would be the need to distinguish between genuine essences that are considered suitable for grounding an Ontological Argument, and arbitrary descriptions that lead to parodies. Special pleading in favour of God (e.g., Anselm's claim in *Monologion* XVII that God's properties all cohere in a uniquely simple essence, or Descartes's claim that 'necessary existence ... forms a part of [God's] essence as it does of no other thing', *Replies* 5 (Descartes (1641: 263)) is a common recourse, but gratuitous unless independently justified: it is up to any would-be Ontological Argument to *prove* that God has a special status, and this cannot properly be taken for granted (cf. Millican (2004: 449n.22)).

should be interpreted as unfolding the implications of a direct revelation of God's nature as *that-TWNG*, but then it ceases to be an Ontological Argument as generally understood.[9] This also seems hard to square with Anselm's language, which explicitly specifies God's nature using a description that he takes to be understood by the sceptical Fool without presupposing any such revelation.

2.2 Concepts and Appropriate Charity

The problems raised in Sections 1.2 and 2.1 above give ample reason to avoid analysing Anselm's reasoning in the naive terms that his own text suggests, involving things that literally 'exist in the mind' and can also – equally literally and without affecting their identity – 'exist in reality'. For if his argument's plausibility turns out to depend crucially on the peculiarities of this framework and the conflations it embodies, then so far from supporting the argument, this will simply confirm suspicions that the framework it builds on is dubious, sanctioning inferences that cannot be verified by other means. To accept an argument that can work *only* within such a problematic framework would be taking philosophical charity too far.

To be fair to Anselm, however, we should avoid being overcritical of his language where it can be interpreted in ways that avoid any serious error or conflation. In most cases this is entirely possible, by understanding 'existence in the mind' in terms of *concept possession*, 'existence in reality' in terms of *concept instantiation*, and *greatness* as a property of concepts.[10] We also have to allow – somewhat in tension with the sensibilities that contemporary philosophers have inherited from Kant and Frege – that a concept's greatness can depend on whether it is actually instantiated (or in Anselmian language 'exists in reality'). This then makes it possible to accept Anselm's account of both the painter and the Fool in appropriate terms. The painter, having completed the anticipated picture, 'both has it in his mind and understands that it exists because he has now made it': the painted picture

[9] For more on non-standard interpretations, see the references in Millican (2004: 440n.5).

[10] In Millican (2004), I preferred the word 'nature' (following the terminology of both Anselm and Descartes) to 'concept', so as to have a technical term that could serve as the basis for a 'theory of natures' designed to maximize the prospects for a valid Anselmian argument. Using a special term also avoided the relatively stark mismatch between Anselm's own language – talking of things that exist both in the mind and in reality – and our modern talk of 'concepts', which seem unambiguously mental. But such choices of theoretical terminology make no difference to the main logical points that follow, as long as appropriate distinctions are respected to avoid absurdities of the kinds already discussed.

is not literally *the very same thing* as the concept of the picture, but is an *instantiation* of it. In the same way, *that-TWNG* 'exists in the Fool's mind' in so far as the Fool possesses that concept, and it can also 'exist in reality' if the concept is instantiated by something real that answers to Anselm's formula.

2.3 'Something' and 'That'

Anselm's switching between *something*-TWNG and *that*-TWNG might be merely harmless 'elegant variation' in wording. It has also been interpreted in a more problematic way, as deviously introducing the unjustified assumption that *there is* some such particular being, with 'that-TWNG' purporting to pick it out. More sympathetically, Anselm's switching terminology has been compared to the use of 'existential elimination' within natural deduction, whereby an existentially quantified variable is replaced with an 'arbitrary name'.[11] On this account, having established that *some* X exists within the mind, Anselm is now referring to *that* X – the very one that is within the mind. Though ingenious, however, this last reading is philosophically problematic given what we have said earlier. For Anselm has not established that some X – i.e., *some particular thing that is an X* – exists within the mind.[12] The most he has any right to claim is that the mind has grasped *the concept of X*, which is a quite different matter. So if this reading faithfully reflects Anselm's thinking, then it would appear to betray a temptation towards the incoherent views dismissed in Sections 1.2 and 2.1 above. The most philosophically charitable approach, therefore, is to adopt the simple 'elegant variation' hypothesis or – almost equivalently – to take 'that-TWNG' to be referring back to the already-identified *concept* 'something-TWNG'. Either way, we should understand these two phrases as intended to refer to the very same mental concept.

[11] As in Campbell (1976: 31–4). Suppose, for example, that I am reasoning from the premises $\exists x Fx$ and $\forall x(Fx \rightarrow Gx)$ to the conclusion $\exists x Gx$. The first step is to use an arbitrary name, say '*a*', for some individual that has the property F, as implied by the first premise. Then from Fa the second premise can be used to deduce *Ga*, and from this $\exists x Gx$ follows.

[12] Theists might be tempted to resist the idea that God is 'a particular thing', and argue that the logic goes differently in His case. But no such special pleading is apparent in Anselm's text, which treats the establishment of God's existence in the mind as a straightforward instance of a general truth, applicable to anything we understand or envisage.

3 'For if it exists solely in the mind, it can be thought to exist in reality also, which is greater. If then that-than-which-a-greater-cannot-be-thought exists in the mind alone, This same that-than-which-a-greater-*cannot*-be-thought is that-than-which-a-greater-*can*-be-thought. But this is obviously impossible. Therefore there is absolutely no doubt that something-than-which-a-greater-cannot-be-thought exists both in the mind and in reality.'

These final sentences of passage (A), in which the Fool is convicted of contradiction and thus supposedly refuted, are especially confusing. We start with the supposition of the concept *that-TWNG* being *uninstantiated*, and are then told that if this supposition were true, it would be possible to think of this same concept's being *instantiated*, and thus being greater than it is. Hence the uninstantiated *that-TWNG* would turn out to be that-than-which-a-greater-*can*-be-thought, a result that looks 'obviously impossible', and thus completes the *reductio* of the Fool's atheism.

3.1 A Crucial Ambiguity: Characterization versus Description

Let us start with the second sentence, which in Charlesworth's translation appears to state that, if uninstantiated, *that-TWNG* would be *that-than-which-a-greater-can-be-thought*: one concept would, apparently, become a different concept entirely. This seems an absurd claim, and therefore philosophical charity should lead us to prefer Logan's translation, according to which *that-TWNG* is threatened not with turning into another concept, but rather (without losing its identity) becoming *something than which a greater can be thought*, on the straightforward ground that if it is uninstantiated, then its greatness would be capable of being exceeded.[13]

This issue illustrates how talking of a concept as *something than which no greater can be thought* can be interpreted in two quite different ways, as referring to either:

(i) that specific concept whose content is: *something-than-which-no-greater-can-be-thought*; or

[13] 'If therefore that than which a greater cannot be thought is in the understanding alone, that same thing than which a greater cannot be thought is [something] than which a greater can be thought' (Logan (2009: 33)).

(ii) whichever concept can be correctly described as being *a concept than which no greater can be thought*.

In the former case, Anselm's formula acts as a *content specification* or *characterization* of the concept in question. In the latter case, the formula acts as a *description* of the concept in question. And when we consider the possibility that *something-TWNG* might be exceeded in greatness and would thus turn out to be *something than which a greater can be thought*, we are mixing together the language of characterization (i.e., identifying the concept in terms of its content as *something-TWNG*) with the language of description (i.e., saying that the concept thus identified is less than supremely great).

Mixing our language in this way need not be philosophically objectionable, but it does require great care if we are to avoid fallacy. Some concepts possess the very properties that characterize them: for example, the concept *widely shared* is itself a widely shared concept, the concept *abstract* is itself abstract, and the concept *sophisticated* is itself sophisticated. But on the other hand, the concept *rare* is not a rare concept, the concept *surprising* is not surprising, and the concept *non-existent* is not non-existent. So we need sharply to distinguish between two quite different kinds of property that can be associated with a concept. On the one hand, the *internal* or *characteristic* properties of a concept define *which concept it is, in terms of its content*: for example, the concept of an omniperfect being, or of an equilateral triangle, or of a winged zebra. On the other hand, the *external, descriptive* properties of a concept do not determine its *identity*: they are typically properties that the concept has in virtue of its relations with other things, for example, that it is present in the Fool's mind, or widely shared, or instantiated in reality.[14] The latter properties can thus be used to identify the concept *descriptively* (e.g., 'the concept that was in my mind just a moment ago', 'the most impressive concept I have thought about this week'), but they do so without specifying its conceptual content. Concepts can also, of course, be referred to using mixtures of internal and external properties (e.g., 'the last geometric concept I thought of').

Given this background, it is crucial to recognize that we have no reason to assume in general that the *characterizing descriptions* of a concept – those that specify its conceptual content – should also correctly *describe* the concept

[14] To avoid absurd consequences, Meinongian theories of objects standardly draw a related distinction between *nuclear* and *extranuclear* properties, whereby the former characterize the nature of an 'entity', and the latter such things as its ontological or modal status (e.g., existent, fictional, mythical, possible or impossible) and whether it is an object of intentional attitudes (e.g., believed or worshipped). See, for example, Parsons (1980: 22–6) and Jacquette (1994: 236–7).

itself; indeed they will do so only in very special cases. And hence if Anselm's argument is found to trade implicitly on such an assumption, it is to that extent fallacious. If, for example, we allow ourselves to conflate characterizing and external descriptions, then we might quickly conclude that the Fool contradicts himself, in having within his mind the incoherent concept of *a-not-really-existing-being-than-which-nothing-greater-can-be-thought. But* this would be quite unjustified, for as Mackie points out (1982: 52), the rational Fool has in his mind the concept whose characteristic content is *a-being-than-which-nothing-greater-can-be-thought*, but he simply denies that it is instantiated (i.e., that anything in reality matches up to that concept). If we thus carefully separate *characterizing* from *external* properties of the key concept, we can see very clearly that the Fool is quite innocent of any such crude contradiction.

3.2 The Aquinas Rebuttal

Thomas Aquinas rejected Anselm's argument, and although his objection to it is notoriously unclear, his words suggest that he might have noticed exactly the fallacy just mentioned. For he states that the following combination of claims leaves the atheist with 'no difficulty':[15]

(i) That which is indicated by the name *God* – i.e., *that-TWNG* – exists only in the intellect and not in reality.
(ii) Something greater can be thought than anything given in reality or in the intellect.

The consistency of this pair of claims would seem to imply that the concept *that-TWNG* can exist in the mind and yet be exceeded in greatness. And this is indeed possible, if the concept's own *surpassable* greatness is taken to be an *external* property of the concept, distinct from the property of being *unsurpassably* great which provides the concept's *content* (and which therefore must be true of anything that falls under it). Hence Aquinas is apparently correct in denying that the atheist can be convicted of self-contradiction, in which case Anselm's *reductio* argument fails.

[15] 'Now, from the fact that that which is indicated by the name *God* is conceived by the mind, it does not follow that God exists save only in the intellect. Hence, that than which a greater cannot be thought will likewise not have to exist save only in the intellect . . . No difficulty, consequently, befalls anyone who posits that God does not exist. For that something greater can be thought than anything given in reality or in the intellect is a difficulty only to him who admits that there is something than which a greater cannot be thought in reality' (Aquinas (1975: 82)).

The point here is subtle, and easily overlooked by those attracted to the Ontological Argument. Lynne Rudder Baker and Gareth Matthews (2010: 47–8), for example, slide seamlessly – and apparently without noticing that a significant move has been made – from 'That than which nothing greater can be conceived is an object that exists in . . . the atheist's understanding' to 'Let S be the object that exists in the . . . atheist's understanding and that is such that nothing greater can be conceived.' The rational atheist may accept *that-than-which-nothing-greater-can-be-conceived* as a *characterization* of an object of his thought, but he should then absolutely deny the supposed implication that this object is *such that* – i.e., *correctly described* as being such that – nothing greater can be conceived.[16] In the same way, *that-than-which-nothing-more-surprising-can-be-conceived* is currently an object of my thought in the sense that I am pondering the concept thus characterized. But it is not itself particularly surprising, and I can easily conceive of things that have been or would be more surprising.

3.3 Kant and Descartes

Kant's famous dictum – often cited in the form 'existence is not a predicate' – occurs within a discussion in his *Critique of Pure Reason* which is in parts confusing and perhaps confused. But the key point is made in terms which resonate clearly with the discussion above:

> 'Being' is obviously not a real predicate; that is, it is not a concept of something which could be added to the concept of a thing. It is merely the positing of a thing . . . If . . . we . . . say 'God is', we attach no new predicate to the concept of God, but only posit the subject in itself with all its predicates, and indeed posit it as being an *object* that stands in relation to my *concept* . . . Whatever, therefore, and however much, our concept of an object may contain, we must go outside it, if we are to ascribe existence to the object. (Kant (1781: 504–6))

Kant can naturally be read here as intending to say that *existence* is to be understood, not as a *characterizing* property of a concept – i.e., one that defines it or determines its content – but rather as an *external* property which applies if the concept is *instantiated* (that is, if some real object 'stands in relation' to it). This seems both sensible and persuasive, explaining why Kant's diagnosis has

[16] In this paragraph, I use the term 'conceived' rather than 'thought', to follow Baker and Matthews.

been so influential, though as we shall see, there are further twists to be negotiated before we can consider Anselm's argument as refuted.

Kant's own primary target was not Anselm's argument but the far simpler Cartesian variant (which had been further elaborated by Spinoza and Leibniz). And Descartes does straightforwardly treat *existence* as a characterizing property of his idea of God, thus putting it alongside omnipotence, omniscience and perfect goodness as one of the definitive divine perfections:

> the idea of God [is that of] a supremely perfect being . . . Hence it is . . . a contradiction to think of God (that is, a supremely perfect being) lacking existence (that is, lacking a perfection) . . .' (Meditation 5, CSM ii 45–6)

Kant overstates his case, however, in implying that it is always and obviously a logical crime to treat 'real existence' as a characterizing property. In thinking of famous monarchs, we might wish to distinguish between those that we know to be fictional (e.g., Tolkien's Aragorn), and those that we consider as real historical figures (e.g., England's Henry VIII).[17] But in context this is a nitpicking detail, because it is clearly the *external* property of real instantiation that is the central issue between the theist and the atheist: the theist believes there to be a real object 'that stands in relation' to the concept in question, while the atheist denies it.[18] This point is closely linked to a crucial difference between the *internal* and *external* properties of our concepts, namely, that the former – but not the latter – are, in general, 'up to us': we can define concepts as we choose, and include within them whatever properties we wish (e.g., we can contemplate the concept of a real historical king with the qualities of Aragorn). But having thus defined them, we cannot then choose whether or not there is a genuine reality that corresponds to them: that is a matter of fact that depends on how the world happens to be. Interpreted along these lines, Kant's critique of Descartes is right on target, but as we shall see, Anselm's argument is harder to pin down and neutralize.

[17] Cases whose historicity is uncertain, such as the legendary King Arthur, raise further complications though without affecting the key point here.

[18] The theist and atheist can agree that the concept of Jehovah purports to be of a real god, and the concept of Zephyrus (from Terry Pratchett's *Discworld*) of a fictional god. What is at issue between them is not what is built into the theist's preferred concept of God, but whether there is a genuine external reality that corresponds to it.

4 Reconceiving Anselm's Argument

So far, we have been following mainstream philosophical tradition in treating Anselm's argument as involving a concept whose content is *something-than-which-nothing-greater-can-be-thought* (*something-TWNG*). This makes it relevantly similar to Descartes's argument, and subject to Kant's critique: *real existence* is being smuggled into the *internal* content of the concept (under the guise of 'greatness'), but for the argument to succeed, it needs to be established as an *external* property of the concept. There is, however, another way of understanding Anselm's argument – generally overlooked in critical discussions – which is quite different from the Cartesian conception and can evade Kantian objections. This involves *consistently* interpreting the Anselmian formula as an external description of the key concept, rather than as an internal specification of its content.

In Section 1.1 above, we saw that Anselm's notion of *greatness* involves some mixture of *power*, *knowledge*, *goodness* and *degree of existence*.[19] We then discovered – leading up to Section 2.2 – that his argument needs to be couched in terms of *concepts*, and later – in Sections 3.1 and 3.3 – that although *power*, *knowledge* and *goodness* can appropriately be considered as characterizing or internal properties of a concept, *real existence* (in the sense that Anselm is trying to prove against the Fool) seems clearly external.[20] Suppose, therefore, that we accordingly recognize *greatness* to be a hybrid property that depends on a combination of a concept's internal and external properties. This enables us to follow Anselm as before, accepting – exactly as stated in Section 1.1 above – that '*x* can be greater than *y* by having more impressive *power*, *knowledge* and *goodness*, and/or by having a higher degree of existence'. Let us now note explicitly, however, that since *greatness* so understood involves an external element, *it is not a property that can be settled by definition*: we may be able to define a concept as we like, but it is not then 'up to us' how *great* that concept will be, because its greatness will depend – at least in part – on the external question of whether or not it 'exists', i.e., is instantiated in reality. Indeed this feature of greatness is crucial if Anselm's argument is to have any chance of success. For the Fool can be

[19] As before (cf. notes 5 and 6), we are here abbreviating the relevant catalogue of great-making properties to simplify discussion.

[20] Again there might be a sense in which 'real existence' can be included as an internal property of a concept, but then it ceases to be the point at issue between the theist and the atheist. See Millican (2004: 453–4) for more on this.

refuted only if the key concept's greatness implies its real instantiation, and this can be so only if its level of greatness depends on that instantiation.[21]

Now let us set out to identify which concept actually satisfies the description: *that-concept-than-which-no-greater-concept-can-be-thought* (avoiding the '*TWNG*' abbreviation to emphasize that this version of the Anselmian formula is intended to be *descriptive* of the concept in question, rather than *characterizing* it). Whichever concept this is, it presumably scores well in terms of the internal properties of *power*, *knowledge* and *goodness*, for otherwise it would surely be possible to think of a greater concept. But also, it seems plausible that this concept must be *really instantiated*, because if it were not, then again it would presumably be possible to think of a greater concept. So at last, perhaps, we have the materials for a proof that the concept which descriptively satisfies the Anselmian formula – *that-concept-than-which-no-greater-concept-can-be-thought* – both combines the godlike internal qualities of *power*, *knowledge* and *goodness*, and also is *really instantiated*. This looks like progress!

4.1 Which Is the Greatest Concept?

A problem emerges, however, if we probe more deeply into the hybrid nature of 'greatness', with its combination of internal and external properties. To focus only on the most central issue, and for the sake of simplicity, let us charitably assume that the relevant internal properties – *power*, *knowledge* and *goodness* – are mutually commensurable, so that any combination of these can be given a single greatness 'score' that enables appropriate comparisons to be made.[22] Again for simplicity, let us assume that the relevant

[21] This simple point alone seems to be enough to wreck any prospect for Anselm's argument if *greatness* is interpreted as purely internal. Thus the approach described in this section – treating the Anselmian formula as a *description* rather than as a *characterization* of the key concept – provides, I suggest, the only chance of vindicating or salvaging anything from it. Note also that modal versions of the Ontological Argument, which are the only versions commonly considered to be valid, likewise standardly evade the Kantian objection by using an *external* definition of the relevant entity (in terms of its status across possible worlds). In thus avoiding invalidity, however, they run into the problem that if the entity is defined in such a way that its existence cannot be contingent, then claiming that it is *possible* simply begs the question against the atheist, while Humean principles (cf. note 35 below) make *impossibility* far more plausible. Such arguments are also subject to parody, since for example a *necessarily existing flying zebra* cannot be contingent (and hence, if possible, must be necessary). For a comment along these lines specifically on Plantinga's argument, see Millican (2004: 469n.44).

[22] Without this assumption, greatness comparisons between concepts could become indeterminate where, for example, concept *x* is characterized as involving more power than concept *y*, but less knowledge or goodness. In Section 1.1 we allowed Anselm to ignore the detail of how greatness is

external quality – *degree of existence* – is straightforwardly binary: either a concept is *really instantiated*, or it is (at best) *only in the mind*.[23] These two assumptions together imply (i) that among all the possible concepts that are actually instantiated, there will be some specific highest level of greatness *MaxI*; and also (ii) that among all the possible concepts that are actually uninstantiated, there will be some specific highest level of greatness *MaxU*.[24] For simplicity, let us now add a third assumption, that there is just one *instantiated* concept whose greatness reaches *MaxI*, and just one *uninstantiated* concept whose greatness reaches *MaxU* – this will allow us, in each case, to refer without ambiguity to 'the concept' which does so.[25] This gives us two possible candidates for satisfaction of our Anselmian formula: *that-concept-than-which-no-greater-concept-can-be-thought*. It seems that the successful candidate must either be the instantiated concept that achieves greatness level *MaxI*, or the uninstantiated concept that achieves greatness level *MaxU*.

The theist and atheist will disagree about the values of both *MaxI* and *MaxU*, and may also disagree about which is higher. But they can agree that the following concept – in virtue of its unsurpassable *characteristic* properties – will feature *either* as the greatest instantiated concept, *or* as the greatest uninstantiated concept:[26]

[God]: [omniperfect, creator of the universe]

The actual greatness of this concept will depend on whether or not it is instantiated; let us suppose that this value is *G* if it is instantiated, and *g* otherwise. Since instantiation is (we are assuming) the only external great-making property, *G* will be the highest level of greatness that any concept could possibly achieve (and *g* is obviously lower). As far as the theist is

constituted, since it seemed clear that the ultimate limit of greatness will be reached only by a really existing omniperfect being. Here we continue to allow him to ignore such detail in respect of internal properties, but can no longer do so when considering the interplay between these and real instantiation.

23 But we shall not restrict our discussion to concepts that are *actually* 'in the mind', because Anselm's 'can-be-thought' clearly suggests that the relevant domain should include all *thinkable* concepts.

24 Note that the values of *MaxI* and *MaxU* will depend on which concepts are actually instantiated, whereas *G*, *g* and *A* (to be introduced shortly) are intended to represent specific levels of greatness.

25 All of these assumptions are intended to be 'friendly' to Anselm's argument, by reducing complications and making it easier for the argument to work, if indeed there is *any way* that it can work. If the following discussion turned out to vindicate Anselm, then it would be appropriate to revisit the assumptions and examine whether they are actually tenable.

26 We here adopt the convention of using square brackets to enclose both the names of concepts and their list of characteristic (i.e., defining) properties.

concerned, then, ($MaxI = G$) and clearly ($MaxU < G$); hence *that-concept-than-which-no-greater-concept-can-be-thought* is [God].

From the atheist point of view, however, things are less straightforward: all we can conclude so far is that ($MaxU = g$), since [God] is then the greatest *uninstantiated* concept, and we do not yet know what value *MaxI* has, nor how this compares with *g*. In order to work these things out, we need to know which concept is the greatest *instantiated* concept, and as far as the atheist is concerned, that cannot be a concept that carries any implication of divinity (for short, not a 'divine' concept). To facilitate our discussion, then, let us suppose that the concept in question is:[27]

> [Aurelius]: [absolute Emperor of the Roman Empire, wise, just, beneficent]

and that the greatness of this concept is *A*. For the atheist, therefore, ($MaxI = A$), and we can now ask, from his point of view: how does *A*, the greatness of the *instantiated* concept [Aurelius], compare with *g*, the greatness of the *uninstantiated* concept [God]? The latter obviously has more impressive *characteristic* properties, but might this advantage be outweighed by the difference between them in *instantiation*?

4.2 The Principle of the Superiority of Existence

Faced with exactly this sort of question, Millican (2004: 451) proposed another simplifying assumption:

> [N]othing that Anselm says makes clear what advantages in other respects, if any, are sufficient to outweigh the additional share of greatness that is conferred on a [concept] which is instantiated in reality as compared with one which is not. At this point, therefore, it will considerably streamline our discussion if we make a simplifying assumption which, though not unquestionably Anselmian, at least has the authority of having been stated by his correspondent Gaunilo without being contested by him. Namely, that among the various criteria for greatness (power, wisdom, goodness etc.), real existence 'trumps' all others, so that any [concept] which has a real archetype, however lowly its characteristic properties may be, will on

[27] For explanation of this supposition, see Millican (2004: 456, especially n.31, and 463). As in the case of [God] – cf. note 19 above – it might be possible to define a greater concept by including further properties such as 'celebrated Stoic writer'. Such complications can be ignored here, but for discussion, see Millican (2004: §5, especially 453n.28).

that account alone be greater than any [concept], however impressively characterized, which does not.

Yujin Nagasawa (2007), in his critique of my analysis, called this assumption *The Principle of the Superiority of Existence* (PSE), disputed its faithfulness to Anselm and suggested that it unfairly weakened his Ontological Argument.

I agree that Anselm might well reject PSE,[28] but deny that the principle weakens his argument, which fails either way. If, on the one hand, PSE is *true*, then [Aurelius] is, according to the atheist, the greatest of all concepts, outscoring [God] on the basis of its instantiation, and hence ($A > g$). PSE accordingly forces the atheist to accept the instantiation of *that-concept-than-which-no-greater-concept-can-be-thought*, thus potentially yielding a valid proof of existence.[29] But this is no real concession, of course, for the concept thus vindicated will not be divine. If, on the other hand, PSE is *false*, then it might well be that ($g > A$), in which case the atheist must accept that [God] can qualify as the greatest of all concepts *even if it is not instantiated.* But this again yields no victory to the theist, for if indeed [God] can qualify as that-concept-than-which-no-greater-concept-can-be-thought even if it is not instantiated, then clearly the atheist cannot be convicted of inconsistency for denying its instantiation. Anselm cannot have it both ways against the atheist: *either* he can accept PSE and thus define 'greatness' in such a way that the greatest of all concepts *must be instantiated*; *or* he can reject PSE and define 'greatness' in such a way that the greatest of all concepts *must be [God].* But he cannot ensure both of these simultaneously unless [God] is indeed instantiated, which is just what the atheist denies.

4.3 Supreme Greatness: Actual and Hypothetical

These conclusions are likely to be intensely frustrating to the advocate of the Ontological Argument. We have highlighted three main levels of greatness to consider:

[28] Smith (2014: 92–3) argues persuasively that the principle is contradicted by the logic of Anselm's reasoning in V of the *Reply to Gaunilo*, and also by a sentence in VIII which he translates: 'very much better than this [something temporal without beginning or end] is that which in no way lacks anything, nor is forced to change or move – whether something of this kind actually exists or not'.

[29] John Duns Scotus adopts PSE in a discussion whose explicit aim is to *strengthen* Anselm's argument: 'The thinkable which exists in reality is greater than that which exists only in a mind. This is not to be understood to mean that one and the same item if it is thought of is a greater thinkable if it actually exists [than if it does not]; rather it means that something which exists is greater than anything which exists only in the mind' (Bosley and Tweedale (2006: 112, *Ordinatio* I, dist. 2, qu. 2.5.2). William of Ockham follows him in this also: see note 34 below.

A: the greatest of the greatest *instantiated non-divine* concept (e.g., [Aurelius]);
g: the greatness of the concept [God] when *uninstantiated*;
G: the greatness of the concept [God] when *instantiated*.

The Anselmian formula, interpreted as a *description* of the relevant concept, purports to refer to *that-concept-than-which-no-greater-concept-can-be-thought*. The atheist can be forced to accept that this formula successfully refers to a concept whose greatness reaches the level of *A* or *g*, whichever is higher (potentially depending on PSE). But this is not enough for the theist, who wants to force the atheist to accept reference to a concept that reaches the ultimate level of greatness *G*. If this could be achieved, then the atheist – in accepting reference to a concept of such immense greatness – would have to admit that this can only be an instantiated concept of an omniperfect being; hence such a being must exist.

The theist's frustration is understandable, because we are evidently able to *think about* the level of greatness *G* that would belong to the instantiated concept [God].[30] This supreme level of greatness would be unsurpassable even in thought, and is therefore *the highest level of greatness that can be thought*. Why, then, cannot the atheist be forced to accept that reference is made to this instantiated concept [God] through the formula *that-concept-than-which-no-greater-concept-can-be-thought*? The answer, of course, is that the atheist does not accept that the concept is, in fact, instantiated. So from his point of view, there is no 'instantiated concept [God]' to be referred to. He can accept that *we are able to think of the concept [God] as instantiated*, but if we do this, we are imagining it within a *different* reality, one in which God exists. Hence the atheist can only accept reference to *that-concept-whose-greatness-is-G* as succeeding *hypothetically*: as applying to

[30] This is the point that Anselm seems to be making when he says: 'For if it [i.e., *that-TWNG*] exists solely in the mind, it can be thought to exist in reality also, which is greater.' As mentioned in note 3 above, in Millican (2004) I preferred a different translation of this sentence, namely 'For if it exists solely in the mind, something that is greater can be thought to exist in reality also.' The latter is less philosophically problematic, because it can be fulfilled – at least if PSE is assumed – by the comparison in actual greatness between [God] and [Aurelius], whereas Charlesworth's translation requires a comparison between [God]'s actual and hypothetical greatness, as discussed below. The avoidance of such complications was helpful in Millican (2004), where a major part of my aim was to show that – despite all the many 'deep' philosophical objections that have been thrown at it – Anselm's argument potentially bears a valid interpretation, albeit one that cannot refute the atheist (e.g., because it proves the instantiation of [Aurelius] rather than [God]). For an interesting discussion of the implications of various readings of the crucial sentence, see Mann (2012, especially III).

that concept which, *if it were instantiated*, would reach that ultimate level of greatness. And this is not enough for the purposes of Anselm's argument, for if the atheist is only considering [God] as reaching greatness of level *G hypothetically*, then he cannot be forced to consider [God] as genuinely instantiated *in reality*.

To put this another way, the theist is attempting to persuade the atheist that reference has been made to a concept of such unsurpassable greatness *G* that it can only be a concept of *instantiated* divinity. Obviously the atheist does not accept that any concept *actually* reaches this level of greatness, but he is persuadable that reference can be made to what the theist has in mind by reference to its *hypothetical* greatness. Thus the concept can be identified – in the thought of both the theist and the atheist – as the concept that *can be thought* to reach such a level of greatness. But having used this ploy to convince the atheist that reference to the concept in question is achievable, the theist cannot *simultaneously* claim that the achievement of reference to such a supremely great concept then inevitably implies that concept's *actual* instantiation. As before, he cannot have it both ways against the atheist: the greatness of the relevant concept can be assessed either *in reality* or *hypothetically*, but not both at the same time. If assessed in reality, the atheist will not accept that any concept at all reaches level *G* of greatness. If assessed hypothetically, the atheist may well accept that the concept [God] *can be thought* to reach such a level of greatness (by thinking of it as instantiated), but since this is only *hypothetical* greatness, he is not forced to accept that such greatness is *really* reached, and hence he cannot be forced to accept that the concept is *really* instantiated.[31]

[31] In Millican (2004: §8) and (2007: §2), I suggest that a similar sort of dilemma can be applied against many other Ontological Arguments (including those of Descartes and Plantinga: see Millican (2004: 469–70)). The arguments in question first purport to make reference to some 'entity' (concept, essence, nature, type, or whatever) whose 'reality' (actuality, existence, instantiation, or whatever) is to be proved; they then aim to demonstrate that the entity in question cannot fail to be real. Critics of such arguments have tended to focus on challenging the theoretical framework within which they are couched (e.g., whether it is legitimate to talk of non-existent things, or to treat existence as a property). But a more straightforward attack is to accept the theoretical framework and then simply ask: 'Is it necessary, in order to qualify as the entity referred to, that the entity in question should *really* exist as described?'. If the answer is 'yes', then there will be serious questions over whether successful reference is achieved in the first place; if 'no', then the inference to reality fails. Insisting on an answer to this dilemma can inhibit the proponent of the Ontological Argument from trying to have it both ways, adopting one interpretation when arguing that reference succeeds, and another when arguing that successful reference implies real existence.

4.4 The Seductive Ambiguity of Anselm's Formula

We have now seen that proper consideration of Anselm's Ontological Argument requires clarity about two important distinctions: between *characterization* and *description* of a concept (in Section 3.1 above) and between *hypothetical* and *actual* greatness (in Section 4.3). It is easy to conflate these, since the characterizing descriptions of a concept X tell us what properties an X will have *if there is one*, while the external descriptions typically pick out the concept in terms of its *actual* properties. But they are not the same distinction, and we have seen that Anselm's argument can be framed without violating the first of them (by unambiguously interpreting his formula in terms of *external* descriptions) yet in a way that trades on a conflation between hypothetical and actual properties.

Most versions of the Ontological Argument fall foul of the first distinction, and can be disposed of relatively straightforwardly once that is recognized. Anselm's version is more tenacious, and his clever wording also makes it especially easy to overlook the second distinction, because the phrase 'can be thought' is interpretable in two quite different ways. When we survey the range of concept-greatnesses that 'can be thought' with a view to identifying the relevant maximum, we might intend to consider:

(i) *the maximum greatness of all thinkable concepts (as they stand)*;

or we might wish to cast our net wider, to:

(ii) *the maximum greatness of any thinkable concept in any thinkable scenario.*

On interpretation (i), *the greatest concept that can be thought* will be whichever concept *is in fact* the greatest, which the atheist (assuming PSE for simplicity here) will take to be [Aurelius]. On interpretation (ii) – superficially more promisingly for the theist – it will be [God], since this concept *can be thought* to be supremely great (i.e., in the thinkable scenario that theism is true). But the atheist can happily accept this too, because if [God] qualifies as *the greatest concept that can be thought* only in virtue of its *hypothetical* greatness, then he cannot be forced to infer that the concept so described must also be supremely great *in reality*. What the atheist should refuse to accept, however, is the theist's mixing of the actual and hypothetical domains, by considering:

(iii) the greatness of that thinkable concept which is (as things stand) at least as great as any concept can be thought to be.

Note the significant change here: whereas interpretations (i) and (ii) straightforwardly select the maximum greatness from some *consistent* domain of concepts and their degrees of greatness, interpretation (iii) purports to select – from a *restricted* domain (i.e., thinkable concepts and their *current* degree of greatness) – a concept whose greatness reaches the maximum that is achievable in a *vastly extended* domain (i.e., the degrees of greatness that any thinkable concepts can be thought to reach, in *any possible* scenario). To suppose that (iii) even succeeds in achieving reference, therefore, is to make a very substantial assumption, namely, that some concept *currently reaches* that supreme level of greatness that could only be reached by an *actually instantiated* concept of an omniperfect being. The atheist can reasonably deny this assumption, and thus insist that (iii) fails to refer: in his view, *there is no concept that great.*

This discussion shows that Anselm's key formula, *that-than-which-nothing-greater-can-be-thought*, can be understood in at least three different ways depending on the implied scope of the phrase 'can be thought'. These different interpretations can be neatly schematized as follows:

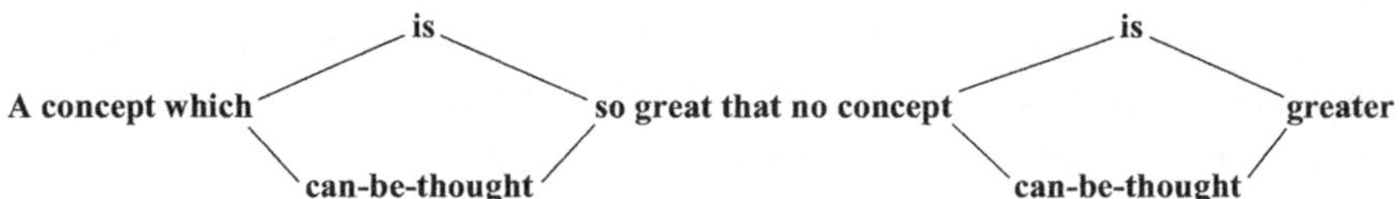

Interpretation (i) involves choosing 'is' at both selection points, thus focusing consistently on the *actual* greatness of thinkable concepts.[32] Interpretation (ii) involves choosing 'can-be-thought' at both selection points, thus focusing consistently on the wider domain of concepts' greatnesses across the entire range of thinkable scenarios. Interpretation (iii) involves selecting 'is' at the first selection point and 'can-be-thought' at the second, thus illicitly taking for granted that some concept *actually* reaches the maximal level of greatness that can be reached in any thinkable scenario. The fact that these three interpretations – of such contrasting philosophical significance – can all be represented so easily within a single structure illustrates the seductive slipperiness of Anselm's formula. If this crucial ambiguity goes unnoticed, then his argument can appear to succeed.[33]

[32] Note that even on this reading, 'can be thought' in Anselm's formula is not redundant, since it clarifies that all thinkable concepts are being considered – we are not restricted to concepts that are *actually* thought.

[33] Logan (2009: 170, 181) argues that Anselm's formula *something-TWNG* – abbreviated to the atomic term 'X' – is intended to provide a uniquely suitable 'middle term of a syllogism that establishes the existence of God', this syllogism taking the form: 'God is X, X is F, therefore God is F.' Interpretatively this seems plausible, especially in the light of Logan's discussion of the prior logical tradition, but even if correct as an account of Anselm's own thinking, it cannot vindicate his argument. For if there is an ambiguity in the formula – which clearly there is – then it cannot

But if he is forced to disambiguate his formula, then the argument decisively fails – albeit for different reasons – under every interpretation.[34]

5 Conclusion

Anselm's Ontological Argument fails, as any such argument must, since it attempts to reach a substantial conclusion about a really existing (and not merely abstract) entity by *a priori* reasoning, starting merely from the understanding of his key formula. It would be astonishing if such an argument could genuinely work, and it is no surprise that few contemporary philosophers take this possibility seriously.[35] But nevertheless Anselm's argument itself deserves to be studied carefully, not only because of its historical influence, but also because it is so subtle and fascinating. It bears interpretation in various ways, highlighting a range of logical issues that have stimulated profound philosophical and logical developments, whether by defenders who have wished to represent it faithfully and sympathetically (e.g., within 'Meinongian' frameworks), or by sceptics who have wished to refute it decisively (e.g., Bertrand Russell).[36]

properly be treated as an unanalysed atomic term which has the same meaning and reference throughout.

[34] William of Ockham may have been the first to detect an ambiguity in Anselm's formula: 'Something's being that than which a greater cannot be thought has two senses: In one sense it means that nothing which can be thought is in fact greater. In another sense it means that it is not possible for something to be thought which would be greater if it existed. In the first sense Anselm's argument proves its conclusion. Formulated as follows, "Nothing which does not exist in reality is in fact greater than what exists in reality; therefore, that than which a greater cannot be thought exists in reality", the inference certainly holds good, on the assumption that in existing things the series of one thing greater than another does not go to infinity. Further, if that than which a greater cannot be thought exists in reality, since everybody agrees that the greatest of the items which are thought is God, it follows that God exists in reality' (*Quodlibet* VII, qu. 15, 5.2.4, Bosley and Tweedale 2006, pp. 119–20). Ockham here clearly identifies interpretation (i), and follows Scotus (note 29 above) in accepting PSE to render it valid. His second interpretation seems most likely to be (ii), but this is less clear because he does not go on to analyse its implications within Anselm's argument.

[35] Despite recent challenges to the orthodoxy inherited from 'Hume's Fork' – the famous distinction between *relations of ideas* and *matters of fact* (Hume (1748/2007: §4.1–2)) – most would agree that *a thought cannot both possess the certainty that comes from being known* a priori *through ideas alone, while also at the same time conveying substantial factual knowledge of the empirical world.* The general failure of attempts to circumvent this – most famously by Kant in his quest for the 'synthetic *a priori*' – justifies serious scepticism about the possibility of a successful Ontological Argument. For discussion of Hume's Fork, Kant and the contemporary challenges, see Millican (2017).

[36] The reference to Russell is in recognition that the Ontological Argument seems to have had a significant impact on his thought, and thus on the development of twentieth-century logic and philosophy (see Millican (2004: §9)).

Some of the objections to Anselm's argument are common to many other variants of the Ontological Argument, and of these perhaps the most important is the one discussed in Section 3 above and anticipated by Kant. This applies to arguments (such as Descartes's) that trade on a conflation between *characterizing* and *external* descriptions, first *defining* the concept that suits them in terms of the desired characteristic properties, and then presuming – usually without observing any logical gap – that the concept itself can therefore be truly *described* as possessing the same properties. The fallacy here is subtle, and especially hard to spot if the properties in question are ones that can plausibly be applied to both concepts and objects, such as *greatness*, *perfection* or *impossibility*.[37] But we have seen that it can readily be exposed by choosing less metaphysical characterizing properties: the concept of the funniest joke imaginable is not itself a joke, nor funny; and the concept of the lowest uninteresting natural number is not itself a natural number, nor uninteresting.[38] Likewise it cannot be assumed that the concept of a being with all perfections will itself have all perfections, nor that the concept of a supremely great being will itself be supremely great. Moreover this problem cannot be evaded by refusing to distinguish between characterizing and external descriptions (for example by insisting that the relevant mental and external entities are literally one and the same and therefore share the same properties), because this will simply open the door to paradox and parody.[39]

What makes Anselm's argument especially intriguing, however, is the tenacity with which it is able to survive recognition of this Kantian distinction. For it can remain seductive even when the descriptive content of Anselm's key formula is interpreted as unambiguously *external* rather than *characterizing*. It does this by exploiting three distinctive tricks. First, the formula identifies the relevant concept as a *superlative*: take all the concepts in

[37] The well-known Conceivability Principle – especially prominent in Hume's philosophy (see Millican (2017: §5)) – implies that a conceptual content which is self-contradictory (e.g., *round square*) is also *inconceivable*, so impossibility of instantiation goes together with impossibility of conception. In Proslogion III and IV, Anselm himself argues in this way, maintaining that God cannot even genuinely be conceived not to exist.

[38] This point is nicely made by a well-known and amusing paradox. Low natural numbers such as 1, 2, 3, 4, 5, 6 etc. are obviously *interesting* in various ways, for example 1 is the multiplicative identity, 2 is the only even prime, 3 is equal to the sum of the numbers below it, 4 is the first composite number, 5 is the hypotenuse of the smallest Pythagorean triad, 6 is a perfect number, and so on. Carrying on in this way, we should presumably eventually encounter a number that is *not* interesting, but 'lowest uninteresting natural number' seems itself to be a very interesting property!

[39] See, for example, the problems discussed in Sections 1.2 and 2.1 above. There are several famous parodies of the Ontological Argument which purport to use similar logic to 'prove' the existence of such implausible entities as a supremely excellent island (Gaunilo), a perfect Pegasus (Gassendi) or an unsurpassably evil being. I call these 'Gaunilo *reductios*' (Millican (2004: 445)).

some domain, rank them by greatness, and take the top scorer (or a top scorer, if there is a tie). As long as the domain is non-empty, and greatness is an acceptable measure, then it looks as though this has to succeed in achieving reference. Secondly, the specified domain includes all concepts that 'can be thought', thus apparently embracing all conceivable degrees of greatness, and ensuring that the top scorer will be truly impressive. Thirdly, as we have just seen, the formula is phrased in such a way that the 'can be thought' operator may be applied with variable scope, yielding a crucial ambiguity. This permits both a *modest* interpretation which confines attention to thinkable concepts with their *actual* degrees of greatness, but also a far more *ambitious* interpretation which aims to persuade us that one of these concepts reaches the maximal degree of *thinkable* greatness. Recognizing this ambiguity is crucial, because until it has been identified and neutralized, it is impossible to pin down exactly where or how the argument fails, which could happen in one of at least three different ways: either proving the *reality* of a non-divine entity, or failing to go beyond the *thinkability* of a divine entity, or simply begging the question.

Schopenhauer (1813: ch. II, §7) aptly described the Ontological Argument as a 'charming joke' or piece of magic trickery. Through his cleverly ambiguous formula, Anselm cunningly smuggles a huge metaphysical rabbit into his hat, only to reveal it at the denouement by supposedly combining the logical force of the modest interpretation with the impressive conclusion of the ambitious interpretation. In any Ontological Argument we know that there has to be a cheat somewhere, but in Anselm's case the trick is so clever as to impress us even after we have seen how it is done.

2 Aquinas

Brian Leftow

Aquinas approaches ontological arguments differently than we do. For us, they try to answer a metaphysical question: should our world-picture include God? For him, that was not a live question. He was quite sure that it should. So was everyone around him. So for him, the interesting question was one of epistemology. Taking it for granted that <God exists> is true, Aquinas wants to know its epistemic status. For Thomas, the significance of ontological arguments is simply that if any work, <God exists> is *per se notum*: known through itself, or self-evident. (As he explains this term, 'analytic' would be a rough equivalent.[1]) The interesting question for him is whether <God exists> has this status. So he always discusses ontological arguments under the heading 'is the existence of God self-evident?' and groups them with arguments for self-evidence that are not arguments for God's existence. Further, when Aquinas discusses Anselm, he is not primarily concerned to rebut the ontological argument. He is primarily concerned to explain the senses in which <God exists> is and is not *per se notum*. Anselm figures only as a foil, and the main distinction Aquinas makes, between being *per se notum* 'in itself' and 'for us', is not primarily a way to counter ontological arguments, though it has often been taken that way.

1 Aquinas on Anselm: First Move

In Aquinas' first major work, a commentary on Lombard's *Sentences*, Anselm appears only in a supporting role. Thomas discusses this argument:

[1] See, e.g., ST Ia 2, 1. This chapter uses the following abbreviations. ESLBDT: *Expositio Super Librum Boethii De Trinitate* (Aquinas); LQS: *Libri Quattuor Sententiarum* (Lombard); QDMT: *Quaestiones Disputatae de Mysterio Trinitatis* (Bonaventure); QDPD: *Quaestiones Disputatae de Potentia Dei* (Aquinas); QDV: *Quaestiones Disputatae de Veritate* (Aquinas); SCG: *Summa Contra Gentiles* (Aquinas); SSS: *Scriptum Super Sententiis* (Aquinas); ST: *Summa Theologiae* (Aquinas).

1. If <P> cannot be thought not to be true, <P> is self-evident.
2. <God exists> cannot be thought not to be true.
3. (Therefore) <God exists> is self-evident.

Anselm comes in to support (2): Thomas recounts *Proslogion III*'s reasoning that God is that than which no greater can be thought, it is greater to be than not to be unable to be thought not to be, therefore ... Thomas replies to Anselm that

> After we understand God, we cannot understand that God exists and can be thought not to exist. But ... it does not follow ... that someone cannot deny God's existence or think God not to exist. He can think nothing of the kind *thing than which no greater can be thought* to exist. And so the argument proceeds from this supposition, that something is supposed to exist than which nothing greater can be thought.[2]

We 'understand God' only if we grasp the divine essence. If we do, we see God's proper mode of being, and so see that if God exists, He is not the kind of thing that can be thought not to exist. But for Aquinas, we do not in this life grasp God's essence.[3] As we do not, we can think God not to be – that is, this is a supposition we are willing to entertain. In the *Summa Contra Gentiles*, Thomas adds that because this ignorance is the reason we can think God not to be, our being able to think this does not imply that we can think of something greater than God.[4] Nothing about God in Himself follows from our own cognitive limitations. Perhaps it's implicit here that intellects weak enough to think that God can fail to exist will be too weak to think up anything greater than a God who can fail to exist.

Thomas' move takes advantage of Anselm's formulating *Proslogion III* in terms of what 'can be thought'. He is right to point out that reasons a proposition can or can't be 'thought' can be found on the side of the thinker, not just the side of the proposition, and reasons from the side of the thinker need not have implications about God. But Anselm's talk of thinking is not just inessential but positively misleading in *Proslogion II* and *III*. As I argue in Leftow (in press), Anselm's reasoning is best understood in terms of whether something *can be greater* than God, not whether something can be thought greater. Aquinas' move actually gives us a reason to believe that this is the most charitable interpretation.

[2] SSS, d. 3, q. 1, a. 2. [3] So, e.g., ST Ia 12. [4] See also QDV 10, 12 ad 2.

2 Aquinas on Anselm: Main Move

The text above suggests a way to think God not to exist. We can think a second-order proposition, that the kind of *thing than which no greater can be thought* (henceforth G) has no instances, or a quantified proposition, that there is nothing of that kind. Either is true just if God does not exist. Thomas has the same thought in the *Summa Contra Gentiles*:

> No difficulty happens to those positing God not to exist. It is no difficulty that, for anything in reality or the mind, something greater can be thought, save to one who concedes there to be in reality something than which no greater can be thought.[5]

<There is nothing than which no greater can be thought> and <for anything in reality or the mind, something greater can be thought> are equivalents. The question is why Thomas thinks that either makes progress against Anselm.

One answer, I think, is this. *Proslogion II* in effect offers the atheist a poisoned pawn: posit some particular item that exists at least in the mind, reason about *that*, and (so Anselm claims) one must in the end grant that it really exists. Aquinas gives the savvy atheist a way to decline the bait. One can deny that God exists without speaking of any individual thing. If one keeps to quantified or second-order propositions, one doesn't posit any individual G. And so there is no starting-point for Anselm's *reductio*.

The *Contra Gentiles* text makes two claims:

1. It is no problem that something greater can be thought than anything that exists in reality, save to one who grants that a G exists in reality.
2. It is no problem that something greater can be thought than anything that exists in the mind, save to one who grants that a G exists in reality.

The reasoning behind (4) is this. If I say that a G exists in reality and something is greater than it is, I imply that something is and is not a G: it is, because I said so, and it is not, because something is greater. But if I say that no G exists in reality and that something greater can be thought than anything that really exists, I am not driven into this inconsistency. There is 'no problem' of this sort with the denial.

The reasoning behind (5), I think, is this. Suppose again that no G exists. If so, surely we can think of things greater than something that exists only in

[5] SCG I, 11, from Aquinas (1930), with an assist from Matthews (1963: 473–4).

someone's mind (if we go in for an ontology of mental existents at all). There is nothing inconsistent about this. But if a G exists, then it is not the case that something greater can be thought than anything that exists in the intellect. For a G exists in the intellect, *per Proslogion II*, and nothing greater than a G can be thought. So it would be 'a problem' for a believer in a G to hold that something greater can be thought than anything that exists in the intellect, but *only* for a believer in a G. Thus (says Aquinas) Anselm's *reductio* displays a problem only for people who already believe in a G, and so in offering it as a problem, Anselm is implicitly supposing that a G really exists.

Proslogion II contends that we can't stop short and posit a G only in the mind: if we go that far, we must go all the way to a G in reality. Aquinas' counter is that atheists need not concede a G in the mind, can state their atheism without doing so, and Anselm's *reductio* has no force against an atheism so stated. He's right. The *reductio* as stated does require a particular G 'in the mind'. Thomas has zeroed in on the crucial role this item plays in *Proslogion II*, and has in effect pointed out that one needn't accept Anselm's assumed ontology of items that exist in the intellect. But it's not hard to reformulate *Proslogion II* without this assumed ontology.[6] Aquinas has a point against *Proslogion II as stated*, but that is not enough to lay it to rest.

3 Is Atheism Consistent?

The previous section might suggest that for Thomas, atheism is in some sense a consistent view.[7] But Thomas treats the existence of God as absolutely necessary. For Thomas, what makes a proposition narrow-logically impossible is a 'repugnance' between its predicate and subject, and he includes in this all cases that 'imply being and not being at once'.[8] Thomas argues that the predicate of <God exists> is identical to its subject: God is His existence, and so in this case 'God' and 'exists' pick out the same thing.[9] Thus Thomas takes <God exists> to be of the form 'A is A'. Its negation, ¬(A is A), may imply being and not being at once. By calling A 'A', it may imply that A is A. But it also imply that A is not A. If this represents Thomas' thinking, then for him, atheism is narrow-logically impossible. If it does not, we can approach <God does not exist> another

[6] See Leftow (2019: ch. 14). [7] Matthews (1963: 475–6). [8] ST Ia 25, 3. [9] ST Ia 2, 1.

way: for Thomas, identity-statements like 'A = A' are predications.[10] This is surely a predication of an essential property, if so. If God and His existence are identical, 'God exists' predicates an essential property, and so 'God does not exist' involves a 'repugnance' between predicate and subject, as 'Leftow is not Leftow' or 'Leftow is not animate' do. Either way, for Thomas, <God does not exist> is absolutely impossible.

Thomas claims that God's existence is self-evident in itself: 'God's existence, in itself, is *per se notum*, because His essence is His existence.'[11] That is, for Thomas, some proposition whose subject-term's *ratio* includes its predicate asserts that God exists.[12] For Thomas, there is such a proposition if the essence of its subject 'contains' its predicate.[13] And for Thomas, God's essence is identical with His existence, and so 'contains' it.[14] For Thomas, this self-evident-in-itself proposition is not self-evident to us, because we do not grasp the divine essence.[15] So Thomas holds that atheism is the denial of something self-evident in itself, but that it is so is not self-evident to us.

Still, for Thomas, it can be made clear. Thomas holds that God's existence is demonstrable, though not in Anselm's way[16], and that arguments by which one can demonstrate this yield conclusions from which one can further demonstrate that God's essence is identical to His existence.[17] So for Thomas it can be shown that atheism is in fact absolutely impossible and in itself self-evidently false. Only initially and apparently is it 'no problem' to the atheist to deny that there is a G. Thomas' 'concession' to the atheist is merely that Anselm's argument is not a good way to make the 'problem' with atheism clear.

4 Summa Theologiae

In the *Summa Theologiae*, Thomas does not repeat his sample ways to say that God does not exist. Instead, he isolates the charge of question-begging: understanding Anselm's phrase commits one at most to seeing a G as existing in the intellect, and:

[10] ST Ia 13, 12. [11] ESLBDT 1, 3 ad 6; Aquinas (1959: 70).

[12] ST Ia 2, 1. As he explicates this, two sorts of proposition have this status. One sort involves indefinable terms, e.g., 'being' and 'non-being' (ST Ia 2, 1). The self-evident proposition 'God exists' might express falls into this category for Thomas, for Thomas denies that 'God' can be defined (really, as vs nominally, in Locke's terms: DP 7, 3 ad 5).

[13] ST Ia 2, 1. [14] SCG I, 11. [15] ST Ia 2, 1. [16] ST Ia 2, 3. [17] ST Ia 3, 1–5.

> Nor can it be argued that it exists in reality, unless it is granted that there exists in reality something than which no greater can be thought, which is not granted by those positing God not to exist.[18]

Thomas' point can be put this way. Suppose we grant that a G is 'in the intellect'. Then that thing has (we can suppose) some degree of greatness. It has the degree appropriate to a G in the intellect. *Proslogion II* supposes that it is maximally great, just as a G existing in reality is. It needs that supposition. Its *reductio* depends on it. *Is* the G in the intellect maximally great? Well, it is if it exists in reality. But to assert at this point that it exists in reality would beg the question. It's unclear, though, that there can be any other reason to say that it is maximally great. So apparently we have no non-question-begging basis to say that the thing in the intellect is maximally great. But if the item in the intellect is not maximally great, there is no contradiction in denying that something could be greater than it is. So (Thomas thinks) Anselm can derive his conclusion only if he begs the question. The only way to get the conclusion that it is maximally great, it seems, is to assume that it exists in reality, is maximally great there, and then is also thought of and so in an intellect. Here Thomas pinpoints the key assumption of *Proslogion II*, that some item in the intellect actually has, in the intellect, the full greatness of a G. He has in effect asked why we should hold this, and challenged Anselm to give a non-question-begging reason to do so. Anselm is not well-placed to reply, since he never gave much reason to believe this.

5 Arguments from Simplicity

In the *Sentence*-commentary, Thomas also brings up this argument:

> Nothing can be thought of without its essence . . . But the essence of God is his own being itself . . . So God cannot be thought not to be.[19]

Thomas replies that this should be dealt with as he had just dealt with Anselm: that is, as involving begging the question.[20] Thomas' riposte, then, is that there is an essence of God to think about only if there is a God who has it. Given his general Aristotelian approach to 'universals', this is precisely the right answer: if attributes exist only if instanced, then there is a divine essence only if God exists. Perhaps Thomas also means us to see that his quantified

[18] ST Ia 2, 1 ad 2; Aquinas (1941), 12b13–17.
[19] SSS; translated partly by Tristan Franklinos.
[20] SSS.

proposition provides a way to think of (a non-existent) God without thinking of His essence.

St Bonaventure's *Disputed Questions on the Mystery of the Trinity* date from somewhere in the period 1253–7, when he and Thomas were both teaching at the University of Paris. Bonaventure argues that:

> When I say that God exists, the existence predicated of God is totally identical with God, because God is His very existence. Therefore, nothing is more . . . evident than that proposition . . . Therefore no-one can think it false or be in doubt about it.[21]

In *Contra Gentiles*, Thomas relates an argument which includes this:

> Those propositions ought to be most evident in which the same is predicated of itself, or whose predicates are included in the definitions of their subjects . . . In God . . . His existence is His essence . . . So therefore when 'God exists' is said, either the predicate is the same as the subject, or it is included in the definition of the subject. So God's existence is self-evident.[22]

Here, however, his reply is a distinction he makes in many places.[23] Some truths are self-evident in themselves but not to us. A truth is self-evident in itself just if its subject-term's *ratio* includes its predicate. ('*Ratio*' is a scarcely translatable term which can mean (roughly) 'meaning' or 'essence' depending on context.) It is self-evident to us just if it is self-evident in itself and we have the concepts its subject- and predicate-terms express. That every whole is greater than its (proper) part is self-evident in itself, but could not be self-evident to someone who could not have the concept of a whole. Similarly, Thomas writes, that God exists is self-evident in itself, because His existence and essence are identical. But we cannot conceive God's essence, and so we cannot access this self-evidence. We cannot 'see' His essence, at least in this life. As he puts it in his *Commentary on Boethius' De Trinitate*:

21 QDMT arg. 28; Bonaventure (1979: 113). Bonaventure's argument may well be derived from Richard Fishacre, a Dominican of the preceding generation.

22 SCG I 10; Aquinas (1930: 23).

23 SCG I, 11; ST Ia 2, 1; QDV 10, 12. In SSS, Thomas made the distinction, but explained it differently. There he said that God's existence is self-evident in itself and known through itself rather than by being made 'intelligible', as happens when we 'abstract' material forms from matter. The thought is perhaps that this is a consequence of His being immaterial. But His being immaterial guarantees that His existence is not self-evident to us, for things self-evident to us are things we learn through sense-experience, and there is no sense-experience of the immaterial.

> God's existence, in itself, is *per se notum*, because His essence is His existence – and Anselm speaks in this way – but not to us, who do not see His essence.[24]

God's essence = God's existence. This is a truth of the form $a = b$. If we see that $a = b$, we cannot also 'think' that $a \neq b$: this is as inconceivable as that $a \neq a$. However, we lack the concepts of both a and b. So we cannot access this proposition, and what it describes is thus not self-evident to us. Putting this in more familiar terms, Thomas thinks that <God exists> is analytic. But he thinks we cannot use this to generate an ontological argument that will persuade anyone.

6 Aquinas on Damascene

Bonaventure's *Disputed Questions on the Mystery of the Trinity* argue at length that God's existence is 'indubitable', and it is plausible that Thomas' treatments of self-evidence target some of Bonaventure's arguments in this work, though he recasts Bonaventure's reasoning in terms of being *per se notum*. Thus Bonaventure argues, for instance, just by citing a theologically authoritative statement from St John Damascene, that the knowledge of God is somehow innately implanted in us.[25] Obviously, we're meant to supply some further premise to reach the conclusion of indubitability. It cannot be a coincidence that Thomas discusses this statement in all five places he raises the self-evidence question.

According to Damascene, we know innately that God exists. Thomas adds the missing premise, that what is innately known is self-evident to us, and draws the conclusion that <God exists> is self-evident. We might today say that what we know innately we in some sense know *a priori*. If so, then if anything we know innately is actually the proposition that God exists in some guise, we know *a priori* that God exists: thus Damascene's point might point to an ontological argument. As Damascene was an 'authority', those who disagreed with him were under some intellectual pressure to 'save' some truth contained in his claim rather than deny the claim outright. This was always Aquinas' move. Aquinas gives the argument from Damascene short shrift in the *Sentences*, just asserting that what are innately known are only truths about God's likeness, not His very nature or being.[26] The answer recurs in *Contra Gentiles*. The Boethius commentary and Thomas' *Disputed Questions*

[24] ESLBDT 1, 3 ad 6; Aquinas (1959: 70). [25] QDMT 1, 1, arg. 1. [26] SSS, d. 3, q. 1, a. 2.

on Truth offer a deflationary account: we can be said to know God's existence innately only in the sense that by innately known principles we can come to see that God exists – i.e., by the use of reason.[27] The *Summa Theologiae* expands the *Sentence*/SCG reply: we know innately that God exists only in a 'general and confused' way, in that we naturally want to be truly happy, what we want naturally is naturally known to us, and God is in fact what will make us truly happy. But to know that we want whatever will make us truly happy, or even (Thomas does not add) that whatever will make us truly happy exists, is not to know in any clear way that God exists; it is compatible with believing that only other things than God will make us truly happy.

7 Conclusion

I have argued that Aquinas had genuinely good points to make against the ontological arguments circulating in his milieu. Few medieval philosophers after Aquinas championed ontological arguments; they more or less went into eclipse until Descartes. This was part of broader shifts in view that I cannot discuss here, but it is entirely possible that later medievals' appreciation of Aquinas' critique contributed too.

[27] ESLBDT 1, 3 ad 6; Aquinas (1959: 70); QDV 10, 12 ad 1.

3 Descartes

Lawrence Nolan

The ontological argument tends to elicit one of two polarized responses from philosophers: fascination or repulsion. Those in the former group are tempted by its boldness, elegance and simplicity, as the ontological argument purports to demonstrate God's existence merely from the concept of such a being. Even if the argument fails, it promises to teach us much about the limits of logic, the nature of existence, and the concept of God. Philosophers in the latter group, by contrast, regard the ontological argument as a cheap parlour trick that is patently invalid, begs the question and falsely assumes that existence is a predicate. This negative assessment has largely prevailed, and the conventional wisdom is that Descartes's version of the argument succumbs to the same criticisms. But this assumption derives from reading Descartes through the eyes of Kant, Leibniz, Russell and other famous critics, who misconstrue both the nature of the argument and Descartes's aims in presenting it. Descartes's discussion is much more sophisticated and nuanced than commonly thought, but to appreciate its virtues one must examine the context in which it appears and the various philosophical doctrines on which it depends. I shall do that here and, more importantly, resolve some of the major interpretive disputes associated with his version of the argument.

I shall address six such disputes, giving some more attention than others. First, I take up the issue of whether the so-called ontological 'argument' is intended as a formal proof or as the report of an intuition. Second, some commentators purport finding multiple *a priori* arguments in Descartes's writings and so have wondered what relation holds between them, whether there is a definitive formulation, and, – if so, where it is located in the text. Third, Descartes sometimes characterizes the ontological argument as a proof from God's essence or 'true and immutable nature'. What does this characterization reveal about the nature of his project? Fourth, it is well known that Descartes presents two theistic proofs in the *Meditations*, with the ontological argument appearing last. Commentators have puzzled over why he reverses this order in the *Principles of Philosophy*. Fifth, the principle of clear and distinct perception plays a pivotal role in many of Descartes's central arguments. But some readers have worried that if the ontological argument depends on this principle then it begs the question. Finally, it is generally believed that the standard objections to the ontological argument are fatal, but I will show that Descartes has the resources for answering some of the most important ones.

1 The Ontological Argument as the Report of an Intuition

The main challenge to understanding Descartes's version of the ontological argument is that he seems to offer conflicting accounts of its status. In some passages he presents a formal argument, a syllogism even. But in other passages in the same context he insists that God's existence is known via intuition, 'without a formal argument' and that it is ultimately as self-evident as an axiom of geometry or a simple truth of arithmetic.[1] Although readers have puzzled over this seeming inconsistency, Descartes's writings provide a simple resolution. There is conclusive evidence that he conceived of the so-called ontological argument as the report of an intuition in the sense of a non-discursive, self-validating, intellectual apprehension.[2] If this is correct, then why does he present a formal proof? And what relation does the syllogism bear to the intuition, if any? The answer to the first question is straightforward. Here one must bear in mind that Descartes is writing for seventeenth-century readers who, owing to their scholastic-Aristotelian philosophical training, would have been used to engaging in syllogistic reasoning and being persuaded in those terms. He also had political motivations for presenting a formal argument, as the Catholic Church had urged philosophers to devise proofs by natural reason for two articles of faith: the immortality of the soul and the existence of God.[3] As for the second question, when we examine the syllogism that Descartes presents in detail we shall find that it can be reduced to a single proposition, namely, that necessary existence is included in the clear and distinct idea of God. This is the axiom that he takes to be self-evident and equivalent to the proposition that God exists. So the

[1] AT 7:163–64, CSM 2:115. This chapter uses the following abbreviations.
AT: Descartes (1964–76), cited by volume number: page number.
CSM(K): Descartes (1984–91), cited by volume number: page number.

[2] Barnes (1972: 16) and Gueroult (1984: 253) were among the first to propose this general reading, though without developing it.

[3] I refer to the Lateran Councils of the sixteenth century, to which Descartes alludes in his 'Dedicatory letter to the Sorbonne' appended to the *Meditations* (AT 7:3, CSM 2:4).

formal version of the ontological argument is merely a dressed-up version of the axiom, and the main reasons he dresses it up are to satisfy the expectations of his readers and to lend it the authority of Aristotle. In the rest of this section and in the next, I examine the main evidence for regarding the Cartesian ontological argument as the report of an intuition. In a later section, we shall discuss Descartes's syllogism and take up its relation to the intuition in greater detail. (NB: I use the expression 'ontological *argument*' throughout this chapter as an expository convenience, given its currency, but this should not be read as retracting my thesis about the intuitive nature of God's existence on Descartes's view.)

There are two kinds of evidence favouring the 'Intuitionist Account', one textual and the other systematic in the sense that it derives from the character of Descartes's philosophical system. I begin with the former. There are three key passages in which Descartes explicitly asserts that God's existence is ultimately self-evident and/or known by intuition. First, about midway through the Fifth Meditation, after formulating a formal argument and answering potential objections, Descartes writes:

> [1] But whatever method of proof [*probandi ratione*] I use, I am always brought back to the fact that it is only what I clearly and distinctly perceive that completely convinces me. Some of the things I clearly and distinctly perceive are obvious to everyone, while others are discovered only by those who look more closely and investigate more carefully; but once they have been discovered, the latter are judged to be just as certain as the former. In the case of a right-angled triangle, for example, the fact that the square on the hypotenuse is equal to the square on the other two sides is not so readily apparent as the fact that the hypotenuse subtends the largest angle; but once one has seen it, one believes it just as strongly. But as regards God, if I were not overwhelmed by prejudices, and if the images of things perceived by the senses did not besiege my thought on every side, I would certainly acknowledge him sooner and more easily than anything else. For what is more self-evident [*quid ex se est apertius*] than the fact that the supreme being exists, or that God, to whose essence alone existence belongs, exists?[4]

This is the most important passage on the ontological argument in the whole of the Cartesian corpus, at least for the purposes of understanding the status of the argument and Descartes's aims in presenting it. Descartes explicitly

[4] AT 7:68–9, CSM 2:47.

affirms that knowledge of God's existence is attained through clear and distinct perception, or what he elsewhere calls 'intuition' (*intuitus*).[5] This affirmation has the effect of subordinating the argument that has come before. But he is not asserting that God's existence is *immediately* self-evident, at least not for most meditators, for that would be patently false and obviate the need for theistic proofs of any kind, including those of the Third Meditation. Descartes would have been keenly aware of Psalm 14:1 (cf. 53:1): 'The fool said in his heart, "there is no God".' St Thomas Aquinas cites this passage as grounds for denying that God's existence is self-evident to us, for if it were then it would be impossible for anyone to refuse belief.[6] When presented with Aquinas' denial elsewhere, Descartes tries to find common ground by agreeing that God's existence is not immediately self-evident *to everyone*.[7] This concession is consistent with his point here, which is that it can *become* self-evident to anyone, so long as one is careful and industrious. In fact, he distinguishes two types of meditators – those for whom God's existence is immediately self-evident and those who must work much harder to attain the same epistemic status. To illustrate this distinction, he invokes one of many geometric analogies in this context. For some meditators, God's existence is akin to the Pythagorean Theorem, where one discovers the truth in question only after considerable practice and mental exertion. But for other meditators, God's existence is as simple and obvious as an axiom or definition in geometry, such as that the hypotenuse of a right triangle subtends the greatest angle. Most meditators presumably fall into the former group, not because they are 'fools' or God-deniers but because even true believers tend to be mired in the senses and 'overwhelmed by philosophical prejudices' and so typically accept God's existence on faith alone.[8] The important point is that *all* meditators ultimately attain knowledge of God's existence via intuition.

[5] See note 14.

[6] *Summa Theologica* I, q.2, art. 1. Aquinas claims that the proposition 'God exists' is self-evident in itself but not to us. When presenting his own version of the ontological argument in the *Proslogion*, Anselm presents himself as refuting the proverbial fool. Aquinas is likely responding to this way of framing the topic.

[7] See First Replies, AT 7:115; CSM 2:82. Historically, it is a common rhetorical strategy of Christian philosophers, indeed of Aquinas himself, to accommodate an opponent's views within one's own, even when there is deep disagreement. It would have been important politically for Descartes to find common ground with the 'the Angelic Doctor' in this context, given the authority Aquinas held within the Catholic Church and given Descartes's efforts to win the Church's sanction of the *Meditations*.

[8] For a detailed discussion of the nature of these prejudices and Descartes's efforts to dispel them, see Nolan (2005) and Nolan and Nelson (2006).

One might start with a formal argument but after much meditative work the existence of God *becomes* self-evident.[9]

Turning to the second passage, Descartes is even more explicit about the self-evident and non-discursive character of our knowledge of God's existence in the Second Replies:

> [2] I ask my readers to spend a great deal of time and effort on contemplating the nature of the supremely perfect being. Above all they should reflect on the fact that the ideas of all other natures contain possible existence, whereas the idea of God contains not only possible but wholly necessary existence. This alone, without a formal argument [*discursu*], will make them realize that God exists; and this will eventually be just as self-evident [*per se notum*] to them as the fact that the number two is even or that three is odd, and so on.[10]

In the third and final passage, from the *Principles of Philosophy*, he writes: 'simply on the basis of its perception that necessary and eternal existence is contained in the idea of a supremely perfect being, the mind must clearly conclude that the supreme being does exist'.[11] The key point of both of these last two passages is that one discovers God's existence simply by perceiving that 'necessary and eternal existence' is contained in the idea of a supremely perfect being. Knowing that God exists does not demand a formal proof; all that is required is an analysis of one's idea of such a being. Again, this perception does not always come easily, but once achieved God's existence is self-evident.

2 The Grounds for Intuitionism in Descartes's Philosophical System

Let us turn now to three systematic considerations, which will reveal why Descartes holds that God's existence is known ultimately through intuition given other philosophical commitments. This discussion will also serve us in the next section, where an appreciation of some of these commitments will enable us to unravel Descartes's syllogism and to analyse some key passages on the ontological argument that are commonly misunderstood.

9 To contemporary ears this sounds odd, as we tend to regard self-evidence as an intrinsic feature of propositions, but Descartes holds that self-evidence is relative to the epistemic status of the meditator, in keeping with the notion of epistemic progress that characterizes the *Meditations*.

10 AT 7:163–4, CSM 2:115. Cf. *Principles* I.15, AT 8A:10; CSM 1:198.

11 AT 8A:10, CSM 1:197–8.

Although Descartes formulates the ontological argument in all three of his central philosophical works – the *Discourse on Method* (1637), the *Meditations* (1641) and the *Principles* (1644) – the most sophisticated and authoritative presentation is to be found in the Fifth Meditation and cognate texts in the First, Second and Fifth Replies to Objections to the *Meditations*. The epistemic project of the *Meditations* is thus highly relevant to the ontological argument, which plays a very special role in that project. The main advertised goal of the *Meditations* is to attain perfect knowledge (*scientia*), and, simultaneously, to show that all of our knowledge depends on knowledge of the existence and nature of God. To use one of Descartes's most familiar metaphors, knowledge of God constitutes the 'foundation' of our knowledge of everything else. In the preface to the *Principles* he identifies God's existence as one of only two first principles constituting his philosophical system, the other being the existence of the soul as a thinking thing.[12] He also asserts that such first principles must satisfy two conditions:

> [3] First, they must be so clear and so evident that the human mind cannot doubt their truth when it attentively concentrates on them; and, secondly, the knowledge of other things must depend on them, in the sense that the principles must be capable of being known without knowledge of these other matters.[13]

The first condition is, in effect, asserting that first principles must be intuitively certain. Elsewhere he says this even more explicitly: 'first principles . . . are known only through intuition'.[14] The second condition explains why they must be known in this way: if the existence of God were not known via intuition, but were instead the conclusion of an argument, then the meditator's knowledge of it would depend on prior knowledge of the premise(s) of that argument. God can play the foundational role that Descartes assigns to him only if his existence is ultimately axiomatic.

Descartes's claim about the dependence of all knowledge on knowledge of God appears twice in the *Meditations*. It is telling that both statements occur toward the end of the Fifth Meditation. Given space constraints, I quote only the first.

> [4] Although it needed close attention for me to perceive this [viz., that God exists], I am now just as certain of it as I am of everything else which appears most certain. And what is more, I see that the certainty of all other

[12] AT 9B:10, CSM 1:184. [13] AT 9B:2, CSM 1:179–80. [14] AT 10:368–70, CSM 1:14–15.

> things depends on this, so that without it nothing can ever be perfectly known [*perfecte sciri*].[15]

This remark occurs just after Descartes asserts that God's existence is ultimately self-evident (see passage [1]). The juxtaposition indicates that he sees a connection between his view that God's existence is self-evident and his claim that the knowledge of all other things depends on knowledge of God. Again, God's existence must be known through intuition in order for this latter claim to be true.

It might be objected at this point that God's existence might be knowable through intuition, but it cannot be knowable through intuition alone, for if that were Descartes's view he would not have mounted a total of three proofs for God's existence – the two causal arguments of the Third Meditation and the syllogistic version of the ontological argument. This objection is easily deflected, however, by appealing to Descartes's distinction between conviction (*persuasio*) and knowledge (*scientia*). When we are merely convinced of some proposition we affirm its truth, but it is consistent with doing so that we later entertain doubts about it. By contrast, when we attain knowledge of some proposition all doubt is impossible. Descartes sometimes indicates that the causal arguments of the Third Meditation yield conviction alone, since the premises of those arguments are still subject to doubt when we are no longer attending to the premises.[16] By contrast, when we intuit God's existence no further doubts can arise. Any attempt to doubt that God exists induces this intuitive state, which Descartes regards as self-validating. This difference helps to explain the order of Descartes's theistic proofs in the *Meditations* and why he introduces another proof in the Fifth Meditation. The causal arguments of the Third Meditation provide the meditator with a means for challenging the hyperbolic doubts of the First Meditation, but they do not yield perfect knowledge of God's existence and that cannot be achieved until one attains the proper intuition of God.[17]

It is often noted that Descartes reverses the order of his theistic arguments in the *Principles*. On the interpretation given here this is easily explained. Descartes wrote the *Principles* using, in part, a method he called 'synthesis', which he associates with the method of Euclidean geometry, where one starts

[15] AT 7:69; CSM 2:48; cf. AT 7:71, CSM 2:49.

[16] See, e.g., Letter to Regius, 24 May 1640; AT 3:64–5; CSMK 147.

[17] Much more could be said here than space allows. I refer the reader to Newman and Nelson (1999) for one fuller treatment of the issues that I find compelling.

from axioms, definitions, postulates, etc. and then derives theorems.[18] In other words, he begins with the ontological argument in that work because he saw himself as taking the axioms of metaphysics as immediately self-evident, as one does with the axioms of geometry – not because the axioms of metaphysics *are* immediately self-evident, but because the method requires treating them as such. This would explain why the syllogistic version of the ontological is absent from the *Principles*. Instead, one finds the statement quoted earlier to the effect that God's existence is obvious.

Although the texts are rather sparse on this point, Descartes likely thought that when we intuit God's existence we also intuit that he is our creator and is no deceiver. If so, this would explain why he would be tempted to hold that the intuition of God's existence is self-validating. It is not possible to doubt the reliability of one's present intellectual state if it is part of the content of that state that one is created by a being who, given his omnipotence and supreme benevolence, created one with a trustworthy intellect.[19]

I turn now to a second systemic consideration favouring the Intuitionist Account relating to Descartes's theory of inference. Like the ancient sceptics, Descartes was highly critical of the Aristotelian syllogism. In fact, in his early work, *Rules for the Direction of the Mind*, and to a lesser degree in the *Discourse*, he repudiates formal reasoning generally which he associates with scholastic 'dialecticians', a term of derision intended to imply that his medieval predecessors were more interested in verbal disputes and sophistry than in discovering the truth.[20] As part of his critique, Descartes explicitly rejects rules of inference and forms of reasoning, which he characterizes as mechanical 'fetters' that 'entrap' our native power of reason. In another striking metaphor he speaks of 'reason's taking a holiday' when it employs such formal devices.[21] '[N]othing can be added to the clear light of reason which does not in some way dim it.'[22] In lieu of the syllogism, Descartes offers up his own non-formal theory of inference. Here he distinguishes two mental operations: intuition and deduction – terms that he acknowledges using in a novel manner. Intuition, which is the central notion, just is our native power of reason. It is also the forerunner of clear and distinct perception. He defines

[18] Second Replies, AT 7:156; CSM 2:110–11.

[19] I owe a debt here to Newman and Nelson (1999), who make a similar point. They also develop what might be regarded as a further systematic consideration favouring the Intuitionist Account: the only way that Descartes can dispel the hyperbolic doubts of the First Meditation and circumvent the putative Cartesian Circle is if God's existence is known through intuition, which they concur is attained in the Fifth Meditation.

[20] See, e.g., AT 10:405–6, CSM 1:36.

[21] AT 10:406, CSM 1:36.

[22] AT 10:373, CSM 1:16.

'intuition' as 'the conception of a clear and attentive mind, which is so easy and distinct that there can be no room for doubt about what we are understanding'. Deduction is defined in terms of this more primary notion: it consists of a chain of self-evident intuitions in which there is 'a continuous and uninterrupted movement of thought' from one intuition to another. A deduction is necessary only when there is difficulty in intuiting something directly: 'immediate self-evidence is not required for deduction, as it is for intuition'.[23] Since deduction involves a movement of thought, it relies on memory and is thus less certain than intuition. To overcome this shortcoming, Descartes insists that one should aim to reduce deductions to single intuitions.[24] A Cartesian deduction is thus very different than a formal proof – syllogistic or otherwise. It is also merely a stepping stone to attaining single intuitions and ultimately dispensable.

The implications of this non-formal theory of inference for Descartes's ontological argument are clear. Some truths are immediately self-evident and thus amenable to intuition. Others are not and must be 'deduced' in his sense by a chain of intuitions, but the goal of reasoning is to reduce these chains to single intuitions as well. This summary is very close to what Descartes says in passage [1] from the Fifth Meditation, where he concedes that God's existence is not immediately self-evident to everyone but can, through careful meditation on one's innate idea of God, *become* self-evident.

I turn now to the third and final systematic consideration, which is metaphysical in nature and grounds the claim that God's existence is ultimately known through intuition. Another distinctive feature of Descartes's version of the ontological argument – aside from the characteristic geometric analogies – is his presentation of it as an argument from the *essence* of God. For instance, in the now familiar passage from the Fifth Meditation, he writes: 'For what is more self-evident than the fact that the supreme being exists, or that God, to whose essence alone existence belongs, exists?' By formulating the argument in these terms, Descartes is self-consciously invoking the traditional medieval distinction between essence and existence. Medieval philosophers drew this distinction in different ways and in fact one of the great intellectual debates of the Middle Ages concerned the precise nature of the distinction. All parties to the debate agreed that God's essence just is his existence, i.e., that they are identical in reality. So the debate focused on the relation between essence and existence in finite, created substances. One of the most influential theories, first articulated by Aquinas, was that there is a

[23] AT 10:368–70, CSM 1:14–15. [24] AT 10:387–8, CSM 1:25.

real distinction between essence and existence in finite beings, such that essence and existence are two distinct things (*res*) or at least two different 'principles of being'.[25] Such a view would seem to lend itself to a proponent of the ontological argument: existence is included in the essence of God but not in the essence of finite beings. So one can demonstrate *a priori* the existence of God but not of creatures. But Descartes rejects the Thomistic view. He holds that there is merely a rational or conceptual distinction between essence and existence in *all* things – both finite and infinite, created and divine.[26] This is a bold claim, but to fully appreciate its import we must place it in the context of Descartes's general theory of distinctions.

The distinction of reason (*distinctio rationis*) is one of three types of distinction that Descartes recognizes, the other two being the more familiar real distinction, which underwrites his substance dualism ('the real distinction between mind and body'), and the modal distinction, which obtains, for example, between a corporeal substance and its determinate shape. Unlike the real and modal distinctions, which obtain in reality independently of our thought and are something we discover, a rational distinction is something that *we produce* by regarding a substance in different ways. Specifically, we produce it by means of intellectual abstraction. Case in point, we 'understand the essence of a thing in one way when we consider it *in abstraction* from whether it exists or not, and in a different way when we consider it as existing; but the thing itself cannot be outside our thought without its existence'.[27]

Descartes's notion of abstraction is best understood in contrast to the notion of another intellectual operation that he calls 'exclusion'. He invokes the latter explicitly when stating the criterion of a rational distinction. In the *Principles* he says that we recognize that two attributes are merely rationally distinct by means of our inability to form a clear and distinct idea of one if we *exclude* or *separate* it from the other.[28] The contrast between these two types of intellectual operation – abstraction and exclusion – turns out to be key to understanding Descartes's ontological argument. This is not surprising. One commentator has shown how this little-known distinction runs like a thread through several Cartesian doctrines and arguments.[29] Like many early modern philosophers, Descartes understands abstraction in terms of selective

[25] See Wippel (1982).
[26] See esp. Letter to an unknown correspondent, 1645 or 1646; AT 4:348–9; CSMK 279–80.
[27] AT 4:349; CSMK 280 (emphasis added). For further discussion, see Nolan (1998).
[28] I.62, AT 8A:30, CSM 1:214. [29] Murdoch (1993).

attention. So when drawing a rational distinction between essence and existence of God, I attend to his essence while ignoring – but not denying – his existence. By contrast, when excluding one attribute from another, I must attend to both and actively deny that each pertains to the other.[30] For example, when proving the real distinction between mind and body, Descartes says that we can mutually exclude the essences of mind and body – viz., thought and extension, respectively – within our thought.[31]

This discussion provides a way of reframing the intuition that constitutes the so-called ontological argument. What one intuits, in effect, is that God's essence and existence are merely rationally distinct – that although one can abstract from his existence and attend to his essence alone, one cannot exclude it. Descartes stresses this last point repeatedly in the context of the ontological argument, sometimes using the word 'separate' as a synonym for exclude. For example, in the Fifth Meditation he writes: 'it is quite evident that existence can no more be separated [*separari*] from the essence of God than the fact that its three angles equal two right angles can be separated from the essence of a triangle . . .'[32] Two paragraphs later he adds:

> [5] . . . from the fact that I cannot think of God except as existing, it follows that existence is inseparable [*inseparabilem*] from God, and hence that he really exists. It is not that my thought makes it so, or imposes any necessity on any thing; on the contrary, it is the necessity of the thing itself, namely the existence of God, which determines my thinking in this respect. For I am not free to think of God without existence (that is, a supremely perfect being without a supreme perfection) as I am free to imagine a horse with or without wings.[33]

Some of Descartes's remarks in this passage bear on issues that will be treated in the next section, and so for now I shall merely mention them in passing. Descartes wants to stress that innate ideas constrain the way that we think of them. This is why he says in the Fifth Meditation that such ideas have 'true and immutable natures' and contrasts them with invented ideas, whose content is up to us to determine at will.[34] Innate ideas are immutable in the sense that they resist efforts by the mind to deform them. We cannot, as he says elsewhere of the idea of God, 'take away anything from it or . . . add

[30] Letter to Gibieuf, 19 January 1642; AT 3:474–6; CSMK 202.

[31] *Principles* I.60, AT 8A:29, CSM 1:213. [32] AT 7:66, CSM 2:46. [33] AT 7:67, CSM 2:46.

[34] For an account of the ontological status of 'true and immutable natures', see Nolan (1997).

anything to it'.[35] So, again, if this idea contains existence, then we cannot exclude this attribute while maintaining a clear and distinct idea of him.

Descartes's claim about the relation between God's essence and existence serves his purposes well in the ontological argument. But this doctrine is intended to be general: essence and existence are merely rationally distinct in all things, which entails that existence is included in the idea of every substance. 'Existence is contained in the idea or concept of every single thing, since we cannot conceive of anything [clearly and distinctly] except as existing.'[36] This position seems to encourage a classical objection to the ontological argument – first raised by Gaunilo against Anselm's version – namely, that if the argument were valid then one could proliferate such arguments for contingent beings such as a supremely perfect island.

Descartes blocks this objection, however, by distinguishing two grades or types of existence, what he calls necessary existence and possible (or contingent) existence, a distinction we first encountered in passage [2]. It is tempting to regard these as modal notions, given the modern connotations of the terms, but that would be a mistake. Descartes understands necessary existence in the same way that medieval philosophers understood the notion of a necessary being (or aseity), i.e., in terms of ontological independence. Such a being does not depend for its existence on anything else; it has being from itself (*a se esse*) and hence is eternal. Descartes indicates that he has this notion of necessary existence in mind in the Fifth Meditation, for when first stating the ontological argument he says 'it belongs to his [God's] nature that he always exists', only later substituting the term 'necessary existence'.[37] And both in the passage from the *Principles* discussed in the previous section and in the French translation of the Fifth Meditation, he speaks of God's 'necessary and eternal existence'.[38] If this is what Descartes means by 'necessary existence' then, given the contrast, it is plausible to suppose that by 'possible or contingent existence' he means *dependent* existence. This is confirmed both by the term 'contingent' (which he uses interchangeably with 'possible') and by the fact that he defines finite substance in terms of ontological *dependence*: finite minds and bodies depend both for their creation and their continual preservation on God.[39]

35 Third Meditation, AT 7:51, CSM 2:35. 36 AT 7:166, CSM 2:117.

37 AT 7:65, CSM 2:45. Cf. First Replies, AT 7:119; CSM 2:85 (discussed below). This is also how Descartes defines 'God' in the *Principles*, as a being who does not depend on anything whatsoever for his existence (AT 8A:24, CSM 1:210).

38 AT 8A:10, CSM 1:197–8. AT 9A:55. 39 *Principles* I.51, AT 8A:24; CSM 1:210.

The distinction between two types of existence enables Descartes to qualify his general claim about the essence–existence relation and thus block the proliferation objection: the clear and distinct idea of God contains independent or eternal existence while the clear and distinct ideas of all finite things contain merely dependent existence. Thus, one can know *a priori* the actual existence of the former but not of the latter.[40] This is one reason that Descartes asks his readers in passage [2] 'to reflect on the fact that the ideas of all other natures contain possible existence, whereas the idea of God contains not only possible but wholly necessary existence'. To know that a finite thing exists *a priori*, one would have to know at the very least that its creator exists and chose to produce it. But seeing as one lacks knowledge of God's volitions (and his purposes in creation) on Descartes's view, one cannot know the latter *a priori*.

3 Descartes's Syllogism and Other Putative Ontological Arguments

Descartes formulates the ontological argument as a syllogism in four different passages and, in two of these, advertises it as such.[41] His presentation varies somewhat, but the general argument can be stated as follows:

1. Whatever I clearly and distinctly understand to belong to the idea or nature of something can truly be affirmed of that thing. (Major premise)
2. I clearly and distinctly understand that necessary existence belongs to the idea or nature of God. (Minor premise)
3. Therefore, God exists.

Given Descartes's repudiation of the Aristotelian syllogism, as detailed in the previous section, it is quite remarkable that he presents his argument in this way. He never rescinds this critique and so by casting one of his central arguments in the *Meditations* as a syllogism, he appears to contradict himself. The problem seems especially acute since one of his principal criticisms of the traditional syllogism is that it begs the question. Ironically, this is a standard

[40] See First Replies, AT 7:116–17, CSM 2:83. Interestingly, Descartes's distinction between possible and necessary existence serves a similar role to that which Anselm's distinction between existing in the understanding (alone) and existing in reality serves in his version of the ontological argument.

[41] AT 7:65, 116–17, 150–1, 166–7; CSM 2:45, 83, 106–7, 117. One commentator has made much of the differences among these formulations of the syllogism, but given Descartes's view that God's existence is ultimately self-evident it is difficult to see how they matter. (See Doney (1978).)

objection to the ontological argument generally: one must assume something exists in order to ascribe properties to it (sometimes called 'the principle of presupposition'). But Descartes's syllogism is circular for reasons unique to his epistemic project in the *Meditations.* Note that the argument begins with a version of his well-known principle of clear and distinct perception.[42] Descartes justifies this principle in the Fourth Meditation, just prior to articulating the ontological argument in the Fifth, but he does so in part by appealing to the results of the causal arguments for God's existence in the Third Meditation. He knows that whatever he clearly and distinctly perceives is true because he was created by a supremely perfect being who is not a deceiver. But if this is right, then Descartes's general argument in the *Meditations* moves from the existence of God to the rule for truth and then back to the existence of God – a second Cartesian circle![43] Surely, given the nature of his critique of the traditional syllogism, Descartes was keenly aware of *this* circle.

What these considerations reveal is that it is highly unlikely that Descartes regarded the syllogistic version of the argument as a genuine demonstration. It is rare for him ever to formulate a syllogism in defence of his own views, let alone advertise it as one. He must have had a very specific goal in mind to resort to one in this case. I suggest it is the goal mentioned above: Descartes frames the ontological argument as a syllogism in order to enhance its appeal among his contemporary readers, who were trained in traditional logic. Doing so, he thinks, will lend it the authority of Aristotle. In a letter to Marin Mersenne, an influential savant and close friend, Descartes writes of his syllogism: 'this method of demonstration is even according to Aristotle the most perfect of all, for in it the true definition of a thing occurs as the middle term'.[44] But even if Descartes tries to mimic a traditional syllogism, the premises fail to meet the standard of categorical propositions. The syllogistic form of the argument is thus just a bit of window dressing. This is an important finding since, given the circularity problem, Descartes cannot avail himself of the major premise. But if his idea of God is self-validating, then he *does not require* the rule for truth or the formal structure of the syllogism to justify his belief that God exists. The syllogism thus reduces to the minor premise, which, not surprisingly, is what Descartes stresses in his writings,

[42] Some commentators have denied that this is a version of the rule for truth, but this strains credulity given the textual evidence. See, e.g., Curley (1978: 161f.).

[43] This point is owed to Edwin Curley (2005). Following Curley, I say 'a *second* circle' here because *the* Cartesian Circle purportedly consists in assuming the rule for truth in the Third Meditation before proving it in the Fourth Meditation.

[44] AT 3:383; CSMK 183–4.

with the formal character of the argument all but dropping out. Again, this premise constitutes the axiom that he takes ultimately to be self-evident.

Although the rule for truth that constitutes the major premise of the syllogism does not play a formal role, it does serve as a useful heuristic. One might notice that the version of the rule that Descartes invokes in the Fifth Meditation differs somewhat from the one he introduces in the Fourth. The principle in that earlier meditation is simply that whatever one clearly and distinctly perceives is true, but the version cited above in premise (1) makes reference to ideational contents.[45] In effect, Descartes is introducing a new method of 'demonstration', one that differs markedly from the Aristotelian syllogism and that simply involves unveiling the contents of one's clear and distinct ideas, in keeping with the notion of intuition that we have already discussed.

The syllogism above is not the only formal version of the ontological argument that readers have found in Descartes's writings. In fact, there is a long line of philosophers, including, most notably, Leibniz and Kant, who claim to discover another proof in the Fifth Meditation, one that they treat either as *the* Cartesian ontological argument or as a sub-argument for the minor premise of the syllogism. This so-called 'Perfection Argument' can be formulated as follows:

1. God is a supremely perfect being, i.e., a being having all perfections.
2. Existence is a perfection.
3. Therefore, God exists.

Both the validity and soundness of this argument are problematic, as critics such as Gaunilo and Kant have made clear. Absent a 'bridge' principle (such as Descartes's rule for truth), the argument makes an illicit logical leap from the mental to the extra-mental. At most, it demonstrates that existence is part of the concept of a supremely perfect being (as Kant noted). As for the truth-value of the premises, any attempt to provide a precise and non-subjective analysis of the concept of perfection – and a compelling defence of why existence qualifies as one – seems doomed to failure. But there are several reasons for thinking that Descartes never intended to articulate this argument. First, it is the only place in his writings where he purportedly formulates it. In every other relevant passage, he invokes some version of the syllogism and/or says that God's existence is self-evident. Second, there is no reference here to the geometric analogies that characterize his treatment of the *a priori*

[45] AT 7:62, CSM 2:43.

argument. Third, the Perfection Argument is closer in character to Anselm's ontological proof than it is to Descartes's.[46] Anselm starts from the definition of God as the greatest conceivable being and then asks whether existence is a mark of supreme greatness. But as Descartes says elsewhere, our natural tendency, given the finitude of our intellect, is to conceive of the divine perfections *separately* rather than under some general rubric such as 'supremely perfect being'.[47] To revisit an earlier discussion, it is because of this tendency that we are prone to draw rational distinctions between the divine attributes by concentrating on one and abstracting from the others. Descartes sometimes uses the term 'supremely perfect being' as an expository convenience, but he is not claiming that this notion of God is epistemically primary and can thus serve as the basis of an argument, as the major premise of the Perfection Argument does. What *is* epistemically basic is God considered under some single attribute or other.

Apart from these considerations, when the passage in question is read carefully, it becomes clear that Descartes is not mounting a second argument but responding to a potential objection to the syllogism that he has already presented.[48] The paragraph begins: 'And it must not be objected at this point that while it is indeed necessary for me to suppose God exists, once I have made the supposition that he has all perfections ... nevertheless the original supposition was not necessary.' As the context indicates, the notion of 'necessity' here and in what follows should be understood in terms of psychological compulsion. On Descartes's view, the objection raises the question of what we are compelled to attribute to God in order to conceive of him clearly and distinctly. Here is his answer:

> [6] Now admittedly, it is not necessary that I ever light upon any thought of God; but whenever I do choose to think of the first and supreme being, and bring forth the idea of God from the treasure house of my mind as it were, it is necessary that I attribute all perfections to him, even if I do not at that time enumerate them or attend to them individually. And this necessity plainly guarantees that, when I later realize that existence is a perfection, I rightly conclude [*recte concludam*] that the first and supreme being exists.[49]

[46] I suspect that some readers are drawn to this proof out of a desire to assimilate Descartes's discussion to Anselm's. Others, like Curley, are attracted to it precisely because it does not appeal to the rule for truth, and thus avoids arguing in a circle.

[47] AT 7:119, CSM 2:84–5.

[48] Doney (1993: 429) was likely the first to propose this.

[49] AT 7:67, CSM 2:46–7.

Readers have struggled to understand this passage, in part because they are innocent of Descartes's distinction between abstraction and exclusion, but by using these notions we can add precision to his claims. Descartes begins by asserting that one is not compelled to attend to the innate idea of God, nor, if one does call forth this idea, is one compelled to attend to any given attribute. In fact, one may never notice that this idea includes some particular attribute such as existence. And even after one has discovered particular attributes one can *abstract* from them. The crucial point, however, is that one cannot *exclude* any of the attributes contained in one's innate idea of God, at least not by a clear and distinct intellectual operation.

So there is no argument in this passage, only an attempt to clarify how innate ideas constrain the way one thinks of them, a topic that runs throughout the Fifth Meditation and elsewhere. Descartes speaks of 'concluding' in the last line of this citation, but he could have used the term 'judging' without loss of meaning. His point is that as a result of clearly and distinctly perceiving that necessary existence cannot be excluded from one's idea of God, one rightly *judges* that God exists.

Some readers purport to find a third and final *a priori* argument in Descartes's writings but, as we shall see, he is again addressing an objection and, more importantly, trying to help his objector intuit that necessary existence is contained in the idea of God. The passage appears in the First Replies where, among other things, Descartes tackles the objection that we discussed in the previous section, namely, that if the ontological argument were valid, one could proliferate such arguments for contingent beings or even imaginary ones. The trick is simply to build existence into the concept, either explicitly (e.g., 'existing lion') or implicitly (e.g., 'supremely perfect island'). In his reply and throughout his discussion of the ontological argument, Descartes emphasizes the difference between ideas like these that have been 'put together by my own intellect' (i.e., invented) and those such as the idea of God that are innate and hence have 'true and immutable natures'. In the case of a supremely perfect island, necessary existence 'does not arise from the other corporeal perfections' and 'can in fact be denied of this body' since in virtue of being finite it lacks ontological independence ('when I examine the idea of a body, I perceive that a body has no power to create itself or maintain itself in existence'). In other words, it is clear that the idea of a supremely perfect island is a mental fiction because necessary existence is not linked conceptually to the island's other attributes, which are corporeal in nature.

The case of God is different, and to illustrate this to the reader he describes a thought experiment. It involves perceiving that necessary existence *is* conceptually linked to God's other attributes, omnipotence in particular.

> [7] Yet if we attentively examine whether existence belongs to a supremely powerful being, and what sort of existence it is, we shall be able to perceive clearly and distinctly the following facts. First, possible existence, at the very least, belongs to such a being, just as it belongs to all the other things of which we have a distinct idea ... Next, when we attend to the immense power of this being, we shall be unable to think of its existence as possible without also recognizing that it can exist by its own power; and we shall infer from this that this being does really exist and has existed from eternity, since it is quite evident by the natural light that what can exist by its own power always exists. So we shall come to understand that necessary existence is contained in the idea of a supremely powerful being, not by any fiction of the intellect, but because it belongs to the true and immutable nature of such a being that it exists.[50]

Descartes appeals here to his distinction between possible and necessary existence. Recall that what he means by these notions is *dependent* and *independent* existence, respectively. He also invokes his doctrine that we cannot distinctly conceive of anything except as existing. So like all clear and distinct ideas, the idea of an omnipotent being must contain either dependent or independent existence. But in virtue of his omnipotence such a being cannot possess merely dependent existence. An omnipotent exists 'by its own power' and hence is eternal. In other words, omnipotence is conceptually linked to the traditional notion of aseity or what Descartes means by necessary existence. (Contemporary philosophers might say that 'omnipotence *logically entails* necessary existence', but given his anti-formalism Descartes would not.) By working through this cognitive exercise, we come to discover that necessary existence *is* properly contained in our innate idea of a supremely perfect being and has not been superadded to it by 'a fiction of the intellect', unlike the idea of a supremely perfect island. Descartes believes that all of the divine attributes are conceptually intertwined in this way, though he seems compelled to grant that the link between omnipotence and necessary existence is particularly salient, which is why he focuses on it here.

So once again there is no argument in this passage, let alone another *a priori* argument. Descartes is committed to the view that God's existence is ultimately self-evident and thus sees his own role as that of Socratic midwife, massaging the intellect of his reader in an effort to induce the relevant intuition. The advantage of this reading over the standard one could

[50] AT 7:118–19, CSM 2:84–5.

not be clearer. Those who see Descartes as presenting an argument in this passage saddle him with an absurd position. Anthony Kenny, most notably, makes it sound as if Descartes's argument is that a supremely powerful being – *as a merely possible entity* – bootstraps itself into actual existence by means of sheer power.[51] Interpreting this passage properly depends on understanding how Descartes uses the notions of possible existence and necessary existence, but the cogency of the reading developed above also confirms that we have parsed these notions correctly.

To be fair to those who claim to find an argument in this passage, Descartes does employ something akin to the procedure of a *reductio ad absurdum* proof. By supposing that the idea of a supremely powerful being contains merely possible existence, one is in effect trying to exclude necessary existence from that idea. But Descartes believes that one discovers that it cannot be excluded. Failed exclusion is like a *reductio* in revealing that one's initial supposition is false.[52]

4 Existence Is Not a Predicate and Other Objections

Two of the most important criticisms of Descartes's ontological argument have been credited historically to Leibniz and Kant, even though credit is owed instead to two of his contemporaries who articulated them in their official objections appended to the *Meditations.* The first objection, attributed to Leibniz, was originally formulated by Marin Mersenne (against Descartes's syllogism). The complaint is that the ontological argument proves too little. It establishes that *if* God's existence is possible or non-contradictory then God exists, but it fails to demonstrate the antecedent of this conditional.[53] The possibility of a supremely perfect being must be proven since the divine attributes could be inconsistent with one another.

Given his account of the relation between the divine attributes, Descartes has an effective reply to this objection. Like other Catholic philosophers, Descartes subscribes to the doctrine of divine simplicity. In fact, he places special emphasis on this doctrine: 'the unity, the simplicity, or the insepar-ability of all the attributes of God is one of the most important of the

51 Kenny (1968: 159). Margaret Wilson (1978, 175–6) responds favourably to Kenny's reconstruction, dubbing it the 'argument from omnipotence'.

52 See Murdoch (1993) for a general comparison of a *reductio* to a failed exclusion.

53 Second Objections, AT 7:127; CSM 2:91.

perfections which I understand him to have'.[54] However, the objection cannot be deflected merely by invoking divine simplicity. Leibniz subscribes to this doctrine too, yet nevertheless holds that the ontological argument requires a supplementary proof of God's possibility. The difference is that Descartes understands this doctrine more strictly than perhaps any other philosopher in the Christian tradition. For example, on the basis of divine simplicity, he asserts that willing and understanding are the same in God, a claim that Leibniz must reject given his view that in creation God chooses among different possible worlds.[55] Unlike Leibniz, Descartes holds that the divine attributes are merely rationally distinct. Properly understood, this means that in reality, God's omnipotence *just is* his omniscience; his benevolence *just is* his immutability, etc. It is only we, with our finite intellects, who draw distinctions in reason where there are no distinctions in reality. But if the divine perfections are identical in God (should he exist) and the distinction between them arises only in our thought, then there can be no problem about their consistency or compossibility.

The most famous objection to the ontological argument is that it falsely assumes that existence is a predicate or property. Although standardly attributed to Kant, the objection was first articulated by Pierre Gassendi, who writes: 'existence is not a perfection either in God or in anything else; it is that without which no perfections can be present'. Gassendi's point is that existence is a precondition for having properties rather than a property itself: 'if a thing lacks existence, we do not say it is . . . deprived of perfection, but . . . instead that it is nothing at all'.[56] To convince us of this point in his own statement of the objection, Kant notes that existence does not add anything to the concept of a thing. For example, there is no difference between the concept of a hundred imaginary dollars and a hundred real dollars.[57] One could take this to mean that there is no difference in idea between the real and imaginary dollars, and this is because whenever we conceive of anything we conceive of it as existing. Hume, for his part, expressly affirms the latter:

> [8] The idea of existence, then, is the very same with the idea of what we conceive to be existent. To reflect on any thing simply, and to reflect on it as existent, are nothing different from each other. That idea, when

[54] Third Meditation, AT 7:50; CSM 2:34.

[55] Letter to Mersenne, 27 May 1630; AT 1:152; CSMK 25.

[56] Fifth Objections, AT 7:323; CSM 2:224–5.

[57] *Critique of Pure Reason* A598–9/B626–7.

> conjoined with the idea of any object, makes no addition to it. Whatever we conceive, we conceive to be existent.[58]

Many philosophers have taken the existence objection to be fatal to the ontological argument, but they fail to appreciate that Descartes largely agrees with his critics about the nature of existence and the role it plays in thought.[59] For example, Descartes insisted long before Hume and Kant that 'we cannot conceive of anything except as existing'.[60] As for the ontology of existence, Descartes also agrees that any putative thing cannot have properties unless it exists. He explicitly affirms the Aristotelian principle that 'nothing has no properties'.[61] It follows from this that existence is not a property, but here one must draw a distinction. One could affirm that existence is a property while denying that it is an accidental or changeable property (i.e., a 'mode' in Descartes's sense). However, Descartes's position is more radical. He denies that it is a property of any kind. This is the force of saying that a substance and its existence are merely rationally distinct. Existence qualifies as an attribute in Descartes's technical sense, but because of the relation they bear to their respective substances, Cartesian attributes are not properties in the traditional sense.

Despite this agreement, there are two key differences between Descartes and his critics about the nature of existence. First, Descartes thinks that one can attend to one attribute of a substance while ignoring any of the others, including existence. This again is what it means to 'abstract' in his sense and thereby produce a rational distinction. Second, and more importantly, he distinguishes two grades of existence – contingent and necessary. The former is contained in our ideas of all finite things, while the latter is contained exclusively in the idea of God. As we have seen, the ontological argument hinges on this distinction. So existence does add something to the concept in the case of God. One could of course reject the distinction but, if so, one must do so on different grounds than whether existence is a property.[62]

Given Descartes's view that God's existence is ultimately self-evident, the best objection to his project is that one lacks the requisite intuition. Much is

[58] *Treatise on Human Nature* I.ii.6.

[59] The objection itself is somewhat controversial. Modern logic treats existence as a quantifier (Russell says it is a property of a propositional function), but that hardly settles the debate since there are alternative systems of logic that treat it as a predicate.

[60] AT 7:166, CSM 2:117. See discussion above.

[61] *Principles*, AT 8A:25; CSM 1:210.

[62] Kant betrays an ignorance of this distinction when he says that the argument shows only that if God exists then he exists necessarily, mistakenly taking the notion of necessity here to be logical necessity (*Critique* A594/B622).

purportedly packed into this intuition, which makes the criticism all the more pointed. To be fair, Descartes anticipates this objection and much of his efforts in the Fifth Meditation and elsewhere are designed to help induce the clear and distinct perception of God's existence in the meditator. But he grants that his efforts might fail. The *Meditations* is written as a guidebook to the truth, but there is no guarantee that readers will attain it. Indeed, Descartes acknowledges that some readers might not discover their innate idea of God even after reading the *Meditations* a thousand times.[63] Readers who are unsympathetic to Descartes's project, however, will find this reply to be unsatisfying, as they will deny that the requisite intuition is possible. They may even deny having an (innate) idea of God.[64]

63 Letter to Hyperaspistes, August 1641; AT 3:430; CSMK 194.

64 I thank Nicholas Jolley and Al Spangler for comments on drafts of this chapter.

4 Leibniz

Maria Rosa Antognazza

The feature of Leibniz's ontological argument most frequently commented upon is its stress on the incompleteness of previous versions.[1] Anselm's and Descartes's proofs, Leibniz objects, only show that 'If God is possible, God exists' (A VI vi 438; A VI iv 588).[2] The conclusion, however, is merely hypothetical. It only allows the claim that *if* God is possible, God exists. But is God possible? To be unconditionally conclusive, the argument must be completed as follows:

1. If God is possible, God exists.
2. God is possible.
3. Therefore, God exists.

Leibniz was not the first to note that God's possibility must be shown. His point belongs to a family of objections contesting that we can argue for the

[1] The following abbreviations are used in this chapter:

A:	Leibniz (1923–), cited by Series (Reihe), Volume (Band) and page. 'N' followed by an Arabic numeral indicates the number assigned to the text by the editors. The superscript '2' after the volume number indicates the second edition of the volume.
A/B:	Kant (1781) (1900–) / Kant (1787) (1900–); translated as Kant (1781/1787/1998).
AG:	Leibniz (1989).
AT:	Descartes (1897–1909); cited by volume and page.
CSM:	Descartes (1988); volume 3 as CSMK; cited by volume and page.
GP:	Leibniz (1875–90), cited by volume and page.
Grua:	Leibniz (1948).
LDB:	Leibniz and Des Bosses (2007).
NE:	Leibniz (1981).
Parkinson:	Leibniz (1992).

[2] Leibniz remained interested in the ontological argument all his life and worked on it in a particularly intense way between 1676 (when he visited Spinoza in The Hague on his way back from Paris) and 1678. Important sets of papers document both his exchange with Spinoza and his sustained discussion of 1677 with Arnold Eckhard, a Cartesian professor of logic, physics and mathematics. A paper of January 1678, probably written for Henning Hutmann, is also especially notable (A II i^2 N. 164). There is a significant body of literature treating his versions of the argument. A detailed and most insightful discussion, including key related issues, is offered by chs. 4–8 of Adams (1994) to which I am indebted. Among other important contributions, see Look (2018), Blumenfeld (1995) and Janke (1963).

existence of God *a priori*, from God's idea, because it is at least doubtful that we have a genuine idea of God, that is, a sufficiently clear understanding of the essence of God. Gaunilo presents the objection to Anselm by wondering how we can have the idea of God since we 'do not know what God is in itself [*rem ipsam quae Deus est*]'.[3] Thomas Aquinas denies that a proper idea of God, grasping his essence, is immediately evident *to us* (*per se nota quoad nos*).[4] In the second objections to his *Meditations on First Philosophy*, Descartes is charged with taking for granted that we possess an idea of God so clear and distinct that we are justified in assuming that it represents a possible essence (AT VII 127). Gassendi raises the same type of challenge in his set of objections to Descartes's *Meditations*.[5] Leibniz, however, is arguably the author who points the spotlight most directly on the issue of God's possibility as the pivot of a conclusive ontological argument.

The argument, he writes in the *Nouveaux Essais*, 'runs more or less as follows':

> God is the greatest [Anselm's version] or (as Descartes says) the most perfect of beings; which is to say that he is a being whose greatness or perfection is supreme, containing within himself every degree of it. That is the notion of God. Now here is how existence follows from that notion. Existing is something more than not existing, i.e. existence adds a degree to the greatness or to the perfection – as M. Descartes puts it, existence itself is a perfection. So this degree of greatness and perfection (or rather this perfection) which consists in existence is in that wholly great and wholly perfect supreme being; for otherwise he would be lacking in some degree, which is contrary to his definition. And so it follows that this supreme being exists.[6]

This is 'not fallacious', Leibniz observes, but tacitly assumes that 'this idea of a wholly great [Anselm] or wholly perfect being [Descartes] is possible and does not imply a contradiction'. That is, the argument has 'the defect of assuming that there is such an idea in us' (NE 437–8).

[3] Gaunilo, *Liber pro insipiente*, in *Patrologia Latina*, T. 158, col. 244. Unless otherwise stated, translations are my own.

[4] Thomas Aquinas, *Quaestiones Disputatae de Veritate*, q. 10, art. 12; *Summa Contra Gentiles*, liber I, capita 10–11; *Summa Theologiae*, I, q. 2, art. 1.

[5] AT VII 287–8 / CSM II 200–1: '[C]an anyone claim that he has a genuine idea of God, an idea which represents God as he is? . . . [W]e have no basis for claiming that we have any authentic idea which represents God; and it is more than enough if, on the analogy of our human attributes, we can derive and construct an idea of some sort for our own use.'

[6] NE 437. See also A VI iv 588.

As Leibniz was well aware, given his support for innate ideas, 'and especially that of God' (NE 437–8), his calling into question that we have the idea of God may be puzzling. These prima facie conflicting claims need to be read in the context of Leibniz's wider metaphysical and epistemological commitments. According to him, we do have an innate, *positive* idea of God – that is, an idea which is not constructed *a posteriori* on the basis of the negation of the limitations of the created beings of which we have experience. Such an *a posteriori* construction is precisely the bottom-up way in which Gassendi thinks we form our idea of God, and which grounds his objection against Descartes.[7] Like other heirs of the Platonic tradition (such as Descartes and Spinoza), Leibniz takes instead a top-down approach.[8] According to him, there is a priority of the perfect over the imperfect. The primitive (and hence unanalysable, irreducible) case is the perfect. It is the imperfect which is formed by a partial negation of the perfect, not the other way round. Limited beings are ultimately intelligible only in relation to the absolute. Finite beings can be understood only when referred to the infinite.[9] We must have, therefore, some positive idea of God as a primitive 'Perfect'.

Crucially, however, this idea is very far from adequate. In Leibniz's taxonomy of ideas and notions, the 'idea' of God as the greatest or the most perfect of all beings appears to be treated as a composite notion in which there may be some distinct elements but mixed with other confused (or even obscure) elements. We may have a *nominal* definition of such a notion, that is, we can explain what we mean by it, but this falls short of a *real* definition, namely, a definition 'from which one establishes that a thing is possible'. Like any such partially confused notion, there could be a contradiction lurking in it. And if this were the case, it would turn out that our alleged idea is not a genuine or 'true' idea at all (that is, it is not the 'essence' of a possible being grasped by us albeit confusedly).[10] Indeed, Leibniz notes, 'we often mistakenly believe that we have *ideas* of things in mind' when, in fact, we do not.[11]

[7] See AT VII 287–8, cited in note 5 above.

[8] On a top-down approach in philosophical theology, see Adams (1994: 116) (2007) and Antognazza (2007).

[9] An explicit formulation of this thesis is offered, for instance, by the Cartesian Eckhard in the context of his exchange with Leibniz on the ontological argument (see A II i^2 488).

[10] Cf. A VI iv 589.

[11] See *Meditationes de Cognitione, Veritate et Ideis*, November 1684 (A VI iv 585–92 / AG 23–7).

For instance, we can think about the words ‘square circle’, and grasp both the notion of circle and the notion of square, but the expression ‘square circle’ does not pick out any possible being; it does not represent any genuine idea or essence. In the same way, the words ‘most perfect being’ or ‘that of which nothing greater can be thought’ may not pick out any possible being, despite our grasp of the individual components of these expressions. If this were the case, these expressions would not correspond to a ‘true’ idea. As Leibniz crisply summarizes in the *Meditationes de Cognitione, Veritate et Ideis*:

> Of course we understand what we say, and yet we certainly do not have an idea of impossible things. And so, in the same way, it is not enough that we think about the *Ens perfectissimum* in order to assert that we have an idea of it; and in the demonstration mentioned above the possibility of the *Ens perfectissimum* must either be shown or presupposed to reach a correct conclusion. Nevertheless, nothing is truer than that we have an idea of God, and that the *Ens perfectissimum* is possible, indeed, necessary. The argument, however, is not sufficiently conclusive. (A VI iv 589)

The following sections will be devoted to unpacking ‘the argument’ in what Leibniz regards as its complete form.

1 First Premise

1.1 If God is Possible, God Exists: From Ens Perfectissimum to Ens Realissimum and Ens Necessarium

Why did Leibniz think that the first premise of his complete version of the argument is true? How did he support the momentous claim that ‘If God is possible, God exists’? Notwithstanding its purely hypothetical import, if properly supported, this claim would undoubtedly constitute a key result for philosophical theology.

According to Leibniz, ‘the possibility of any thing’, or its ‘possible existence’, are ‘inseparable’ from ‘the essence of that same thing’. That is, ‘for there being an essence of a thing is the same as the thing being possible’. As for any other being, to say that God is possible is equivalent to saying that there is an essence of God. Assuming for the moment that God is possible and that there is, therefore, an essence of God, the key step in a demonstration of God’s existence from his essence would be to show that ‘the essence of God and his actual existence are inseparable’. From this step, the conclusion would follow that ‘the possible existence or Possibility of God and his actual existence are inseparable, *or, what is the same*, on the assumption that God is possible it follows that God actually exists'.[12] Some thirty years later, in a letter of 10 November 1710, the same reasoning is neatly summarized as follows:

> *If a Being, from the essence of which existence follows, is possible* (*or if it has an essence*), *it exists* (this is an identical or indemonstrable axiom). *God is a Being from the Essence of which existence follows* (this is a definition): *Therefore if God is possible, he exists.* Q. E. D. (GP VII 490)

One way in which Leibniz tries to shore up the most difficult passage of this proof, namely that 'the essence of God and his actual existence are inseparable', follows a well-trodden Cartesian path. 'Whatever follows from the idea or definition of something', Leibniz writes in 1684, 'can be predicated of that thing.' If God is defined as '*Ens perfectissimum*' (or, he adds, as 'that than which a greater cannot be thought'), existence follows, 'for the *Ens perfectissimum* involves all perfections, in the number of which is also existence'.[13]

But is existence a perfection? This version of the argument, which Leibniz seems to endorse uncritically,[14] immediately faces another family of objections all denying in various forms that existence is a property which can be included into the concept of something. The ontological argument does not have to go further than Gaunilo to be confronted with this objection. Things cannot be defined into existence. If it were acceptable to insert existence into the definition of something, it would be as easy to demonstrate the existence of the most perfect island or of the winged horse as to demonstrate the existence of God.[15] The same objection is raised by Gassendi against Descartes (AT VII 323 / CSM II 224–5). Well past Leibniz, the objection keeps returning. Existence is not a 'real predicate' or 'determination' (*Bestimmung*) which enlarges a concept, Kant teaches, and (in case someone still doesn't get the point) one hundred dollars in my mind are very different from one

[12] A II i[2] 588 (January 1678: *Probatio existentiae Dei ex ejus essentia*) and A II i 545. Trans. by Adams in *Leibniz*, pp. 136–7. I have omitted Leibniz's own numbering of these steps of his proof.

[13] A VI iv 588. Cf. A II i[2] 589.

[14] Note that the objection by Leibniz which immediately follows this passage is not that the existence of something cannot be drawn from its definition, but that 'we cannot safely use definitions for drawing conclusions unless we know first that they are real definitions, that is, that they include no contradiction' (A VI iv 588 / AG 25). That is, we *could* conclude to the existence of God from the definition of God as *Ens perfectissimum* if we had established that the *Ens perfectissimum* is possible. A similar absence of the classic objection to regarding existence as a perfection is noticeable in NE 437.

[15] Cf. Gaunilo, *Liber pro insipiente*, in *Patrologia Latina*, T. 158, cols. 246–7 and Gassendi, *Fifth Objections* to Descartes's *Meditations* (AT VII 324 / CSM II 225).

hundred dollars in my pocket, although their concept does not change.[16] Yet, Leibniz's considerate view seems to remain unmoved. He continues to think that God's essence, his 'idea', involves existence.[17] To see why and how, we have to look at his conception of a 'perfection' and of *Ens perfectissimum*.

In a key paper of November 1676, which (according to Leibniz) Spinoza found 'solid',[18] a perfection is defined as

> every simple quality which is positive and absolute, or that expresses without any limits whatever it expresses. But a quality of this kind, since it is simple, is for that reason unanalysable, or indefinable, for otherwise either it will not be one simple quality but an aggregate of a plurality [of qualities], or, if it is one, it will be circumscribed by limits, and so it will be understood through negations of further progress, contrary to the hypothesis, for it is assumed to be purely positive. (A VI iii 578)

In brief, a perfection is a quality which is simple and purely positive. As we will see in Section 2.1 below, of these two features of a perfection – simplicity and positivity – it is positivity which will emerge as Leibniz's most important conceptual tool for the demonstration of the possibility of the *Ens perfectissimum*.[19] As regards simplicity, a simple quality is for Leibniz a quality which cannot be resolved into, or reduced to, other qualities. As regards positivity, a purely positive quality involves no negation whatsoever. Since any limitation is a negation of some 'further progress' or further degree of that which is limited,[20] pure positivity involves having no limitation at all. In turn, pure positivity captures, for Leibniz, what it is to be absolute. To be absolute is to be free from any condition and any limitation.[21] Only what is purely positive can be absolute since any condition is a sort of limitation, and any limitation is a negation. Hence, an absolute quality must be a purely positive quality.

The *Ens perfectissimum* is, quite obviously, the Being that has *all* perfections. Setting aside some important open questions concerning which

[16] Kant, *Critique of Pure Reason*, A 598–9/B 626–7. [17] Cf. *Monadology*, §44 (GP VI 614).

[18] Leibniz reports having presented this paper to Spinoza while he was in The Hague in November 1676 (A VI iii 579).

[19] Adams (1994: 113) notes that 'the most durable feature of Leibniz's conception of perfections is that they involve no negation at all'.

[20] Cf. A VI iii 578, cited above.

[21] On the meaning of 'absolute', cf. Adams (1994: 115), referring to texts in which Leibniz explicitly opposes 'absolute' to 'limited' or uses 'absolute' in the sense of 'unconditioned' or 'unqualified'. On Leibniz's conception of the absolute as beyond any determination or qualification, and on its relation to pure positivity and to divine infinity see Antognazza (2015).

qualities can be divine perfections,[22] let us proceed on Leibniz's assumption that the nature or essence of the *Ens perfectissimum* is constituted by the conjunction of all simple and purely positive qualities which count as perfections.[23] With this conception of perfections and *Ens perfectissimum* in place, we can now return to the vexed question of whether existence can be a perfection.

Despite early formulations to the contrary,[24] if one takes a closer look at Leibniz's more mature texts on the matter, it becomes reasonably clear that, according to him, existence is not a perfection amongst other perfections or properties. In a text penned around 1677, he writes: 'it is indeed true that what exists is more perfect that the non-existent, but it is not true that existence itself is a perfection, since it is only a certain comparison of perfections amongst themselves.'[25] Thus, existence can be defined in terms of perfection without being itself conceived as a perfection. This is precisely what Leibniz proposes to do in a text dating around 1680 in which a 'real definition' of existence is offered: 'The *real definition* of existence consists in this, that that which is maximally perfect, or which involves more essence, exists amongst those which could otherwise exist, so that it is the nature of possibility or of essence to demand [*exigere*] existence. If it were not this way, it would not be possible to give the reason of the existence of things.'[26]

This is a 'real' definition insofar as it seeks to explain the nature of existence through the identification of the reason or cause that any existence would have. Leibniz's short answer is as follows: the reason of existence is *perfection*.[27]

[22] For a brief discussion see Section 2.1.

[23] Leibniz writes in 1676: 'from the conjunction in the same subject of all absolute forms or possible perfections arises the *Ens perfectissimum*' (A VI iii 521); 'Essence is all that is conceived per se in the thing, that is, the aggregate of all attributes' (A VI iii 572).

[24] See especially *Quod Ens Perfectissimum existit*, November 1676 (A VI iii 579) and *Probatio existentiae Dei ex ejus essentia*, January 1678 (A II i^2 589). Later texts such as the *Meditationes de Cognitione, Veritate et Ideis* (1684) and the *Nouveaux Essais* (1703–5) indicate that the formulation according to which existence is a perfection is Descartes's rather than Leibniz's ('as M. Descartes puts it, existence itself is a perfection' NE 437). It is significant, however, that Leibniz does not appear to be particularly worried about pushing back on this Cartesian formulation, although by this time he had come to reject the view that existence can be regarded as a property on a par with other properties of an essence.

[25] *Existentia. An sit Perfectio*, A VI iv 1354. Cf. also *De veritatibus primis*, *c.* 1680 (A VI iv 1443) where Leibniz objects that existence cannot be conceived as 'superadding something new to things'. This objection is very much in line with the classic family of objections according to which (in its Kantian version) existence cannot be a property which 'enlarges' a concept.

[26] A VI iv 1443. Cf. A VI iv 1363.

[27] Cf. also a text of 1672 in which Leibniz suggests that 'to exist' is nothing else than being sensed (by God) as 'Harmonious' (A VI iii 56) – and harmony is, for Leibniz, an expression of perfection.

More precisely, each possible being or essence has a 'propensity [*propensio*]'[28] or a 'claim [*exigentia*]'[29] to existence in proportion to its degree of perfection. Degrees of perfection are identified, therefore, with the reason or the 'source of existence [*principium existentiae*]' (rather than with existence itself).[30]

Around 1685, however, Leibniz denies that existence can be defined, at least in the sense of reducing it to some 'clearer notion'. Nevertheless, he still gives the same account, in terms of degrees of perfection, of why some possible things exist while others do not:

> *Existent* cannot be defined, any more than Entity [*Ens*] or the purely positive, that is, in such a way that some clearer notion might be shown to us; one should know, however, that every possible will exist if it can, but since not all possibles can exist, as some hinder others, those exist which are more perfect. Therefore, it is certainly established that what is most perfect exists. (A VI iv 626)

But how does Leibniz justify what has been called the 'principle of essence's demand for existence' underpinning the whole proposal? This principle, intended as the claim that each essence will exist unless there is a reason preventing its existence, is for him a corollary of the principle of sufficient reason.[31] As he writes around 1680, 'if in the nature of the essence itself there was not a certain inclination toward existence, nothing would exist; for to say that some essences have this inclination, and some do not, is to say that something is without a reason, since existence is regarded in general as referred to every essence in the same manner'. (A VI iv 1443) Leibniz indicates here that existence, rather than non-existence, is the easier, and hence the default status. As we will see in Section 2.2 below, this claim plays an important part in Leibniz's version of the ontological argument.

Granted (on the basis of the principle of sufficient reason) that all possible things have a claim to existence, those compossible things exist which, together, have a greater degree of perfection in relation to competing sets of things which are incompossible with that most perfect set.

[28] *Elementa verae pietatis, sive de amore Dei super omnia*, c. 1677–8; A VI iv 1363.

[29] *De veritatibus primis*, c. 1680; A VI iv 1442. See also GP VII 303.

[30] *De rerum orginatione radicali*, 23 November 1697; GP VII 304.

[31] This point is highlighted by Adams (1994: 173), citing GP VII 194 (A VI iv 1443) as evidence that the principle 'every possible demands to exist' was intended by Leibniz in this way. As Adams (1994: 175) argues, there is, therefore, a sense in which the principle of sufficient reason is required also for Leibniz's *a priori* argument for the existence of God insofar as it is needed to account for the necessity of the divine essence.

(The existence of incompossible things is obviously blocked by the principle of non-contradiction.) As Leibniz puts it:

> Therefore, existence will be the superiority of the degrees of reality of one thing over the degrees of reality of an opposite thing; that is, that which is more perfect than all things incompatible among themselves *exists*, and, on the other hand, what exists is more perfect than the remaining things. (A VI iv 1354)

It is important to note that degrees of perfection are equated in this passage to quantity or degrees of *reality*. Leibniz formulates the same thought very succinctly in other texts ('*More perfect* is that which has more *reality* or positive entity'; '*Perfection* is degree of reality').[32]

This equation between degrees of perfection and degrees of reality is in line with the proposal advanced by Arnold Eckhard in his exchange with Leibniz on the ontological argument.[33] A few months after the discussion with Spinoza in which Leibniz endorses the view that existence is a perfection,[34] in April 1677 we find him questioning this very point in his debate with Eckhard. 'Perfections', Leibniz objects, 'seem to be qualities in a way that existence is not.'[35] Eckhard retorts, however, that perfection for him 'is Being [*Entitas*] in so far as it is understood to depart from non-Being'.[36] Presented with this conception, Leibniz declares himself happy to drop his objection to considering existence as a perfection. More precisely, he adds, 'as I would prefer to define it, *perfection* is degree or quantity of reality or [*seu*] essence' (A II i^2 543).

The same reason of existence which applies to possible limited beings – namely, perfection, intended now as 'degree or quantity of reality' – applies to God. As the most perfect of all beings, God's essence must involve existence. The pivotal point here is the metaphysical claim that the existence of a possible being is prevented by its incompatibility with a more perfect possible being which, precisely insofar as it is more perfect, has a greater claim to existence. However, by definition, no competing essences or set of essences would have greater perfection than the *Ens perfectissimum*. (Insofar as they are *not* the *Ens perfectissimum*, all other essences or sets of essences must involve limitation of some sort.) If one grants that the reason of existence is

32 A VI iv 867; A VI iv 1429. See also *Elementa verae pietatis*, *c.* 1677–8, quoted below (A VI iv 1358).

33 See II i^2 N. 140, N. 142, N. 143, N. 146, N. 148.

34 *Quod Ens Perfectissimum existit*, November 1676 (A VI iii 579): 'existence is included in the number of perfections'.

35 A II i^2 488. See also A II i^2 494, 499.

36 A II i^2 543. See also A II i^2 488 ('perfection is every attribute, or every reality') and A II i^2 494.

perfection, and that a possible being exists unless its existence is incompatible with a more perfect possible being, it follows that the nature of the *Ens perfectissimum* (assuming this is a possible nature) must involve existence – and, indeed, necessary existence.[37]

In sum, existence is treated not as a property simpliciter but as a second-order property, that is, as a property of properties or as a property of a conjunction of properties. That is to say, existence, or more precisely, *necessary* existence, is a property of properties which are absolutely unlimited or purely positive qualities. Thus, this is not a case of inserting existence into the definition of something, or of treating existence as a property to be added to an essence on a par with the other properties of which such an essence is a conjunction. Necessary existence is a property which supervenes, as it were, only upon the conjunction of all properties expressing whatever they express absolutely, without any limitation. Conversely, this is not a property which the properties of a most perfect island or a winged lion could have. For instance, the most perfect island may well have all the best compossible qualities of an island in their highest degree – but this degree will still be a *limited* degree of a *limited* number of compossible qualities, as opposed to being an unlimited conjunction of all unlimited properties. It is their very nature as unlimited that requires existence since 'existence [is] the superiority of the degrees of reality of one thing over the degrees of reality of an opposite thing' (A VI iv 1354). The *Ens perfectissimum* is, therefore, also the *Ens realissimum*.[38] Assuming the

[37] That this would be necessary existence should be clear from the definition of God as *Ens perfectissimum* and the 'real definition' of existence proposed by Leibniz. If anything, one could wonder whether the same necessary existence would then apply to the most perfect set of compossible (limited) beings amongst all possible sets, leading to a necessitarianism which Leibniz would surely want to avoid. One way to avoid such necessary existence of the best set of limited beings would be its incompatibility with a more perfect being, namely God. But if this were the case, the result would not be the contingent existence of the best set of compossible limited essences, but the impossibility of its existence. This impossibility would not stretch to logical impossibility – it would still be a set of logically possible (and compossible) beings, like any other, less perfect, set of compossible essences – but it would lose its metaphysical possibility in the sense of possibly having actual existence. A more promising way out of necessitarianism is to stress that the essences of limited beings constitute the *formal* cause of their existence but not their *efficient* cause, and that in order to have actual existence also an efficient cause (namely God) is needed. In other words, essences are *reasons* which *influence* God's choice, but God's free choice to create is still needed. Only the divine essence constitutes a reason which excludes non-existence – hence only in the case of God is there no need of efficient cause. On essences as formal (as opposed to efficient) causes of existence see Adams (1994: 176).

[38] See for instance *Elementa verae pietatis*, *c.* 1677–8 (A VI iv 1358): '*God* is the *Ens perfectissimum*. *Perfection* is degree or quantity of reality. Hence *perfectissimum* is what has the highest degree of reality.' In his exchange with Leibniz on the ontological argument, Arnold Eckhard insists that *perfectissimum* can be substituted with *realissimum*, the latter being a rougher way to express what the former expresses in a more sophisticated manner (cf. A II i^2 527, 541).

Ens realissimum is a possible being, it *must* involve existence since it is the *only* being whose nature is to have unlimited reality as the conjunction of all qualities expressing absolutely, without any limitation whatever they express.

The backbone of the first part of the argument, as Leibniz sees it, is *not*, therefore, whether existence can be treated as a perfection. As noted above, no later than 1680 he recognizes the obvious problems of considering existence as a first-order property of God's essence. Despite this acknowledgement, however, in the later *Meditationes de Cognitione, Veritate et Ideis* (1684) and in the *Nouveaux Essais* (1703–5), he does not abandon the view that Anselm's and Descartes's versions are basically equivalent, although Anselm's definition of God does not mention perfections or the *Ens perfectissimum*. This seems to indicate that, according to Leibniz, the objection targeting the link between existence and properties misses the crucial point, since existence can still be construed as some kind of property, albeit not a first-order one 'enlarging' the essence on a par with other first-order properties.

The crux of the matter is, instead, whether God's essence (conceived either as the greatest being or as the *Ens perfectissimum*) involves existence.[39] Leibniz never abandons the view that it does. And the reason for this is that any essence (that is, any possible being) has a claim (*exigentia*) to existence in proportion to its degree of perfection (or degree of reality). In other words, what does the work is the notion of degree of perfection as reason for existence. Any essence will exist unless it is incompatible with the existence of an essence of greater perfection, and having, as such, a greater claim to existence. This is the principle which governs, in general, the grand competition for existence among possible worlds, resulting in the victory of the best (that is, the richest in perfection or reality) of them all. The same principle also explains the necessary existence of the *Ens perfectissimum* or *Ens realissimum*. By definition, no competing being of greater perfection could hinder its existence. The *Ens perfectissimum*, or *Ens realissimum*, is therefore also the *Ens necessarium*, that is, the Being involving not only existence but necessary existence. For Leibniz, the only way in which existence can be involved in an essence is by its being *necessary* existence. Leibniz seems indeed quite happy

[39] The Cartesian Eckhard notes: 'that being [*ens*] which involves necessary existence in its concept, exists. God is the being [*ens*] which involves necessary existence in its concept. Therefore God exists. This is the very argument of Descartes [*Hoc est ipsissimum Cartesii argumentum*]' (A II i^2 497). In his reply of 28 April 1677, Leibniz concedes that the Cartesian argument is consistent with this interpretation and can be reduced to that 'of the forefathers' (presumably Leibniz means Anselm), despite its being formulated as a claim that existence is a perfection (cf. A II i^2 501).

to slide from *Ens perfectissimum* to *Ens necessarium* as if these were two equivalent notions,[40] since on his account of perfection the *Ens perfectissimum is* the *Ens necessarium*. And being the *Ens necessarium* makes all the difference, given that (if possible) this is the being with the unique privilege of existing by conceptual necessity.

1.2 If God is Possible, God Exists: *Ens Necessarium* and Existence

For Leibniz, there is therefore no problem, in principle, with the claim that an essence has the unique privilege of involving existence.[41] Likewise, if properly understood, there is no problem with a (much maligned) passage from the ideal order to the real order.[42] After all, correct mathematical calculations do translate, in the real order, into audacious skyscrapers which do not fall. Or, as Leibniz puts it in *Quid sit idea*, 'although the idea of a circle is not similar to a circle, it is possible to draw truths from it which, without any doubt, will be confirmed by the experience of the true circle' (A VI iv 1371). Nevertheless, he is sensitive to the benefit of avoiding altogether treating existence as a property.[43] He tries in fact to support the first premise of his complete argument also without reference to existence as a perfection. This move yields, in modern parlance, a modal argument for the existence of God.

Starting from a definition of God as the *Ens necessarium*, we have the following proof:

> The essence of God involves necessity of existence (for by the name of God we understand a necessary Being). If the essence of anything involves a necessary existence, its essence is inseparable from existence (for otherwise it is a merely possible or contingent thing). Therefore, the essence and existence of God are inseparable. Finally therefore we have concluded that, if God is possible, he actually exists, and therefore it need only be proved that a most perfect Being [*Ens perfectissimum*], or at any rate a necessary Being [*Ens necessarium*], is possible.[44]

[40] Cf. for instance A VI iv 589. [41] See A II i^2 590.

[42] See A VI iii 583 and GP IV 406, quoted below.

[43] See for instance A II i^2 486, 501, 589; GP VII 490.

[44] January 1678; A II i^2 589 (trans. by Adams in *Leibniz*, p. 138). In one of the annotations to this proof, Leibniz defines the *Ens necessarium* as '*Ens a se*' 'whose existence necessarily follows, or is inseparable, from its very essence' (A II i^2 591; translated in Adams: (1994: 138)). See also GP IV 405.

In a paper written roughly one year before, around December 1676, Leibniz takes the same kind of approach:

> *Ens a se* is the same as a Being from whose essence existence follows, namely a Being to which it is essential to exist, or which exists through its own essence.
>
> Again, a necessary Being is the same as a Being from whose essence existence follows. For a necessary Being is one which necessarily exists, such that for it not to exist would imply a contradiction, and so would conflict with the concept or essence of this Being. And so existence belongs to its concept or essence. From this we have a splendid theorem, which is the pinnacle of modal theory and by which one moves in a wonderful way from potentiality to act: If a necessary Being is possible, it follows that it exists actually, or, that such a Being is actually found in the universe.[45]

The 'splendid theorem', which Leibniz regards as the 'pinnacle of modal theory', corresponds to the characteristic axiom of the system of modal logic S5 'if possibly *p*, then necessarily possibly *p*' ($\Diamond p \rightarrow \Box\Diamond p$). This axiom is logically equivalent to the formula directly relevant to the modal argument for the existence of God: 'if possibly necessarily *p*, then necessarily *p*' ($\Diamond\Box p \rightarrow \Box p$), as shown below:[46]

The S5 axiom can be expressed in the following form, with the propositional variable negated:

$$\Diamond{\sim}p \rightarrow \Box\Diamond{\sim}p$$

By transposition, this is equivalent to:

$${\sim}\Box\Diamond{\sim}p \rightarrow {\sim}\Diamond{\sim}p$$

Substituting now the equivalencies of the modal operators ($\Diamond p \equiv {\sim}\Box{\sim}p$ and $\Box p \equiv {\sim}\Diamond{\sim}p$) in the antecedent and consequent, we obtain:

$${\sim}{\sim}\Diamond{\sim}{\sim}\Box{\sim}{\sim}p \rightarrow \Box p$$

Eliminating the double negations in the antecedent we have

$$\Diamond\Box p \rightarrow \Box p$$

45 *Definitio Dei seu Entis a se* (A VI iii 583 / Parkinson 107, trans. slightly modified). Cf. A II i^2 587 and GP IV 406.

46 The equivalence is shown by Look (2018) in endnote 15, from which I am drawing.

S5 is, of course, only one of the systems of modal logic, and there are systems in which its characteristic axiom is not valid. However, in the context of Leibniz's argument, S5 does seem to be the appropriate system since we are concerned with the logical necessity and possibility of ideas.[47]

The same result can be obtained in a system of modal logic containing Brouwer's axiom[48] $p \rightarrow \Box\Diamond p$ expressed as $\sim p \rightarrow \Box\Diamond\sim p$

Substituting the possibility operator with the equivalent necessity operator ($\Diamond p \equiv \sim\Box\sim p$) we obtain:

$$\sim p \rightarrow \Box\sim\Box\sim\sim p$$

and applying the double negation rule

$$\sim p \rightarrow \Box\sim\Box p$$

Next, let us translate Leibniz's claim 'Ens necessarium est possibile' as $\Diamond\Box p$.

Substituting the possibility operator with the necessity operator, this is equivalent to:

$$\sim\Box\sim\Box p$$

We can now use the claim 'Ens necessarium est possibile' as the first premise of a proof in which the existence of God follows directly from this premise and Brouwer's Axiom via the application of the *modus tollens* (3) and double negation (4) rules of inference:[49]

1. $\sim\Box\sim\Box p$
2. $\sim p \rightarrow \Box\sim\Box p$ (Brouwer's axiom)
3. (Therefore) $\sim\sim p$
4. (Therefore) p

In Leibniz's words, we have here the 'splendid theorem', 'pinnacle of modal theory', according to which 'if a necessary Being is possible, it follows that it exists actually'

$$(\sim\Box\sim\Box p \rightarrow p).$$

[47] On the appropriateness of S5 in the context of modal arguments for the existence of God, see Adams (1997: esp. 234–5). As Adams notes, similar considerations can be made for the Brouwersche system.

[48] This result has been proved by Adams in the context of a discussion of Anselm's modal argument in Adams (1997: 232–6), from which I am drawing. The Brouwer's axiom is characteristic of the Brouwersche (or 'B' for short) system of modal logic but is also a provable theorem in S5.

[49] See Adams (1997: 236), where this proof is formulated (with a different formal notation).

There are at this point only two alternatives: either there is an essence with the unique privilege of involving existence, or there is not such an essence. If the second alternative is the case, the *Ens necessarium* is 'an impossible fiction' (A II i^2 591): that is, not only it does not exist (as a matter of fact or contingently), but it is impossible for it to exist. Leibniz offers different versions of an argument based on a *reductio ad absurdum*.[50] It starts from the premise that the *Ens necessarium* does not exist, reaching the contradictory conclusion that the *Ens necessarium* is not the *Ens necessarium*. This conclusion may be true or false. (Leibniz notes that, contrary to what is normally thought, a contradictory conclusion may be true when it concerns something impossible, e.g., a square circle.)[51] If it is true, it amounts to a demonstration that the notion of *Ens necessarium* implies contradiction and is therefore impossible. If it is false, the premise 'the *Ens necessarium* does not exist' must be false. 'Therefore, we conclude that the *Ens necessarium* either is impossible, or it exists' (A II i^2 586).[52]

In sum, according to Leibniz, the conclusion that the *Ens necessarium*, if possible, exists, 'is a corollary which follows immediately' from the definition of God as 'a Being from itself [*un Estre de soy*] or primitive *Ens a se*', and which indeed 'almost does not differ at all' from this very definition.[53] 'Those who maintain that one can never infer actual existence from mere notions, ideas, definitions, or possible essences', Leibniz notes, 'fall back in fact' on 'the only thing one could say against the existence of such a Being, namely, deny its possibility' (GP IV 406).[54] It is time to turn, therefore, to the issue that Leibniz regards as the only real objection, namely, the issue of God's possibility.

[50] A II i^2 585–8. See also GP IV 406.

[51] On the issue of impossible things in Leibniz's logic, see Lenzen (2017).

[52] Leibniz's reasoning is in line with present-day work on the modal argument. It is generally accepted that the *Ens necessarium* could not exist contingently because such a being would not be the *Ens necessarium*. Moreover, it could not not-exist contingently because contingent non-existence equates to possible contingent existence ($\Diamond p \equiv \sim\Box\sim p$), and contingent existence is ruled out by the very notion of *Ens necessarium*. Therefore, either the *Ens necessarium* exists necessarily or it does not exist and its non-existence is necessary (that is, its existence is impossible).

[53] GP IV 405. The *Ens a se* is the being 'which exists by its essence', that is, the *Ens necessarium* ('The *necessary Being* and the *Being by its Essence* are the same thing' GP IV 406). See also A VI iii 583 and A II i^2 591, quoted above.

[54] Leibniz is well aware of the objection that one could insert 'necessary' into the definition of anything (e.g., 'necessary man') and thereby prove its existence. Once again, his reply is that the issue revolves around showing that this definition is a consistent one, namely that it picks out a possible being (see A II i^2 587).

2 Second Premise

2.1 God is Possible: *Ens Perfectissimum* and Pure Positivity

Above, we saw that, according to Leibniz, the *Ens perfectissimum* or the being of maximal greatness, implies a logically necessary being. Further, we have seen that a logically necessary being, if possible, necessarily exists. Assuming Leibniz has been successful in establishing these two points (that is, assuming he has shown that the *Ens perfectissimum* is the *Ens necessarium*), he can then focus on the possibility of the *Ens perfectissimum* without further worries that its essence, even if it does not involve logical contradiction, may still fail to involve existence.

The pivot of Leibniz's argument for the possibility of the *Ens perfectissimum* is the notion of 'pure positivity'. As he puts it in the briefest of forms around 1685: 'There is however some *Ens perfectissimum*, or the most perfect Being is possible, because it is nothing other than pure positivity [*Ens summe perfectum est possibile, quia nihil aliud est, quam pure positivum*]'.[55]

As we have seen, Leibniz conceives the *Ens perfectissimum* as the conjunction of all purely positive qualities, that is, all qualities which express without any limits whatever they express (A VI iii 578). Their being 'purely positive' implies the lack of any negation whatever. Leibniz's key point is that, from a logical point of view, that which is purely positive cannot contain any formal contradiction. There would be a contradiction if two incompatible qualities (or, broadly speaking, properties) are attributed to the same subject (say, 'being square' and 'being round'). Such incompatibility implies a negation. More precisely, it implies that one property is the negation of the other property not merely in the sense that a property A (e.g., extension) is not another property B (e.g., thought) but in the sense that A ('being square') excludes B ('being round'). This exclusion or incompatibility can be expressed as an identity: A = not-B.[56] A = not-B, however, is directly against the hypothesis of the pure positivity of all perfections (property A cannot be purely positive if it is equal to not-B). Hence the *pure positivum*, since it does not involve any negation, cannot involve any contradiction. If it cannot involve any contradiction, this means that it must be possible. In short, according to Leibniz, purely positive qualities must be compatible because, as purely positive, they cannot involve negation and they cannot, therefore, involve contradiction.[57]

55 *Definitiones notionum metaphysicarum atque logicarum*; A VI iv 626.

56 See esp. A VI iii 575. Cf. Adams (1994: 145).

57 See A VI iii 572, 575, 577 and 578–9. Interestingly, the same type of argument is employed by Eckhard in his exchange with Leibniz (see letter of 19 April 1677; A II i^2 495–6).

In paragraph 45 of the *Monadology* (1714), Leibniz advances very briefly a similar argument but with a metaphysical slant.[58] Since 'nothing can prevent the possibility of that which is without any limits, without any negation, and consequently without any contradiction' (GP VI 614), the *Ens perfectissimum* must be possible. In other words, that which is without limits cannot be limited, that is, partially negated, by anything. Therefore, nothing can restrict it or hinder its possibility. This argument, presented by Leibniz at the end of his life, echoes an earlier note of March 1676 in which the compatibility of purely positive (or 'affirmative') properties is seen as directly implied by their lack of any negation, which in turn implies their being unlimited or absolute:

> For the rest, I demonstrate that all attributes are compatible in no other way than by their being absolute, pure, and unlimited. For if they were modified by limits, they would not be affirmative but negative in a certain manner. (A VI iii 396)

One can object, however, that the possibility of a purely positive being constituted by the conjunction of all purely positive qualities can still be doubted. To start with, although all perfections are, for Leibniz, simple and purely positive qualities, it is not immediately clear whether all simple and purely positive qualities should count as perfections, that is, as God's properties. If there were, for instance, *sensible* simple and purely positive qualities, it would be at the very least untraditional to attribute them to God.[59] And if God were to miss some purely positive quality, then his essence could no longer be regarded as the conjunction of *all* purely positive qualities. One could try to show, however, that no sensible quality, or no quality which does not traditionally belong to God, is purely positive since they all involve some kind of negation or limitation.[60]

Assuming one was able to show this, as well as showing that all purely positive properties are compatible, one would still have to face the objection that a plurality of perfections implies some sort of negation for the very fact that perfection A, although compatible with perfection B, is *not* perfection B.

[58] Cf. Adams (1994: 173).

[59] Leibniz himself objects to Eckhard that pain could be regarded as a reality and hence as having (metaphysically) a positive ontological status as opposed to being mere privation of pleasure (A II i^2 488). If so, it would follow that pain should also be attributed to the Being that encompasses all reality, that is, all positive qualities.

[60] Cf. Eckhard's reply to Leibniz (A II i^2 494), which convinces Leibniz (A II i^2 499, 543), and Adams (1994: esp. pp. 114, 119–22).

In other words, as Spinoza and Hegel point out, *omnis determinatio est negatio*:[61] any determination implies some kind of negation (being *this* perfection and *not that* perfection). Hence the notion of a purely positive being constituted by a plurality of perfections is not a coherent notion since any plurality implies negation.

Finally, there is the problem of clarifying whether all the qualities or properties which are traditionally attributed to God can be purely positive. In this regard, a particularly difficult case is omniscience. Since omniscience implies knowledge of limited beings, and hence representation of beings which involve negation, one may object to a conception of omniscience as a purely positive attribute. If it is not purely positive and yet it belongs to God, it seems that some form of negation is being introduced in what is supposed to be the purely positive nature of God.[62]

In fact, in 1677, Leibniz himself challenges with the following objection Eckhard's claim that the *Ens perfectissimum*, as *Ens realissimum* or *pure positivum*, is the Being which does not participate in any non-Being, since non-Being implies negation and, therefore, imperfection:[63]

> The concept of Being [*ens*] which does not participate in non-Being [*non-ens*] involves two aspects, one: to be [*esse*], the other: *no not to be any thing*, that is, to be all things [*nihil non esse*, seu omnia esse] ... But it seems impossible for there to be a Being which is all things; of such a Being it could be said that it is you, and that it is me as well; something which, I take, you will not admit. (A II i^2 500)

At least part of Leibniz's objection involves the question of how a Being that embraces all reality ('*nihil non esse*, seu omnia esse') can exclude all negation since any determinate thing implies the negation of other determinate things (in Leibniz's own example, 'me' is not 'you').

[61] Cf. Spinoza to Jarig Jelles, Epistola 50 in Spinoza (1925: Vol. 4, and Hegel's 1816 review of Jacobi's *Werke* in Hegel (2009: 9).

[62] Cf. Adams (1994: 122–3).

[63] See for instance Eckhard to Leibniz, 19 April 1677 (A II i^2 494–5): 'philosophers do not distinguish perfect from Being [*ens*] if not as a mere distinction of reason. Indeed Being and positive are opposed to non-Being [*non ens*] ... where there is some positive entity, there is also perfection ... pain is not something positive but non-Being [*non ens*] and negation, and indeed also imperfection ... to be an entity, to be real, to be positive, and to exist do not differ among themselves ... Being [*Ens*] and perfect do not differ from one another, as it is shown above. Accordingly, *ens perfectissimum* is identical to *ens purum*, or that which in no manner is non-Being [*non ens*].'

Eckhard replies, basically, that embracing all reality does not mean to be all things in their determinate essences – that is, it does not mean that God is 'man, brute, horse, lion, dog, Peter, Paul, you, me and so on'.[64] It means that in God there is all the *perfection* or *reality* of all these things.[65] In other words, as the scholastics would say and as Leibniz notes *en passant* in his own reply, all things are in God not *formally* but *eminently*, that is, not in their own determinate form (as horse, lion, dog and so on) but in a superior form which implies, while at the same time surpassing, the degree of perfection or reality of these determinate essences.[66] It seems Eckhard's point convinced Leibniz. In a note of 1695, he explicitly states:

> In the divine essence, things are contained eminently; in the intellect, they are contained somewhat more widely, indeed representatively, because in the divine intellect are represented also the imperfections or limitations of things. . . . Hence it is manifest that all things are in God. (Grua 355–6)

Later on, in a remark of 1706 meant for his friend, Bartholomew Des Bosses, Leibniz adds: 'there is a *hypercategorematic infinite*, or potestative infinite, and active power having, as it were, parts eminently but not formally or actually. This infinite is God himself' (LDB 52–3). In order to protect the pure positivity of God, Leibniz seems to turn to a metaphysical model inspired by the Neoplatonic 'One'. Only a Being which is *beyond* all determinations (or, as Leibniz puts it, which is *hyper-categorematic*), while containing *eminently* all determinations, can be the ontological grounding of all things (*omnia*) without being tainted by the negation which comes with any determination. Indeed Leibniz also seems to need some version of the Neoplatonic distinction between One and Intellect to counter the objection mentioned above that God's knowledge of limited things introduces negation in God. In brief, he seems to think that focusing on the *essence* of God as still beyond any determination (thanks to its containing all things purely eminently) is sufficient to ensure the absolute positivity of God's own nature.[67]

[64] A II i^2 515. Eckhard's letter of reply of May 1677 stretches over almost forty pages (A II i^2 505–41).

[65] For instance, in an earlier exchange, Eckhard notes that if there is something metaphysically real or positive in pain, pain will be *materially* in God, that is, that reality and positivity will be in God (A II i^2 488). It is implied that, on the contrary, pain *as such* (that is, *formally*) is not in God.

[66] Cf. Leibniz to Eckhard, summer 1677 (A II i^2 543): 'The concept which you assign to the *Ens perfectissimum* not only does not imply contradiction, but produces, or contains *eminently*, every other perfection' (my emphasis).

[67] For a detailed discussion of these issues see Antognazza (2015). The conception of God as *pure positivum* (that is, as absolutely perfect, unlimited, infinite), far from being an ad hoc trick needed

On the other hand, Leibniz follows also a different path to God's possibility by offering an *a posteriori* argument based on a version of the 'cosmological' argument. In 1701 he writes:

> If the *Being-from-itself* [*Etre de soy*] is impossible, all the beings-by-another [estres par autruy] are also impossible, since they are, ultimately, only by the *Being-from-itself*: so nothing could exist. This reasoning leads us to another important modal proposition, equal to the previous one [*if the necessary Being is possible, it exists*], and which joined to it completes the demonstration. It could be stated thus: *if the necessary Being is not, there is no possible Being.* (GP IV 406)

As required by the principle of sufficient reason, the existence of something contingent is possible only if also a necessary being is possible. We know by experience that some contingent being is possible because some contingent being exists. Therefore, the necessary being must also be possible.

The argument, however, has at least two shortcomings. Firstly, it introduces an *a posteriori* element in an argument which Leibniz would certainly wish to be strictly *a priori* to maintain all its strength of a demonstration solely from the essence of God.[68] Secondly, it turns only on the *Ens necessarium.* Any claim that the *Ens necessarium* is also the *Ens perfectissimum* would need to be supported independently.[69] Still, one can imagine Leibniz thinking that, for the purpose of arguing for the existence of God, this is a supplementary argument well worth having.

2.2 God is Possible: Presumption and Possibility

At any rate, in addition to the *a posteriori* approach just mentioned, Leibniz pursues also a weaker strategy to support the thesis of God's possibility. Namely, he argues that, in the absence of a demonstration, possibility should be presumed until impossibility is proved. In quasi-juridical terms, a claim of possibility is innocent until proved guilty.[70] Despite his confident assertions

by the ontological argument, is a fundamental feature of Leibniz's conception of God and his relation to creatures.

[68] Cf. GP IV 406. Contrary to Kant's famous assertion that the cosmological argument is based on the ontological argument, in this case, the ontological argument is based on the cosmological argument.

[69] In a note written around 1702, Leibniz observes: 'The necessary Being truly exists and is possible, otherwise nothing would exist; but something else is needed to prove that the necessary Being must have all perfections. I agree, however, that this can certainly be proved' (GP II 450).

[70] The juridical inspiration of Leibniz's notion of presumption is explicitly acknowledged, for instance, in the *Nouveaux Essais* (A VI vi 457) and in the *Theodicy* (GP VI 69).

of the possibility of the *Ens perfectissimum*, perhaps he did feel that his demonstration was not as watertight as one would need. Or perhaps he simply wished to provide yet another argument *ad abundantiam*. Whatever the case, if adequately established, the thesis that, metaphysically, presumption favours possibility would provide a powerful argument for the rational justification of belief in God's existence, despite falling short of a demonstration of his existence.

In the context of his discussion of the ontological argument in the *Nouveaux Essais*, Leibniz writes:

> We are entitled to assume the possibility of any being, and above all of God, until someone proves the contrary; and so the foregoing metaphysical argument does yield a demonstrated moral conclusion, namely that in the present state of our knowledge we ought to judge that God exists and to act accordingly. (NE 438)

In a text of 1702, he advances a similar claim, presenting it more explicitly as a general metaphysical thesis which has the power to shift the burden of proof onto those who deny possibility:

> . . . any being must be judged possible, *donec probetur contrarium* [until the contrary has been proved], until it is shown that it is not [possible]. This is what is called *presumption*, which is incomparably more than a simple *supposition*, since the majority of suppositions should not be admitted unless they are proved: but all that has presumption on its side must be taken as true until it is refuted. . . . possibility is always presumed and must be held as true until impossibility is proved. Thus this argument has the power to shift the *onus probandi in adversarium*, or of charging the opponent with the burden of proof.[71]

Leibniz's claim about presumption favouring possibility is situated in a broader metaphysical framework in which non-existence, as well as existence, needs a sufficient reason.[72] Indeed, contrary to the more famous dictum of paragraph 7 of the *Principles of Nature and Grace* (1714), according to which 'nothing [*le rien*] is simpler and easier than something', and there must be, therefore, a sufficient reason for the fact that 'there is

[71] *Raisons que M. Jaquelot m'a envoyées pour justifier l'Argument contesté de des-Cartes qui doit prouver l'existence de Dieu, avec mes reponses*, 20 November 1702; GP III 444.

[72] See GP VII 194–5, quoted above in Section 1.1.

something rather than nothing' (GP VI 602), Leibniz indicates that the easier or default status, as it were, is existence rather than non-existence.[73] The absence of a sufficient reason for non-existence becomes a sufficient reason for existence. There is, therefore, a metaphysical bias or presumption in favour of existence rather than non-existence.[74] In Leibniz's system of thought, a thing's existence is grounded in a reason provided by the essence of that thing. In turn, 'the essence of a thing is the specific reason of [its] possibility'.[75] In short, essences are reasons for possibility and hence for existence. They all express some degree of reality. On the contrary, there is no essence of 'nothingness' or of total absence of reality. Therefore, there is no *primitive* reason for it.[76]

In this metaphysical framework, it makes sense for Leibniz to think of existence rather than non-existence as the default status since existence has its own specific reason (the essence) whereas non-existence does not. However, it is unclear that the metaphysical presumption in favour of existence, grounded in the possibility of a thing, justifies also a metaphysical presumption in favour of *possibility* itself. Why not think that, metaphysically, there is complete neutrality as regards possibility or impossibility, that is, no presumption in favour of there being or not being an essence?

It seems that the claim Leibniz could defend is, therefore, considerably weaker than the one suggested at the outset of this section, namely that, in the absence of proof to the contrary, there is a metaphysical presumption in favour of God's possibility. At best, Leibniz could claim that believers are rationally justified in holding on to a presumption of God's possibility until proof to the contrary is forthcoming. This claim would be an epistemological rather than a metaphysical thesis. However, notwithstanding its (comparatively) weaker status, many theists may well think that this is a claim very much worth having.

[73] Adams (1994: 173–6) argues persuasively that 'treating existence rather than nonexistence as the default status, so to speak, for any possible being' (175–6) is more in line with the overall thrust of Leibniz's metaphysics than the opposite view expressed in the famous paragraph §7 of the *Principles of Nature and Grace*.

[74] See Adams (1994: 176), as well as the entire chapter 8, offering a magisterial discussion of Leibniz's 'Presumption of Possibility'.

[75] A II i^2 588. See also A VI iii 583: 'the essence of a thing and the specific reason of [its] possibility are the same'.

[76] See Adams (1994: 211). Cf. *De rerum originatione radicali* (GP VII 304).

3 Conclusion

If one is able to establish the truth of the premises '1. If God is possible, God exists; 2. God is possible', the conclusion '3. God exists' follows.

As we have seen, Leibniz tries to support the first premise by defining God as the *Ens perfectissimum*, and by arguing, in turn, that a most perfect being implies necessary existence. According to his account, the only way in which existence can be involved in an essence is indeed by its being *necessary* existence. The pivotal point of the argument is that any essence has a claim to existence in proportion to its degree of perfection and will exist unless incompatible with the existence of an essence of greater perfection. Once perfection is conceived, with Leibniz, as degree of reality, the *Ens perfectissimum* is also the *Ens realissimum*. In turn, the Being which must involve existence is the *Ens necessarium*. As Leibniz persuasively argues, the conclusion that the *Ens necessarium*, if possible, exists, 'is a corollary which follows immediately' from the definition of Necessary Being, and which 'almost does not differ at all' from this very definition.[77]

The really crucial issue is proving the second premise, namely, that God is possible. Leibniz's favourite strategy is to argue for the 'pure positivity' of the *Ens perfectissimum*. The *Ens perfectissimum*, as the conjunction of all purely positive qualities, that is, all qualities which express without any limits whatever they express (A VI iii 578), does not involve any negation whatsoever. Therefore, it cannot involve any contradiction. If it cannot involve any contradiction, it must be possible. In other words, according to Leibniz, purely positive qualities must be compatible because, as purely positive, they involve no negation and, therefore, no contradiction. In addition, in order to support the possibility of God, he offers an *a posteriori* approach based on a version of the cosmological argument and turning on the notion of *Ens necessarium*. Finally, he proposes also a weaker strategy based on the claim that, in the absence of a demonstration, possibility should be presumed until impossibility is proved.

All these arguments for God's possibility face objections which seriously challenge Leibniz's claim to have succeeded in filling the gap which prevents the ontological argument from being complete, and concluding therefore in an unconditional way to the existence of God. For instance, one could still challenge the coherence of the notion of a purely positive being constituted by a plurality of perfections on the ground that any plurality implies

[77] GP IV 405.

negation. Moreover, the success of establishing possibility *a posteriori* on the basis of a version of the cosmological argument will depend on the success of that argument. Finally, it could be objected that there is no metaphysical presumption in favour of possibility. But whatever one may think of the level of success enjoyed by Leibniz's attempts, his discussion is one of the most penetrating explorations of the multi-layered richness of this classic argument, in the context of one of the deepest metaphysical reflections on the nature of God.

5 Kant

Lawrence Pasternack

There is perhaps no more famous objection to the Ontological Argument (OA) than Immanuel Kant's contention that existence is not a predicate. Kant first advances this objection in his Pre-Critical work *The Only Possible Argument in Support of a Demonstration of the Existence of God*, though it appears in its most developed and best-known form in the *Critique of Pure Reason*'s Transcendental Dialectic. In its original form, it serves as a propaedeutic to Kant's own proof for God's existence, one that argues in its own way for the existence of an absolutely necessary being. While this argument is withdrawn under the strictures of Transcendental Idealism, the 'existence is not a predicate' objection (E ~ P) is nevertheless repurposed in the Critical Period to be used as a crucial step within the Dialectic's critique of all transcendental theology.

However, in its repurposing, it is no longer offered as the one and only objection against the Ontological Argument, but instead becomes part of a more comprehensive attack on the OA, one that contains at least four distinct arguments, only one of which involves (E ~ P). Because of all the attention given to this most famous of his objections, the other three have received by comparison minimal attention in the literature; and yet, as we will discuss, there are good reasons for taking them, or at least the first two, to more closely reflect the intended structure of the OA. For unlike the second two objections which render 'God exists' as a synthetic judgment, the first two are based upon a rendering of the judgment as analytic.

Hence, this chapter will not only explore Kant's case for (E ~ P), but will examine all four objections proffered by the *Critique of Pure Reason*. To prepare the way for this analysis, we will begin with a brief discussion of a few key concepts found in the Transcendental Dialectic's treatment of the Ideal of Pure Reason. We will then move on to the text's four objections to the OA. Finally we will sample three approaches found in the secondary literature which seek to reinforce Kant's case for (E ~ P).

1 Some Preliminaries: The Ideal of Pure Reason

The *Critique of Pure Reason*'s treatment of the OA appears within one of the three main divisions of the Transcendental Dialectic. Overall, the Dialectic's aim is to establish that we can neither have knowledge (*Wissen*) nor theoretical cognition (*Erkenntnis*) of things-in-themselves. This critique begins with the 'Paralogisms' whereby Kant targets 'transcendental psychology'. The 'Antinomies' then target cosmology. Then, lastly, Kant turns to theology in 'The Ideal of Pure Reason', where he begins with an etiology of the metaphysical conception of God (the *ens realissimum*) before then moving on to the traditional proofs for God's existence. Given our limited space, we unfortunately will have to forgo a detailed discussion of this fascinating etiology.[1] But before moving straightaway to Kant's treatment of the OA, let us briefly discuss a few points of key significance for the arguments to come.

First, at the opening of 'The Ideal of Pure Reason', Kant differentiates between objects, concepts, ideas and ideals by way of their respective levels of 'determination' (*Bestimmung*). An individual object is 'thoroughgoingly determined', in that of 'every two contradictorily opposed predicates only one can apply to it' (A571/B599). For example, an actual human being is either male or female (understood as having either at least one Y chromosome versus having only X chromosomes). In contrast, concepts, ideas and ideals (in most cases) fall short of this level of determination. Most concepts and ideas are general, and thus are indeterminate with regard to paired opposed predicates. The idea of human being, for example, does not have either male or female as one of its determinations, though of course, since individual humans are either male or female, the general idea of human being includes the general determination of being gendered. In other words, while being gendered is what Kant calls an 'internal mark' (*Merkmal*) or conceptual component of the idea of human being, specific gender remains indeterminate at the level of the general idea.

Like ideas, the determinations which comprise the conceptual content of ideals are general. Ideals, moreover, are constructed by us using the determinations which comprise their underlying ideas. We have, for example, the idea of academic scholarship, and thus we may construct the ideal of the

[1] More extensive discussions of the Ideal of Pure Reason can be found in: Wood (1978: 25–63); Grier (2001: 230–56); Allison (2004: 396–412); Hong (2012). Citations to Kant will be to the Akademie Ausgabe (abbreviated as 'AA') by volume and page, except for the *Critique of Pure Reason*, where citations will use the standard A/B edition pagination. Unless otherwise noted, English quotations will be from Guyer and Wood (1992–).

perfect scholar. Like the idea of academic scholarship, the ideal of the perfect scholar contains determinations such as punctiliousness, erudition, dedication, humility, and so forth. Further, like the underlying idea, the ideal is indeterminate with regard to various features of an actual individual. Actual (human) scholars are male or female. But as the idea of scholarship does not involve a specific gender as one of its internal marks, so likewise the ideal, as composed solely by the marks of the idea, does not include a specific gender.

As we shall later discuss more fully, note that Kant uses 'determination' to refer to both the actual properties of things as well as to the marks which comprise the contents of each concept or idea. Consider, then, the determination of being male. When used to describe an individual human being, Kant uses the term ontically. It refers to a property of the individual. When used as part of an idea, such as the idea of Catholic priesthood, one can say that being male is among its conceptual contents or internal marks. In addition, as Kant later discusses in the *Critique*, the determinations which comprise our concepts only roughly correlate with the actual determinations of things (A727/B755–A728/B756). This is particularly evident with natural kinds. For example, there are numerous properties borne by chemical elements beyond those we know. Hence, the determinations which comprise our concept of iron only partly overlap with iron's actual determinations. As we shall see later, this is a point of considerable importance to Kant's treatment of the OA.

By way of this framework, Kant then advances the Ideal of Pure Reason, an ideal that is distinctive in that unlike other ideals, it is thoroughgoingly determined, and, moreover, thoroughgoingly determined *a priori*. Kant calls this the *ens realissimum*, or most real being. Kant's account of how this ideal is constructed is quite involved, but in short, he proposes that out of 'every two contradictorily opposed predicates' one 'belongs absolutely to being' while the other involves a negation. Accordingly, only the former are real in the sense that only they reflect an actual reality. Where there is a negation, the predicate 'signifies a mere lack' (A575/B603). Hence, as ideals are functions of ideas, the ideal of the most real being is constructed as a function of the idea of the sum total of all positive predicates.[2] Moreover,

[2] Some predicate pairs clearly contrast the positive to the negative: omnipotent versus not-omnipotent, for instance. Some predicate pairs have an implicit negative within them. For example, being gendered depends upon having a body, which then depends upon being limited to having at any point in time a singular spatial location. Hence, once one winnows away all predicates that have any explicit or implicit negative, we are then left with just those predicates that belong

as this ideal is constructed through a function that picks out *all* positive predicates, it is therefore, Kant explains, thoroughgoingly determined via this *a priori* procedure for predicate selection. Finally, as this being is conceived of as the most real being, Kant takes it to be the metaphysical tradition's conception of God and the object of the traditional theological proofs.

2 Kant on the Ontological Argument

A key goal of Kant's critique of transcendental theology is to establish that there is no viable way to prove God's existence through theoretical reason. But rather than developing independent criticisms of the various proofs, he instead contends: (a) that they all ultimately depend upon the OA; (b) that there is a component of the OA common to each of its various formulations, namely an inference to the 'existence of a highest cause entirely *a priori* from mere concepts' (A590/B619); and (c) the inference is flawed in such a way that brings down all arguments which employ it. So, while Kant mentions in particular the Cartesian formulation of the OA (as well as a Leibnizian supplement to the Cartesian OA), he nevertheless targets what he regards as the core feature of the OA, a feature that is common to all its formulations.[3]

Kant's analysis of the OA focuses almost exclusively on the statement 'God exists.' This is because, as Kant renders the OA, it is through our grasp of the subject term, God, that we must affirm the predicate term, exists. While his contention that existence is not a (real) predicate is certainly the best known of his objections, there are nevertheless three other objections advanced in the *Critique*'s Ideal of Pure Reason, all of which grant for the sake of argument that existence is a predicate (E = P). Moreover, two of these three objections are developed by way of an analytic rendering of 'God exists,' while a third, as well as (E ~ P), are based upon a synthetic rendering of the statement at issue. We will now consider these four arguments, following their order of appearance in the *Critique*'s 'Ideal of Pure Reason'.

'absolutely to being'. The *ens realissimum* is constructed by way of this winnowing process, such that it contains all and only the 'absolutely' positive predicates. As such, it is, according to Kant, unique among ideals, for by having as its internal marks *all* such predicates, it is thereby thoroughgoingly determined.

3 Numerous defenders of the OA have argued that Kant's critique, especially his thesis that (E ~ P), does not apply to all versions of the argument. See, for example, Plantinga (1966), Forgie (2008). See also Van Cleve (1999: 189).

3 Analytic Objections

The first objection to the OA offered by Kant is contained in the following:

> To posit a triangle and cancel its three angles is contradictory; but to cancel the triangle together with its three angles is not a contradiction. It is exactly the same with the concept of an absolutely necessary being. If you cancel its existence, then you cancel the thing itself with all its predicates; where then is the contradiction supposed to come from? (A594/B623–A595/B624).

As discussed by Beatrice Longuenesse, we may understand 'posit' [*setzen*] and 'cancel' [*aufheben*] as having somewhat different meanings when used in relation to a subject versus a predicate. Following her account of these terms, when one posits a subject, one is asserting that that subject exists; when one posits a predicate, one is attributing the predicate to the subject (Longuenesse 1998: 352).[4] A similar distinction may be drawn between uses of 'cancel'. When one 'cancels' a subject, its existence is being denied; when one 'cancels' a predicate, it is being denied as an attribute of the subject.

Cancelling a subject, however, has significant carry-over for the predicate, since, as Kant writes, when one 'cancels' a subject, one has 'at the same time cancelled everything internal [to it]' (A595/B623). What Kant means here is somewhat unclear, and his examples unfortunately do not offer adequate direction. If we follow Longuenesse, then to cancel *a* triangle would be most naturally understood as a singular negative existential statement: some particular triangle under consideration does not exist. One might for example ask: 'Is that a triangle I see on the side of the building?' One answers: 'No, there is no triangle there.' However, there is a problem: such 'cancelling' of *a* triangle does not entail the cancellation of each and every predicate that triangles have. The queried object may still be a polygon, for instance, or it may even still be three-angled (an arbelos, for example).

A second option, though, may be drawn from *The Only Possible Argument*, where Kant correlates cancellation with the absence of '*datum*, to be thought' (2:78). He then asserts that 'there is no internal contradiction in the negation of all existence' because when all that exists is cancelled 'there is no

[4] This account of positing oversimplifies since not all propositions advance the existence of the subject. Kant writes, for example: 'That all bodies are extended is necessarily and eternally true, whether they exist now or not' (8:235). Hence, just as modern logic's universal quantifier does not have existential import, Kant does not presume that universal judgments commit us to the existence of the subject. These further considerations are certainly relevant to a proper analysis of Kant, but for this exposition of his critique of the OA, please excuse the simplification.

material element for anything which can be thought' (2:78). Without getting into the intricacies of the text, we may nevertheless extract from it a different treatment of 'cancel' than the one discussed above. When one cancels a subject, one withdraws from consideration its *datum*. Hence, by this reading of the term, when one cancels a triangle, one cancels each and every internal mark that comprises the concept borne by the subject term. Assuming we are to take Kant's claim in the *Critique* that when one cancels a triangle, one cancels even the individual mark or predicate three-angles, it seems that 'cancel' is not symmetric with 'posit' if the latter is not just putting forth a *datum* but advancing the existence of that which is thought through the *datum*. By contrast, 'cancel' withdraws the *datum* rather than advancing the *datum* while denying the existence of that which is thought through the *datum*.

Kant may or may not have intended the latter in the *Critique*, but it does more fully explain why the cancellation of the subject carries over to the predicate – or more precisely, to each and every predicate that is an internal mark of the subject. Understood in this way, we have here Kant's first objection to the OA. When 'God exists' is taken as analytic, such that <exists>[5] is an internal mark of God, when one cancels the subject, one cancels 'everything internal' to it. In doing so, there is no longer any material for thought through which a contradiction can arise. Let us call this the Complete Cancellation Objection (CCO).

Kant's second objection is developed by way of a possible rebuttal to CCO. Since CCO depends upon the cancellation of the subject term, what if 'there are subjects that cannot be cancelled' (A595/B623)? Kant's use of 'cancel' here is not, however, the same as its use in *The Only Possible Argument*, since it hardly could be contended that there is some *datum* that one cannot but think. Here, instead, we seem to have a use better reflected by Longuenesse's account, since what is now being considered by Kant is whether or not there is some subject whose existence cannot be denied. Initially, Kant dismisses this proposal on the grounds that it merely restates the issue at hand: whether or not there are beings whose existence is 'absolutely' necessary.[6] But he then recasts it in a manner that draws from a supplement that Leibniz offers on behalf of OA.

[5] We will use '<. . ..>' to denote reference to the concept/predicate-candidate of existence.

[6] By an 'absolutely necessary being' Kant means a being that cannot not exist. The contrasting notion is that of a being whose existence is necessary, given that some other being exists. See Pasternack (2001).

According to Leibniz, the OA needs to be supplemented with the additional premise that the idea of a being whose essence involves <existence> is internally consistent and thus possible.[7] Hence, for Leibniz, the OA involves the movement from the possibility of an absolutely necessary being to that being's actuality. Kant acknowledges that he has 'consented up to this point' (A596/B624) that the idea of a being whose essence involves existence is internally consistent, and thus he recognizes that he has given to the defender of the OA a possible rebuttal to the CCO.

Duly adjusted to reflect the Leibnizian supplement, the defender of the OA may contend that the denial of God's existence (i.e., its cancellation) would violate Kant's concessions that the concept of God in play (a) includes <existence> as one of its predicates, and (b) is the concept of a being internally consistent and logically possible. For if such a being is 'cancelled' then 'the internal possibility of the thing is cancelled' (A597/B625) – making then the being out to be one that is (contrary to the concession) not internally consistent.

Of course, denying the existence of a possible being does not on its own (absent the principle of plentitude) entail that the concept of that being is contradictory. Hence, in the spirit of charity, it is better to unpack the OA's defence by attending to what is supposed to be unique about the subject at issue, i.e., God. So long as Kant continues to grant (E = P) and grant that 'God exists' is analytic, the OA defender's point gains far more force when the contradiction is taken to arise from considering the combination of (a) <exists> as a predicate that 'lies in the concept' of God and (b) a 'cancelling' by which part of what 'lies in the concept' is denied.

In other words, so long as Kant continues with the concession that <existence> is 'comprehended within the range of its ["God"'s] meaning' (A594/B622), the defender of the OA can protest that Kant is barred from cancelling the subject, for in doing so, Kant would deviate from his concession that the subject concept is internally consistent. Kant thus cannot deny the existence of a being that, by definition, exists unless he either denies the internal consistency of the subject concept or denies that existence can be part of that concept. Since, at least for now, Kant has granted both of these, he cannot deny/cancel the subject.

Kant eventually responds that this move on the part of the OA's defender creates no more than 'the illusion of a victory' (A597/B625), and his reason

[7] See Leibniz's notes 'That the Most Perfect Being is Possible' (A 6.3 675–80) and 'That the Most Perfect Being Exists'.

for this serves as his second objection to the OA. While the Leibnizian supplement to the OA does seem to make a compelling case against CCO, Kant protests that it turns the OA into no more than a 'mere tautology' (A597/B625), for if <existence> is part of what it is to be the most real (or most perfect) being, <existence> is then already granted along with all the other internal marks of the subject when the subject is posited. Let us call this the Mere Tautology Objection (MTO): since non-cancellable subjects are those which putatively include <existence> as already contained in the subject, the predicate <exists> just restates part of what is already contained in the subject.[8]

4 An Initial Synthetic Objection

Kant's third objection comes on the heels of MTO, and is offered by way of a dilemma for the OA's defender. Kant asks whether the proposition 'This or that thing exists' is analytic or synthetic. If the former, we return to MTO: the predicate adds nothing new, nothing already in the subject, and thus is a 'miserable tautology' (A597/B625). Kant then proposes that in light of the problems with the analytic rendering of 'God exists,' the defender of the OA would opt for the concession that 'every existential proposition is synthetic' (A598/B626). But, Kant now points out, having made this concession, the defender of the OA can no longer claim that the denial of God's existence is a self-contradiction, for self-contradiction 'pertains only in the analytic' (A598/B626). Let us call this the Synthetic Contradictionless Objection (SCO). It serves as the third objection against the OA and the last offered prior to Kant's turn to the most famous (E ~ P) objection.

To recap, Kant's initial two objections to the OA gave the OA's defender the home-field advantage, so to speak. Both CCO and MTO treated 'God exists' as analytic, and, further, approached <existence> as if it were a predicate. But with these mounting criticisms against the analytic rendering of the statement, Kant has the defender of the OA concede some ground, and accept 'in all fairness' (A598/B626) that 'God exists' is more aptly read as synthetic. Accordingly, what then remains is the final contested principle, namely, whether or not existence is a (real) predicate.

[8] According to defenders of the OA 'God exists' is, once one understands the meaning of the terms, self-evident. For Kant to then raise the objection that a putatively self-evident truth is tautological will hardly be considered a problem for those sympathetic to the OA. In fact, Kant's account of the non-cancellability of the subject could, despite its intent, just as well be used in defence of the OA.

5 Types of Predicates

To set the stage for his fourth and final objection, that existence is not a predicate, Kant begins by distinguishing between a logical and a real predicate. 'Anything', he writes, 'can serve as a logical predicate,' since 'logic abstracts from every content' (A598/B626). That is, in the statement 'Every A is a B', 'B' is the logical predicate. It is the second term, along with the subject term of a complete, well-formed proposition. A logical predicate thus understood reflects a syntactic distinction between the two necessary elements of a complete proposition. Content is abstracted from it not because the term that serves as the logical predicate has no content, but rather because a logical predicate simply picks out the term's syntactic function.[9] A real predicate, by contrast, is distinguished by its semantic function. As Kant describes it, a real predicate carries content 'which goes beyond the concept of the subject and enlarges it' (A598/B626).

From the above, we should recognize that logical and real predicates involve two different orders of analysis, one syntactic, one semantic. As such, we should recognize that the two need not be considered mutually exclusive.[10] They instead distinguish between two different roles that one and the same term can have. For example, in the statement 'Labrador Retrievers are friendly,' friendly is both a logical and a real predicate. Like all real predicates, it is a logical predicate merely by virtue of syntactic function. Secondly, it is at the same time a real predicate because it 'goes beyond the concept of the subject'. That is, it is not analytically contained in the definition of 'Labrador Retriever'. By contrast, in the statement 'All triangles are three-angled,' three-angled is a logical but not a real predicate, for it is analytically true that triangles have three angles.[11]

A real predicate, therefore, is necessarily also a logical predicate, though the reverse does not always hold. Sometimes, a logical predicate is also a real predicate, sometimes it is not. Accordingly, it would be an error to assume that Kant's (E ~ P) objection amounts to the claim that because 'exists' is a logical predicate, it is therefore not a real predicate. While it is certainly a logical predicate, whether or not it is a real predicate remains to be seen.

9 See also Gardner (1999: 239).

10 This point is also recognized in Abaci (2008: 572).

11 While Kant regards arithmetic and geometry as synthetic *a priori*, note that the example here used is of an analytic claim – a triangle has three angles.

To better understand the logical/real predicate distinction, let us add a third option, one that will make clear that the distinction is also not exhaustive.[12] Consider again the example: 'triangles have three angles'. As real predicates go beyond the concept of the subject, the predicate in this statement is not real. But the predicate still has content. Hence, while it serves the syntactic role of a logical predicate, it is not merely a logical predicate. In a formal system, where terms have no 'material' semantic content, the predicate can be merely logical. But in natural language, this will not be the case.

To capture the semantic value of predicates that are not real, we may appeal to Kant's distinction between analytic and synthetic judgments. Synthetic judgments are 'ampliative' since the concepts carried by their predicates are not contained in the concepts of their subjects. That is, the predicates of synthetic judgments are real – they 'go beyond the subject'. Analytic judgments, by contrast, are merely 'explicative' in that the concepts carried by their predicates are already contained in the concepts carried by their subject terms. The predicates of analytic judgments thus do not 'go beyond the subject'. However, though Kant does not discuss this point within his treatment of the OA, it should be recognized that the predicate of an analytic judgment still has semantic content. It does not collapse into nothing more than a logical predicate. Clearly, there is meaning to the terms 'unmarried' and 'men' in the statement 'all bachelors are unmarried men'.[13]

Given that the semantic contribution at issue pertains to the predicates of analytic judgments, let us refer to these predicates as 'explicative'. While real predicates add new content to the proposition beyond what is contained in the subject concept, explicative predicates do not add any further content. Nevertheless, they still have specific semantic content relevant to the proposition. This content differs depending upon which feature or mark of the subject concept they pick out.

As noted earlier in this chapter, and as more fully explained in the Jäsche Logic, we may divide our concepts into various parts or marks. When we

[12] Kant scholarship has of late been more actively exploring his distinction between real and logical possibility. This distinction does not, however, track with the real/logical predicate distinction. This is in part because logical possibility is still informed by conceptual content, whereas logical predication 'abstracts away from every content' (A598/B626).

[13] Allison (2004) presents the logical/real predicate distinction as exhaustive. Despite Kant's own account of logical predication as abstracted away from content, Allison correlates it with the non-ampliative character of predicates in analytic judgments. Hence, for Allison, logical predicates play no role in the 'content to be judged' or 'content that can be thought' (86). As such, by Allison's measure, there is no semantic difference between 'bachelors are unmarried' and 'bachelors are men'.

reflect on the contents of a concept, we do so by surveying the marks which as an aggregated whole comprise the concept (9:59). When we compare concepts, we consider which marks they have in common and which marks are present in one but not the other. When we make an analytic judgment, we pick out one or more of the marks already contained in the concept of the subject term. When we make a synthetic judgment, we attach a mark that is not contained in the subject (9:58–9).

An explicative predicate thus identifies one or more marks which comprise the subject concept, and depending upon the specific predicate, different marks of the subject are thereby rendered. Hence, while the following judgments are both analytic, there is nevertheless a semantic difference between 'All bachelors are unmarried' and 'All bachelors are men.' Each picks out a different mark within the subject concept.[14]

Additionally, the same mark can be utilized as either a real or explicative predicate, depending upon its semantic relationship to the subject concept. In the statement 'All bachelors are unmarried,' 'unmarried' is an explicative predicate since it is part of the meaning of the subject. Whereas, in the statement 'All new employees are unmarried,' 'unmarried' is a real predicate. It is not contained in the subject and thus adds new content.

Since the same mark can be not only logical and real, but also real and explicative, depending upon its relationship to the subject, Kant faces the challenge that even if in one instance <exists> is not a real predicate, it does not immediately follow that it is never a real predicate. Further, since the distinction between logical and real is not exhaustive, it is hardly a foregone conclusion that the naive rendering of (E ~ P), where 'exists' is denied predicative meaning, is enough to have it stand as a decisive objection against the OA. Perhaps, 'exists', particularly where the subject term is 'God', a being that according to much of the theological tradition is unique in having

[14] This point should highlight the importance of a third form of predication other than logical and real. Although Allison, as noted above, takes the distinction to be exhaustive, a predicate that is not real (i.e., not enlarging) is not by virtue of that merely then a logical predicate. 'Men' and 'unmarried' are both marks of 'bachelor', but they are semantically distinct. Accordingly, I have put forth the term 'explicative predicate' for predicates that are internal marks of the subject concept. This supplement is of further significance because the internal marks of our concepts of objects are not to be put forth as real but only explicative predicates. Consider 'gold is a yellow metal'. By Kant's accounting, 'yellow' and 'metal' are not real predicates of 'gold'. See A727/B755: the marks which comprise our empirical concepts are 'explicated' in our judgments. That is, they are not, semantically speaking, real predicates, but are instead what I am calling 'explicative' predicates. But, again, this is a semantic distinction, not syntactic, and as I will discuss in the next section, also – and more importantly – not ontic.

<exists> within the scope of its meaning, remains as a semantically significant predicate, one that may not be real (i.e., ampliative), but is still explicative.

6 Predication and Determination

Before moving on to Kant's alternative treatment of how 'exists' operates in statements, let us take a moment to consider whether or not we should understand 'real predicate' as synonymous with 'determination'. As Kant sets the stage for his (E ~ P) objection, he writes 'determination is a predicate, which goes beyond the concept of the subject and enlarges it. Thus it must not be included in it already' (A598/B626). If we strictly follow Kant's definition here, then explicative predicates are not determinations. Since, however, whether or not a predicate is ampliative or explicative depends upon the subject term, it would be a mistake to conclude that what in one instance is not a determination is never a determination. While unmarried is not a determination of bachelor, it is a determination of one of my colleagues. Similarly, while three-angledness is not a determination of a triangle, it is a determination of the corner printer stand in my office, even while this stand's shape is that of a triangle. What this further illustrates is that as here used by Kant, 'determination' is not about properties, about the actual constituents of objects, but rather concerns just propositional contents. A predicate is a determination when its semantic content is ampliative of the semantic content of the subject term. Hence, so far construed, the denial that <existence> is a real predicate or determination does not on its own touch the metaphysical thesis behind the OA, that <existence> is a property (or consequence of a property) of the divine essence.

Let us thus recall that Kant elsewhere uses 'determination' to indicate not just conceptual relata, but properties of actual objects. This was seen in our earlier discussion, such as when Kant claims that individual *things* are subject to the principle of thoroughgoing determination. It is also Kant's primary use of the term throughout his *Metaphysical Foundations of Natural Science.* Hence, we need to distinguish between these two uses, the ontic and semantic. Whether or not a concept is thoroughgoingly determined is a semantic point, in that our concept of a horse may include the concept of gender, but is indeterminate regarding which gender. Since, however, actual horses will always have a gender (i.e., either have a Y chromosome or only X chromosomes), actual horses have specific genders as among their determinations. Accordingly, when used ontically, the issue of conceptual enlargement is not applicable. Having three angles is a property (ontic determination) of a triangle. Yellow is a property (ontic determination) of gold.[15] This is of grave importance to the OA, since if the Kantian limits 'determination' to just a technical semantic function such that it is no longer about properties, Kant's objection (E ~ P) could easily be dismissed.

7 Positing versus Predication

After Kant distinguishes between logical and real predicates, he proposes that 'exists', rather than signifying a real predicate, indicates 'merely the positing of a thing or of certain determinations' (A598/B626). This, of course, informs us of how Kant reads 'God exists'. For Kant, <exists> neither offers a new mark to be added to the subject, nor even serves to explicate a mark already given in the subject. Instead, he treats 'exists' in a manner now commonly understood as equivalent to the existential quantifier. That is, for many who agree with Kant on (E ~ P), 'God exists' quite simply states: $\exists x\ (Gx)$.

This certainly is a legitimate way of modelling the statement. However, on its own, it does not constitute an argument against existence being a predicate, for it does not follow that 'exists' cannot confer both a positing and a predicate. Accordingly, Kant must show not only that 'exists' can serve to posit a subject, but that that is its only viable use. With this in mind, let us now turn to Kant's well-known example of a hundred dollars.

8 Object and Concept

Kant writes: 'the actual contains nothing more than the merely possible. A hundred actual dollars do not contain the least bit more than a hundred possible ones' (A599/B627). Kant then clarifies: 'the latter signifies the concept and the former its object' (A599/B627), and then concludes that the former cannot contain more than the latter because otherwise 'my concept would not express the entire object and thus would not be the suitable concept for it' (A599/B627). Unfortunately, though, a problem immediately arises, for as discussed above, according to Kant, actual existing things are fully determined whereas concepts, or at least general concepts, are not. An actual hundred dollars, if understood as a bill, has specific wrinkles, print date,

[15] Kant (notoriously) characterizes the statement 'gold is a yellow metal' as analytic (4:276 – see also A727/B755–A728/B756). Hence, by this accounting, 'yellow' and 'metal' are not real predicates or semantic determinations of 'gold'. Yet, hardly do we want to treat 'yellow' and 'metal' as if they were not in fact properties of gold. We will return to this issue below.

serial number, ownership history, etc. Likewise, an actual hundred dollars, understood as a bank account value or ledger entry, has a deposit or entry date, is part of a specific account, etc. Hence, there will inevitably be a difference in determinations between the concept of a hundred dollars and an object that is a hundred dollars.[16]

This concern may be addressed in a number of ways. First, it may be argued that the actual hundred dollars is just a particularization of the general predicates of its general concept. For example, one's general concept of a possible hundred dollars includes the predicate of having serial numbers, though only an actual bill has a particular serial number. Accordingly, Kant's claim may be defended on the grounds that all the determinations of a specific object that make that object a particular instance of a general class correlate to the determinations of the general class as well.

Yet, insofar as the concept at issue is the concept of a general class, will there not still be determinations of the particular that do not exemplify the marks which comprise this specific class concept? For example, there may be a sticky raspberry jelly stain on a particular hundred dollar bill, even though taking on a breakfast condiment is hardly an internal mark of the general class of *one hundred dollars* – or its genus, *legal tender*. Likewise, a ledger entry of a hundred dollars may have been made in error, may document an extorted sum, or just simply serve to record a payment for goods received. These determinations are borne by the particular and can further serve to distinguish it from others of the same class. However, none of these reflect the marks that comprise the general concept of a hundred dollars, especially once one takes that class to include more than paper instruments.

What these concerns help to bring out is that perhaps there is a conflict between two elements of Kant's analysis of how concepts and objects are related. On the one hand, Kant here deems a concept 'suitable' [*angemessene*] to its object only if it 'express[es] the entire object' (A599/B627). Yet, this is a

[16] One retort is that Kant's argument is specifically meant to target the Leibnizian 'conceptualist metaphysician' (Anderson: 2015), for whom the concepts of objects are thoroughgoingly determined. While this may be so for the Ideal of Pure Reason, there is no clear indication that Kant's example of a hundred dollars is intended to be a thoroughgoingly determined concept. Moreover, at the opening of 'The Ideal of Pure Reason', Kant writes that with the exception of this Ideal, only objects and not concepts are thoroughgoingly determined.

See also Proops (2015), who argues that the hundred dollar example only succeeds as a ledger entry referent since, as discussed here, a material object such as a hundred dollar bill will have determinations not contained within the general concept. Note, however, that even with a ledger entry as referent, the referent is still more than just a monetary value. As a particular entry, it also fixes ownership, date of transaction, and other properties not part of the general concept.

standard at odds with his previous account of how determinate concepts are by comparison to their objects: with the exception of the concept of the *ens realissimum*, Kant claims that only objects and not their concepts are thoroughgoingly determined (A573/B601). Accordingly, our concepts of objects will, as a matter of course, not include all the determinations of the objects that fall under them.[17] Further, in his discussions of our empirical concepts of natural kinds, he notes that we should not even expect 'the exhaustive concept of a thing' (A727/B755).

Let us then consider an alternative way to satisfy Kant's desideratum that the concept must 'express the entire object'. While our discussion so far has compared (as seems intended by Kant's hundred dollar example) a general concept against a particular object, we may further explore whether we might fare any better through a comparison between our concept of the particular object and the object. In other words, if Kant wants the actual and the possible to be properly matched, such that the actual does not contain anything not in the possible, the match may be alternately understood as a comparison between the concept of a particular and a particular object.[18] Such a comparison, moreover, more aptly parallels the target of the OA: the Ideal of Pure Reason (as a thoroughgoingly determined concept) and its object, the most real being, i.e., God.

So, rather than limit ourselves to the *Critique*'s hundred dollars example, where Kant seems to be considering the general concept of a hundred dollars, let us add into our inquiry his earlier treatment of (E ~ P) in *The Only Possible Argument*, and its example of Julius Caesar. There, he contrasts the actual Julius Caesar with all his predicates 'not excepting even those of space and time' (2:72) and the very same catalogue of predicates, though as not actually instantiated. Accordingly, the complete concept of Julius Caesar includes such trivia as on what hour of the day the infant Gaius first smiled, whether on his forty-third birthday he ate more than 2,000 calories, whether he breathed his last breath facing west, etc. As Kant portrays the scope of the Julius Caesar concept, it is to include all such details. Hence, at least ideally, we have here a concept that is supposed to 'express the entire object'. Let us then consider, by way of this comparison, whether or not Kant has provided an argument to answer for us whether <exists> is or is not an ontic and/or semantic determination.

[17] For a further discussion of the significance of this point to the OA, see Plantinga (1966).

[18] While it is common to explore Kant's examples as a comparison between particular object and concept of that particular (e.g., Abaci (2008), Anderson (2015)), Stang (2015) argues that for Kant, there are no concepts of non-existing particular objects. We will consider Stang's position in section 10.

9 Is Existence a Predicate?

According to Kant, if <existence> were an ontic determination of Julius Caesar, then the Julius Caesar concept would not be able to express the entire object. Yet this shortcoming would no longer be because of a concept–object mismatch as we saw between the general concept and the particular. Rather, the pairing here, as between the Ideal of Pure Reason and the most real being, intends a pairing between a thoroughgoingly determined concept and thoroughgoingly determined object. Is Kant then correct that if existence were an ontic determination, the concept would necessarily fall short? That is, would it fall short even if we were to compare a thoroughgoingly determined concept and thoroughgoingly determined object? This seems to be the point at issue in the following:

> [W]hen I think a thing, through whichever and however many predicates I like (even in its thoroughgoing determination), not the least bit gets added to the thing when I posit in addition that this thing is. For otherwise [i.e., if existence were an ontic determination] what would exist would not be the same as what I had thought in my concept. (A600/B628)

We may understand the first sentence as follows. If my thought of a thing rose to a level of thoroughgoing determination, no further predicate, so Kant contends, would be added when I posit that this thing exists. Of course, this is not itself an argument, just a restatement of Kant's thesis that (E ~ P). The argument seems instead to come in the second sentence. If when we posit an object, we ascribe to the object the ontic determination <exists>, then the object is taken to have a predicate that is not part of the thoroughgoingly determined concept of the object.

Kant is certainly quite correct that (a) if <existence> were taken as an ontic determination, and (b) if the marks of the object's concept did not include this determination, then (c) the concept would not be the same as what had been thought. Yet, the obvious rebuttal is: if <existence> were taken as an ontic determination, why couldn't it then be included among the marks of the object's concept? Kant's argument again is that if <existence> were an ontic determination, we would have a mismatch in determinations between concept and object, something that should not be so where the concept is thoroughgoingly determined. Hence, the force of the objection rests on Kant allowing for the sake of the argument that <existence> is an ontic determination and yet excluding existence from the marks of the concept.

While Kant may very well be correct that existence is not a predicate (either ontic or semantic), the merits of his argument(s) remain a matter of considerable debate. There is, moreover, little consensus as to how Kant ultimately argues for (E ~ P), with some wildly different reconstructions offered through the years. In the little space that remains, let us sample from recent literature three of the more sophisticated attempts to strengthen Kant's case. With each, one or more potential objections will also be tendered for consideration.

10 Further Arguments in Defence of (E ~ P)

In *Problems from Kant*, James Van Cleve (1999) offers an analysis of real predication that renders conceptual enlargement in terms of logical non-entailment. He writes:

> A predicate P *enlarges* a concept C $=_{\text{df.}} \Diamond\exists x\ (Cx\ \&\ {\sim}Px)$.

If C = triangle and P = red, P would be, following this definition, a real predicate, since it is possible that there exists an x which is a triangle and is not red. By contrast, if P = three-sidedness, then we do not, by this definition, have a real predicate of C, since there are no triangles that are not-three sided. In other words, where C = triangle and P = three-sidedness, since $\forall x\ (Cx \supset Px)$, P fails to meet the test for conceptual enlargement of C.

By way of this analysis, <existence> will fail to meet the definition above since for any concept C, $\exists x\ (Cx \supset \langle exists\rangle x)$. That is, if there exists some x such that x is a C, then x exists. Unfortunately, however, despite the apparent similarities, the reason why <existence> fails to meet the above definition is relevantly different from the reason why three-sidedness fails.

Consider that $\Diamond\exists x\ (Cx\ \&\ {\sim}Px)$ was offered in order to define conceptual enlargement – whether the concept P is or is not already contained in concept C. Where C = triangle and P = three-sidedness, P's failure is meant to show that P is conceptually contained in C. By contrast, <exists> fails for a different reason. The entailment within $\exists x\ (Cx \supset \langle exists\rangle x)$ is not secured by virtue of C's conceptual containment of <exists>. The entailment does not capture, as it did with the concept triangle, anything about what is contained in the concept C. The entailment is rather just due to the existential quantifier.

Van Cleve acknowledges this point. He recognizes the shifting ground. But even more adroitly, he recognizes a second difficulty. As he remarks, the above argument for (E ~ P) comes as a consequence of 'letting the existential quantifier express existence' (Van Cleve 1999: 188). This is not a minor point, nor is it by any means a nonsensical challenge to logic itself. The challenge, rather, is the same as made by the Free Logic Movement flowing, most notably, from Hintikka (1959) and Lambert (1960), a movement that recognizes how the *conventions* of our notational systems can be misused to establish substantive philosophical claims. Of course, standard predicate logic will yield incoherent and contradictory results when it formalizes propositions which treat existence in ways that conflict with the existential quantifier. But it is a misuse of our formal logical systems to read off from them substantive philosophical claims.

Despite, then, the impression that demonstrations through logical notation are decisive, such demonstrations, as seen in light of the Free Logic Movement, should not be assumed to be incontrovertible logical truths, but rather contestable insofar as they involve the non-philosophically neutral conventions of a given formal system. A nice irony here is that Kant makes the very same point against Wolffian Logic, which, as Kant explains, sought to secure out of the 'canon for judging' an 'organon' of 'objective assertions' (A61/B85).

A second strategy found within Kant scholarship is to argue that <existence> does not enlarge our concept of any object because it is already 'the predicate that applies to every object there is' (Stang (2015: 599)).[19] Under the assumption (of Actualism, and contrary to Possibilism, Meinongianism, etc.) that there are no non-existent objects, '*exists* applies to every object, it does not distinguish some objects from other objects' (Stang 2015: 599).

While this point may accurately capture Kant's view of objecthood, it offers a peculiar reason why <existence> is not a (real) predicate. Consider that the argument here presents <existence> as contained within our concepts of objects. That is, *it is a predicate*, a 'predicate that applies to every object there is' because it is an internal mark of our concept of objecthood itself. Reprising Van Cleve's definition, we now have a conceptual containment model for why <existence> is not a real predicate. Where C = object and P = <exists>, P fails ◊∃x (Cx & ~Px) for the intended reason. Nevertheless, the failure of P does not mean that existence is not a predicate of any sort. It is just that it is not a real predicate (i.e., a difference-making predicate), for it is a predicate of all objects. It is, in other words, an explicative predicate of our concept of objects.

[19] This may be seen as a corollary to the preceding, and so may be vulnerable to the same rebuttal. As Stang (2015) argues, if existence were not 'the concept that necessarily every object falls under. . . it would follow that it is possible for there to be non-existent objects' (597). Of course, this is allowed in Meinong as well as in possible worlds semantics. It fails for Stang, though, precisely for the reasons that the Free Logicians regard as illicit. He takes ◊∃x (Cx & ~<exists>x) to imply ◊∃x ~ ∃y (y = x) because he defines exists(x) as ∃y (y = x).

There are a number of unfortunate consequences of this view. One in particular is that if our concept of objects includes the predicate <existence>, then the Ideal of Pure Reason (as it is the concept of the object the *ens realissimum*) now includes the predicate <existence>. Surely, Kant would not be happy with this.[20]

The third and final strategy of our brief survey is found in R. Lanier Anderson's *The Poverty of Conceptual Thought* (Anderson 2015). His analysis of what he calls Kant's 'Master Argument' against transcendental theology is very much guided by his book's broader examination of Kant's critique of Leibnizian/Wolffian 'conceptualist metaphysics'. Yet, Anderson seeks as well to show more generally that we philosophers need to follow Kant's case for (E ~ P) in order to preserve our contemporary use of modal terms. He offers one initial argument in support of (E ~ P) that specifically challenges the compatibility between the Leibnizian's commitment to the thoroughgoing determination of all concepts of objects and the modal category of possibility.[21] But for the sake of space, let us consider only his second argument, one that extends beyond just what he regards as Kant's critique of Leibniz.

According to Anderson, if our modal terms (existence, possibility, necessity) were predicates, then a change in modal terms would demand a change in the contents of our concepts of objects. The result of this is that the concept

[20] One could retort, as does Stang (2015), that since there are no non-actual objects, our thoughts of non-actual possibilia are just thoughts of general concepts and not objects (621). But if that is so, then the shift in thought from non-actual possibilia to an actual object does add something. It adds objecthood; and since in the line of reasoning here, <existence> is an internal mark of objecthood, <existence>, then, does in fact get added.

[21] In brief, his first argument is that if we grant that existence is a predicate, then a thoroughgoingly determined concept must either include <exists> or <not-exists>. But if that is so, then we could have no thoroughgoingly determined concept of a merely possible object. One way or another, its existence must already be settled by virtue of which of the pair <exists>/<not-exists> is set as one of its determinations.

Anderson is quite correct that if (contrary to the preceding Actualist reading of Kant seen in Stang) there were non-actual possible objects, and our concepts of these objects were thoroughgoingly determined, then they must be determined between the predicate pair <exists> or <not-exists>. According to Anderson, this move allows Kant to reject Leibnizian conceptual metaphysics, given that Leibniz allows both thoroughgoing determination and possible objects.

There is, however, an unintended consequence of Anderson's move. Assuming that the mature Kant still allows one instance of a thoroughgoingly determined concept, i.e., the Ideal of Pure Reason, then the claim that it must be determinate between the predicate pair <exists> and <not-exists> helps rather than hurts the defender of the OA. Since, then, this Ideal is the concept of the most real being, the being that for each predicate pair bears the predicate that represents a positive reality, it is, thus, determined as <exists> – and at least *de dicto* necessarily so. In other words, if it is granted that the Ideal of Pure Reason is the unique instance of a thoroughgoingly determined concept (a point that some but not all Kantians would allow), Anderson has helped make the case that it would be a contradiction to claim that the *ens realissimum* does not exist.

of a possible object would not be the same as the concept of the actual object. Accordingly, Anderson's second argument is intended to reflect what was previously explored as Kant's generalized conclusion from his hundred dollars example: 'what would exist would not be the same as what I had thought in my concept' (A600/B628).

Earlier, we discussed how, given that objects are more determinate than their concepts, it is inevitable that there will be determinations in the former lacking in the latter. Anderson's point, though, is different. He claims that the difference here is not about different degrees of determination, but contrary marks of determination. If our modal terms were predicates, then the non-actual possible would have as one of its marks <non-actual possibility>; whereas the actual would have as one of its marks <existence>. As a result, if I were to consider the actualization of some non-actual possible P, P-*actualized* would no longer be the same P as the P of P-*non-actual possible.* As Anderson explains: 'the supposition that <existence> would determine the concept of a thing is incompatible with its logical function of a modal category, which is to separate the actual objects from the merely possible ones *without altering the contents of the things' concepts*' (Anderson 2015: 322).

This is a legitimate, though overstated, challenge to (E = P). It is legitimate because if modal terms were used as predicates of objects, then the object P would not be qualitatively identical across ◊P, <exists>P, □P. It is, though, overstated for two reasons. The first is because the qualitative identity across these modal terms depends upon further commitments, such as trans-world identity and rigid designation, neither of which would hold either for Kant or Leibniz (perhaps with the exception of God).[22]

Second, Anderson overstates his claim that modal categories could no longer perform their role of 'separating the actual from the merely possible' (Anderson 2015: 321) if they functioned as real predicates. He is correct that they could not under some particular set of axioms. But, if we grant that 'in the room' is a real predicate, then it takes little to recognize how in a possible worlds semantics our modal terms can be rendered as real predicates while still functioning to separate the actual from the merely possible. Likewise, a Counterpart Theorist could introduce the class of objects P whose members

22 This is assuming that Kant is an Actualist (i.e., there are no non-actual objects). That is, if, for Kant, there are no objects that are non-actual possible object, then the P of ◊P and <exists>P may not be the same. In order for P to be the same in both statements, we either must forgo Actualism, or take the P of <exists>P to be other than an object. Leibniz similarly would not allow for trans-world identity for contingent objects. (See: G II 41–2/AG 72–3, A VI iv 1576/AG 61.)

vary merely by the addition of a predicate denoting their indexed world. As such, P can continue to have a stable referent across ◊P, <exists>P, □P. The referent, though, is just the modally generic class. That certainly does not seem too much of a deviation from our naive modal judgments.[23]

The point here is the same as made earlier regarding the Free Logic Movement: change the substantive philosophical commitments informing one's formal systems, change what substantive philosophical commitments may be read off the formal system. While Anderson may nevertheless want to limit his point to Kantian modal semantics, how best to interpret his modal semantics, object ontology and much else of salience to (E ~ P) remains a matter of considerable debate.

11 Conclusion

Senior Kantians have been known to remark that the philosophical community by and large sides with Kant that existence is not a predicate.[24] But as our logical apparatus has through the years become more diverse, support for (E ~ P) has softened. Even among Kantians, there is increasing division – both with regard to the merits of his analysis as well as whether a decisive philosophical case can be made.

To many, as well, the charge that existence is not a predicate is ultimately irrelevant to the OA. For some, this is because the arguments used to establish (E ~ P) offer results too narrow, showing that existence is not a predicate of just one particular technical sort. So circumscribed, it is thus rebutted that (E ~ P) neither touches the idea of ontic determination (i.e., a property), nor what in this chapter has been called an explicative predicate. Others, particularly those who advance a Modal Ontological Argument, often dismiss (E ~ P) either on the grounds that properly handled, the OA does not depend upon (E = P), or that what is predicated of God is not existence simpliciter, but the more plausibly difference-making predicate of necessary existence.

Lastly, insofar as the OA's defender would contend that 'God exists' is most appropriately read as analytic, the question of whether or not <exists> enlarges our concept of God stems from a more fundamental (and perhaps question-begging) distortion of the OA. Accordingly, for those who want to

[23] In fact, this can even hold for the Leibnizian since modal terms apply not only to objects, but to classes, laws, propositions, etc. Hence, while the extension of a class will necessarily vary across worlds (since there is no trans-world object identity), the necessary and sufficient conditions for class membership may remain stable across either some or all worlds.

[24] See for example Wood (1978: 110), Allison (2004: 414).

preserve the analytic rendering of 'God exists,' there is good cause to see this as where the battle must ultimately be fought. If there is, in this chapter, a final philosophical judgment on Kant's treatment of the OA, it is that (a) there is and will be no definitive argument as to whether or not existence is a predicate; (b) Kant's overall treatment of the OA depends upon objections beyond just (E ~ P); and (c) CCO and MTO are of distinctive and unrecognized importance, since it is they, rather than (E ~ P), which most directly address how the OA is conventionally understood by its defenders. Perhaps, then, it is time for CCO and MTO, the *Critique*'s first two objections to the OA, to receive their due.

6 Hegel

Michael Inwood

Hegel attached great importance to the ontological proof of God's existence, and doggedly resisted Kant's criticism of it. Yet the version of the proof that he endorsed remains elusive. The reason for this is that he radically re-fashioned the traditional ontological proof to suit his own purposes. The proof is no longer a proof in anything like the traditional sense. Nor is it concerned with the existence of God in the traditional sense. It is concerned with the existence of the world, of nature and human beings, with – in theological terms – God's creation and redemption of the world. It provides the underpinning of Hegel's whole system.

1 Proofs of God's Existence

Several proofs of God's existence were current in Hegel's day, especially the cosmological proof from the contingency of finite things, the teleological proof or argument from design, and the ontological proof. Kant had questioned their validity, while champions of 'immediate' faith, such as F. H. Jacobi, had argued that they – primarily the cosmological proof – distort the nature of God, making him dependent on contingent things, and therefore finite rather than infinite. The purpose of the opponents of the proofs, or at least of those who interest Hegel, was not to question the existence of God, but to ensure that we have the right sort of God. Hegel, by contrast, wants to resuscitate the proofs, because he believes that, properly interpreted, they provide us with the right conception of God, with a rich (or 'concrete') conception instead of the excessively thin conception supplied by, for example, faith. The proofs supposedly reveal properties of God, such as absolute necessity (the cosmological proof) and wisdom (the teleological proof), that are not available to mere faith. In Hegel's view, there cannot be several alternative proofs of God's existence that simply do the same job in different ways, as there are different alternative proofs of, say, Pythagoras' theorem. The proofs make different, but complementary, contributions to our overall conception of God. Hegel sometimes implies that there are other, indeed many other, proofs of God's existence than the three mentioned above. One suggestion is that characterizations of God are presented throughout his own Logic. If a certain concept or 'thought-determination' is applicable to the world, then the correlative of that concept applies to God. For example, if worldly things are characterized as 'being-there' (*daseiend*), that is, as determinate beings, then God can be seen as pure being with no determinacy; if worldly things are finite, then God is infinite; if they are effects, then God is their cause; and so on.[1] Hegel is trying to determine *what* God is, as well as *whether* God is. He does not regard the concept of God as a clear-cut concept available in advance, and is exploring various ways of filling out our hazy conception of him. Another reason for his strategy, or perhaps a part of the same strategy, is that an adequate conception of God must account for his relation to the highest worldly things. It is of little use if God is correlative to and explains only lowly things such as contingent entities or the seemingly purposive interconnections of nature, if we leave out of account human beings and their doings. This does scant justice both to the world and to God himself. Thus, 'nature itself as merely alive is still not really that in terms of which the genuine *determination* of the Idea of God can be grasped; God is more than living, he is spirit. Insofar as thinking adopts a starting point and wants to adopt the closest one, *spiritual* nature alone is the worthiest and most genuine starting point for the thinking of the Absolute.'[2]

2 The Ontological Proof and Non-ontological Proofs

The three proofs that Hegel explicitly discusses fall into two distinct types, which proceed in contrary directions. The cosmological and teleological set out from 'being' and advance to the 'abstraction of thinking'[3] or to the 'thought of God' or the 'concept'.[4] The being at issue here is the being of the world, the contingency of finite things and their purposive interrelations respectively. By contrast, the ontological proof sets out from the 'abstraction of thinking'[5] or the 'thought of God' or the 'concept'[6] and proceeds to being.

[1] See, e.g., Hegel (1966: 84).

[2] Hegel (1991: §50). The suggestion, in this quotation, that the physico-theological proof implies that God is living is an indication of Hegel's tendency to conflate God and the world. The standard proof argues that God *designs* living creatures. This does not entail that God himself is living or alive in the way that his creatures are. If anything, it implies that God is 'spiritual', as an intelligent designer must presumably be.

[3] Hegel (1991: §50). [4] Hegel (1966: 75). (All translations from this work are my own.)

[5] Hegel (1991: §51). [6] Hegel (1966: 75).

If the transitions of the two types of proof are the exact inverse of each other, then the being to which the ontological proof proceeds should be the being of the world, the starting-point of the first two proofs. The traditional ontological proof, however, proceeds not to the being of the world, but to the being of God. It is intended after all to be a proof of God's existence, not of that of the world. Hegel has more than one reason for blurring this distinction, apart from a desire for symmetry. One is that he has a persistent tendency to conflate God and the world. This conflation in turn depends on at least two features of his thought. Firstly, he regards man's quest for God as an enterprise of thinking about the world. We begin, for example, by regarding the world as a mass of contingent entities, but '[t]hinking of this fullness of being means stripping it of the form of the singularities and contingencies, and grasping it as a universal being, necessary in and for itself, one that is self-determining and active in accordance with universal purposes, one that is diverse from that singular and contingent collection: [i.e.,] grasping it as God.'[7] Thinking about the world need not lead us to equate the world with God. It might lead us to postulate God as a separate entity, distinct from the world, but whose activity on the world removes its merely contingent character. This move is blocked, however, by Hegel's conviction that whatever else God is, he is infinite, and infinite in a sense that excludes his being simply one entity distinct from other entities. In his Logic, Hegel distinguishes between true infinity and bad or spurious infinity. He gives two accounts of this distinction that are not easily reconcilable. One is that whereas bad infinity proceeds in an infinite progression – as do, say, the series of natural numbers – true infinity returns to its beginning in a circular movement. It is, as we might say, finite but unbounded. The other is that while one spuriously infinite entity might be quite distinct from another spuriously infinite entity – as, say, the infinite series of odd numbers is distinct from the infinite series of even numbers – a truly infinite entity is all-inclusive. It cannot be distinct from anything else, since otherwise it would be bounded or limited by it and therefore not truly infinite. The first of these accounts is more properly applicable to mathematical infinity, though, as we shall see, the idea of circular infinity does have a place in Hegel's religious thought. The second account is applicable to God. If God is truly infinite, then he cannot be

[7] Hegel (1991: §50). The conflation is also evident elsewhere, e.g., Hegel (1991: §193). Remark: 'the *object* is quite generally the *One* whole that is inwardly still undetermined; it is the objective world in general, God, the absolute object'.

distinct from the world, whether the world of nature or the world of human beings. The question of God's infinity leads us to Hegel's response to Kant.

3 Hegel vs Kant on the Ontological Proof

Kant objected to the ontological proof that 'being' is not a 'real predicate' and cannot form part of the concept of something. He illustrated this with the 'concept' of a hundred dollars, which cannot be conjured into existence by adding 'being' to their concept. Hegel of course agreed with Kant's treatment of this example, but countered it with two objections of his own: firstly, that the 'concept' of a hundred dollars is not properly called a 'concept', and secondly, that while Kant's objection holds against a finite entity, it does not hold against an infinite entity, such as God: 'what makes everything *finite* is this and *only* this: that its *being-there* [*Dasein*][8] *is diverse from its concept*. But God has to be expressly that which can only be "thought as existing",[9] where the Concept includes being within itself. It is this unity of the Concept and of being that constitutes the concept of God.'[10]

Why the infinitude of God should make a difference is unclear, but Hegel's train of thought may be this. A finite entity is bounded or 'limited' by other entities, and its existence and character depends on these other entities:[11] the existence, survival and demise of a horse depends on its parents, on grass and on the wolf that preys upon it. But God is unbounded and unlimited, and so his existence can depend on nothing except his concept. Hence God is 'that which can only be "thought as existing"'. There are at least two senses of 'concept' in play here. In one sense a concept is *our* concept, the concept we form of God, such as 'the greatest conceivable thing' or 'the perfect being'. Even if such a concept were to entail the existence of God, it could hardly be said to produce or sustain God. Compare how the application of the concept 'bachelor' to someone *entails* that he is unmarried, but does not *explain why*

[8] Hegel's switch from *Sein* ('being') to *Dasein* ('being-there') may also be significant. *Dasein* sometimes amounts simply to 'being' or 'existence', but sometimes has the more technical sense of 'being with a determinacy': see Hegel (1991: §90).

[9] Hegel (1991: 318n.61) suggests that this refers to Spinoza's definition of the *causa sui* in *Ethics* I, Definition 1: *Per causam sui intelligo id*, cuius essentia involvit existentiam, sive id, cuius natura non potest concipi, nisi existens. It is quoted by Hegel in his note to §76.

[10] Hegel (1991: §51). The translators of Hegel (1991) capitalize 'Concept' when it is 'used in the singular and absolute sense' (p. xxviii), that is, when it refers to Hegel's Logic, considered as a single concept. Since the German word, *Begriff*, is always capitalized, there is no explicit warrant in Hegel's text for this distinction, but the distinction is nevertheless a real one.

[11] See, e.g., Hegel (1991: §§91ff.).

he is unmarried. If a believer wants to explain the existence of God, he would do better to say that it is uncaused, or that God is the cause of himself, than to appeal to *our*, or *his*, concept of God. In another sense, the 'concept' of something is conceived as a power immanent in it, responsible for its growth and structure. It is comparable to DNA or, less anachronistically, to the plan in the seed of an organism or perhaps to an Aristotelian form. A concept in this sense is not the same as *our* concept of the thing, nor need it correspond to it very closely. Similarly, a horse has a concept in this sense, an immanent concept that plays a part in its existence, nature and growth, and which is distinct from, and may be quite different from, the concept that *we* form of a horse.[12] (*Our* concept of a whale once classified it as a fish, when in fact it is a mammal.) However, since the concept of a horse is of something finite, it does not have sole responsibility for the existence, etc. of the horse. It is fairly clear, however, that a hundred dollars does not have an immanent concept even of this type: my concept of a hundred dollars plays no part in their existence, except in the sense that it may motivate me to acquire them. If the ontological argument is satisfied by God because God is infinite, it is this second sense of 'concept' that is required. God's immanent concept generates him and sustains him, because there is nothing else that can do it – and nothing else that can hinder the operation of the concept. We might object: 'I can see how *if* God *were* to exist, he *would* be more closely related to his concept than finite entities are. Finite entities fall short of their concept, whereas God would not. But why should I accept that there is a God, or that there is a concept that, as it were, generates him? There is a horse-generating concept, but no unicorn-generating concept. Might there not be a world-generating concept, but no God-generating concept?' The objector is then claiming that *the* concept of God may be only *our* concept of God, and no more object-generating than the 'concept' of a hundred dollars or of a bachelor is. Before we consider this objection, however, we need to ask: Why should God be 'infinite'?

4 The Infinity of God

We may well agree that if God is truly infinite, infinite, that is, in Hegel's sense, then he necessarily exists. But why must we accept that God is infinite? Hegel is, after all, averse to simply presupposing such claims. He seems to level such a charge against previous proponents of the ontological proof: '[t]he defect in Anselm's argumentation, however, which is also shared by

[12] Compare Locke's distinction between real essence and nominal essence.

Descartes and Spinoza . . . is that this *unity* [viz., of subjectivity and objectivity], which is proclaimed as what is most perfect (or subjectively as the true knowing), is *presupposed*'.[13] Moreover, there is no obvious contradiction in claiming that God, let alone a god, is merely finite. Hegel himself agrees that the teleological proof does not establish God's infinity. He followed Kant in accepting that the purposiveness we observe is very great and implies great wisdom and power in its cause, but not absolute wisdom or absolute power (*Allmacht*).[14] So someone who believes in God on the basis of this proof alone may well believe that God is only finite. Nevertheless, it is at this point that the ontological proof requires the cooperation of another proof, namely the cosmological proof. For in Hegel's view it is this proof that establishes God's infinity and thereby provides the concept of God from which the ontological proof can begin. The cosmological proof begins from the observation that the world consists of an aggregate of finite 'contingent' entities, and these are supposed to require a necessary entity in order to ensure their maintenance.[15] It is, in Hegel's view, the oldest of the proofs of God's existence: the first 'determination' of God is not the wisdom manifested in his design of the world and exploited by the teleological proof, but power, the power to create and sustain a world at all.[16] Early versions of the proof are impaired by ignorance of science, of, for example, the conservation of matter (or of energy), which ensures that finite entities are not independent of each other and do not simply pop into and out of existence on their own. However, Hegel takes account of this. He agrees that the emergence and demise of finite entities depends on other entities and on laws establishing a necessary connection between them. But this is not enough to undermine the cosmological proof. Chains of causes and effects extend to infinity without support. 'But above this pile of contingencies, above the necessity enclosed in them that is only an external and relative necessity, and above the infinite that is only a negative [i.e., bad infinity], the spirit ascends to a necessity that no longer goes beyond itself and is in and for itself, self-enclosed, completely determined intrinsically, a necessity by which all other determinations are posited and on which they depend.'[17] This is 'absolute necessity'[18] or

[13] Hegel (1991: §193: 271). One of Aquinas' objections to the ontological proof is that 'not everyone who hears this word "God" understands it to signify something than which nothing greater can be thought, seeing that some have believed God to be a body' (*Summa Theologiae*, I.2, 1: reply to objection 2).

[14] Hegel (1966: 162). [15] E.g., Hegel (1991: §50).

[16] Hegel (1966: 158), from Hegel's lectures on religion of 1831. [17] Hegel (1966: 90).

[18] Hegel (1966: 86), etc.

'the absolutely necessary (essence)',[19] a necessity that is self-supporting and dependent on no condition. But an absolutely necessary essence must be truly infinite.[20] It is wholly self-enclosed and independent. If it were finite, it would itself need explanation in terms of other entities and would therefore not be *absolutely* necessary. Thus the cosmological proof, if it is sound, secures a concept of God as infinite, which can then serve as an appropriate starting-point for the ontological proof. Hegel rejects Kant's claim that the cosmological proof presupposes the ontological proof. It is the other way round: the ontological proof presupposes the cosmological proof.[21]

5 The Relation between the Cosmological and Ontological Proofs

We saw earlier that Hegel denies that there might be alternative proofs of the existence of God, as there are alternative proofs of geometrical theorems. He accepts the coexistence of the cosmological proof and the teleological proof, since these are not alternative proofs of one and the same proposition. The cosmological proof establishes God's existence as an absolutely necessary being, but not as a purposeful designer. This is established, if at all, by the teleological proof, which, in turn, does not establish that God is infinite or absolutely necessary. But now we seem to have two proofs that establish exactly the same conclusion. The cosmological proof concludes that God as an infinite, absolutely necessary being exists, and the ontological proof establishes, albeit in a different way, that God, as characterized by the cosmological proof, exists. The solution to this apparent duplication is as follows. With respect to the non-ontological proofs Hegel maintains that the traditional versions of them were mistaken in supposing that the starting-point of the proof, e.g., the contingency of the world and of the entities in it, still remained in place after the conclusion, e.g., the existence of a necessary being, was drawn from it. On the contrary, the starting-point, and the transition from it, is 'sublated' (*aufgehoben*) by the conclusion of the proof. What he means by this is not that the world is now seen to be necessary in virtue of its divine source, but that 'the very fact that the world is *contingent* implies that it is only something *incidental*, phenomenal, and in and for itself *null and void*'.[22]

[19] Hegel (1966: 89), etc. [20] Hegel (1966: 102), etc.

[21] Hegel (1966: 138ff.). This appeared in a now lost manuscript on Kant's criticisms of the cosmological proof, found by Hegel's first editors and inserted in his Lectures on the Proofs, and printed as a supplement by Georg Lasson to his 1930 edition.

[22] Hegel (1991: §50). Cf. Hegel (1966: 103): 'If we begin from the contingent, we must not set out from it as something that is supposed to stand fast, so that it is left as being in our advance ... but

Hegel applies this point more conspicuously to the cosmological proof than to the teleological proof, since contingency more obviously detracts from full being than does purposive organization. But it applies to the teleological proof as well, and indeed to any proof whose starting-point is some feature of finite, worldly entities. He has at least two reasons for this move. The first is that it answers an objection to the proofs raised, among others, by F. H. Jacobi, namely that the proofs make God dependent on finite things.[23] Hegel notes the difference between ontological dependency and epistemic dependency: 'The whole course of the connection is only in the proving; only our *cognition* of the absolutely necessary being is conditioned by this starting-point: the absolutely necessary does not emerge by elevating itself out of the world of contingency and needing this world as its starting-point and presupposition in order to arrive at its being from it.'[24] But it is nevertheless a defect of the traditional proofs that their 'form' conflicts with their 'content', that the course of the proof does not reflect or track the actual relationship between God and the world. This problem is solved if we see the proofs as treating the world as a ladder by which we reach God and which God then pulls up and absorbs into himself once we have ascended by it. Hegel's second reason is that, as we have seen, since God is truly infinite, he cannot be distinct from the world. God and the world are not, however, straightforwardly identical, as are, say, Cicero and Tully. They take different predicates, God being infinite, while the world is, as yet, finite. We might, provisionally, compare God to the collection of molecules of which a material object consists or perhaps to the soul or mind of the world, related to the world in a way analogous to that in which a human mind is related to a human body.[25] In these cases the objects identified compete for space. One or the other of them must be less than fully real and be subordinate to the other. This dilemma, and Hegel's solution to it, emerges most clearly in his account of Spinoza, who continually intrudes into his consideration of the proofs.

6 Hegel and Spinoza

Spinoza held that everything that exists is a 'mode' of a single substance, which he referred to as 'God or nature'. This was commonly regarded as a

posit it with its complete determination, that non-being equally pertains to it, and that it thereby enters into the result as vanishing. There is absolute necessity not because the contingent is, but rather because it is a non-being, only appearance, its being is not genuine actuality; absolute necessity is its being and its truth.'

[23] Hegel (1966: 101). [24] Hegel (1966: 101). [25] See Ellis (2010).

pantheistic doctrine amounting to atheism, the denial of God's existence. Hegel notes that, although Spinoza cannot accommodate the existence of *both* God *and* nature, i.e., the empirical world, he leaves room for the alternative view that while God exists, the world does not. He prefers to regard Spinoza not as an atheist, but as an 'acosmist', a denier of the existence of the world.[26] Hegel sometimes speaks as if he himself is an acosmist,[27] but he is not an acosmist in Spinoza's way and it is the ontological proof that preserves him from acosmism. What troubles Hegel is that Spinoza does not draw an adequate connection between the one substance and the modes, the empirical world:

> The One [viz. substance] is not explicated as self-developing necessity – not, as the concept has been specified, as the process that mediates itself with itself . . . Now besides this One there just happens to be found the contingent world, being with the determination of the negative, the realm of restrictions and finitudes – and here it makes no difference whether this realm is represented as a realm of external being-there [*Daseins*], of appearance [*Scheins*] or, in accordance with the determination of superficial idealism, as a merely subjective world, a world of consciousness. This manifoldness with its infinite entanglements is initially separate from that substance, and we have to see what relationship to this One is assigned to it.[28]

But no such account is forthcoming in Spinoza, because 'what is recognized as the absolute itself, the One, the substance, is not supposed to be living, not the moving principle therein, not the method – for substance lacks determination'.[29] This leaves the world of appearance unstable and unsupported and even as a merely apparent and not genuinely real world.[30] This consequence can be averted only if substance is also seen as 'subject', that is, if it has

[26] See, e.g., Hegel (1991: §50: 97): 'the world is determined in the Spinozist system as a mere phenomenon without genuine reality, so that this system must rather be seen as *acosmism*.' For earlier accounts of Spinoza as an acosmist, especially Moses Mendelssohn's, see Bell (1984: 26, 46, 48 and 60).

[27] E.g., Hegel (1991: §6): 'we have to presuppose that the reader has enough education to know, not just that God is actual – that he is what is most actual, that he alone is genuinely actual – but also (with regard to the formal aspect) that quite generally, what is there [i.e., empirical entities] is partly *appearance* and only partly actuality'. Hegel is explaining his controversial dictum, in the preface to his earlier *Philosophy of Right*: 'What is rational, is actual, and what is actual, is rational.'

[28] Hegel (1966: 134). See also Hegel (1832/95: III: 142f.) and Hegel (2007: §573), where Hegel associates Spinoza's Judaism with Islam and makes similar criticisms of both.

[29] Hegel (1966: 135).

[30] See also Hegel (1976: §17), and Hegel (2010: 278, 466, 473), at the last of which Hegel takes *Ethica* I, Definition iv – *Per attributum intelligo id quod intellectus de substantia percipit tanquam eiusdem essentiam constituens* – to imply that the attributes of substance depend on the intellect.

sufficient vitality to generate the empirical world in a rationally intelligible manner.[31] So now there are two ontological arguments in play. One is Spinoza's own argument for the existence of substance, namely, that it can only be 'thought as existing'.[32] This is a truncated version of the traditional ontological proof. The other is the quite different argument, that substance, given that it exists, must also be a 'subject' and manifest itself in the empirical world that it generates. This argument is lacking in Spinoza, but Hegel purports to supply it himself. This leaves two questions, however. Is this second argument really an ontological proof of the existence of *God*? And did Hegel *regard* it as an ontological proof of God's existence?

7 The Second Ontological Proof

An ontological proof must satisfy two requirements. It must proceed from a thought or concept, and it must conclude with the existence of God. This second ontological proof meets the first requirement, since Hegel believes that it proceeds from the concept of God established by the cosmological proof. It also satisfies the second requirement, since, although it seems to be a proof of the existence of the world rather than that of God, Hegel does not regard God and the world as distinct. God is truly infinite and therefore comprises nature and human beings. Moreover, nature and human beings are essential to God. God cannot be complete without the world of nature and humanity.[33] It does not follow, however, that Hegel regarded this argument as *the* ontological proof, not at least as the ontological proof that he attempted to defend against Kant. At a pinch, his objections to Kant might be read as an attempt to defend this second proof, but that is not the most natural interpretation of them. Again, in relating the formal ontological proof to the faith of the non-philosophical believer, Hegel says: 'the trivial remark that thought and being are diverse may, at the most, hinder, but not abolish, the movement of man's spirit from the *thought* of God to the certainty that God *is*. Moreover, it is this passage, the absolute inseparability of the thought of God from his being,

[31] See Hegel (1976: §17): 'everything turns on grasping and expressing the True, not only as *Substance*, but equally as *Subject*'.

[32] See note 9 above.

[33] Without man's knowledge of God, God would lack self-consciousness: God knows himself in man, just as man knows himself in God. See, e.g., Hegel (1966: 45, 49), and esp. Hegel (1832/95: vol. I: 217f.), where Hegel approvingly quotes Meister Eckhart: 'The eye with which God sees me is the same eye by which I see him. My eye and his eye are one and the same. In righteousness I am weighed in God and he in me. If God did not exist, nor would I; if I did not exist, nor would he.' (I have modified the translation.)

that has been restored to its rightful position by the theory of "immediate knowing" or "faith" ...'[34] This surely refers to the traditional ontological proof rather than to Hegel's proposed new version. There would seem, therefore, to be some confusion, or a sleight of hand, on Hegel's part, if what he is really defending is this new version. Nevertheless the evidence that this version is the primary object of Hegel's defence is compelling. There is, firstly, his general claim that the ontological proof proceeds in the reverse direction from that of the cosmological and teleological proofs, that whereas they proceed from being to thought, it proceeds from thought to being. This only applies if the being to which the ontological proof proceeds is the finite being of the world, not that of God. That, in Hegel's view, the ontological proof proper proceeds from the thought of infinite God to the being of the finite world, becomes clearer in his manuscript on Kant's criticism of the cosmological proof.[35] In this elaborate account of the relationship between the cosmological and the ontological proofs, he says:

> But if in the indicated transition of the finite into the infinite the finite appears as the starting-point for the infinite, then accordingly the other, merely reversed proposition or transition seems to have to determine itself likewise as a transition from the infinite into the finite or as the proposition: the infinite is finite ... For the infinite, in that it opens up into being [*sich zum Sein entschliesst*], hereby determines itself into an Other of itself; but the Other of the infinite is in general the finite.[36]

This results in a pleasing circularity, that is, in Hegel's view, a mark of true infinity. The cosmological proof ascends from the being of the world to the infinite God, and God descends into the world again, thereby providing the premise required by the cosmological proof. However, the second ontological proof gives the finite world a secure status that, in Hegel's view, Spinoza failed to provide. The world is now represented not simply as a disorderly aggregate of worldly things, but 'as nature, by which we understand, roughly, an intrinsically systematic whole, a system of orders and stages, and especially of laws'.[37]

[34] Hegel (1991: §51). But cf. Hegel (1991: §193), where Hegel criticizes Jacobi's comparison of immediate belief in God to our immediate belief in finite things: 'if the principle of this faith also takes the representations of external finite things in the inseparability of the consciousness of them and of their being (because they are bound up with the determination of existence *in our intuition*), that too is quite correct. But it would be mindless ... if this were supposed to mean that in our consciousness existence is bound up with the representation of finite things in the same way as it is with the representation of God.'

[35] See note 15 above. [36] Hegel (1966: 154f.). [37] Hegel (1966: 80).

8 What about the First Ontological Proof?

Sceptics may well feel cheated by Hegel's brusque defence of the first ontological proof. They brushes Kant's objection aside with remarks such as: 'it would be very odd if spirit's innermost core, the Concept, or even if I, or above all the concrete totality that God is, were not rich enough to contain within itself even so poor a determination as being is – . . .'[38] Hegel might be suspected of confusing 'If God exists, then he is' and 'God is.' But that suspicion is unwarranted. In his 1831 lectures he distinguished two types, or senses, of 'being':

> Being is the poorest of abstractions: the concept is not so poor that it does not contain this determination. We have to consider being not in the poverty of abstraction, in bad immediacy, but being as the being of God, as the wholly concrete being, distinct from God. Finite spirit's consciousness is concrete being, the material of the realisation of the concept of God. We shouldn't speak here of the addition of being to the concept or merely of a unity of the concept and being – such expressions are askew. The unity is rather to be conceived as absolute process, as the vitality of God, in such a way that the two sides in it are also distinct, but that it is the absolute activity of producing itself eternally. We have here the concrete representation of God as spirit.[39]

Being is, on the one hand, an abstract determination that is contained in the concept of God or in the Concept with which Hegel tends to identify God. This is impoverished and does little to advance the argument.[40] Being is, on the other hand, the concrete reality of nature and the human spirit, which is initially distinct from God, but comes to be seen as the expansion or realization of God. Nature and human beings are what Spinoza regarded as mere modes of substance. Now it is God himself, the substance that has become subject, that generates them as other ('distinct') than himself and then reclaims them as the realization of himself. The reclamation is achieved by human beings, who are the pinnacle of God's creation, but also an aspect of God himself.

A problem still remains, however. Why did Hegel not give a more adequate defence of the traditional ontological proof that Kant criticized? The answer to this is two-pronged. On the one hand, the concept of God tends to become excessively thin, especially because, in the hands of Enlightenment

[38] Hegel (1991: §51: 99). On the capitalization of 'Concept', see note 10.

[39] Hegel (1966: 176); Hegel (1985: 356).

[40] Incorporating being or existence into the concept of God may make it hard to *deny* God's existence, since 'God does not exist' will be a contradictory statement and that whose existence is denied cannot be God. But it makes it no easier to *affirm* God's existence.

(and medieval) thinkers, it excludes all negation and involves only undiluted reality. As the 'essential sum of all realities or as the supremely real Essence, [it] becomes the *simple abstraction*'.[41] In Hegel's view, therefore, it is not worth proving its existence. There is no point in proving the existence of something of which we can then say no more than that it exists. This deficiency is repaired by the proofs that proceed from the being of the world to the being of God, since they fill out the concept of God: his various relations to the world generate properties of him, such as necessity and wisdom. But this hardly helps the traditional ontological proof unless the results of these other proofs are presupposed. On the other hand, Hegel radically transforms the traditional conception of God. God is no longer a non-conceptual entity of which we have a concept, but God is himself a concept: 'God is one concept, which is essentially an intrinsically unitary, inseparable concept.'[42] This transformation has several sources. One is Hegel's own belief that God, since he is infinite, cannot be an entity distinct from the world.[43] This suggests, though it may not entail, that God is the concept of the world. Other pressures come from within the tradition itself. God cannot simply have properties or take predicates in the way that a finite entity does. The unity of God requires that he be identical with the qualities predicated of him, that he be, e.g., not simply wise in the way that Socrates is wise, but that he be wisdom itself.[44] Hegel adds to this that when we apply predicates to God as the subject, all the information about God is given by the predicates, while the subject-term, 'God', is really dispensable: 'when we say: "God is infinite, eternal, etc.", God is initially, as subject, a mere presupposition in representation, of which we say what it is only in the predicate. In the subject we do not yet know what it is, i.e. what content, content-determination, he has.'[45] He makes the same point in the *Encyclopaedia*, adding that the 'form of the proposition, or more precisely that of the judgement, is incapable of expressing what is concrete ... and speculative'[46] and, again, '[b]ecause the thought, the matter which is all that we are here concerned about, is contained only in the predicate, the propositional form, as well as the subject [of the proposition], is something completely superfluous ...'[47] The upshot is that instead of presenting concepts, such as being, as explicit 'metaphysical

[41] Hegel (1991: §49, and also §36). [42] Hegel (1966: 73). [43] See especially Hegel (1966: 60).
[44] E.g., Aquinas, *Summa Theologica*, 1.3. 3 ad 1.
[45] Hegel (1966: 148f.). This doctrine is not intended to apply to ordinary predications, such as 'Socrates is wise' or 'The cat sat on the mat.' It seems quite plausible in the case of God, however, both because of the haziness of the term and because of the intimate relationship, amounting to identity, between God and his properties.
[46] Hegel (1991: §31). [47] Hegel (1991: §85).

definitions of God',[48] Hegel focuses exclusively on the concepts themselves. All these factors enable Hegel, with some plausibility, to identify God with the elaborate network of interconnected concepts that unfolds in the Logic, concepts which hang together to form what Hegel regards as a single concept. As a whole, this 'Concept' can be seen as an 'exposition of God as he is before the creation'.[49] Unlike the conception of God as the 'essential sum of all realities', this conception does not collapse into a 'simple abstraction', since it involves negation and difference. In his seventh lecture on the proofs, where the transformation of God into the Concept is primarily undertaken, he compares the Concept to a living organism, each of whose organs is distinct from the others, but inseparable from them and an essential ingredient in the process that constitutes the life of the whole.[50] Unlike Spinoza's substance, the Concept is, in Hegel's view, dynamic and capable of explaining the emergence of nature and of human beings. What reason do we have for supposing that the Concept exists? There is no room for anything like the traditional ontological proof of its existence. Initially, it simply emerges in the mind of the steadfast logician, thinking in the appropriate way. Later it receives confirmation in nature, whose underpinning it proves to be, and in human beings, who gradually ascend towards the concept and eventually become logicians themselves. But before we come to that, we need to consider what happens within the Concept itself.

9 Inside the Concept

Hegel's Logic has three parts, the doctrines of being, of essence and of the concept. Each part is in turn divided, and subdivided, into other thoughts or concepts. Many, though not all, of these concepts may be regarded as 'metaphysical definitions of God',[51] even if Hegel sees no point in retaining the word 'God'. Most prominently, God may be regarded as being or as essence ('the supremely real Essence'). These are relatively traditional characterizations of God, which, though not entirely inappropriate, are not wholly adequate. Hegel regards the notion of God as problematically indefinite. He needs to find out what God is, as well as whether God is, and so he tries out various definitions on God for size. The most adequate of the three mentioned is the concept itself. Hegel considers many subsidiary themes in the Doctrine of the Concept, such as various types of judgments and of 'syllogisms'. But its main interest, from our point of view, is that it represents the logic as a whole, 'the Concept', within logic itself. Logic is thought about thoughts, and thought about thoughts is

[48] Hegel (1991: §85). [49] Hegel (2010: 29). [50] Hegel (1966: 63). [51] Hegel (1991: 85).

itself one of the things we can think about. It is therefore under the heading of the concept that Hegel returns to the ontological proof.[52] (A truncated version, closer to the tradition, of the way in which the Logic arrives at the concept as a suitable starting-point for the ontological proof, is seen above in the relationship between the cosmological and the ontological proofs.)

The proof begins when the 'subjective concept' – consisting of the concept itself, judgment, and the syllogism – 'breaks through its own barrier, and opens itself up into objectivity by means of syllogism'.[53] This repairs a deficiency in the 'logic of the understanding', where 'thinking is taken to be a merely formal and subjective activity, and the objective world that confronts thinking counts as something fixed and present in its own right'.[54] Hegel's idea is that *within logic* the thought of subjectivity or the concept is correlative to the thought of objectivity or the object. Given the all-inclusive nature of the concept, 'the *object* is quite generally the *One* whole that is inwardly still undetermined; it is the objective world in general, God, the absolute object. But . . . as objective *world* it falls apart inwardly into [an] undetermined manifoldness – and each of these *isolated* [bits] is also an object, or something-there that is inwardly concrete, complete, and independent.'[55] There is therefore, initially, a mismatch between the concept and the object. The concept is infinite, while the object is finite and dispersed in separate bits. But:

> The finite is the sort of objectivity which is at the same time not adequate to its purpose, to its essence and concept, but diverse from it; or it is the sort of representation, the sort of subjective something, that does not involve existence. This objection and antithesis is only removed by showing that the finite is something-untrue, or that these determinations are on their own account one-sided and null, and that their identity is therefore one into which they pass over by themselves and in which they are reconciled.[56]

Cognition needs to overcome the antithesis between subjectivity and objectivity by removing the alien character of the objective world, 'tracing . . . what is objective back to the Concept, which is our innermost Self'.[57] The two sides converge:

> The Concept, which is initially only subjective, proceeds to objectify itself by virtue of its own activity and without the help of an external material or stuff. And likewise the object is not rigid and without process; instead, its process

[52] Hegel (1991: §§192ff.: especially 193); Hegel (2010: 620ff., especially 625–8).
[53] Hegel (1991: §192 Addition). [54] Hegel (1991: §192 Addition). [55] Hegel (1991: §193).
[56] Hegel (1991: §193). [57] Hegel (1991: §194 Addition 1).

> consists in its proving itself to be at the same time subjective, and this forms the advance to the Idea [viz. the reconciliation of subjectivity and objectivity].[58]

Hegel transforms Anselm's argument beyond recognition. The two sides in Anselm's argument – the thought of God and God – were both infinite and God did not require any additional cognitive processing by the Concept. But Hegel postulates a process whereby the 'finite', which initially falls short of the Concept, is shown to be 'something-untrue' and finitude and infinity are reconciled in the Idea. Hegel is speaking not about the existence of God, but about the descent of God into the world and about the elevation of the world to God, or the divinization of the finite. To the concern that 'it might appear that the transition from the concept into objectivity is quite another thing than the transition from the concept of God to God's existence',[59] Hegel responds, firstly, that the content, God, makes no difference to the logical course of the argument, that the ontological proof is just an application of this logical course to a particular content, and secondly that it is the predicates applied to the subject, 'God', that prevent it from being just an empty name. This response seems not to concern the difference between Anselm's and Hegel's proofs, however, since the remainder of the Logic identifies the object with the world and presents its progressively higher determination – in terms of mechanism, chemism, teleology, etc. – until it attains to the 'Idea' (*Idee*), a harmonious reconciliation with God or the Concept. All of this happens within the Concept, however. What happens in the world outside?

10 Outside the Concept

Hegel's Logic ends with the 'absolute idea', which involves the harmonization of the Concept and the object.[60] He concludes with a brief account of the transition to nature. The absolute idea '*resolves to release out of itself* into freedom the moment of its particularity or of the initial determining and otherness, [i.e.,] the *immediate Idea* as its reflexion, or itself as *Nature*'.[61] Or more expansively:

> The transition is to be grasped in the sense . . . that the idea *freely discharges* itself, . . . But what is posited by this first resolve of the pure idea to determine itself as external idea is only the mediation out of which the concept, as free concrete existence that has come to itself, raises itself up, completes this self-liberation *in the science of spirit*, and in the science of

[58] Hegel (1991: §194 Addition 1). [59] Hegel (2010: 626).
[60] Hegel (1991: §§236ff.); Hegel (2010: 732ff.). [61] Hegel (1991: §244).

> logic finds the highest concept of itself, the pure concept conceptually comprehending itself.[62]

That is to say, the idea first passes into nature, which is initially alien to the concept,[63] and then proceeds to the science of spirit, which gradually reclaims nature conceptually (and practically) and also records humanity's rise above nature. The advance of spirit culminates in its discovery, or rediscovery, of the science of logic or the concept, and thus its return to the beginning. Hegel's account of the transition to nature is somewhat perfunctory, because he assumes that it is adequately accounted for by the transition from concept to object *within* the concept, an 'infinite' concept with an unimpeded tendency to actualize itself. The concept itself incorporates a dress rehearsal of its emergence into the physical world. He is, in any case, less interested in the emergence of nature than in its subsequent reclamation, or 'sublation', by spirit. After all, Spinoza had got as far as postulating nature, even though, in Hegel's view, he gave no adequate account of it or of its emergence, and left it tied to the apron strings of substance. Moreover, Spinoza gave no account whatsoever of the conceptual reclamation of nature by 'spirit'. Hegel's transformation of the proofs provides this:

> The so-called proofs that God is there have to be seen simply as *descriptions* and analyses of the inward *journey of the spirit*. It is a *thinking* journey and it thinks what is sensory. The *elevation* of thinking above the sensible, its *going out* above the finite to the infinite, the *leap* that is made into the supersensible when the sequences of the sensible are broken off, all this is thinking itself . . .[64]

This journey takes place on more than one level. At a mundane level, we gradually bring conceptual order into our view of nature, discovering laws and teleological relationships. We also establish orderly societies, which are, in Hegel's view, a better reflection of God than nature is. At the level of religion, Christianity represents God's becoming man, and the subsequent descent of the Holy Spirit into the Christian community. Hence Hegel regards the ontological proof as specifically Christian: 'The standpoint on which we find ourselves is the Christian standpoint. Here we have the concept of God in its entire freedom; this concept is identical with being . . . In the Christian

[62] Hegel (2010: 753).

[63] Hegel's own account of nature, Hegel (1970), is structured in terms of Hegel's own conceptual system, since he cannot, of course, describe nature without conceptualizing it.

[64] Hegel (1991: §50).

religion it is known that God has revealed himself, and the very being of God consists in revealing himself.'[65] Hegel frequently refers to the human journey described by the proofs as the 'elevation of (our) spirit to God'.[66] God and man gradually converge, and theism converges with humanism. In this sense, Hegel's ontological proof might be seen as a *disproof* of God's existence. But as Hegel knew, it all depends on what we mean by 'God'.[67]

[65] Hegel (1966: 176); Hegel (1985: 356f.). [66] Hegel (1966: 14), etc.

[67] See also Inwood (2002: xviiiff.) on Hegel's theology, and Inwood (2002: 348ff.) on the relationship between logic and nature.

7 Gödel

Alexander Pruss

Kurt Gödel came up with an ontological argument for a perfect being around 1941, but it was not circulated until the 1970s. The argument is elegant, precise and valid. I will begin by sketching a simplified version of the original argument that still shares the main flaw of the original version, skip forward to improved versions and then proceed to a philosophical discussion of some of the improved versions.

1 The Arguments

1.1 Preliminary Formulations

All the versions of the argument are based on the intuitive notion of a 'positive property'. Exactly what that is shall be discussed below. In the original version of the argument, this is taken to be governed by three axioms.

Axiom F1 A property A is positive if and only if its negation ~A is not positive.
Axiom F2 If A is positive and A entails B, then B is positive.
Axiom F3 If A is positive, then necessarily A is positive.

Here, a property A entails a property B provided that necessarily everything that has A has B. Throughout the paper we assume that if A is a property, then there is a negated property ~A that is possessed by all and only the things that do not possess A. I also assume throughout that axioms hold at all possible worlds.

The original version of the argument then adds a definition:

Definition D1 x is God-like provided that all of x's essential properties are positive and that all positive properties are essential properties of x.

Here, A is an essential property of x provided that necessarily if x exists, x has A. And finally the argument needs two substantive or non-formal axioms specifying that certain properties are positive:

Axiom N1 The property of being God-like is positive.

Axiom N2 Necessary existence is positive.

Given S5-based modal logic (i.e., modal logic assuming that what is necessary cannot vary across possible worlds, so what is possibly necessary is simply necessary), it follows that there is a God-like being, as we shall shortly see. Throughout the paper, I will do modal logic in terms of possible worlds, as that is more intuitive than proceeding axiomatically.

The central 'trick' to the argument is this observation:

Lemma L1 Given F1 and F2, any pair of positive properties is compossible, where two properties are compossible provided that it is possible for something to exist that has them both.

To prove L1, note that if A and B are positive but not compossible, then necessarily anything that has B would fail to have A, and hence B would entail ~A, so that by F2 the property ~A would be positive, which would violate F1 given the positivity of A.

An immediate corollary of L1 is that given F1 and F2, every positive property is possibly exemplified.

It follows from N1, N2 and L1 that it is possible for there to be a necessarily existing God-like being. Let w be a possible world at which there is such a being, call it g. Then at w it is true that g exists at every possible world, and so g exists necessarily at the actual world (this step implicitly uses S5).

The only remaining thing to show is that g is actually God-like. This requires checking two different things, namely that all of g's essential properties are positive and that all positive properties are g's essential properties. But these statements are true in w, and (a) what essential properties an object has does not vary between possible worlds (this uses S5) and (b) what properties are positive does not vary between possible worlds (this uses F3 and, again, S5). So these statements are also true at the actual world, and hence g is indeed God-like.

Thus we have proved:

Theorem T1 Given F1, F2, F3, N1 and N2, there is a necessarily existing God-like being.

However, the premises of this Gödelian argument have an unfortunate consequence. They imply that there is no contingency, given the plausible assumption:

Axiom N3 For any proposition p there is a property S_p of being such that p is true.

Theorem T2 Given F1 and N3, if there is a necessary God-like being and p is true, then p is necessarily true.

To see this, suppose p is true and g is a necessary God-like being. Observe that S_p either is or is not positive. If S_p is positive, then g has S_p essentially. But a God-like being exists in all possible worlds, so in every possible world g has S_p, and hence p is true in every possible world. Suppose now that S_p is not positive. Then by F1, $\sim S_p$ is positive. Hence just as before, g has $\sim S_p$ in every possible world, and hence p is not true in any possible world.

But p is true at the actual world, so the option of S_p not being positive is absurd. Thus, p is true in every possible world.

Given T2, we see that the Gödel argument in T1 leads to the conclusion that all truths are necessary truths, and so modality collapses. This is generally taken to be an unacceptable consequence, so there is something deeply wrong here.

Fortunately, T2 also indicates a diagnosis of the problem. The problem is with F1. Given F1, for every property A, either A is positive or A is negative, where a property A is negative if and only if ~A is positive. This means that for any proposition p, a necessary God-like being will either necessarily have S_p or will necessarily have $\sim S_p$.

The fix is also straightforward and improves the argument. As Anderson (1990) notes, it is not plausible that every property is positive or negative. There might be some indifferent properties that are neither positive nor negative. To allow for that possibility, all we need to do is drop the right-to-left conditional in F1 and get:

Axiom F1a If A is positive, then ~A is not positive.

The proof of L1 in fact only used the left-to-right conditional in F1, and hence also showed:

Lemma L1a Given F1a and F2, any pair of positive properties is compossible.

Moreover, it is easy to check that the proof of T1 also only used the left-to-right conditional in F1 and hence showed:

Theorem T1a Given F1a, F2, F3, N1 and N2, there is a God-like being.

This revised argument is essentially that of Anderson (1990).

The proof of T2 requires the right-to-left conditional in F1, and hence does not go through given only F1a, so the argument for modal collapse is blocked.

1.2 Some Refinements

Although the revised Gödelian argument encapsulated in T1a does not appear to lead to modal collapse, it does suffer from at least one intuitive deficiency. Let A be any property, and let EA be the property of having A essentially.

Now observe this. Assume F1a, F2, F3, N1 and N2. Then by T1a, there is a God-like being g. If A is positive, then g has EA. But by S5, if something has EA then it has EA essentially: what essential properties a being has does not vary between the worlds where the being exists. Hence, g essentially has EA, and since all the essential properties of a God-like being are positive, it follows that EA is positive. Thus:

> *Theorem T3* If F1a, F2, F3, N1 and N2 are true, then every positive property is strongly positive

where a property A is strongly positive provided that EA is positive. (Since EA entails A, by F2 every strongly positive property is positive.)

But it is not plausible that every positive property is strongly positive. For instance, a being that essentially creates kangaroos does not have the ability to refrain from creating kangaroos, an ability that appears to be positive. Thus essentially creating kangaroos does not appear to be positive, even though creating kangaroos intuitively seems to be a positive property.

It turns out that we can avoid the argument that every positive property is strongly positive provided that we replace N2 with:

> *Axiom N4* God†-likeness is positive[1]

where

> *Definition D2* x is God†-like provided that x has all strongly positive properties.

Then:

> *Theorem T4* Given F1a, F2, F3, N2 and N4, there is a necessarily existing God†-like being.

I will give a proof shortly. But first note that it would be nice to reduce the controversial axioms further. For instance, one may have some worries about F3. Couldn't it be a contingent matter that some property is positive? Perhaps

[1] Pruss (2012) instead works with God**-likeness, where x is God**-like provided that x has all strongly positive properties essentially and all of x's essential properties are strongly positive. God**-likeness entails God†-likeness, and so, given F2, Axiom N4 is weaker than the claim that God**-likeness is positive. As there is little loss in proving the existence of a God†-like over a God**-like one, I will proceed with the simpler case of God†-likeness.

in worlds where the earth is round it's positive to believe that it's round, but, in worlds where it's cubical, it's negative to believe that it's round.

It turns out that there is a very nice result that doesn't assume F3, but has a conclusion weaker than T4:

> *Theorem T5* Given F1a, F2 and N2, if A is strongly positive, then there is a necessarily existing being that has A essentially.

To see this, observe that by L1a, N and EA are compossible. Thus there is a world w at which there is a being g that exists necessarily and has EA. Then, g will necessarily exist at the actual world as well (this uses S5). Moreover, what properties something has essentially cannot vary between worlds where it exists (again, by S5), so g has EA at the actual world, too, which completes the proof of T5.

Given T5, Theorem T4 follows from the following lemma:

> Lemma L2. Given F2 and F3, if God†-likeness is positive, it is strongly positive.

To see this, let $G^{\dagger}$ be God†-likeness. By F2, it's enough to show $G^{\dagger}$ entails $EG^{\dagger}$. Suppose that x exists and has $G^{\dagger}$ at some possible world w. Then we need to show that x has $G^{\dagger}$ at all worlds where x exists. Let w' be a possible world and let A be a strongly positive property at w', so EA is positive at w'. Then EA is positive at w as well by S5 and F3 (axioms hold at all worlds). Furthermore, by S5, EA entails EEA, so by F2 the property EEA is positive at w', and hence EA is strongly positive at w'. Since x has all strongly positive properties at w as it has $G^{\dagger}$, it must have EA at w. Thus x has EA essentially (by S5 essential possession doesn't vary between worlds where an entity exists), and hence it has A at w' as well. Hence, x has all strongly positive properties at w', and hence it has $G^{\dagger}$ at w'. Since w' was an arbitrary possible world, it follows that x essentially has $G^{\dagger}$ if x has $G^{\dagger}$ at any world, so $G^{\dagger}$ entails $EG^{\dagger}$.

In fact, T5 is the root of some very interesting ontological arguments. For instance, it is very plausible that each of omniscience, omnipotence and moral perfection is strongly positive. If this is right, then given nothing more than this and F1a, F2 and N (with our constant assumption of S5 modal logic), we conclude that there is an omniscient being, an omnipotent being and a morally perfect being. Each of these is a very interesting conclusion in its own right. And we never used F3 here.

There is one last Gödel-style argument I want to consider (Pruss 2012). Say that a property is uniqualizing provided that it is impossible for there to exist two things that have that property. For instance, being the tallest woman is uniqualizing: necessarily, if x is the tallest woman and y is the tallest woman, then x = y. We now need one more substantive axiom:

Axiom N5 There is a strongly positive uniqualizing property.

This axiom is very plausible. For instance, the property of being the creator of everything other than oneself is uniqualizing (since creation cannot be circular) and is very plausibly strongly positive. Unlimited power is, plausibly, also uniqualizing: if there were two beings of unlimited power, the powers of one would limit those of the other, which would be a contradiction. And unlimited power (or omnipotence) seems to be strongly positive. Being wiser or better or more beautiful or more awesome than anyone else are also each an example of a property that is uniqualizing and appears to be strongly positive. We then have:

Theorem T6 Given F1a, F2, N2 and N5, there is exactly one God†-like being.

To see this, suppose that U is a strongly positive uniqualizing property. Then by T5, there is a necessary being g that has U essentially. I now show that g is God†-like. Let A be any strongly positive property. Then by L1a, there is a world w at which there is a being h that has EA and U. But g also exists at w, and has U at w since it actually has U essentially. Since U is uniqualizing, at w we have g = h, and hence g also has EA at w. But then g has A at the actual world (this uses S5). It follows that g has every strongly positive property at the actual world, and hence is God†-like. Thus there is at least one God†-like being. But every God†-like being will have U since U is strongly positive, and as U is uniqualizing it follows that there is at most one God†-like being.

The merit of the ontological argument encapsulated in T6 is twofold. First, it does not assume the positivity of any grand complex properties such as God†-likeness. By L1a, to assume the positivity of such properties is to assume their possible instantiation, and that's a non-trivial assumption. It only assumes that there is some uniqualizing strongly positive property, and a lot of plausible examples come to mind so the probability that there is an example that works is high. Second, the argument not only yields the existence of a being that can be plausibly called 'God', but it also yields the uniqueness of such a being, which in the case of most theistic arguments requires further steps.

Let us end this survey with the simplest argument:

Theorem T7 Given F1a, F2 and N2, there is a necessary being.

For by L1a and N2, possibly something has necessary existence and necessary existence. Hence, possibly something has necessary existence. By S5, actually something has necessary existence.

1.3 Recapitulation

We have five ontological arguments encapsulated in T1, T4, T5, T6 and T7. The assumptions behind the original Gödelian T1 imply modal collapse, leaving T4, T5, T6 and T7.

All four of these arguments suppose the formal axioms F1a and F2, which say that the negation of a positive property is positive and that anything that follows from a positive property is itself positive.

They all also suppose the substantive assumption N2 that necessary existence is positive, an assumption going back to Anselm's idea that a perfect being couldn't be thought of as non-existent (Anselm 1078/2001: ch. 3).

Arguments T5 and T7 make no further assumptions beyond F1a, F2 and N2. Argument T7 concludes modestly that there is a necessary being, while T5 concludes that for any strongly positive property – any property such that possessing it essentially is positive – there is a necessary being having that property. The conclusion of T7 is somewhat controversial: a nominalist atheist is likely to hold that all beings are contingent. But, nonetheless, the conclusion of T7 is not enough to easily yield anything like theism.

On the other hand, T5 is likely to trouble all atheists, given plausible auxiliary hypotheses that properties like omnipotence, omniscience, moral goodness or even agency are strongly positive. For according to T5, for each strongly positive property, there is at least one necessary being having that property.

If one wants to establish something like full-blown theism, one will want something like the stronger conclusion of T4 or T6 that there is a God†-like being. The cost of T4 is that T4 assumes N4, the positivity of God†-likeness, as well as F3, the necessary positivity of positive properties, while T6 instead only assumes N5, that there is a strongly positive uniqualizing property. The assumption of N5 is intuitively quite plausible given that there are many plausible candidates for such a property.

In my evaluation of the Gödelian family of arguments, I will henceforth focus on T5 and T6, which appear to have the most plausible axioms and a more interesting conclusion than T7. First, we will discuss the formal axioms F1a and F2 and then the substantive axioms N2, N5 and their relatives.

2 Positivity and the Formal Axioms

All our arguments require a notion of positivity together with axioms F1a and F2. We could simply take the notion as primitive and governed by the axioms. But we can also consider five accounts of positivity.

The first is the comparative view and comes from Maydole (2003). A property A is positive if and only if it is better to have the property than not to. Axiom F1a is then immediate. Axiom F2, however, is less clear. Plausibly, it's better to have overcome an addiction than not to have done so. This intuition remains even if it's made clear that one way of not having overcome an addiction is not to have had one in the first place. To have an addiction and overcome it is, plausibly, better than not to have had one at all, as it exhibits greater moral achievement. However, overcoming an addiction entails having had an addiction. By F2 on this definition it follows that it would be better to have had an addiction than not to have. But this is implausible.

Further, Oppy (2009) notes that by F2 the disjunction of a positive property with any other property is positive. But now consider the disjunctive property of being smart or sick. It is far from clear that it would be better to be smart or sick than to be neither. It intuitively depends on the case. If Jim is in fact smart and healthy, then for him it seems better to be smart or sick than to be neither, since in his case to be smart or sick is to be smart. But if he were sick and stupid, then for him to be smart or sick would be to be sick, and it wouldn't be better for him to be smart or sick than to be neither.

So the first comparative view is implausible if we are to have F2.

The second view is the excellence view: a positive property is one that in no way detracts from its possessor's excellence, but its negation does. Again, F1a is immediate. But now F2 is more plausible than it was on the comparative view. For suppose A doesn't detract from excellence and ~A does. Now suppose A entails B. Then ~B guarantees ~A, so it's plausible that since ~A detracts from excellence, so does ~B. It remains to argue that B doesn't detract from excellence in any way. But if B detracted from excellence in some way, then A by entailing B would do so as well.

What about the counterexamples to the comparative view? Having overcome an addiction does detract from excellence. Even if it turns out to be better to have overcome an addiction than to have never had one, there is an excellence that is ruled out by having overcome an addiction, the excellence of perfect essential self-control. Thus, having overcome an addiction is not positive, and the first counterexample fails. On the other hand, being smart or sick is simply positive, since having the disjunction does not detract from excellence, but the negation would preclude excellence in respect of intelligence.

Next, we have the anti-negative view: a property is positive if and only if its negation is negative. Negative properties are then governed by two plausible axioms:

*Axiom F1a** If A is negative, then ~A is not negative.
*Axiom F2** If B is negative and A entails B, then A is negative.

It is easy to check that on this definition of 'positive' the conjunction of F1a* and F2* entails F1a and F2.[2] Of course, this shifts the question of definition to negativity. We could take negative properties to be primitive, but we could also say that a property is negative provided that it limits its possessor in some way. It is plausible that if a property limits the possessor, then lacking that property does not, and hence we have F1a*. Still, at the same time, there is a genuine worry: What if every property in some way limits its possessor? If so, then it would be unsurprising that both a property and its negation were negative. There is a kind of optimism in F1a*, thus. Different people will find this optimism plausible to different degrees. On the other hand, it is generally plausible that anything that entails something that limits a thing also limits the thing, and hence we have F2*.

Fourth, we have a Leibnizian view: a positive property is a conjunction of simple, positive and absolute properties, or anything entailed by such a conjunction. Axiom F2 is now trivial, but it is less clear that if A is entailed by some conjunction of simple, positive and absolute properties, then ~A is not entailed by some (perhaps other) conjunction, as F1a would require. Leibniz's own story here would be that there are no non-trivial logical relations between simple, positive and absolute properties (cf. Leibniz 1965).

Finally, we have a no-entailed-limit view: a positive property is one that does not entail being limited but its negation does. This view has a unique

[2] Pruss (2012) incorrectly claimed that the conjunction of F1a and F2 also entails F1a* and F2*. That is false. Suppose that the only properties are A; ~A; ~~A; . . . Suppose both A and its negation are possibly exemplified. Suppose that A is negative and so is $\sim^{n}A$ for odd positive integers n, where '$\sim^{n}$' is a string of n negations, while all the other $\sim^{n}A$ are not negative. Then $\sim^{n}A$ is positive for all even non-negative integers n, including zero, since $\sim^{n}A$ is positive if and only if $\sim^{n+1}A$ is negative. And $\sim^{n}A$ is non-positive in all other cases. It is easy to see that F1a and F2 are satisfied. But F1a* is not satisfied, since A is negative and so is ~A. The issue is that because 'A' doesn't have a negation in front of it, it is never used to define anything positive, and hence the aberrant choice to make A negative doesn't affect the satisfaction of F1a and F2. Fortunately, none of the ontological arguments in Pruss (2012) relied on the faulty direction of implication.

advantage: it makes it possible to prove F1a and F2. It is clear that A and ~A can't both be positive on this definition: hence F1a is true. And if A is positive and entails B, then, first, B cannot entail being limited as then A would as well, and, second, if ~B failed to entail being limited, so would ~A since ~B entails ~A if A entails B. Thus, B is also positive and F2 follows. However, the no-entailed-limit view can strike one as somewhat stipulative in nature, gerrymandered to ensure F1a and F2 hold (and akin to Oppy's 'natural' parody in Oppy 2009).

The views of positiveness that are most friendly to the Gödelian ontological argument then appear to be the excellence view, the anti-negative view and the no-entailed-limit view. The last of these has the merit of *proving* the needed formal axioms.

2.1 The Compossibility of Positives

The most important fact about Axioms F1a and F2 for purposes of Gödelian arguments is that they enable one to prove the conclusion of Lemma L1a. We could simply take this conclusion to be an axiom, and drop F1a and F2:

Axiom F4 If A and B are positive, then they are compossible.

It is easy to check that the arguments T5 and T6 only need F1a and F2 to establish F4. But F4 is intrinsically less intuitive than F1a and F2.

At this point, one could have two reactions. The first is that F1a and F2 are plausible, and once we learn that F4 follows, it inherits their plausibility. The second is that although F1a and F2 are initially plausible, once we learn that F4 follows, their plausibility is decreased.

In favour of taking F4 to inherit plausibility is the fact that F1a and F2 appear to capture a significant part of the logic of positivity.

In favour of the opposite conclusion is that there appear to be counter-examples to F4. For instance, perfect mercy and perfect justice seem to be both positive, but appear incompatible. Likewise, omnipotence and moral perfection, essential omniscience and possibly creating free beings, and so on. It is interesting that these kinds of cases are also problem cases for any S5-type ontological argument based on the premise that a maximally great being is possible (see versions by Hartshorne, Malcolm and Plantinga in Plantinga 1965), since both of the properties in each apparently conflicting pair are ones that we would expect a maximally great being to have.

One can try to show that in each case there is no actual incompatibility. If the primary aggrieved party completely forgives a malefactor, she thereby shows perfect mercy, but once the malefactor has been forgiven then there is no imperfection of justice in a failure to punish. Aquinas has argued that the ability to do wrong is more a weakness than an instance of power (Aquinas 1947: I.25.3 reply 2) and likewise the recent Pearce and Pruss (2012) account of omnipotence also resolves the apparent tension between omnipotence and moral perfection. There are many well-known ways of resolving the conflict between foreknowledge and free will: compatibilism, Ockhamism, taking the omniscient being out of time, and backwards causation of the omniscient being's beliefs by the free action.

There is, however, another response to the counterexamples available as a backup. Of the above apparent counterexamples to F4, the most compelling seems to be that of perfect mercy and perfect justice. Suppose we grant that indeed perfect mercy and perfect justice are incompatible. It's not unreasonable to conclude from this that at least one of the two is not actually positive. It seems quite reasonable, for instance, to say that justice tends to be a good thing, but an insistence on perfect or complete justice to the detriment of mercy is not. Thus, perfect justice is an imperfection. One might then say that perfect mercy is positive but perfect justice is not, or also say the same thing about mercy as we just said about justice: perfect mercy is not positive. In other words, it seems quite reasonable to use the fact that a pair of apparently positive properties would violate F4 as evidence that at least one of them is not actually positive. In fact, the reasonableness of this approach is some evidence directly for F4.

Finally, there is one more thing one might say about the case of perfect mercy and perfect justice. There are two ways to understand 'perfect' justice, say. First, it could be complete as justice. Second, it could be a morally perfect variety of justice. It could be that a morally perfect variety of justice isn't actually complete justice; it leaves room for mercy. Similar approaches may be available in other cases.

3 The Substantive Axioms

The substantive axioms used in the Gödelian arguments tell us something about the existence of positive or strongly positive properties. Thus, N2 says that necessary existence is positive, N4 says that God†-likeness is positive and N5 says that there is some uniqualizing strongly positive property.

Given our formal axioms F1a and F2, we know from Lemma L1a that every positive property is possibly exemplified. Thus N4 is actually a quite strong claim: its claim that God†-likeness is positive entails that possibly there is a God†-like being. Whether it is possible for there to be a maximally great being is precisely the contentious question in the discussion of S5-based ontological arguments, so assuming something which easily implies an affirmative answer to a very similar question may seem problematic.

At the same time, assuming N4 is not the same as assuming that possibly there is a God†-like being. The conclusion that possibly there is a God†-like being makes use of the plausible axioms F1a and F2. We could, thus, see the Gödelian approach as providing an argument for something close to that contentious premise of the standard S5-based arguments, much as Leibniz (1965) famously hoped he was able to do.

It seems a distinct point of superiority that the T5 and T6 arguments do not assume from the outset that a particular highly complex property like God†-likeness is positive. Instead, they assume simply that necessary existence is positive and that some uniqualizing property is strongly positive.

That necessary existence is positive is an intuition that, as noted, goes back to Anselm: there is a robustness of existence and independence that only a necessary being has that appears to be quite positive. The fact that every positive property is automatically possibly exemplified does not appear to count much against the intuitive positivity of necessary existence. Granted, it follows from S5 that if possibly something exists necessarily, then something actually exists necessarily. But there are no strong arguments against there being something that exists necessarily. Such arguments would not only rule out classical theism but also almost every variety of Platonism. Whether there is a necessary being seems exactly the sort of question where we philosophers should start with reasonable premises – say, that necessary existence is positive – and see what answers we get to, rather than starting with an answer to whether there is a necessary being and seeing what axioms fit with that.

With just N2 on board, plus our formal axioms, we get to conclude via T5 that every strongly positive property is instantiated by a necessary being. That already yields an interesting ontological argument, given very plausible auxiliary claims about properties like omniscience, omnipotence or moral perfection being strongly positive. And adding N5 does not seem to burden the argument significantly, given the plausible examples of uniqualizing strongly positive properties like omnipotence or being creator of everything but oneself.

4 Parody: Naturalness

A weak parody of an ontological argument is meant to establish a conclusion that is absurd or at least very unlikely to be true (e.g., there actually is a maximally great island); a strong parody establishes something incompatible with the existence of the perfect being that the ontological argument aims at proving the existence of (e.g., there is an all-powerful evil being).

Graham Oppy (2009) has given a strong parody based on the notion of naturalness. I will simplify Oppy's parody to give a strong parody for a number of our ontological arguments. Stipulate a natural property as one that does not entail that there is something supernatural.[3] (This stipulation is akin to the no-entailed-limit account of positivity.)

Now assume a pair of plausible non-formal axioms:

Axiom N6. Some property is natural.

Axiom N7. Any God†-like being is essentially supernatural.

A plausible example of a property that is natural is non-supernaturalness.

Then:

Theorem T8 Given N6 and N7, there is no necessarily existing God†-like being.

For if there were a necessarily existing God†-like being, necessarily there would be a supernatural being by N7. But a necessary truth is entailed by all truths. So there would be no property that doesn't entail that there is a supernatural being, and hence there would be no property that is natural.

Furthermore:

Theorem T9 Given F2, N2, N6 and N7, there is no God†-like being.

For given F2 and N2, necessary existence is strongly positive (necessary existence entails essential necessary existence given S5, so if the former is positive by N2, the latter is also positive by F2). But a God†-like being would have to have all strongly positive properties, thus including necessary existence, while by T8 there is no necessarily existing God†-like being given N6 and N7.

Thus, the very weak assumption N6 about natural properties, given some very plausible auxiliary assumptions, undercuts our arguments for a God†-like being. We have a strong parody.

4.1 Evaluation

There is only one controversial axiom in the parody to evaluate, N6. Expanding out the definition of 'natural', N6 says that some property does not entail that there is something supernatural. This seems to be a very weak (and hence plausible) assumption: like N5 it claims the mere existence of a property.

[3] Oppy adds the condition that its negation does. But for the purposes of strong parody, we don't need that. Axiom N6 below would be more controversial with Oppy's added condition, so we get a better parody without the extra condition.

Here is a useful fact:

Theorem T10 Assume there is at least one property. Axiom N6 holds if and only if possibly both: something exists and nothing is supernatural.

To see this, first suppose that the right-hand side of the biconditional is true. So there is a world w at which something, x, exists but nothing is supernatural. Let A be a property that x has at w (it was assumed that there is at least one property B; if x has B, then let A = B; otherwise, let A = ~B). Then A does not entail the existence of anything supernatural, since x has A at w but there is nothing supernatural at w. Hence, A is natural. Conversely, suppose A is a natural property. Then A does not entail the existence of anything supernatural. Thus, there is a world w at which something has A (and hence something exists) and yet nothing is supernatural.

So the apparently innocent assumption that there is a natural property (say, because it seems that non-supernaturalness is natural) is equivalent to there being a non-empty world without anything supernatural. If God is essentially supernatural, the assumption is a little stronger logically than that of the standard parody argument against the S5-ontological argument based on the claim that possibly there is no God. We could worry, thus, that N6 begs the question against theism and other forms of necessary supernaturalism. But the proponent of the parody argument can respond: 'Not at all. Instead we should take ourselves to have learned from N6 that there is a non-empty possible world free of the supernatural.'

Moreover, the parody argument has the merit that it needs only one controversial assumption, namely N6. Apart from the less interesting ontological argument T7 that concludes only that there is a necessary being, all our arguments have more than one substantive assumption, and except on the no-entailed-limit account of positivity they all further have two formal axioms, F1a and F2. It appears, thus, that the parody argument is more plausible than our Gödelian ontological arguments.

But we shouldn't be so quick to agree with this. A reasonable way to read the Gödelian arguments is that they start with an intuitive notion of a positive property (or an excellence or an anti-negative property[4]), and attempt to formalize that property. The axioms are then attempts to codify our understanding of positivity. The notion of positivity maybe also comes along with,

[4] The no-entailed-limit view of positivity is perhaps different. It is a stipulation crafted to make the axioms F1a and F2 automatically come out as true.

or perhaps flows from, a philosophical analysis of the concept of God as a being that is God†-like, a being that has all strongly positive properties.

On the other hand, the notion of naturalness operative in our parody (as well as the more complex notion in Oppy 2009) is stipulative. What makes a property A natural isn't even primarily what it says about the objects that have A: rather, a natural property is one that can be exemplified in a world where nothing is supernatural. The existence of a necessary supernatural being that has nothing to do with the possessor of the property A is enough to make A not be natural.

If we wish to avail ourselves of such stipulated properties, we can make an ontological argument more exactly parallel to the parody than the Gödelian arguments earlier. Say that a property is God-friendly provided that it does not entail the non-existence of God. Then consider this assumption:

Axiom N8 There is at least one God-friendly property.

Then:

Theorem T11 Axiom N8 holds if and only if possibly there is a God.

(The proof of this is similar to that of T10, except that we don't need to worry about empty worlds, since no empty world has a God in it.) But as is widely accepted in ontological argument circles, God would be a necessary and essentially supernatural being, and so by S5 if possibly God exists, then necessarily an essentially supernatural being exists. And by T10 this is incompatible with there being a natural property in the stipulated sense.

It seems reasonable to think of the naturalness parody and the God-friendliness ontological argument as cancelling each other out epistemically. But if these two arguments cancel out, that leaves Gödelian argument based on an attempt to account for positivity standing. This response crucially depends on seeing the notion of positivity in the Gödelian argument as non-stipulative, a genuine non-gerrymandered concept.

5 Conclusions

A number of Gödelian arguments can be given, and the better ones avoid modal collapse. A defence of a Gödelian argument requires a story about positivity that makes axioms F1a and F2 plausible. Moreover, the story needs to make plausible substantive axioms such as that necessary existence is positive and that there is a uniqualizing property having which essentially is positive.

A Gödelian argument is superior when it is based on a notion of positivity that captures genuine philosophical intuitions rather than being a gerrymandered stipulation. There are two general ways in which this could be done. One way starts with a primitive notion of positivity and claims that it satisfies the axioms offered. The second way, of which several instances were considered, offers a non-gerrymandered account of positivity, and argues that it satisfies the requisite axioms. Unfortunately, it is a difficult to settle in a principled way the question of how gerrymandered a given account is or how much it reflects an intuitive concept, so this is simply left to each reader's judgment.

Based on Oppy (2009), an elegant parody can be given based on the idea of a natural property as one that does not entail the existence of something supernatural. However, that parody seems more directly a parody for a different ontological argument, one based on the existence of a God-friendly property.

8 Lewis

Michael J. Almeida

In 'Anselm and Actuality', David Lewis argued that the assessment of Anselm's ontological arguments is best achieved when the familiar modal expressions in which the arguments are typically formulated are translated into counterpart theory. Once the arguments are translated into the language of counterpart theory – into non-modal, ordinary reasoning about possible things – then we can apply our well-known and widely accepted standards for validity. We can then determine – ideally once and for all – whether these perennially debated arguments are successful.

> Given an obscure modal argument, we can translate it into a non-modal argument – or into several non-modal arguments, if the given argument was ambiguous. Once we have a non-modal argument, we have clear standards of validity; and once we have non-modal translations of the premises, we can understand them well enough to judge whether they are credible. Foremost among our modal headaches is Anselm's ontological argument.[1]

The distinctive advantage of Lewis's approach to Anselm's ontological argument is that counterpart theory combined with the vast domain of Lewis's pluriverse makes a perfectly extensional interpretation of the ontological argument possible. On Lewis's approach, modal operators are replaced with quantifiers ranging over worlds and possibilia, modal propositions occurring in Anselm's ontological arguments are translated into non-modal propositions, and Anselm's modal arguments are translated into the familiar lexicon of non-modal arguments. The modal reduction puts us in a better position to assess the credibility of Anselm's premises. The translation of Anselm's ontological argument into one – or many, as it happens – non-modal arguments permits the application of well-known and widely accepted

[1] See Lewis (1970: 175).

standards of validity – the standards of classical logic – to determine the cogency of Anselm's argument.

It is indeed a fruitful and fascinating project to translate Anselm's ontological arguments into the extensional language of counterpart theory. But translating Anselm into counterpart theory – granting that there is a good translation – is much less philosophically neutral than Lewis suggests.

Lewis's translations of premises (2) and (3) of Anselm's argument are extraordinarily strong propositions. Indeed, they are much stronger propositions than are required for the ontological argument. Lewis concludes that the necessary counterpart theoretic translations of premise (3) – his premises (3A) and (3C) – are not credible. And indeed many will find them incredible. But (3A) and (3C) are not necessary to a valid formulation of the ontological argument. There are weaker translations of premises (2) and (3) available that many will find credible.

In Sections (2–4) I present Lewis's formulation of the ontological argument in Anselm's *Proslogion II.* Section 2 focuses primarily on the translation of premise (1) into the language of counterpart theory, and Sections 3–4 focus on translations of premises (2)–(3) respectively. In Section 3, several translations of premises (2) are advanced – (2.1)–(2.6). It is argued (2.1)–(2.6) improve in a variety of ways upon Lewis's translation of Anselm's premise (2). In Sections (4–6), Lewis's translation of premise (3) in (3A) is discussed in detail. It is argued that the ontological arguer should replace Lewis's (3A) with (3A') or, perhaps better, (3E). The corresponding conclusion of Anselm's ontological argument is (C"). The argument in translation is valid and its premises are all plausible – far more plausible than those offered in Lewis's original translation. Some concluding remarks are offered in Section 7.

1 Premise (1)

The version of the ontological argument that Lewis considers is from *Proslogion II.* Lewis formulates the argument in English as follows.

Premise 1. Whatever exists in the understanding can be conceived to exist in reality.

Premise 2. Whatever exists in the understanding would be greater if it existed in reality than if it did not.

Premise 3. Something exists in the understanding, than which nothing greater can be conceived.

Conclusion. Something exists in reality, than which nothing greater can be conceived.

Premise (1), premise (2) and the conclusion all employ the locution 'exists in reality'. Lewis renders the locution 'x exists in the understanding' as 'x is an understandable being.' He does not commit himself on the existence of understandable beings, but leaves the analysis of that phrase to the ontological arguer. Concerning premise (1), Lewis argues that its proper translation into counterpart theory is in (1)

1. $\forall x(Ux \supset \exists w(Ww \,\&\, Exw))$

In quasi-English, (1) states that, for any understandable being x, there is a world w such that x exists in w. Lewis does not talk explicitly of beings existing in the understanding, and indeed regards quantificational talk in relation to the understanding as ill-advised.

> It is ill-advised to speak of them as existing in the understanding: they do not bear to the understanding the same relation which something existing in a world bears to that world! Let us simply call them understandable beings.[2]

Beings that exist in the understanding are just those beings – merely possible or actual – that have the property of being understandable. According to premise (1), every understandable being exists somewhere in reality.

Existing in reality, as Lewis translates that phrase in premise (1), is *existing in some world or other in the pluriverse.* The pluriverse is the totality of metaphysical reality and is the largest domain of quantification. So, the quantifiers in (1) are absolutely unrestricted, quantifying over the largest domain of discourse. The largest domain of discourse for Lewis includes everything in every world, and perhaps much more than that.[3] It is conceivable that x exists, according to (1), just in case (unrestrictedly) x exists. The locution that (unrestrictedly) x exists is true just in case x exists somewhere in metaphysical space. x exists, that is, just in case x inhabits (or just is) some possible world, including of course the actual world.

> It is our plan to reason explicitly about possible worlds and possible things therein. These possible beings will be included in our domain of discourse.

[2] Lewis (1970: 177).

[3] In addition to items that exist in possible worlds, there are items that exist partly in possible worlds (e.g. cross-world objects), and there are items that exist in the pluriverse but do not exist even partly in possible world (e.g. numbers, properties, propositions and the like).

> The idioms of quantification, therefore, will be understood as ranging over all the beings we wish to talk about, whether existent or non-existent.[4]

The worlds in question are *conceivable worlds*, which may not coincide with the metaphysically possible worlds or with possible worlds simpliciter.[5] So, premise (1) comes to the assertion, on Lewis's rendering, that understandable beings are among the beings in the broadest domain of discourse. It is difficult not to see that assertion as trivial. Could there be an understandable being that is *not* in the broadest domain of discourse? (1') is just the negation of (1), so (1) is false just in case (1') is true.

1'. ∃x(Ux & ~∃w(Ww & Exw))

(1') states that there *exists an understandable being that exists nowhere in reality*. But given Lewis's understanding of quantification, (1') is either trivially false or incoherent. It misunderstands the univocity of quantificational idioms.

> We of the establishment think that there is only one kind of quantification. The several idioms of what we call 'existential' quantification are entirely synonymous and interchangeable. It does not matter whether you say 'Some things are donkeys' or 'There are donkeys' or 'Donkeys exist' – you mean exactly the same thing whichever way you say it. The same goes for more vexed cases: it does not matter whether you say 'Some famous fictional detective uses cocaine,' 'There is a famous fictional detective who uses cocaine' or 'A famous cocaine-using fictional detective exists'; whether true or whether false, all three statements stand or fall together.[6]

If there are understandable beings, then they must exist in the largest domain of discourse. (1') therefore seems trivially false, and (1) trivially true. And if understandable beings exist somewhere in the totality of reality, then, they exist in the same way that any actual being exists. If a round square or the largest prime enjoys the property of being understandable – if round squares and largest primes are understandable objects – then a round square and a largest prime exists somewhere in reality. These objects exist, again, in the very same way that any actual object exists. For Lewis,

4 Lewis (1970: 176).

5 Lewis initially includes among the conceivable worlds the set of impossible worlds. He retracts this view in Lewis (1983a: 21ff.).

6 See Lewis (1990: 23f.).

quantificational idioms are univocal. There isn't *existence* on the one hand, and other sorts of *being* on the other.[7]

If the largest domain includes objects that exist in no possible world at all, then it might be that (1) is false. Lewis acknowledges that numbers and propositions – and perhaps cross-world objects – do not exist in any possible world, though they are no doubt understandable objects.

> When we evaluate the truth of a quantified sentence, we usually restrict the domain and quantify over less than all there is. If we evaluate a quantification at a world, we will normally omit many things not in that world, for instance the possible individuals that inhabit other worlds. But we will not omit the numbers, or some of the other sets. Let us say that an individual exists from the standpoint of a world iff it belongs to the least restricted domain that is normally – modal metaphysics being deemed abnormal – appropriate in evaluating the truth at that world of quantifications. I suppose that this domain will include all the individuals in that world; none of the other individuals; and some, but not all, of the sets. There will be many sets that even exist from the standpoint of all worlds, for instance the numbers. Others may not; for instance the unit set of a possible individual might only exist from the standpoint of the world that the individual is in. Thus we have three relations: being in a world, i.e., being part of a world; being partly in a world, i.e., having a part that is wholly in that world; and existing from the standpoint of a world. Postulate 2, the principle that nothing is in two worlds, applies only to the first of these.[8]

[7] The principle of classical possibilism contrasts the *being* of possible objects and the *existence* of possible objects. The principle states that all possible objects – indeed everything simpliciter – have *being*, or in some sense *are*, though not all possible objects exist. There is a brief and clear exposition of classical possibilism in Russell:

'*Being* is that which belongs to every conceivable term, to every possible object of thought . . . Numbers, the Homeric gods, relations, chimeras, and four-dimensional spaces all have being, for if they were not entities of a kind, we could make no propositions about them. Thus being is a general attribute of everything, and to mention anything is to show that it is. *Existence*, on the contrary, is the prerogative of some only amongst beings.'

See Russell (1903: § 423); and cf. Menzel (2015). According to classical possibilism, at least some non-actual objects are contingently non-actual. Such objects have being, but they fail, as a matter of contingent fact, to be actual objects. These are objects, in general, that have being and that might have been actual. Golden mountains have being, for instance, and it is a matter of contingent fact that there are no actual golden mountains. There are possible golden mountains, and if golden mountains had existence in addition to having being, then they would be actual golden mountains.

[8] See Lewis (1983b: 40ff.).

Objects that *exist from the standpoint of* all possible worlds – things such as numbers, properties, propositions and events – do not *exist in* any possible worlds. The distinction is a particularly important one for the Anselmian argument, since God might be among the objects that exist in reality – that exist from the standpoint of every possible world – but do not exist in any possible world. We might also want to acknowledge those understandable beings that do not wholly exist in any possible world, but that have parts in various possible worlds. So, the largest domain of discourse might include understandable individuals that do not exist in any possible world: individuals that, strictly speaking, are not possible individuals. It might include understandable objects, too, that exist from the standpoint of every world but do not exist in any world. These sorts of objects would render (1) false as well.

2 Premise (2)

According to premise (2), whatever exists in the understanding would be greater if it existed in reality than if it did not. Beings that exist in the understanding, recall, are just the understandable beings. So, premise (2) states that if x is an understandable being, then x would be greater if it existed in reality than if it did not.

Premise (2) entails that existing in reality is what we might call a *great-making property* of understandable beings. Since, according to (1), every understandable being exists in some world or other, Lewis urges that every understandable being conceivably has the great-making property of existing in reality. The great-making property of existing in reality is a property that objects exemplify in certain possible worlds – those in which they exist – and a property that objects fail to exemplify in certain possible worlds – those in which they fail to exist. There are, according to Lewis's rendering of premise (2), no objects that are simply greater than others. The greatness of objects is relativized to possible worlds. For objects x and y, it is not true that x is simply greater than y, but it might be true that x in w is greater than y in w'. So, according to Lewis, the proper translation of premise (2) into counterpart theory is in (2).

2. $\forall x\ \forall w\ \forall v\ (Ux\ \&\ Ww\ \&\ Wv\ \&\ Exw\ \&\ {\sim}Exv \supset xwGxv)$

In quasi-English, (2) states that, for any understandable being x, and for any worlds w and v, if x exists in w but x does not exist in v, then the greatness of x in w exceeds the greatness of x in v.

It's important to observe that Anselm's premise (2) does not talk explicitly about greatness relative to worlds or the *greatness of object x in w*.

Premise (2) states that whatever exists in the understanding would be greater if it existed in reality than if it did not. The reading of premise (2), taken at face value, is that if x exists in reality then x is *greater* simpliciter than if x does not exist in reality. And Anselm certainly seems to mean by *x's existing in reality* that *x actually exists*. If x *actually exists* then x is greater than if x does not. For Lewis, this is equivalent to saying that if x exists in our particular region of metaphysical space, then x is greater than if x does not exist in our region. Actual existence is a great-making property and merely possible existence is not.

The quantificational idiom, existing in reality, as Anselm is using the phrase, is a restricted quantifier. Something exists in reality just in case it actually exists. For any understandable object x, then, if x actually exists then x is greater than if x merely possibly exists. And it is not implausible to maintain, quite generally, for any objects x and y, if x actually exists and y merely possibly exists then x is greater simpliciter than y.

Indeed, merely possible beings of any sort barely exemplify any greatness at all. Anselm might exchange Lewis's (2) for (2.1) which makes actual existence a great-making property and replaces the relativized greatness-in-a-world with greatness simpliciter.

2.1. $(\forall x\forall w((Ux \& Ww \& xEw \& w = @) \supset Vx)) \& (\forall y\forall w((Uy \& Ww \& {\sim}yEw) \supset V'y)) \& \forall x\forall y(Vx \& V'y \supset xGy)$

The proposition in (2.1) states that actually existing things are greater simpliciter than merely possibly existing things. Being actual is the property that confers greatness on existing objects.

Of course a merely possible being x might be quite a wonderful being in world w. It might be *true in* w that x is among the best beings that we can imagine. But it does not follow from the fact that it is *true in* w that x is among the greatest beings we can imagine that it is true simpliciter that x is among the greatest beings we can imagine. If it is true that x is a merely possible being, for instance, then x is not among the greatest beings we can imagine. Merely possible beings exemplify very little greatness.

But then, contrary to (2), x in world w might not be greater than x in world v. It is perfectly possible that x does not actually exist. So, x's existence in some possible non-actual world w is at best dubiously greater – from the point of view of the actual world – than x's non-existence in some other possible non-actual world v. It is not obvious in any case that Anselm is committed to taking any stand at all on that claim. And this is consistent with the fact that it is true in w that x is a much greater being than any being y not in w.

But the ontological arguer need not advance any principle as strong as (2.1) for her ontological argument. She might argue instead that, for any two understandable objects x and y that are otherwise indiscernible with respect to their great-making properties, if x actually exists and y merely possibly exists, then x is greater than y. So, we have a restricted version of (2.1) that is even more credible than (2.1).

2.2. $\forall x \forall w((Ux \,\&\, Ww \,\&\, Px \,\&\, xEw \,\&\, w = @) \supset Vx)) \,\&\, \forall y((Uy \,\&\, Py \,\&\, \forall w (Ww \,\&\, {\sim}yEw \supset V'y)) \,\&\, \forall x \forall y(Vx \,\&\, V'y \supset xGy$

The proposition in (2.2) states that any actually existing being that exemplifies all of the great-making properties in P is greater than any merely possibly existing things that exemplify all of the great-making properties in P.

It is true that unrestrictedly existing beings exemplify many properties including many great-making properties. But according to (2.2) – and certainly intuitively – exemplifying the property of omniscience in some non-actual region of metaphysical space is less impressive and less significant than actually exemplifying the property of omniscience. It is not a very impressive or significant property of Jones that he is possibly omniscient, if Jones is in fact mostly ignorant.

Of course, Anselmians might be persuaded that *absolutely unrestricted existence* is a great-making property rather than actual existence. An Anselmian might be persuaded that, if x is an understandable being, then x is greater if it exists in some world in the pluriverse than if x does not exist in the pluriverse at all. Existing in the pluriverse – existing in some possible world – makes everything that does so greater than it would be were it to exist in no possible world at all. Premise (2) on such a reading amounts to the claim that if x is a possible being then it is greater than it would be were x an impossible being.

In that case, we could render premise (2) as stating that if x and y are understandable beings and x exists in some possible world and y exists in no possible world, then x is greater than y.

2.3. $\forall x \forall y(Ux \,\&\, Uy \,\&\, \exists w(Ww \,\&\, xEw) \,\&\, {\sim}\exists w(Ww \,\&\, yEw)) \supset xGy)$

In quasi-English, (2.3) states that, for any understandable beings x and y, if x exists in reality and y does not exist in reality then x is greater than y. Any possible thing – whether or not it is actual – is greater than any impossible thing, or, equivalently, any (unrestrictedly) existing thing is greater than any (unrestrictedly) non-existing thing. Here we have the greatness of beings not relativized to possible worlds, but relativized to the pluriverse or the largest domain of discourse.

We might again find some reason to restrict (2.3) to possible beings that exemplify all of the great-making properties P. We might find it more credible to substitute (2.4) for (2.3).

2.4. $\forall x \forall y(Ux \ \& \ Uy \ \& \ Px \ \& \ Py \ \& \ \exists w(Ww \ \& \ xEw) \ \& \ {\sim}\exists w(Ww \ \& \ yEw)) \supset xGy)$

(2.4) states that, for any understandable beings x and y, if x and y exemplify all of the great-making properties in P and x exists in reality and y does not, then x is greater than y. Any possible being that exemplifies all of the great-making properties in P – whether or not it actually exists – is greater than any impossible being.

If a greatest conceivable being is one that exemplifies all of the great-making properties and exists in reality as a whole – and not necessarily in our particular region of it – then theists have reason to celebrate the absolutely unrestricted existence of a greatest conceivable being.

If something like (2.4) is true, then an unrestrictedly existing God exists in *the right way* for theists; it would be no better were it to actually exist. If an unrestrictedly existing God exists in the right way for theists, then we should expect it to have the properties of being worthy of devotion and worship, worthy of veneration, praise, love, petition and prayer. It would not be more worthy of praise, devotion and worship were it an actually existing being.

Of course it might be urged that no merely possible God is the proper object of any of those attitudes or a worthy object of those practices. Perhaps those attitudes are appropriate only if God exists in our particular region of reality. Merely possible Gods stand in no causal relation to our world; they cannot be the creator of our world or respond to petitions in our world or take responsibility for conditions in our world. Of course such a God would know everything about our world, would know our petitions and prayers. Nonetheless perhaps merely possible Gods are not the proper object of those attitudes and practices. If so, that is just as well. We might better conclude that God exists in just the right way, then, only if he actually exists – only if he exists in our neighbourhood of reality.

There is another version of premise (2) that is worth considering. Perhaps it is a great-making property that something *exists from the standpoint of* every possible world. It might be that anything that exists from the standpoint of any world is greater than anything that doesn't. Anselmians do have reason to believe that the proper object of creation for a being than which none greater is conceivable is the *totality of reality*, the entire pluriverse. It is greater to create all of reality – all possibilia and all possible worlds – than to create just part of reality. Each possible world constitutes a mere part of total reality.

Each candidate for the greatest being existing in each world creates, at most, the possible world in which he exists.

Every object that exists in any possible world, exists simpliciter. So, (2.3)–(2.4) distinguish possible beings from impossible beings: any *possible* being is greater than any *impossible* being. But (2.5) distinguishes objects that exist from the standpoint of every possible world from objects that do not. Beings that exist from the standpoint of all worlds are greater, according to (2.5), than beings that do not. We let 'E!x' stand for x exists from the standpoint of every world.

2.5. $\forall x \forall y((Ux \ \& \ Uy \ \& \ E!x \ \& {\sim} E!y) \supset xGy)$

According to (2.5), anything that exists from the standpoint of every possible world is greater than anything that doesn't.

If something like (2.5) is true, then if God exists from the standpoint of every world, then God exists in the right way for theists. A God that exists from the standpoint of every world would have the properties of being worthy of devotion and worship, being a proper object of veneration, praise, love, petition and prayer.

And there is a rationale for the view that a God that exists from the standpoint of every world is the proper object of any of those attitudes. A God that creates all of reality – that creates all possibilia in all worlds – cannot exist restrictedly. Everything that exists restrictedly exists in some possible world or in some sub-region of worlds. But anything that *exists in* some world w creates, at most, the contingent beings in w. So everything that exists restrictedly creates at most some sub-region of all reality.

Of course there is the alternative of assuming that God exists in every possible world. This is the view that all possible worlds overlap with respect to God. There are lots of unnecessary costs in the assumption that worlds overlap with respect to God.[9] But there seems to me the insurmountable cost that if the same God literally exists in every possible world, then it is a direct consequence of the indiscernibility of identicals that God in any arbitrarily

[9] There is the alternative of allowing worlds to overlap with respect to God. See, for instance, McDaniel (2004). But the other costs of this account include compositional pluralism, the view that there's more than one fundamental part–whole relation. The view also threatens a failure of modal reductionism. On this account, x is a part of y at w iff there is some space–time region R such that x is a part of y at R and R is a part of w. But of course y might be a part of no proper subregion R of w and be a part of w. For instance, y might be a musical event that occupies all of w. In that case, x is a part of y at w iff x is a part of y at w. So, we are not offered an analysis of objects existing at worlds that does not appeal to possible worlds. Indeed, we do not have here an analysis of objects existing at worlds.

chosen world w must be indiscernible from God in any other arbitrarily chosen world w'. But if God in w is indiscernible from God in w', for any arbitrarily chosen worlds w and w', then God has all of his properties essentially. The hyper-essentiality conclusion is untenable.

If God creates all of metaphysical reality, then God exists from the standpoint of every world. There is again a restricted and more plausible version of (2.5) available to the ontological arguer. (2.6) restricts (2.5) to beings that exist from the standpoint of every possible world that otherwise exemplify all of the great-making properties.

2.6. ∀x∀y((Ux & Px & Uy & E!x &~E!y) ⊃ xGy)

According to (2.6), anything that exemplifies all of the great-making properties in P and exists from the standpoint of every possible world is greater than anything that doesn't exist from the standpoint of every possible world.

3 Premise (3)

Anselm's third premise says that there is some understandable being x whose greatness is not conceivably exceeded by the greatness of anything. The greatness of x is not exceeded by the greatness in any conceivable world w of any being y. Because Lewis relativizes the greatness of things to possible worlds – there is no greatness simpliciter, but only greatness-in-world-w – Lewis finds Anselm's premise (3) to be multiply ambiguous. Lewis offers at least three ways to disambiguate premise (3) in counterpart theory.

We have seen that greatnesses, as thought of by the ontological arguer, belong to beings paired with worlds; according to the third premise, no such pair has a greatness exceeding the greatness of a certain understandable being x. But if greatnesses belong to beings relative to worlds, what are we talking about when we say: the greatness of x? Which greatness of x? The greatness of x in which conceivable world? Different answers to the question yield different non-modal translations of premise (3).[10]

We might consider a non-modal translation of premise (3) according to which there is an actual object whose greatness in the actual world is not exceeded by the greatness of anything in any other possible world. On this understanding of premise (3), there is an understandable being x whose

[10] Lewis (1970: 170).

greatness in the actual world is unexceeded by the *greatness of any other being in* any other possible world. Lewis calls this version of premise (3), 3A.

3A. ∃x (Ux & ~∃w ∃y (Ww & ywGx@))

According to (3A), there is an understandable being x, such that for no world w and being y does the greatness of y in w exceed the greatness of x in the actual world.

(3A) might be a welcome translation to the ontological arguer – it does entail the preferred conclusion that God actually exists – but it is an extraordinarily strong claim. It is indeed a much stronger claim than the ontological arguer needs. Recall that the ontological arguer in (2.2) claims that a being x that otherwise exemplifies all of the great-making properties P and actually exists is *greater than* any being y that exemplifies all of the great-making properties P and does not actually exist. According to (2.2), actual existence is a great-making property. And recall that the fact that x is greater than y does not entail that x in @ is greater than y in w. For instance, an actual dog might be a greater being than a merely possible griffin, even if in the *great chain of being* an actual griffin is greater than an actual dog. So, it might be true that the greatness of the griffin *in his own world* w exceeds the greatness of the dog *in his own world* @. It might be true in w, for instance, that the value of the griffin is V on the scale of greatness and true in @ that the value of the dog is V', and necessarily true that anything with value V is greater than anything with value V'. The value of the griffin in his own world is greater than the actual value of the griffin. But in the actual world, the griffin doesn't have much value at all. It is a merely possible being.

The view that actual existence confers greatness on beings that existence in other regions of the pluriverse does not is not a mere bias on the part of ontological arguers. The pluriverse, after all, does not differ ontologically from region to region. Griffins in a non-actual region of the pluriverse exist in the very same way as dogs do in the actual world. It is not as though non-actual griffins have a diminished form of existence that affects their greatness and actual dogs have an enhanced form of existence that affects their greatness. So, the distinction in greatness between actual beings and non-actual beings can seem invidious.

The ontological arguer has a persuasive response. The proper response to the fact that you might have discovered the calculus is not to offer you the Fields Medal. You might have discovered the calculus and no doubt you do discover the calculus in some other region of the pluriverse. But that possible, non-actual achievement is not worthy of the Fields Medal. The actual discovery of the calculus, by contrast, is worthy of accolade. Why so? Your possible, non-actual achievement is not ontologically any different from your actual achievement. The difference is that, despite the ontological symmetry, it is *false* that you discovered the calculus. Mathematicians are not awarded for what might have been.

The response is the same for possible, non-actual, Gods. If there is no actual God, then it is false that there is a being that exemplifies all of the divine attributes. There might have been such a being, and no doubt there is such a being existing in some region of the pluriverse, but there isn't such a being. Such a being, despite the ontological symmetry with actual beings, is unworthy of worship, honour and praise. An actual God does in fact exemplify all of the divine attributes, and therefore is worthy of worship, honour and praise.

Lewis urges that (3A) is a candidate translation of premise (3), but it is not credible without independent evidence. Why believe (3A)? The ontological arguer might accept (3A) on the basis of (G).

G. $\forall v(Wv \supset \exists x(Ux \;\&\; \exists w\exists y(Ww \;\&\; ywGxv)))$

> G states that, for any world v, there is an understandable being x such that for no world w and being y does the greatness of y in w exceed the greatness of x in v . . . Why might he accept G? . . . Unless inferred from 3C, G does not seem credible. Let v be a bad world – say, one containing nothing but a small chunk of mud – and let w be the most splendid conceivable world. Then according to G there is some understandable being whose greatness in v is unexceeded by the greatness in w of anything – even the greatest of the inhabitants of w. What could this understandable being be?[11]

The principle in (G) is just the generalization of (3A). It entails that, in every possible world w, there is a being whose greatness *in w* is unexceeded by the greatness of any other being *in any other world v*. (G) is true just in case there are unexceeded beings, x, y, z, and so on, in possible worlds, w, v, u, and so on, such that the greatness of x in its world equals the greatness of y in its world equals the greatness of z in its world, and so on.

Lewis's counterexample to (G) invites us to consider a possible world w that contains nothing except a small chunk of mud and a possible world v that is the most splendid conceivable. What being in w is such that its greatness in w is unexceeded by the greatness of any being in the splendid world v?

[11] Lewis (1970: 183).

Certainly the greatness of the mud in w is exceeded by the greatness of almost any being in v. But the ontological arguer can offer some resistance to the chunk-of-mud counterexample. If (G) is true, the ontological arguer might insist, then there are no possible worlds like w. There are no possible worlds that include only chunks of mud. Lewis's counterexample is only as good as his evidence that there are mud worlds. Is there better reason to believe that there are mud worlds than there is to believe that (G) is true? It's not obvious, so there are epistemological reasons for resisting. Still, it might be urged, if there are no mud worlds, then perhaps there are worlds that contain no rational beings at all or inorganic worlds which contain no living matter at all or metaphysically nihilistic worlds that include no concrete objects at all. Similar counterexamples can be generated on the assumption that there are such worlds.

Lewis notes that one natural way to argue for (G) is on the basis of (3C), the third non-modal translation of premise (3).

3C. $\exists x(Ux \& {\sim}\exists v \exists w \exists y(Wv \ \& \ Ww \ \& \ ywGxv))$

According to (3C), there is an understandable being x such that for no worlds v and w and being y does the greatness of y in w exceed the greatness of x in v.

(3C) is true just in case there is some being x such that the greatness of x in any world whatsoever is unexceeded by the greatness of any being y in any world. If (3C) is true, then there are no counterexamples to (G). Indeed, if (3C) is true, then we have a direct argument for (3A). On the trivial assumption that the actual world is a possible world, (3C) entails (3A).

Is there a reason to believe (3C)? One reason to believe that (3C) is true follows from the fact that we understand *maximal greatness.* Maximally great beings are essentially maximally excellent. Plantinga, following Findlay, urges that the greatness of a being in a possible world w does not depend merely on the properties of that being in w.

> . . . what it is like in other worlds is also to the point. Those who worship God do not think of him as a being that happens to be of surpassing excellence in this world but who in some other worlds is powerless or uninformed or of dubious moral character.[12]

Plantinga distinguishes between the properties of greatness and excellence. He allows the excellence of a being in a world w to depend on its

12 See Plantinga (1974: 214ff.).

(non-world-indexed) properties in w. But the greatness of a being in any world w depends on *both* the excellence of that being in w and its properties in other possible worlds. We will say that the property of maximal excellence entails the following properties.[13]

> ME. Maximal excellence entails omnipotence, omniscience, rational perfection and moral perfection.

(ME) just tells us that, necessarily, something is maximally excellent in a world w only if it is omnipotent, omniscient, rationally perfect and morally perfect in w. Presumably, something might be maximally excellent in some worlds and not in others. (ME) tells us nothing about whether a being that is possibly maximally excellent in w enjoys any excellence at all in w. We'll say that a being has maximal greatness only if it is essentially maximally excellent.

> MG. Maximal greatness entails maximal excellence in every possible world.

According to (MG), a being is maximally great only if it exists in every possible world and is essentially maximally excellent. It follows from (ME) and (MG) that a being is maximally great only if it necessarily exists and is essentially omnipotent, essentially omniscient, essentially morally perfect and essentially rationally perfect.

There is also good reason to believe that there is ontological space for maximally great beings under Lewisian modal assumptions. Ross Cameron confirms the view expressed above, that God is the creator of reality, not merely particular regions of reality.

> Either each God created the world He exists at, or He didn't. If the former, then there is no sense in which God is responsible for all of creation since, for the modal realist, all of creation is the pluriverse of worlds, not just the actual world. But if there are Gods that didn't create the world they exist at then it's not clear why they deserve to be called 'God'; being the creator is essential to God if anything is, so a God that didn't create the world He exists at would seem not deserve the title, thus undercutting the claim that He is in fact a counterpart of the actual God, and hence undercutting the claim that God is a necessary existent. But there is no need for the theist

[13] When I speak of a property P entailing another property Q, I mean that in every world in which x exemplifies P, x also exemplifies Q or $(\forall x)(Px \supset Qx)$. There are interesting weaker entailment relations among properties. We might also say that P weakly entails Q just in case, necessarily, something is P only if something is Q or $(\forall x)(\exists y)(Px \supset Qy)$.

> modal realist to go the route of postulating distinct counterparts of our actual God at each non-actual world.[14]

But might possible worlds – possible regions of reality – overlap with respect to God? Might God – the very same God – exist in every possible world? There are no objections to that view from modal realism. If God has all of his intrinsic properties essentially, then God might well exist in every possible world. Lewis allows that possible worlds might overlap with respect to universals precisely because universals have all of their intrinsic properties essentially.

> If two worlds are said to overlap by having a coin in common, and if this coin is supposed to be wholly round in one world and wholly octagonal in the other, I stubbornly ask what shape it is, and insist that shape is not a relation to worlds . . . I do not see any parallel objection if worlds are said to overlap by sharing a universal. What contingent, non-relational property of the universal could we put in place of [the] shape of the coin in raising the problem? I cannot think of any.[15]

Of course, one may doubt whether God does have all of his intrinsic properties essentially. God's anger and disappointment are presumably intrinsic properties, but it is hardly an essential property of God to be angry and disappointed.

In any case, Lewis would no doubt grant that we understand maximal excellence, so by premise (1) there are maximally excellent beings in some worlds. But how could we understand maximal excellence and not understand maximal greatness? A maximally great being just is a maximally excellent being that exists in more than one world. Despite these observations, Lewis simply rejects the thesis that a maximally great being is understandable.

> [The ontological arguer] might assume that for every description he understands, there is some understandable being answering to that description. But what of such well-understood descriptions as 'largest prime' or 'round square'?[16]

The point presumably is that there is not an understandable being for every understandable description. And if it were insisted that, for some plausible notion of understandable, there is an understandable being for every understandable description, then Lewis urges that he would have to reject premise

[14] See Cameron (2009: 98ff.). [15] Lewis (1999: 11n.5). [16] Lewis (1970: 182).

(1) in Anselm's argument. He would reject the thesis that every understandable being exists in some world or other. So, either there are understandable descriptions for which there are no understandable beings or there are understandable beings for which there are no (unrestrictedly) existing beings. Either way, the fact that maximal greatness is understandable does not entail that there (unrestrictedly) exists a maximally great being.

Ontological saturation principles – and perhaps, principles of plenitude – are also ineffective approaches to supporting (3C). Consider the principle of saturation that any sentence saying that there exists an understandable being of so-and-so description is true unless provably false. It follows directly from such an ontological saturation principle that (3C) is true. But that is no reason to believe (3C). Lewis urges that saturation principles prove too much. (*) also follows from such an ontological saturation principle.

(*) $\exists x \exists w \exists v$ (Ux & Ww & Wv & Vy (y $\neq$ x $\supset$ xwGyw) & $\exists$y(yvGxv))

> If the Principle of Saturation supports 3C, it should equally well support (*); otherwise it makes a discrimination unjustified by any visibly relevant difference between 3C and (*). But (*) is incompatible with 3C. So if the Principle of Saturation supports 3C, then it is a bad principle.[17]

(*) states that there is an understandable being which is greater than anything else in some world, but is exceeded in greatness in another world. So, clearly, (*) is inconsistent with (3C). But it is also true, as Lewis notes, that (*) is no less supported by the saturation principle than (3C). The principle of saturation entails inconsistent propositions and ought to be rejected.

4 A Better Translation of Premise (3)

According to Lewis, the translation in (3A) is necessary to any valid rendering of Anselm's argument in counterpart theory. Only the translations in (3A) and (3C) make the argument valid, and (3C) entails (3A). Since Lewis argues that there is no non-circular reason to believe (3A), he concludes that Anselm's argument is unsound.

But we noted that the ontological arguer might well reject (3A), too. (3A) expresses a much stronger claim that the ontological arguer needs, and perhaps much stronger than the ontological arguer believes. According to (3A), there is an understandable being x, such that for no world w and being

[17] Lewis (1970: 183).

y does the greatness of y in w exceed the greatness of x in the actual world. The ontological arguer in (2.2) claims that a being x that otherwise exemplifies all of the great-making properties P and actually exists is *greater than* any being y that exemplifies all of the great-making properties P and does not actually exist. According to (2.2), actual existence is a great-making property. And the fact that x is greater than y does not entail that x in @ is greater than y in w. The ontological arguer might therefore wish to replace (3A) with (3A').

3A'. ∃x(Ux & @Ix & ∀y~(yGx))

According to (3A'), there is some actual being whose greatness is unexceeded by any other existing being. The quantifiers in (3A') are all unrestricted. The greatness of x exceeds – actually exceeds – the greatness of all other existing beings – all beings that exist anywhere in metaphysical space, any beings that exist anywhere in reality. If there is a greatest conceivable being, it would have to have the property of being actual.

(3A') does not make the strong claim that there actually exists a being x whose greatness in the actual world is unexceeded by the greatness of any other being y in its world w. That extreme claim, we have found, is otiose. The ontological arguer wants to show that there is some actual being whose greatness is actually unexceeded by any other existing being.

But what reason is there to believe (3A')? There is an understandable being x that exemplifies all of the great-making properties P. According to (1), x exists in some possible world or other. According to (2.2) any actually existing being that exemplifies all of the great-making properties in P is greater than merely possibly existing things that exemplify all of the great-making properties in P. So, x exemplifies all of the great-making properties only if x actually exists.

But, once again, why does actual existence confer greatness on x while possible existence does not? The answer is not far to seek. Only an actually existing God has the properties of being worthy of devotion and worship, worthy of veneration, praise, love, petition and prayer. No being in any other world – no matter how great that being is *in its world* – is great enough to be worthy of devotion, worship, praise, honour, love or prayer. No being in any other world – no matter how great that being is in its world – is the proper object of these religious attitudes. It is the actual existence of God that makes these attitudes appropriate to the actually existing God. It is the possible non-actual existence of other great beings that makes these attitudes inappropriate to the possible non-actual beings.

Concerning the conclusion of Anselm's ontological argument, Lewis observes the following:

> So our non-modal translation of the conclusion resembles 3A, our first version of Premise 3:
>
> C. ∃x(Ex@ & ~∃w∃y (Ww & ywGx@))
>
> (There is a being x existing in the actual world such that for no world w and being y does the greatness of y in w exceed the greatness of x in the actual world.)[18]

But as we have been at pains to show, the ontological arguer does not want to show anything like (C). The conclusion in (C) is much too strong a claim for the arguer to establish. The premises (1), (2.2) and (3A') do not establish (C). Rather the premises (1), (2.2) and (3A') establish the conclusion in (C').

C'. ∃x(Ex@ & ∀y~yGx)

There is a being x existing in the actual world such that for no being y does y's greatness exceed x's greatness.

5 Existing from the Standpoint of Every World

We noted in Section 3 above that, if God creates all of metaphysical reality – all possible worlds and all possibilia – then God must exist from the standpoint of every world.[19] But then if God exists from the standpoint of every possible world, then God exists in the right way for theists. A God that creates all of reality and exists from the standpoint of every world might well be greater than any being – however great that being is in its own world(s) – that *exists in* some possible world or other in metaphysical space. A God that creates all of reality and exists from the standpoint of every world might well be greater than any being existing in the actual world, however great that being actually is.

A being that exists from the standpoint of every world would have the properties of being worthy of devotion and worship, being a proper object of veneration, praise, love, petition and prayer. And, as we have noted, there is a

[18] Lewis (1970: 181).

[19] The alternative is to claim that God exists in every possible world. This requires either the assumption that God exemplifies all of his intrinsic properties essentially, which seems false, or threatens the failure of modal reductionism. See McDaniel (2004).

rationale for the view that a God that exists from the standpoint of every world is the proper object of any of those attitudes. A being that exists from the standpoint of every world can create all of the pluriverse – all of creatable reality.

There is again a restricted and more plausible version of (2.5) available to the ontological arguer. (2.6) above restricts (2.5) to beings that exist from the standpoint of every possible world and otherwise exemplify all of the great-making properties. Recall that, according to (2.6), anything that exemplifies all of the great-making properties in P and exists from the standpoint of every possible world is greater than anything that doesn't exist from the standpoint of every possible world.

If existing necessarily – existing from the standpoint of every possible world – is a great-making property, rather than merely actually existing, then (2.6) might be found appealing. Corresponding to (2.6) is (3E).

3E. $\exists x \forall w(Ux \,\&\, E!wx \,\&\, {\sim}\exists y(yGx))$

According to (3E), there is an understandable being existing from the standpoint of every world whose greatness is unexceeded by any other existing being. The quantifiers in (3E) are all unrestricted. The greatness of x exceeds the greatness of all other existing beings y – all beings that exist anywhere in the totality of creation, anywhere in metaphysical reality. And our corresponding conclusion is (C").

C". $\exists x(E!x@ \,\&\, {\sim}\exists y(yGx))$

There is a being x existing from the standpoint of the actual world such that for no being y does y's greatness exceed x's greatness.

6 Concluding Remarks

The interest and advantage of Lewis's approach to Anselm's ontological argument is that it makes a perfectly extensional interpretation of the argument possible. The modal reduction puts us in a position to assess the credibility of Anselm's premises. The translation of Anselm's ontological argument into a non-modal argument permits the application of the standards of classical logic to determine the cogency of Anselm's argument.

The central difficulty in Lewis's versions of Anselm's ontological argument is his translations of premises (2) and (3). According to Lewis, (2) states that, for any understandable being x, and for any worlds w and v, if x exists in w but x does not exist in v, then the greatness of x in w exceeds the greatness of x in v. That is, whatever exists in some world is greater in that world than it is in any world in which it does not exist. (2) is a claim about the greatness of objects in worlds. But because (2) is formulated in terms of greatness in worlds, Lewis's greatest conceivable being in (3) requires a formulation as strong as (3A). According to (3A), there is an understandable being x, such that for no world w and being y does the greatness of y in w exceed the greatness of x in the actual world.

But Anselm is offering an argument that does not rely on such radical and implausible premises. Anselm is arguing from the premise that actual existence is a great-making property. For any beings x and y sharing all of the divine attributes P, the actual existence of x and mere possible existence of y makes x greater than y. That can be true though the greatness of x in the actual world does not exceed the greatness of y in w.

9 Plantinga

Joshua Rasmussen

Plantinga constructs an ontological argument using twentieth-century developments in modality. He begins with a premise he thinks can be plausible to someone *a priori*: that maximal greatness (worthiness or value) is possible. He then brings the resources of contemporary logic and metaphysics to deduce that maximal greatness is actually instantiated in our world. From maximal greatness, he unpacks the traditional 'worthy-making' attributes of God: maximal knowledge, maximal power, and moral perfection. Astonishingly, Plantinga labels his argument 'victorious', and he suggests that one can rationally accept its conclusion on the basis of the argument.[1]

I shall examine the potential merits of Plantinga's ontological argument. I will begin by reviewing Plantinga's assessment of previous ontological arguments, which lead him to his own formulation. I will then present Plantinga's ontological argument and show how it fits within his larger metaphysical framework. Next, I will pose a pressing and popular type of objection: the problem of 'reverse' parallel arguments *against* the existence of God. I will consider Plantinga's general remarks about this objection, and then I'll explore a new strategy for potentially breaking symmetry. In closing, I'll consider whether, or in what sense, someone could consider Plantinga's ontological argument to be successful.

1 Arguments That Went Before

Plantinga searches for an ontological argument that avoids the pitfalls of previous ontological arguments. He starts by examining Anselm's ontological argument and then turns to a contemporary formulation. In this section, we will review Plantinga's assessment of these ontological arguments as they prepare the stage for Plantinga's version.

[1] Plantinga (1974: 221).

Here is a formulation of Anselm's argument:

A1. Assume God exists in the understanding but not in reality.
A2. Existence in reality is greater than existence in the understanding alone.
A3. Therefore, if God did exist in reality, then he would be greater than he is.
A4. God's existence in reality is conceivable.
A5. Therefore, it is conceivable that there be a being greater than God is ((A3) and (A4)).
A6. Therefore, it is conceivable that there be a being greater than the being than which nothing greater can be conceived (A5), by the definition of 'God').
A7. It is false that it is conceivable that there be a being greater than the being than which none greater can be conceived.
A8. Therefore, it is false that God exists in the understanding but not in reality.

Plantinga adds, 'So, if God exists in the understanding, he also exists in reality; but clearly enough he does exist in the understanding, as even the fool will testify; therefore he exists in reality as well.'[2]

Does Anselm's argument, as stated above, succeed? Plantinga thinks not. He draws out two problems. First, there is the problem of seeing how to make sense of premise (A2) – that *existence in reality is greater than existence in the understanding alone*. What does that even mean? Plantinga offers the following translation:

A2*. For any worlds W and W* and any object x, if x exists in W and x does not exist in W*, then the greatness of x in W exceeds the greatness of x in W*.

This translation has the advantage of taking a standard logical form. It has a serious disadvantage, however: premise (A2*) implies that things can have features in worlds where those things don't even exist. For example, a horse could have legs in a world where that horse doesn't exist. The result is that things can *be* in worlds where they *don't exist*. Plantinga rejects this distinction between *being* and *existence* (with an argument), and so he is committed to rejecting (A2).[3]

Nevertheless, Plantinga thinks that Anselm's argument also fails for another reason, even if we grant (A2*). The reason is that the rest of the argument must be rewritten to fit with (A2*), yet Plantinga finds no way to do that successfully. He explores a few possible ways of rewriting the argument. His first attempt leaves him with a premise that explicitly presupposes that God exists in the actual world. Clearly, that won't work. Plantinga then considers whether we might develop Anselm's core strategy using a more modest premise: that God *could* exist. But the same two problems re-emerge:

[2] Plantinga (1974: 197). [3] Plantinga (1974: 145–63).

(i) the resulting argument involves the idea that there are or could have been non-existent things, and (ii) it requires a premise which, when properly understood, explicitly presupposes God's existence. According to this analysis, Anselm's argument is doomed.

Plantinga then turns his attention to a more contemporary version of the Ontological Argument given by Hartshorne and Malcolm.[4] He summarizes their argument as follows:

B1. There is a world W in which there exists a being with maximal greatness.
B2. A being has maximal greatness in a world only if it exists in every world.
B3. Therefore, there is a being with maximal greatness in the actual world.

This argument has two advantages over Anselm's argument. First, it doesn't require that there are, or could have been, non-existent things. Second, it doesn't have a premise which, when properly understood, explicitly presupposes God's existence.

Even still, Plantinga finds a fatal flaw. He points out that just because a being may be maximally great in some world W, it doesn't strictly follow that this being is maximally great in *every* world at which it exists. Thus, even if a being which is maximally great in W exists in our world, it doesn't follow that this being is maximally great in our world. In short, their argument fails to be formally valid.

2 A 'Victorious' Version

Plantinga proposes a way to fix Hartshorne and Malcom's argument. He begins with the observation that one's greatness in a world depends upon which features one has in other worlds. For example, a being that is wise in a single world is not as great, other things being equal, as a being that is wise in every possible world. From this observation, Plantinga develops his own ontological argument.

We may summarize the Plantingian Ontological Argument (POA) as follows:

C1. There is a possible world W in which there exists a being with maximal greatness.
C2. A being has maximal greatness in a possible world only if it has maximal greatness in every possible world, including the actual world.
C3. Therefore, there is a being with maximal greatness in the actual world.

[4] Plantinga (1974: 212ff.).

Is this argument sound? Plantinga thinks so. Regarding (C1), Plantinga thinks it is true that maximal greatness is possibly instantiated. He takes this premise to be equivalent to the premise that there is some *essence* which includes maximal greatness. Plantinga suggests, moreover, that someone could find that premise reasonable without presupposing that God exists.

What about (C2)? This premise is largely motivated by Plantinga's understanding of *greatness*. Plantinga suggests that, in general, a being is greater if its greatness spans more worlds. So, for example, suppose there is a being which has the great-making features of wisdom and power in some, but not all, worlds. Such a being would not be as great, other things being equal, as a being which has wisdom and power in all worlds. If that is correct, then a *maximally* great being – a being with the highest conceivable degree of greatness – would have great-making features in every world. It would thus be maximally great in every world. To use Anselm's terminology, a being *than which none greater can be conceived* would be great in every possible world, if it were great in any.

Implicit in the argument is a technical assumption about the logic of possibility. In particular, the argument requires that the actual world would still be *possible* (i.e. logically consistent with the metaphysically necessary facts) were any of the possible worlds actual. To illustrate this principle, suppose unicorns are possible creatures. We observe that foxes are actual creatures. So the principle predicts that the foxes of our world would be possible creatures if unicorns were actual creatures. Here is how the principle applies to POA. Suppose a maximally great being exists in a possible world W. Then given the premise that such a being would span all possible worlds, it follows that a maximally great being exists in all worlds that are possible relative to W. The actual world is possible relative to W (per assumption). Therefore a maximally great being exists in the actual world.

Although this understanding of possibility is not incontestable, one could perhaps sidestep worries about the correct logic of possibility by treating the logic as part of an implicit definition of the term 'possible'.[5]

The idea here is that one may focus on just those possible worlds relative to which the actual world is also possible. Suppose, for the sake of argument, that there is a sense of 'possible' according to which there are possible worlds relative to which the actual world is *not* possible. Put those worlds aside. There remains a vast array of possible worlds relative to which the actual world is possible. If we define 'possible' in terms of those worlds and 'maximal

[5] More precisely, we may treat 'it is necessary that' as a modal operator '$\Box$' that obeys the following S5 axioms: **M:** $\Box p \rightarrow p$; **K:** $\Box(p \rightarrow q) \rightarrow (\Box p \rightarrow \Box q)$; **4:** $\Box p \rightarrow \Box\Box p$; **5:** $\Diamond p \rightarrow \Box\Diamond p$.

greatness' in terms of having greatness in those worlds, then the second premise is true by definition. Meanwhile, the first premise amounts to the claim that a maximally great being exists in one of the relevant possible worlds – that is, in a possible world relative to which the actual world is also possible.

I should note that my talk of possible worlds here is merely heuristic. We need not assume that there *really are* possible worlds in order to develop POA. Instead, we may make use of twentieth-century developments in the logic of possibility and necessity. Specifically, we can show that 'X is necessary' follows from 'possibly, X is necessary' using standard modal logic.[6] Reference to worlds is not required.

Let us recap the argument. Suppose maximal greatness is possibly instantiated (premise (1)). And suppose that *if* maximal greatness is possibly instantiated, *then* maximal greatness is instantiated in every possible world (premise (2)). Then it follows that maximal greatness is instantiated in every possible world. The actual world is among the possible worlds. Therefore, maximal greatness is instantiated in the actual world. For the sake of neutrality, let 'being' stand for whatever reality or realities instantiate maximal greatness in our world, and we reach the conclusion that there is a maximally great being.

3 The Problem of Parallel Arguments

In my estimation, the most serious and significant objection to POA is that it is plagued by the problem of parallel arguments which have an *opposite* conclusion. (We will consider other sorts of objections later.)

[6] Here is one way to show the inference:
Let 'N' abbreviate '∃x (N(x)', where 'N(x)' reads '□ (∃!(x))'.

1. Assume ◊N.
2. Then: ◊□N. (□(N → □N), by axioms 4 & 5)
3. Now suppose (for the sake of argument) that ◊~N.
4. Then: □◊~N. (by axiom 5)
5. Then: ~◊~◊~N. (by substituting '~◊~' for '□')
6. Then: ~◊~~□~~N. (by substituting '~□~' for the second '◊')
7. Then: ~◊□N. (because '~~X' is equivalent to 'X')
8. But (7) contradicts (2).
9. So: (3) is not true. ((3) → (7))
10. So: ~◊~N.
11. So: □N. (by substituting '□' for '~◊~')
12. So: N. (□X → X, by axiom M)

13: So: if ◊N, then N.

Consider, for example, the following argument:

D1. There is a possible world W in which there is *no* being with maximal greatness.
D2. A being has maximal greatness in a possible world only if it has maximal greatness in every world.
D3. Therefore, there is no being with maximal greatness in the actual world.

The parallel argument's conclusion contradicts the conclusion of Plantinga's ontological argument. So it can't be that *both* arguments are sound. Yet the two arguments are strikingly similar. Both arguments have the same valid structure, and both rely on the inference from *a maximally great being is possible* to *a maximally great being is actual*. The only salient difference is the first premise: (C1) invites us to imagine that there *could be* a maximally great being, whereas (D1) invites us to imagine that there *could fail to be* a maximally great being. Does a non-theist have a reason to favour the possibility of a maximally great being over the possibility of no maximally great being? If not, then it seems the intellectually respectable thing for the non-theist to do is to withhold judgment about both possibilities. In this situation, the epistemic force of the parallel argument *cancels* the epistemic force of Plantinga's argument. The arguments wash out.

Plantinga is aware of the problem of parallel arguments, and he offers a few considerations. First, he suggests that a parallel argument need not *automatically* defeat his argument. For it could be that someone is perfectly rational in accepting the 'possibility' premise in POA while rejecting the 'possibility' premise in the parallel argument. To motivate this point, Plantinga mentions other contested philosophical propositions, such as Leibniz's law of identity. He observes that one can certainly be within one's epistemic rights in accepting a proposition that others contest; otherwise, no one could rightfully accept any philosophical proposition. Plantinga proposes, then, that someone who thinks the 'possibility' premise in POA argument is true could in principle be within their rights in thinking so.

On the other hand, Plantinga does not show, or attempt to show, that the 'possibility' premise in POA actually is more credible than the parallel premise. His proposal appears to be more modest. I take him to be suggesting that someone who is aware of the parallel argument can – at least in principle – still be rational in accepting the salient premise of POA. Although not explicit, he may be thinking something like this:

> I personally find the premises in my argument quite plausible, and, indeed, I think they rise to the estimable status of being *true*. My argument doesn't seem to presuppose the existence of God in my own mind: I do not see that *my* acceptance of these premises depends, explicitly or implicitly, on my prior belief

> in God. So, I don't see that my argument is circular (explicitly or implicitly). Also, I seem to be perfectly within my rights, as far as I see, to think the premises are true. I assume others could be like me in this respect. Thus, even though there can certainly be rational disagreement here, it seems clear enough that it is at least *rational* to accept the conclusion on the basis of the premises.

A question remains: should someone who doesn't already think God exists find the 'possibility' premise in POA to be more credible (or probable or plausible) than the parallel premise?

Speaking for myself, I find it difficult to *just see* that the possibility of God's existence is more credible (or probable or plausible) than the possibility of God's non-existence. Sure, it may be tempting to think that God's existence is at least *possible*. But when I consider whether God's *non-existence* is at least possible, I find it difficult to *just see* that the one possibility is more plausible than the other. Perhaps I simply cannot see well enough into these scenarios to tell whether either one is genuinely possible.

Here is a little anecdote suggesting that even Plantinga may be sympathetic with the difficulty of seeing such possibilities. When I was Plantinga's student at the University of Notre Dame, he advised me to be careful not to confuse *seeing that something is possible* with *failing to see that it is impossible*. He added that in his younger days he hadn't fully distinguished these two epistemic states in his own mind. The distinction is clearly relevant to POA. For when one is tempted to think that God's existence is possible, it could be that one doesn't actually *see* that such a situation is possible. Rather, perhaps one merely *fails to see* that God's existence is impossible. Failing to see that God can't exist is not the same as seeing that God genuinely can exist.

Suppose one's temptation to think that God can exist rests merely on one's failure to see that God can't exist. Then one should resist the temptation to think that God's existence is possible. Similarly, if one's temptation to think that God can fail to exist rests merely on one's failure to see that God can exist, then one should resist that temptation, too. The conclusion is this: in the absence of an *independent* reason to think that God's existence (or non-existence) is genuinely possible, the proper response is to withhold judgment about such a possibility.

4 The Prospect of an Unparalleled Path

I shall introduce a new 'ontological-type' argument about value. It begins with the premise that some value is possible and concludes that the greatest conceivable value is possible. I call the argument 'the Value Argument'.

The conclusion of the Value Argument is relevant to Plantinga's argument. For if maximal greatness is itself a conceivable degree of value, then the conclusion of the Value Argument entails the crucial 'possibility' premise in Plantinga's argument. In other words, the Value Argument promises a way to break the stalemate between POA and the reverse, parallel argument. In this section, then, I will unpack the Value Argument and then consider whether it might stand any stronger against the general problem of parallel arguments.

Here is an outline of the Value Argument:

E1. Some degree of value can be instantiated.
E2. If *some* degree of value can be instantiated, then *each* degree of value can be instantiated.
E3. Therefore, each degree of value can be instantiated (E1, E2).
E4. Maximal greatness is a degree of value.
E5. Therefore, maximal greatness can be instantiated.

If this argument is sound, then it breaks the stalemate in the battle over Plantinga's 'possibility' premise. So let us consider what reasons there may be in support of its premises.

Start with (E1): some value can be instantiated. Perhaps the strongest reason to accept (E1) is that some value *is* instantiated. For example, you exist, and you instantiate great value. If you agree, then you have reason to infer that value *can* be instantiated. (Note that by appealing to *actual* value, the Value Argument may stray from typical ontological arguments, whose premises are normally not based on what *actually* exists. On the other hand, one could argue that value judgments are themselves ultimately justified *a priori*, rather than from sensory experience, and perhaps that licenses classifying the Value Argument as an ontological argument.)

To be clear, I make no assumptions here about the *nature* or *source* of value. Maybe the constructivists are right: value depends in a certain way upon idealized thinking. Or maybe value is a basic and unanalysable feature of certain states or things. Or perhaps value is analysable in terms of thoughts or emotions. There are many options on the market. If you think any of them are 'worthy' of attention, then you may accept that there is value in our world.

Not everyone will accept value realism, of course. Some philosophers deny that anything has genuine value. I respect these philosophers, and in fact, I value their thinking. Rather than enter the trenches with value nihilists, I'll mention two reasons I think the Value Argument could still be of interest to philosophers despite the nihilist escape. First, most philosophers, whether theist or atheist, do not accept value nihilism (they reject it), and so the nihilist escape is not open to most philosophers.[7] Second, value nihilists are already committed to denying that Plantinga's God exists, since such a God would be *great* – and so have value. It remains open at the outset, then, that the Value Argument could appeal to someone who is a neutral agnostic or who thinks the existence of God is unlikely due to lack of evidence. In the next section, I will return to the question of to whom, if anyone, the Value Argument may appeal.

Consider, next, (E2): if *some* degree of value can be instantiated, then *each* degree of value can be instantiated. Why might someone think that is true? Here is one reason. You might think that mere differences in degree of value are *irrelevant* to a difference with respect to exemplifiability. If some particular degree of value is possible, then why isn't any other? What difference could there be between one degree of value and another that could explain why the one is possible but the other is impossible? It may seem no difference could make a difference.

This reasoning flows from a more general principle of *modal continuity*, which says that classes of properties that differ merely in degree tend to be modally uniform – either all possible or all impossible.[8] To be clear, there can be breaks in modal continuity. For example, there can be a *three*-sided triangle, but there cannot be a *two*-sided triangle. Nevertheless, where modal breaks occur, there is some *relevant difference* between the respective properties accounting for the break. In the case at hand, the idea is that a mere difference in *degree of value* doesn't account for the possibility or impossibility of a value of that degree, as far as anyone can see.

We may express the principle of modal continuity in terms of defeasible reasoning. Modal continuity is a defeasible default position. So, for example, given any degrees of value one considers, one has a defeasible reason to consider those degrees of value to be modally uniform. If that is right, then one may enjoy a defeasible reason to think the class of all degrees of value is modally uniform. In the next section I will consider whether there may be defeaters, which suggest that degrees of value are *not* modally uniform.

Let us consider now the final premise: maximal greatness is a degree of value. My argument for this premise is simple. Maximal greatness is a

7 According to Phil. surveys (2013), 56.4 per cent of philosophers accept or lean toward moral realism.
8 Rasmussen (2014).

determinate of value; it is a *maximal* value. Every determinate of value is a degree of value. Therefore, maximal greatness is a degree of value.

The above argument falls out of my understanding of a degree of value. In the most general terms, I am thinking of a degree of value as any *determinate* of the property, *being valuable.* Here are some examples: *being somewhat valuable, being tremendously valuable,* and *being valuable to degree N,* where *N* is some arbitrary unit. We can grasp different degrees of value by comparison with each other. For example, let us say Timothy is valuable to degree *N.* Then we may define other degrees of value relative to Timothy's value. Perhaps, for instance, a certain crowd of people is valuable to degree $14 \times N$. (In case someone worries that not all degrees of value are comparable to each other, we may limit our scope to those determinates of value that are less than or equal to maximal value.)

Here, then, is how someone might use the Value Argument as a means of justifying the key 'possibility' premise in POA. One starts by seeing that there is value in the world. One then recognizes that mere differences in *degree* of value don't apparently make a difference with respect to possible instantiation. One thereby gains a reason to infer that each degree of value *can* be instantiated. Maximal greatness is a degree of value. Therefore, one has reason to infer that maximal greatness can be instantiated. Therefore, one has reason to think there can be a maximally great being.

We have so far considered possible reasons in support of the Value Argument. Let us now consider whether there may be parallel reasons in support of a *reverse* value argument. Two reverse arguments come to my mind.[9] Here is the first:

F1. Some degree of value can fail to be instantiated.
F2. If some degree of value can fail to be instantiated, then each degree of value can fail to be instantiated.
F3. Therefore, each degree of value can fail to be instantiated (F1, F2).
F4. Maximal greatness is a degree of value.
F5. Therefore, maximal greatness can fail to be instantiated.

[9] I will concentrate on reverse arguments about *value*. Yet, there may be other reverse arguments that are less parallel but which follow the same basic reasoning as the Value Argument. One example that comes to mind is the Subtraction Argument, which has a premise that for any given number of concrete things there could be, there could be fewer. The conclusion of this argument is that there could have been *no* concrete things – hence: there is no maximally great concrete being which spans all worlds. In the end, I don't think the Subtraction Argument is sufficiently parallel, for it seems to me that best explanation for why there are some concrete things rather than none is that there couldn't be none. This explanation provides me with an independent reason to think there couldn't be no concrete things. That said, others may have a different assessment or bring to light better reverse arguments.

This argument has a conclusion that is incompatible with the conclusion of POA. Yet the premises of this argument may seem to be no less plausible than the premises in the Value Argument. So why favour the Value Argument over this reverse argument?

There is an important difference between (F1) (from the parallel argument) and (E1) (from the Value Argument), however. The justification I offered for (E1) is based upon one's experience of *actual* value. The idea is that one infers that some degree of value *can* be instantiated from the experience-based premise that some degree of value *is* instantiated. Consider, by contrast, that one cannot support (F1) merely by appealing to one's experience of the *lack* of some value. For even while one may *fail to experience* the presence of some degree of value around them, one doesn't thereby experience the complete absence of that degree of value in all places. Perhaps every degree of value is instantiated somewhere.

In fact, one could theorize that the greatest conceivable value *entails* every degree of value. This proposal is an instance of the general theory that greater degrees include lower degrees, where the lower degrees are positive, modally continuous degrees. A ten-dollar bill, for example, *includes* the value of nine dollars: after all, you could use a ten-dollar bill to buy something that cost nine dollars. Similarly, a ball that has mass of 1 kg also has mass of 0.5 kg. The greater mass includes the lesser mass values. Suppose this 'greater includes lesser' theory is correct. Then the value of the greatest conceivable being would include the values of all lesser conceivable beings. In other words, God would have *all* conceivable value. The result is that if there were a greatest conceivable being, then all values would be instantiated, regardless of the *lack* of values you and I may experience.

My purpose here is not to provide an unassailable defence of the 'greater includes lesser' theory. My point is merely that the experience-based consideration in support of the first premise in the Value Argument is *not parallel* to the sort of considerations that would be required to support the first premise in the parallel argument. I conclude, therefore, that the Value Argument enjoys a kind of support that is missing from the reverse value argument. The arguments are not alike.

Here is a second reverse argument:

G1. Some degree of value can be instantiated.
G2. If *some* degree of value can be instantiated, then *each* degree of value can be instantiated.
G3. Therefore, each degree of value can be instantiated (G1, G2).
G4. Some degrees of value preclude maximal greatness.
G5. Therefore, maximal greatness can fail to be instantiated.

This argument hinges upon premise (E4). Are there degrees of value that preclude maximal greatness? Plantinga considers two candidates. First, he uses the term 'near-maximality' to refer to a property that, by stipulation, could only be instantiated by a nearly maximal being whose greatness is not exceeded by any being. Second, 'no-maximality' is his name for the property of being such that there is no maximally great being (Plantinga (1974: 218). If either of these properties could be instantiated by something, then maximal greatness couldn't be instantiated by anything. So, if either of these properties is a degree of value, then (G4) is true.

The properties just mentioned are not degrees of value, however – or at least they are not 'degrees' in any ordinary sense. Degrees are differentiated by a quantity or magnitude. For example, such properties as *being four feet tall*, *being five feet tall* and *being six feet tall* differ by a quantity of feet. By contrast, the property of *being four feet tall, such that there are no pigs*, adds a non-quantitative, propositional element. The non-quantitative, propositional add-on disqualifies this property from being a genuine degree of height. After all, there is no way to *compare* the add-on with other degrees of height: is *being four feet tall, such that there are no pigs* a greater or lesser height than *being four feet tall*? The question is nonsense. Similarly, there isn't a genuine *value* comparison between *being such that there is no maximally great being* and ordinary degrees of value. The propositional add-on – *such that there is no maximally great being* – disqualifies the properties Plantinga considers from being genuine degrees of value. I conclude, then, that Plantinga's examples do not reveal that (G4) is true.

Note that even if (G4) is justifiable, (G4) isn't really *parallel* to any premise in the Value Argument. It is not as though (G4) is simply an obvious, uncontroversial truth. In fact, the Value Argument is itself a reason to doubt G4. Consider that the Value Argument includes every premise of the parallel argument minus (G4). In place of (G4), the Value Argument has the premise that *maximal greatness* is a degree of value. So, if you think maximal greatness is a degree of value, and if you accept the rest of the premises in the *parallel* argument, then you have a reason to reject (G4).

To recap, the Value Argument is an auxiliary argument, whose conclusion is the crucial 'possibility' premise in POA. If the Value Argument is sound, then maximal greatness is *possibly* instantiated. And if POA is sound, then maximal greatness is actually instantiated. So, the arguments fit together to produce an extended version of POA. Let us call the combination of POA together with the Value Argument 'Plantinga's Ontological Argument Extended' (POAE).

5 Objections

Let us begin to test POAE with some objections.

Objection 1: There is a significant difference between *finite* degrees of value and *infinite* value. POAE requires that every degree of value can be instantiated. Maybe each finite degree of value can indeed be instantiated, but why think *infinite* value is possible?

Reply. The objection rightfully inspires caution. We want to avoid hasty generalization from familiar cases to the unfamiliar, infinite case. On the other hand, there is a cluster of considerations that leads me to be cautious about being too cautious:

- The difference between finite and infinite isn't *automatically* modally relevant. For example, suppose co-location of any finitely massive objects is impossible. Then co-location of any infinitely massive objects would (clearly) also be impossible. The difference between finite and infinite mass is plainly irrelevant to the possibility of co-location.
- It is far from obvious that the difference between finite value and infinite value could be relevant to modal continuity. According to the general principle of modal continuity, the default position is that mere differences in degrees are not modally relevant. So, unless one has reason to think that infinite value is impossible, there is a presumption to think that infinite value, like any other value, is possible.
- Infinite value is (arguably) implied by a conceptually simple feature: *absolute perfection*. Consider that any finitely valuable being could be surpassed by a more perfect being – a being with greater knowledge or power. If so, then a perfect being would not be a finitely valuable being; it would have infinite value. The simplicity of perfection counts in favour of its exemplifiability. (Can you think of any simple feature that *can't* be exemplified?)

Objection 2: There is a tradition of arguments designed to show that the notion of a maximally great being is incoherent. For example, there are arguments that purport to expose conceptual problems with features – such as omniscience, omnipotence and moral perfection – that have been traditionally thought to be entailed by maximal greatness. If any of those arguments are sound, then Plantinga's 'possibility' premise – *that maximal greatness is possible* – is false.

Reply. Right: if there are sound arguments against the coherence of maximal greatness, then Plantinga's argument is unsound. More generally, if any argument against the existence of God is sound, then no argument for God's existence is sound. Nevertheless, we can bracket the arguments against the existence of God and see how strong POAE is in its own right. In general, there are potentially infinitely many arguments against every philosophical proposition P. If one had to rebut every argument against P in order to successfully defend an argument *for* P, then one could never successfully defend any argument. Fortunately, we can evaluate an argument according to its own merits. Maybe POAE provides some weight in support of its conclusion, while other arguments provide overwhelming counterweights against it. In the final section, we will return to the question how much weight, if any, POAE carries.

Moreover, it is worth highlighting that the arguments against this or that divine attribute do not generally target the coherence of maximal greatness. Even if particular attributes are incoherent, it doesn't follow that maximal greatness itself is incoherent. Perhaps the arguments for the incoherence of various divine attributes help us to navigate past incoherent conceptions of a perfect being. For example, perhaps a being than which none greater can be *coherently* conceived would lack the power to create unliftable rocks; perhaps it couldn't know a future that doesn't exist; perhaps it wouldn't automatically have reflective knowledge of its own knowledge (to avoid set-paradoxes); and so on. Rather than show that there cannot be a maximally great being, perhaps these various arguments helpfully rule out faulty concepts of what such a being would be if there were one.

Objection 3: Many bad events appear to be gratuitous – permitted for no good reason. (More carefully: many bad events are such that there does *not* appear to be a reason for their allowance.) Now putting aside whether any of the bad events are in fact gratuitous, it is at least *conceivable* that some bad event is gratuitous. Conceivability is evidence for possibility. So, we have evidence that possibly some bad event is gratuitous. Yet POAE presses against that possibility. For if POAE is sound, then there is a maximally great being in every possible world. Surely a maximally great being *would* and *could* prevent all gratuitously bad events. So, if there were a maximally great being in every possible world, then gratuitously bad events would exist in no possible world. In other words, if POAE is sound, then gratuitous bad is not even possible. Gratuitous bad is possible. Therefore, POAE is not sound.

Reply. I begin with a cautionary note based upon the distinction between *seeing that something is possible* and *failing to see that something is impossible*. When we conceive of a bad event that is permitted for no reason, do we actually *see* that such an event is possible? Or do we merely fail to see the factors that would make it impossible?

Consider parallel reasoning with respect to H_2O. You think water is H_2O. But Jeb objects, 'It is surely *possible* this watery stuff in lakes and rivers is not H_2O. And, given the necessity of identity, if water *were* really H_2O, then it would not be possible that this watery stuff is not H_2O. Therefore, water is not H_2O.' Jeb is wrong, of course. The problem is that Jeb is not *seeing* into the nature of water. He is therefore unable to tell that water is possibly not H_2O. Similarly, when one imagines a gratuitous bad event, one fails to see that the event *must* have a good reason. It doesn't follow that one thereby *sees* that the bad event possibly doesn't have a good reason. One might fail to see into the factors, if there are any, that would make it impossible for a bad event to be gratuitous. As far as anyone sees, there *might* be factors that would prevent the event from being gratuitous. In particular, there might be a maximally great being. Unless we beg the question at issue and assume that there is no maximally great being, it doesn't seem we are in a position to *just see* that there could be gratuitously bad events. More modestly: you could be someone who fails to just see that there could be gratuitously bad events.

Consider, moreover, that the argument from gratuitous evil doesn't specifically target any *premise* of the POAE. Rather, it targets the conclusion. So, even if the argument from gratuitous evil is sound, that argument doesn't show that POAE carries no weight in its own right.

Objection 4: POAE proves too much. We can use the same reasoning to show that there is a perfect island (à la Gaunilo). First, we show that a perfect island *can* exist:

H1. Some degree of valuable island can be instantiated.
H2. If *some* degree of valuable island can be instantiated, then *each* degree of valuable island can be instantiated.
H3. Therefore, each degree of valuable island can be instantiated (H1, H2).
H4. Maximally great island is a degree of valuable island.
H5. Therefore, a maximally great island can be instantiated.

Then we add a Plantingian ontological argument to deduce that a perfect island actually exists:

H6. There is a possible world W in which there exists a maximally great island.
H7. An island is maximally great in a possible world only if it is maximally great in every world.
H8. Therefore, there is an island that is maximally great in the actual world.

It gets worse. By similar reasoning we can deduce that there are maximally great *fairies*, *unicorns* and *spaghetti monsters*. These results are absurd. Therefore, the reasoning that delivers them is problematic.

Reply. I have two replies. The first is from Plantinga. He suggests that the 'island' argument isn't parallel because we have independent reason to think there can't be a maximally great island. The reason is that for every island one can imagine, one can imagine a *greater* island – one with more fruit trees or exotic animals. So the concept of an island fails to admit of an *intrinsic maximum*. It follows that *maximally great island* is either not a genuine degree of valuable island (contra (H4)) or not a degree which can be exemplified (contra (H2)).

In response to this reply, someone might think POAE is in the same boat. For they might have independent reason to think *maximal greatness* is either not a genuine degree of value (contra (E4)) or not a degree which can be exemplified (contra (E2)). This reason would then defeat POAE.

On the other hand, someone could lack adequate reasons to think maximal greatness is not a genuine property or that it is a degree of value which cannot be exemplified. Speaking for myself, maximal greatness seems to be a genuine property, if anything is. I also have deep reservations about the usual arguments against the exemplifiability of maximal greatness; none are decisive to my mind. In principle, at least, someone could have reasons that defeat the 'maximal island' argument but not the 'maximal being' argument.

Here is a second reason one might think the arguments are importantly different. The 'island' argument requires that necessary existence contributes to the greatness of an *island*, whereas the Value Argument requires that necessary existence contributes to the greatness of a being. Is an island a greater *island* in virtue of existing in more worlds? It seems clear to my mind that necessary existence makes a thing greater with respect to being a *being*, not with respect to being some specific sort of being. If my mind is not misleading me here, then being a maximally great island doesn't by itself entail necessary existence. (In view of the above distinction, one might try modifying the 'island' argument so that 'maximally great island' is short for 'maximally great *being* that happens to be an island'. But this modification doesn't deliver a counterargument because being maximally great *and an island* is not a degree of anything.)[10]

It is worth adding that greatness with respect to *being* is a simpler, more natural concept than greatness with respect to *island*. Consider that one way in which a concept is incoherent is that it has multiple parts that can't go together. For example, the concept of a square-circle is built from two simpler concepts which can't go together (except perhaps in one's mind). Sometimes it is less obvious that concepts can't go together (such as when one combines

[10] I owe this consideration to Rachel Rasmussen.

extension with partlessness, for example, to form the concept of an *extended simple*), but the greater the complexity of a concept the greater the potential for incoherence. Likewise, the simpler the concept the lesser the potential for incoherence. The concept of maximal greatness with respect to being is not nearly as complex in terms of the number of concepts it combines as the concept of a maximally great island. For that reason it has less 'opportunity' to be impossible. More to the point, there is less 'opportunity' to break modal continuity along degrees of greatness simpliciter than along degrees of great islands.

6 Assessment

What shall we make of POAE? Is it successful?

In order to assess whether a given argument is successful, it would help if we had some *standard of success* by which to measure the argument. What makes an argument successful? John Keller has proposed that an argument's success is *relative* to different people.[11] Building on his ideas, I will articulate one measure of 'success' based upon an argument's ability to lead people to see the truth of its conclusion.

I begin by noticing that the success or failure of a given argument depends upon the *purpose* or *purposes* for which the argument is given. My sense is that most of us philosophers are interested in (among other things) increasing our stock of true beliefs, while minimizing our stock of false beliefs. Our purpose as *philosophers* is not primarily to persuade someone. Rather, we wish to expand our understanding of reality. We are truth-seekers. Thus, we deliver arguments in order to *test* their soundness, not in order to win converts. Although we may become invested in an argument, we value peer review because we realize how easily our own biases prevent us from seeing accurately. One central purpose, then, of a philosophical argument is to help people see reality more accurately.

In view of the truth-seeking purpose of arguments, we could say that an argument is successful to the extent that it helps people see more truth. On this account, there are two ingredients to the success of an argument. First, there is *persuasive power*: the argument is such that one who understands it may reasonably become more confident in its conclusion or come to believe its conclusion for the first time. Second, there is *soundness*: the premises are true, and a true conclusion follows from them.

[11] Keller (2016).

Since the soundness of any philosophical argument is typically in dispute, I will focus on the success of an argument at persuading reasonable people. I'll therefore give a 'persuasive power' account of success. There are three salient features of my account:

- First, an argument's success comes in *degrees.* An argument is more successful if it can move more people more. On this account, every argument probably has at least *some* minimal degree of success.
- Second, persuasive power comes in different degrees relative to different people. The argument for the Pythagorean theorem has high persuasive power; and we call it a 'proof'. Some arguments are highly persuasive to some people but not to others. For example, here is an argument that is highly persuasive to me but which probably won't persuade many others:
  1. Joshua Rasmussen has never gone fishing.
  2. If Joshua Rasmussen has never gone fishing, then he has never caught any fish as a result of having gone fishing.
  3. Therefore, Joshua Rasmussen has never caught any fish as a result of having gone fishing.

  This argument is highly successful relative to *me.* The first premise strikes me as obvious given my particular memories, and the second is trivially true. Meanwhile, those who don't have *my* memories will not have my reason for accepting (1). I could testify to my memories, but unless I do that, most people would have no good reason at all to accept premise (1). So, much as I personally like the argument, its success is quite limited.
- Third, an argument's persuasive power depends upon a person's *state of mind.* For example, someone who is in a hurry may consider the premises of an argument quickly without much thought or reflection. Some arguments may be more (or less) persuasive relative to a hurried state of mind. Similarly, if you examine an argument while you are in a state of depression, the argument may appeal differently to you than if you consider it while feeling jovial. So, the persuasive power of an argument is not merely relative to people. It is more generally relative to mental states of people.

To be clear, I am not suggesting that 'persuasive power' is the only feature that contributes to the success of an argument. I'm simply stipulating one 'success'-contributing feature of arguments. My thought here is that an argument that has a high degree of persuasive power is successful in an important respect.

So, is POAE successful in the above sense? Like any argument, there is probably someone somewhere who *could* be moved somewhat by considering its premises. So, the argument probably has at least minuscule success. But does it have more than minuscule success? Could POAE appeal to reasonable people who don't already accept its conclusion?

These are empirical questions which, unfortunately, I cannot answer from my favourite armchair. Plantinga's argument is a pathway of reason that, for all I know, might appeal to some people. I confess that when we supplement his argument with the Value Argument, the resulting pathway presently appeals to my mind to some extent. On the other hand, there may be unforeseen problems with the argument; it is rather new. My biggest worry is that there may be an equally appealing parallel argument for an opposite conclusion. Perhaps someone will spot a reverse argument – other than the ones we considered – that is no less plausible than POAE. Alternatively, people will find parallel arguments which are no less likely *to them* but which will, for various reasons, strike others as importantly different. In that case, POAE could be successful to *some* extent (to some people), even if it lacks the power to distribute knowledge of God to all who consider it. Or: perhaps a parallel argument will indeed be brought to light which virtually everyone would – or should – consider no less plausible than POAE. If that happens, then the argument will become another relic of history rather than an animated force of knowledge or reasonable belief. Time may tell.

10 Tichý

Graham Oddie

Ontological arguments force us to confront questions about the nature and value of existence. My aim in this chapter is to present a little-known analysis of the nature of existence – within a general ontology of offices – and outline its relevance for the soundness of two ontological arguments – one well known, the other somewhat less so.[1] Descartes's much discussed argument has long been criticized for committing some kind of category error, from Kant to Frege. There are two quite different categorial criticisms and between them they are decisive. Anselm's argument in *Proslogion II* has also been much discussed and criticized, but Anselm presents a rather more promising and succinct argument in *Proslogion III*, one which has suffered relative neglect.[2] The *Proslogion III* argument, which commits neither of the two errors that jointly cripple Descartes's, turns out to be logically valid but axiologically unsound.

1 Existence

Descartes takes the concept of God to be that of a being possessing all 'perfections', and he cites as examples of perfection the properties of being 'eternal, infinite, immutable, omniscient, omnipotent'.[3] To this list he notoriously adds *existence*:

> There is not any the less repugnance to our conceiving of a God (that is, of a Being supremely perfect) to whom existence is lacking (that is to say, to whom a certain perfection is lacking) than to conceive of a mountain without a valley.[4]

1 Office theory has been expounded in many papers by Pavel Tichý, starting with Tichý (1971).

2 For example, the mammoth Sobel (2004) devotes considerable space to ontological arguments in general, and to Anselm's *Proslogion II* in particular. Anselm's argument in *Proslogion III* barely rates a mention. Tichý's novel analysis of *Proslogion III*, which I reconstruct and develop here, is presented in Tichý (1979).

3 Descartes (1911). 4 Descartes (1911: 181).

Anselm is more circumspect about our grasp of God's nature or essence. He posits just one rather modest *constraint* on the divine essence – namely, that whichever one it is, nothing outstrips it in greatness. Thus the central term in Anselm's argument is not 'God', but rather 'that than which nothing greater can be conceived'.[5]

> [That than which a greater cannot be thought] exists so truly [really] that it cannot even be thought not to exist. For there can be thought to exist something whose non-existence is inconceivable; and this thing is greater than anything whose non-existence is conceivable. Therefore, if that than which a greater cannot be thought could be thought not to exist, then that than which a greater cannot be thought would not be that than which a greater cannot be thought – a contradiction.[6]

Descartes assumes that *existence* is a property the possession of which enhances the value of its bearer. Anselm assumes that *necessary existence* is such a property. One perennially popular objection to both takes a cue from Kant in denying that existence is any kind of property (or a 'predicate') of a thing. It does not, according to Kant, add to the concept of a thing. This objection is sometimes attributed to Frege as well. The Kantian and Fregean objections are in fact quite different and it is important to disentangle them in order to show that Anselm's argument falls foul of neither.

According to Frege, *first-order concepts* are functions which take objects to True or False. For example, *being an Apostle* or *being a planet* are first-order concepts, functions that take the individuals that fall under the concept to True and the rest to False. When applied to *Matthew*, the concept *Apostle* yields True; when applied to *Trump* it yields False. When applied to *Mars* the concept *Planet* yields True, when applied to *Pluto* it yields False. First-order concepts must be distinguished from second-order concepts, functions which take first-order concepts to True or False. Numbers – like *Twelve* – are second-order concepts. *Twelve* applies to a first-order concept just in case the first-order concept takes exactly twelve individuals to True. *Twelve* takes *Apostle* to True and *Planet* to False. *Existence*, according to Frege, is also a second-order concept, one that is closely related to the numbers:

[5] From here on I will abbreviate 'Anselm's *Proslogion III* argument' to 'Anselm's argument'.

[6] Anselm (1078/2001: 94).

> Affirmation of existence is in fact nothing but denial of the number nought. Because existence is a property of concepts the ontological argument for the existence of God breaks down.[7]

While Frege denies that existence is a property or concept applicable to individuals, he does hold it to be a second-order property or concept, one that applies non-trivially to first-order concepts. Existence claims – like *horses exist but unicorns don't* – are clearly meaningful and some are true, but their subjects are first-order concepts. To apply a second-order concept to an individual results in a straightforward category error.

This is a theory of general existence and non-existence (*existence*^{G}). What does Frege have to say about singular existence and non-existence (*existence*^{S})? In particular what does he say about the existence of *individuals*?

Let *A* be an individual, and consider these two claims: *A exists* and *A doesn't exist*. The second-order concept of existence clearly cannot be intended, on pain of a category error. For these claims to make sense, it seems there must be a quite different, first-order concept of existence. But what concept could that be? Once an individual *A* is given, or presented, in thought or language there is no additional question as to whether *A is*. And if no individual is given then no first-order concept can be either applied or withheld. Frege does concede that one could entertain such a first-order concept of existence, one that applies to individuals rather than to concepts, but he notes that it would be a bit pointless to introduce it. For it would apply of necessity to every individual, and would fail to apply to nothing. Frege notes that there are concepts, like *being self-identical*, that apply of necessity to every individual, and perhaps that is all one means by *individual existence*. This is close to a well-known suggestion – that *A exists* be symbolized in first-order ideography as: $(\exists x)(x = A)$. But on either proposal the first-order concept of existence would apply pleonastically to every individual, and to deny existence of an individual would be to affirm a necessary falsehood.[8] As Frege says:

> Neither in '*A is identical with itself*' nor *in* '*A exists*' does one learn anything new about *A*. Neither statement can be denied. In either you can put anything for *A*, and it still remains true. They do not assign *A* to one of

[7] Frege (1950: § 53).

[8] $A = A$ is necessarily true, and $(\exists x)(x = A)$ follows by existential instantiation. So on both analyses *A exists* expresses a necessary truth, and *A doesn't exist* a necessary falsehood. Neither account explains how *A doesn't exist* might turn out to be both true and informative. At best it might turn out to be a comment not on any individual, but rather on the name '*A*', to the effect that it does not designate anything. Existence as a genuine property of things would still not figure in the analysis.

> two classes in order to mark it off from some *B* which does not belong to that class.[9]

Russell, following Frege, eventually subscribed to this view too, after an early dalliance with Meinongianism.[10] It is a consequence of the Frege–Russell view that if there is a coherent concept of first-order existence, it must apply to all individuals of necessity.

Neither the general second-order concept nor the singular first-order concept can be usefully employed in characterizing God's nature. Using the second-order concept involves a straightforward category error. This is Frege's objection. The first-order concept applies to every individual of necessity, so including it in a list of properties that constitute God's nature would add nothing. This is Kant's objection. Further, on neither proposal could existence constitute a *good* property for an individual to have. On the second-order reading it is not a property of an individual at all. On the first-order reading, it is a property that every individual has of necessity – and having such a property isn't something to brag about.[11]

There is, however, a problem with this otherwise neat twofold analysis. Some existence claims seem to be neither of the general (second-order) kind nor of the necessary (first-order) kind. Some seem both singular and contingent – like *God exists but Satan doesn't.* In the next section I will lay out an analysis that is Fregean in spirit – although Frege himself never embraced it – and show how it naturally accommodates singular existence and non-existence claims.

2 Offices and their Occupants

Consider what many consider to be an identity claim:

1. Donald Trump is the American President.

[9] Frege (1980: 62).

[10] Russell (1903) is more or less a Meinongian. The famous Russell (1905) marked his apostasy. He was not entirely consistent on the subject of existence thereafter but in his best moments he embraces the Fregean position.

[11] It is something of an irony that critics who claim that existence is not a property that things can have or lack often go on to denounce the cosmological argument for trafficking in the concept of a *necessarily existing* being. Their objection is not that necessary existence, like existence, is something that every individual lays claim to, and that because of this all individuals are necessary beings. Nor is it that *contingent existence*, like existence and necessary existence, involves a category error. Rather they claim that *all* individuals that exist exist contingently. But this is either a category error (on the second-order construal) or a necessary falsehood (on the first-order construal).

If (1) is an identity claim then, since it is true, Donald Trump and the American President must be *one and the same entity*. But there are myriad features which set the two apart. Trump and Clinton were both vying to *be* the American President (hereafter *the President*) but neither was vying to be Donald Trump. The President is elected every four years, whereas Trump will be elected at most once more. Because of term limits, the President cannot be the numerically same individual for more than eight years. But Trump not only *can*, but *must* be the numerically same individual, even after he ceases to be the President. It isn't possible for anyone, even Trump, to be the President without being an American citizen (natural born, of course). But it is entirely possible for Trump to be *Trump* without being an American citizen. It is entirely *possible* for Trump not to have been a natural born citizen (had he been born, say, in Scotland), and had he not been natural born, that would have disqualified him from being the President. But it wouldn't and couldn't have disqualified him from being Trump. Not even the most enthusiastic advocate of the thesis of the necessity of origins claims that the *location* of one's birth is an essential property of an individual.[12]

Many philosophers seem perplexed by the discrepancies between *Trump* and *the President*, because they are convinced that there can only be one entity at issue here, and that that one entity has to be an individual. But there is nothing perplexing once we understand that they are not only distinct entities, but two entirely different *types* of entity. *The American President* is an *office*, occupied by different individuals in different possible circumstances, while *Trump* is an *individual*, one who occupies that office in the actual circumstances in 2018. It would hardly be necessary to be labour this if it had not been the subject of such confusion over the course of a century. We are often told that the phrase 'the American President' *denotes*, or *refers to*, or *stands for*, or even *names* an individual – the individual Trump, the one who

[12] Super-essentialists hold that all the properties that an individual has – apart from existence – she could not have failed to have. Leibniz, Meinong and Lewis are super-essentialists. Leibniz and Meinong are explicit about this while Lewis is coy. For Lewis each individual is world-bound, existing literally in only one world. Since Lewis was born in Oberlin, OH, there is no possible circumstance in which *that very individual* was born in Cleveland, OH. Lewis gives the (literally false) claim, that *Lewis himself might have been born in Cleveland*, a figurative reading, viz., that there are non-actual worlds in which neither Lewis nor Cleveland exists but in which there does exist some person more or less like Lewis in sundry respects, who was born somewhere more or less like Cleveland in sundry respects. On the view of first-order existence presented here, the domain of individuals does not and cannot vary from world to world. It is a fixture of the logical space. This view was argued for in multiple papers by Tichý, starting with Tichý (1971). There are extensive passages dedicated to it in Tichý (1988). It has recently been revived by Williamson (see, for example, Williamson (2002)) but he does not cite Tichý's papers.

is of course the current occupant of the office of the American President. But the office and its occupant are undeniably distinct items. As we have seen, there are a plethora of properties to set the two apart. That Trump and the American President appear to have quite different properties is often considered a deep and intractable *puzzle*, the solution of which requires drastic measures. One measure involves the positing of systematic ambiguity in the meaning of phrases as apparently straightforward as 'the American President';[13] another involves denying that anything at all is denoted by 'the American President';[14] another involves the positing of two *distinct* individuals who currently happen to be in the very same location;[15] another involves the abandonment of, or some kind of restriction on, Leibniz's principle of the indiscernibility of identicals; finally, as a final desperate response the discrepancies between Trump and the American President could be reconciled with their identity by embracing them as a rich source of true contradictions.[16]

None of these extreme proposals is mandated by the phenomena. All we need is the simple distinction between individuals and the offices they occupy, the roles they play. Trump is an individual; the American President is an office that Trump currently occupies.

There is, however, one rather plausible-sounding argument in favour of identifying the American President with a certain individual rather with than an office. (2) is true (at least as I am writing this, at the beginning of Trump's second year in office):

2. The American President is arrogant.

Individuals, not offices, are arrogant. It seems to follow that for (2) to be true *the American President* has to be an individual, and an arrogant one.

[13] This is the approach favoured in Frege (2000), and the 'systematic ambiguity' he posits in contexts that clearly set the office apart from its occupant has become something of an entrenched dogma in contemporary philosophy.

[14] This is the approach advocated in Russell (1905). A definite descriptive phrase disappears on proper analysis. There is no 'term' corresponding to it. It does not have a sense, it does not denote a Meinongian pure object, and it does not stand for the individual, if there happens to be one that satisfies the description. The problem with Russell's theory is that it gives the wrong truth-conditions in many contexts, e.g., when a definite description occurs within the scope of a non-propositional attitude.

[15] Here I am extrapolating from a class of solutions to the puzzle of the statue and the lump of clay. The puzzle has a simple solution in office theory, but it has spawned many dualist theories which posit two distinct particulars, one of which is a statue and one of which is a lump of clay. When applied to Trump and the President, such theories ought to posit two distinct but co-located individuals in the Oval Office, although rarely is the theory taken to this startling conclusion.

[16] Although I don't know any para-consistentists who have solved the puzzle in this way; doubtless this, too, will come to pass.

This argument sounds plausible but it ignores the fact that we routinely make claims about the instantiation of individual properties without referring to the particular individual whose instantiation of those properties makes those claims true. For example:

3. There is a rich person sitting in the Oval Office, and he's arrogant.

The state of affairs (**S**) that consists in the individual Trump's being a very rich and arrogant person sitting in the Oval Office is a truth-maker for (3), but (3) does not require that **S** obtain. For example if, at Trump's invitation, David Koch were to sit alone for a while in the Oval Office, (3) would still be true without **S**'s obtaining, as would (4):

4. There is exactly one rich person sitting in the Oval Office, and he's arrogant.

(4) clearly does not predicate arrogance of Trump. On Russell's analysis of definite descriptions, (4) is the correct analysis of (5):

5. The rich person sitting in the Oval Office is arrogant.

If Russell is right then, since (4) doesn't predicate arrogance of Trump, neither does (5). And (2) and (5) either both predicate smartness of Trump or neither does. Obviously what (2) affirms is that a certain office, *the President*, is occupied by an arrogant person. Similarly (5) affirms that a quite different office, *the rich person sitting in the Oval Office*, is also occupied by someone arrogant.[17]

In the actual circumstance, the office of the President is occupied by Trump. Had Trump lost the 2016 election, Clinton would have been the occupant (and (5) might not have been true). And at some future moment Trump will be replaced by a new occupant. So there are two parameters that affect office occupancy – what possible world is actual and what time it is. An office induces a mapping from world-time pairs to individuals. The mapping takes each world-time to the occupant of the office at that world-time (if there is one), and is *undefined* at world-times at which there is no such occupant. *The King of France* maps the actual world at any moment during 1714 to Louis XIV. Since that office is now vacant, it does not map the actual world at any moment in 2018 to any individual. It is a partial mapping. Partial

[17] Russell's theory isn't quite right. Whenever (4) is true so is (5) and vice versa. However, when there is no, or more than one, rich, arrogant politician in the Oval Office, (4) is false while (5) is truth-valueless.

functions are perfectly good functions, and they are, of course, indispensable elements of any general theory of functions.[18]

Each office singles out a unique function from world-times to individuals. Perhaps each such function singles out a unique office. If so we may as well identify an office with the associated function. This, at any rate, is the core of Tichý's office theory.

3 Existence, Requisite and Essence

Certain office claims, like (2), say of an individual office that it is currently occupied by an individual of a certain sort. We can call these *de re* attributions.[19] Other claims – like *the American President is elected every four years* – do not. Some offices are filled by election at four-yearly intervals; others are not. This is a property that *offices* have or lack; *the American President* has it and *the wife of Donald Trump* lacks it. The latter office loses its occupant from time to time, and acquires a new one, but not by popular vote. We can call claims that attribute *office* properties to offices *de dicto* attributions.[20]

Being occupied and *being unoccupied* are office properties. Consider: *the American President* and *the American Dictator*. As of my writing, the first is occupied and the second is not. (If things go badly by the time of publication, their occupancy status may flip.) The claim that *the American President exists* is simply an affirmation of office occupancy. The claim that *the American Dictator doesn't exist* is a denial of office occupancy. Neither claim attributes a property to an individual, either directly or indirectly. This is obvious for the second claim. It would be fatuous to try to gloss it as: *whoever is the occupant of the office of the American Dictator fails to have the property of existence.* But it would be just as fatuous to try to gloss the former claim as: *whoever is the occupant of the office of the American Dictator has the property of existence.* If an office has an occupant, then there is no further question of

[18] We do not have to start with an ontology in which sets are fundamental and functions are derivative. In fact it is far more natural, though less common, to start with functions as fundamental. This is the Fregean approach as developed by Church (1940). Tichý essentially developed Church's extensional theory of types into a partial intensional type theory that added worlds and times to Church's individuals and truth-values (see Tichý (1971), and subsequent papers). The logical apparatus is outlined in Tichý (1982). Tichý (1988) developed it further into a ramified theory that solves the problems of hyper-intensionality in a transparent way within a possible-worlds framework.

[19] For a formal account of the *de re*/*de dicto* see Tichý (1978a).

[20] I am not proposing this as an analysis of *de dicto* claims. There are other *de dicto* claims. See Tichý (1978a).

whether the individual occupant has the first-order property of existence. And if that office doesn't have an individual occupant then the question of whether the occupant has the property of existence or not simply doesn't arise.

Office theory happily combines the Frege–Russell view of *general* existence claims (that existence is not a first-order-property that *particulars* contingently have or lack) with the obvious fact that there are interesting singular existence and non-existence claims. But in all such cases the subject of the existence claim is an office, and the claim is that the office in question has the property of being occupied.[21]

In order to occupy a particular office an individual has to have properties that are essentially linked to that office. To occupy the office of the American President an individual has to be, inter alia, an American citizen. These properties are *requisites* of the office. Of necessity anything that occupies an office has to have all the requisites of the office. Call the conjunction of all requisites of an office its *essence*. Being the unique bearer of an office's essence is sufficient for one to occupy it. Unlike *being a natural born American citizen*, the property of *being rich* is no part of the essence of *the American President* (though it may be a contingent requirement as things stand). However, being rich is a requisite of the office of *the rich person sitting in the Oval Office.*

By definition of *requisite*, the occupant of an office, at each world-time, is guaranteed to have all the requisites of the office at that world-time. Because of this it may be tempting to endorse the following inference schema concerning requisites:

(+) *P is a requisite of O. Therefore, the occupant of O possesses P.*

Let *P* be *rich* and let *O* be the office of *the rich American Dictator.* The premise of (+) is true, but is the conclusion, *the rich American Dictator is rich*, true? Interpreted as a claim ascribing a requisite to that office it is true, but interpreted as a *de re* claim about the nature of the occupant of the office, it is not true. Compare it with *the rich American Dictator has very small hands.* This clearly is not currently true because no one currently occupies the office of *the rich American Dictator*, though with certain developments it may

[21] Why not just eliminate offices in favour of certain properties? After all for each office there is the property of uniquely instantiating the conjunction of its requisites. In fact this is very close to Russell's proposal, and it suffers many of the shortcomings of that. I do not have space here to deal with those, but one obvious defect is that it deems the extension of *the present King of France* to be a set (either a singleton or the empty set) and that just seems wrong. If *the present King of France exists*, the extension of *the present King of France* is an individual, not a singleton of an individual. If *the present King of France* does not exist then it has no extension. Office theory preserves this intuition, the property proposal does not.

become true. It is a matter of debate whether *the rich American Dictator has very small hands* is false (Russell) or truth-valueless (Strawson). Whether Russell or Strawson is right about this, (+) is invalid. There is, however, a closely related valid schema, one with an additional occupancy premise:

> (++) *P is a requisite of O. O is occupied (O exists). Therefore, the occupant of O instantiates P.*

The conflation of (+) with (++) leads to many of the unacceptable consequences in Meinong's theory of pure objects, including the affirmation of contradictions. Meinong postulates pure objects – objects that are 'indifferent to existence' – and these function both as the bearers of individual properties and the subjects of contentful existence and non-existence claims. Meinong proclaims, rather boldly: 'Not only is the much heralded golden mountain made of gold, but the round square is as surely round as it is square.'[22] The golden mountain is an object that fails to exist, according to Meinong, precisely *because* it *has* the properties being golden and a mountain – whereas no *existent* object has those two properties.

Meinong's pure objects are not quite as absurd as they are often made out to be. A pure object is, according to the first component of the theory, whatever entity functions as the subject of interesting and informative singular existence claims – and, for the reasons already given, that cannot be a concrete individual. It might, however, be an office that concrete individuals may or may not occupy or embody. But if he were to embrace this idea, Meinong would have to drop the second component of the theory of pure objects. *Being golden* would then be a requisite (rather than a property) of the office of *the golden mountain.* Since (+) fails, Meinong cannot infer from this that *the golden mountain is golden.* And to apply (++) Meinong would need, in addition, the premise that *the golden mountain exists* – a patently false existence claim that Meinong himself keenly denies.

If pure objects are identified with offices, and their essential properties are construed rather as office requisites, many of the problematic features of Meinong's theory either disappear or are rendered harmless. The incompleteness of *the golden mountain*, for example, is just the obvious fact that its requisite set is sparse. Further, it is not at all contradictory to assert that *there are* things (like *the golden mountain*) that *don't exist* (viz., are not occupied or embodied by any individual). Furthermore, an office can have contradictory requisites (like *being round* and *being square*) without having contradictory

[22] Meinong (1960: 82).

properties, thereby violating the law of non-contradiction. Contradictory requisites do render an office impossible, but only in the sense that it is logically impossible for such an office to be occupied. There could be no object that is both round and square, and so the office remains necessarily vacant, necessarily unembodied.

4 Greatness and God's Nature

The claim that *God exists* is meaningful and contentful, as is its negation. This is unproblematic if 'God' stands not for an individual but rather for an office. *God exists* predicates occupancy of the divine office. But which office is that? What are its requisites? Anselm, unlike Descartes, does not presume to know the precise contours of God's nature. He appeals to just one obvious fact about it, one that even the Fool grasps: namely that, of necessity, *whichever nature it is*, it is greater than any other. The items being compared for greatness here are those that can be said to exist or not exist. So the greatness relation doesn't order the domain of concrete individuals – at least not in the first instance.[23] Rather, it is an ordering of offices.

We routinely compare offices for greatness. Few would dispute, for example, that *the President of the United States* is greater than *the Prime Minister of New Zealand*. This is not because Trump, the current occupant of the former office, has some wonderful individual properties that Jacinda Ardern, the current occupant of the latter office, lacks. Their relative greatness depends at least in part on features of the two offices, regardless of who occupies them. Likewise, *the New Zealand Prime Minister* is greater than *the New Zealand Minister of Finance*, since the latter serves at the pleasure of the former and cannot implement fiscal policies without the former's approval. However, when Muldoon became the Prime Minister in 1975 he promptly appointed himself Minister of Finance. His co-occupancy of the two offices didn't alter the fact that the former is greater than the latter. Co-occupied offices can possess different levels of greatness. (*The President of the United States* and *Stormy Daniels' most notorious customer* are distinct offices that are, currently, co-occupied, though the former is still greater than the latter.) Finally, offices can be compared for greatness even if one or other or both are unoccupied. It is quite coherent to claim that the occupied office of *the American President* is greater than the unoccupied office of *the American Dictator*, on the grounds that an

[23] An individual may of course have greatness conferred on her through her occupation of a great office.

office whose occupancy requires a democratic mandate is, other things being equal, greater than an office whose occupancy would require acts of despotism. Of course, the ordering of offices may be sensitive to changes in occupancy. It is not incoherent to claim, as some do, that Trump is grossly diminishing the greatness of the office of the American President. And it is certainly not insensitive to other matters of fact. If Trump starts a nuclear war that reduces the USA to rubble while leaving New Zealand intact, the relative standings of the American President and the New Zealand Prime Minister might well be reversed. So the greater-than relation is best regarded as contingent. Its extension (a mapping from pairs of offices to truth-values) may differ from world-time to world-time.

Just as there are offices for individuals to occupy, there are also offices for offices to occupy. Consider *the most powerful office in the world.* Currently this is *the American President*, but if dissatisfied Trump supporters successfully stage a coup after his impeachment for obstruction of justice, *the American Dictator* may well become that instead. Something that different individual offices can be or become cannot itself be an *individual* office. One individual office cannot become another distinct individual office. Rather, *the most powerful office in the world* is a second-order office, an office first-order offices can occupy. It is currently occupied by *the American President*, but in the nineteenth century it was arguably occupied by *the Queen of Great Britain* and it may well become occupied by *the American Dictator.*

The *greater-than* relation undergirds a rather special second-order office: *that individual office such that no individual office is greater than it.* Or simply: *that than which none is greater*. Let this office be **H**. The occupant of **H**, if there is one, depends on the extension of the greater-than relation. It is this second-order office, Tichý claims, that Anselm's phrase *that than which a greater cannot be thought* denotes. What relation does *God* bear to the second-order office **H**?

> As for the term 'God itself', it is best reserved for the divine office, i.e., for whichever individual-office (if any) happens to occupy the second order office **H**. This at any rate seems to be Anselm's construal of the term. For he admits readily that when he – let alone the Fool – speaks of God, he does not quite know what he is talking about. Yet he is absolutely positive that even the Fool can grasp 'that than which nothing greater can be conceived'.[24]

Individual offices form the first order of an infinite hierarchy of orders. Order-1 offices are occupied by individuals (which we stipulate are 0-order entities) and

[24] Tichý (1979: 414).

these have as requisites individual properties – properties that individuals have or lack. Order-n+1 offices are occupied by order-n offices, and have as requisites properties that order-n offices can have or lack. Just as individual offices (order-1 offices) instantiate office-properties and have as requisites individual properties, order-n+1 offices have properties of order-n offices as requisites, while themselves instantiating order-n+1 properties. Among the properties that order-n offices have or lack is order-n existence, ($\mathbf{E}_n$). $\mathbf{E}_n$ is the property instantiated by an order-n office just in case it is occupied. As a property of an order-n office $\mathbf{E}_n$ cannot function as a requisite of order-n offices. However, it can serve as requisite for an order-n+1 office. For example, since $\mathbf{E}_1$ is a property individual offices have or lack, $\mathbf{E}_1$ cannot serve as a requisite of an order-1 office, but it is perfectly appropriate for it to feature among the requisites of a second-order office. It is, for example, explicitly incorporated in the requisites of the following office: *the greatest occupied political office in America.* This is a second-order office which is occupied by an individual office only if that first-order office itself is occupied by some individual.

Just as there are things that exist or fail to exist as a matter of contingent fact, so too there are things that exist or fail to exist of necessity. *He who loves all and only those who don't love themselves* necessarily lacks existence at every world-time. It is a necessarily vacant office. An office possesses existence of necessity if it possesses existence at every world-time. An individual office is necessarily occupied ($\mathbf{N}_1$) just in case it possesses $\mathbf{E}_1$ of necessity. And if an individual office possesses $\mathbf{N}_1$ at any world-time, then of course it possesses $\mathbf{N}_1$ at every world-time. The same goes, of course, for higher-order offices and higher-order necessary existence. Like $\mathbf{E}_1$, $\mathbf{N}_1$ is a perfectly good property for an individual office to have, and it makes perfect sense to ask whether or not $\mathbf{N}_1$ is among the requisites of a second-order office like **H** – *that than which none is greater.*

5 The Argument in *Proslogion III*

Anselm's desired conclusion (C) is:

(C) That than which none is greater exists of necessity.

Because **H** is a second-order office and there are existence/occupancy properties for each order, (C) is ambiguous. It could be construed as the (*de dicto*) claim about **H** itself, that **H** is necessarily occupied. That, however, is not the ultimate conclusion that Anselm is seeking. In fact as we will see, he does need the proposition that **H** is occupied – that **H** possesses $\mathbf{E}_2$ – as an intermediate step, but he does not require the *necessary* occupancy of **H** (that **H** possesses $\mathbf{N}_2$).

The ultimate conclusion (C) is more plausibly construed as the (*de re*) claim that whatever office occupies **H** must itself be occupied. In order to establish (C), Anselm makes the following bold axiological claim:

> ... something whose non-existence is inconceivable ... is greater than anything whose non-existence is conceivable.

Something whose non-existence is inconceivable is simply an office that possesses necessary existence, $\mathbf{N}_1$. So Anselm is committing to the following axiological claim:

(A) Any first-order office **O** that has $\mathbf{N}_1$ is greater than any first-order office that lacks $\mathbf{N}_1$.

At first blush, (A) does support Anselm's requisite claim:

(B) $\mathbf{N}_1$ is a requisite of **H** (*that than which none is greater*).

Suppose, for the sake of a *reductio*, that (A) is true and (B) false. Then there is an office O that occupies **H** at some world-time but which lacks $\mathbf{N}_1$. Note that an office lacks $\mathbf{N}_1$ at one world-time just in case it lacks $\mathbf{N}_1$ at all world-times. So O lacks $\mathbf{N}_1$ at every world-time. Let O^* be an office that has $\mathbf{N}_1$ at some (hence all) world-times. From (A) it follows that O^* is greater than O at all world-times, including the world-time at which O occupies **H**. (Contradiction.)

This argument makes a tacit appeal to the following auxiliary premise:

(N) There is an office O^* that possesses $\mathbf{N}_1$.

If (N) is false then (A) is vacuously and necessarily true, and at any world-time at which a second-order office like **H** is occupied, its occupant must lack $\mathbf{N}_1$. But then (B) is necessarily false provided only that **H** has an occupant at at least one world-time. In the first part of the passage above Anselm does affirm a proposition that entails (N): namely, that it is *possible* that there be something that has necessary existence. For suppose at some world-time O^* possesses $\mathbf{N}_1$ – then O^* itself possesses $\mathbf{N}_1$ at every world-time.

However, there is a much more direct argument for (N) within office theory. An office is a function from world-times to individuals. A necessarily occupied office is a total function from world-times to individuals. It is defined at every argument. And there are, of course, a plethora of those.[25]

[25] What if there are world-times at which no individuals exist? In that case won't every office be empty at such a world-time? But by now the reader will discern the error lurking in this objection. Hint: it assumes a first-order property of existence that individuals can have or lack.

(A) and (N) yield (B). However, the step from (B) to (C) is an instance of the fallacious schema (+) the tacit appeal to which crippled Descartes's argument. To apply the valid schema (++) we need an additional premise:

(E) **H** *is occupied* (i.e., **H** possesses $\mathbf{E}_2$).

(E) is not the question-begging claim that *God* (or the office that occupies **H**) exists, but rather the claim that *the greatest office* itself exists (viz., that there is some office that in fact occupies **H**). If **H** is occupied then **H**'s occupant has to have all of **H**'s requisites. In light of (B), one such requisite is $\mathbf{N}_1$. (C) follows from (B) and (E).

Anselm does give an argument for (E) in an earlier work, the *Monologion*. Grant that the *greater-than* relation is transitive, asymmetric and connected. Then there are just two ways that **H** might fail to be occupied. It might be that for every office *O* there is some office that exceeds *O* in greatness. Or it might be that there is more than one office that no office exceeds in greatness, where these optimally great offices are equally great. In the *Monologion*, Anselm argues against these two possibilities. His argument against the first is a *reductio* – it would imply an infinity of offices which he takes to be absurd. The argument against the second is more obscure and although I believe it can be given an interesting office-theoretic analysis there is no space for that here. Whether or not Anselm successfully blocks these two possibilities, he seems to have seen the necessity for a supremum in the order of natures, in order to forestall an embarrassing objection to his argument. In fact his arguments, if sound, would appear to establish not just that **H** is occupied (i.e., **H** possesses $\mathbf{E}_2$ in fact), but that it is necessarily occupied (i.e., **H** possesses $\mathbf{N}_2$). Although Anselm does not need this, it is nevertheless interesting.

(A) and (N) entail (B), and (B) and (E) entail (C) by the valid inference schema (++). On this reconstruction Anselm's argument is valid. If Anselm's argument fails in the end it is not because he made some elementary error in logic or committed an egregious category error.

6 Anselm's Axiology of Existence

Is Anselm's argument sound? Perhaps the most controversial premise in the argument is the axiological claim (A). Anselm simply asserts it, but is it plausible? What argument might be given for it?

Let's assume that the greatness of a first-order office depends in some systematic way on the values of the properties of the office. One set of properties that will be relevant is the office's requisites. The following general principle suggests itself.

Requisite: If *P* is a valuable property for an individual to have then having *P* as requisite is a valuable property for an office to have.

We need a principle to connect valuable office properties with the relative greatness of the offices of which they are requisites, but here we have to tread carefully. The contribution to greatness that *having P as requisite* confers on an office will depend on the value of property *P* itself. Let omnipotence (**P**) be the sole requisite of the office $\mathbf{O^P}$ (*the omnipotent one*). Now add *omniscience* (**K**) as an additional requisite and we obtain the office of *the omnipotent and omniscient one* ($\mathbf{O^{P\&K}}$). If being omniscient is a valuable property too, then **P&K** is more valuable than **P**, and so $\mathbf{O^{P\&K}}$ is greater than $\mathbf{O^P}$. Or so it would seem. In fact, because the value of a conjunction may not be the simple sum of the values of its conjuncts, we need to add (an admittedly vague) *ceteris paribus* clause.[26]

Difference: If *P* is a valuable property for an office to have then, *ceteris paribus*, an office that has *P* is greater than one that does not.

Given some rather obvious and fairly natural value assumptions, the following properties increase in value in the following order:

L: at least as knowledgeable as anyone else
K: all-knowing
A: all-knowing, all-powerful and all-loving

This ordering of properties, in conjunction with *Requisite* and *Difference*, entails that (other things being equal) $\mathbf{O^A}$ is greater than $\mathbf{O^K}$, which in turn is greater than $\mathbf{O^L}$. Now, one might be tempted to derive (A) from *Difference* and the premise that $\mathbf{N_1}$ is a good property.

[26] Suppose knowledge and moral depravity come in degrees and consider the following:

D: *being morally depraved exactly to the degree that one is knowledgeable*
K: *being all-knowing*

Consider $\mathbf{O^D}$. This is not a great office by any means. Add **K** as requisite obtain the office $\mathbf{O^{D\&K}}$. The occupant of $\mathbf{O^{D\&K}}$ is morally depraved exactly to the degree that she is knowledgeable and she is maximally knowledgeable, so she is also maximally morally depraved. It would be difficult to argue that $\mathbf{O^{D\&K}}$ is greater than $\mathbf{O^D}$. Any additional value that being omniscient bestows is presumably undermined by the disvalue of the additional depravity to which it is yoked in $\mathbf{O^{D\&K}}$. These two changes pull with equal force in opposite directions so that, at best, $\mathbf{O^{D\&K}}$ is no greater than $\mathbf{O^D}$.

Suppose $\mathbf{N}_1$ a good property. By *Difference*, it follows that, other things being equal, possessing $\mathbf{N}_1$ makes an office greater. But how can two offices, one of which is only occupied at some world-times and the other of which is occupied at all world-times, be otherwise equal?

Here is one proposal. Where *O* is a partial function, call any total function O^* that delivers the same occupant as *O* wherever *O* is defined, a *total extension* of *O*. A total extension of *O* possesses $\mathbf{N}_1$. A total extension O^* of *O* is thus just like *O* except that it possesses $\mathbf{N}_1$. Unfortunately even if $\mathbf{N}_1$ itself is a good office property, O^* might well possess bad requisites that undermine any additional value that $\mathbf{N}_1$ confers. Let **A** be some really valuable property, like being *all-knowing, all-powerful and all-loving.* $\mathbf{O}^{\mathbf{A}}$ is *the all-knowing, all-powerful, all-loving one.* Assume that **A** is only contingently instantiated and that $\mathbf{O}^{\mathbf{A}}$ is thus only contingently occupied. Consider **Worst** – the property of *being no less morally depraved than any other individual* – and let *Pick* be a choice function, one that selects one individual from each non-empty collection of individuals. Let $\mathbf{O}^{\mathbf{A*Worst}}$ be the following total extension of $\mathbf{O}^{\mathbf{A}}$: at a world-time at which $\mathbf{O}^{\mathbf{A}}$ is vacant the occupant of $\mathbf{O}^{\mathbf{A*Worst}}$ is the pick of the worst. $\mathbf{O}^{\mathbf{A*Worst}}$ is total and so it possesses $\mathbf{N}_1$ but it is considerably less great than $\mathbf{O}^{\mathbf{A}}$. $\mathbf{O}^{\mathbf{A*Worst}}$ has a property as requisite that is logically weaker than **A**, namely **A*Worst**: *either being all-knowing, all-powerful and all-loving, or, in the absence of anything having those properties, being the pick of the worst.* But **A*Worst** is not as valuable a property as **A**. Imagine, for example, that you are given a choice between possessing **A** and possessing **A*Worst.** The transition from $\mathbf{O}^{\mathbf{A}}$ to $\mathbf{O}^{\mathbf{A*Worst}}$ does ensure necessary occupancy, but only at the cost of sacrificing some of the greatness of $\mathbf{O}^{\mathbf{A}}$. So *Difference* does not ensure (A) even given the assumption that $\mathbf{N}_1$ is a good office property.

What we need to derive (A) is not the relatively plausible *Difference* principle governing *good* properties, but rather a Trumping principle governing *great* properties.

> *Trumping*: *P* is a *great* office property if and only if any office with *P* is greater than any office without *P*.

The concept of a great property is a coherent one and there are provable instances of it. For example, for any office *O* the property of *being at least as great as O* is clearly a great property, and is so of necessity. There are also contingently great properties. The property of *enjoying greatness parity with O* is a great property at those world-times at which *O* is no less great than any office, and isn't great at the rest. Lest one think that all great properties trade on an already given greatness ordering on offices, consider the property of being both occupiable and having **A** as requisite. One could easily be forgiven for thinking this is a great property. Any office that boasts **A** amongst its requisites seems greater than any that does not.[27]

Greatness is thus a genuine property of office properties, and (A) is the claim that $\mathbf{N}_1$ is great. Let $\mathbf{O}^{\mathbf{Worst}}$ be the office of *the pick of the most morally depraved.* $\mathbf{O}^{\mathbf{Worst}}$ is everywhere occupied – it possesses $\mathbf{N}_1$ – and $\mathbf{O}^{\mathbf{A}}$ lacks $\mathbf{N}_1$. So if $\mathbf{N}_1$ is great, *the pick of the most morally depraved* is greater than *the all-knowing, all-powerful and all-loving one.* That's not a result a theist should quickly embrace.

The last example may beg the question against ontological arguments – by assuming that no sound argument can succeed in establishing the necessary occupancy of $\mathbf{O}^{\mathbf{A}}$. To make the same point without begging any questions, consider the obviously contingent property of *discovering the incompleteness of arithmetic* (**I**). $\mathbf{O}^{\mathbf{I}}$ is the office of *the discoverer of the incompleteness of arithmetic.* $\mathbf{O}^{\mathbf{I}}$ is quite high up in the ranking of offices by greatness, and it is only contingently occupied. But *the discoverer of the incompleteness of arithmetic* is surely no less great than *the pick of the worst.*

Anselm's axiological principle (A) is thus *deeply* implausible. But perhaps he does not need anything nearly as strong. Perhaps there is some weaker and more plausible principle in the ballpark of (A) that will serve as well. (A) entails the principle that if *O* is partial then every total extension of *O* is greater than *O*. That, as we have seen leads to unacceptable results. But consider the following very much weaker consequence of this:

(G) If *O* is partial then some total extension of *O* is greater than *O*.

(G) is sufficiently strong to entail (B): that the greatest office, if there is one, is necessarily occupied. And (B), together with (E) – that the greatest office is occupied by some first-order office, God – entails the desired conclusion (C) – that God exists of necessity.

(G) is obviously very much weaker than (A) but is it true? Let's agree that $\mathbf{O}^{\mathbf{A}}$ is great. If one were to learn of an individual that she is the occupant of $\mathbf{O}^{\mathbf{A}}$ – that she and she alone instantiates that wonderful trio of requisites – it would be entirely appropriate for one to be in awe of her. At every world-time at which $\mathbf{O}^{\mathbf{A}}$ is occupied, it is occupied by an individual who is undeniably, and quite literally, *awesome.* There are lots of world-times at which $\mathbf{O}^{\mathbf{A}}$ is vacant.

[27] With the caveat that if a requisite set includes **A** but also includes properties, like being maximally morally depraved, that are logically incompatible with **A** then the resulting office (which is necessarily unoccupied) is not greater than all offices that lack **A** as requisite.

Let's extend $\mathbf{O}^{\mathbf{A}}$ to $\mathbf{O}^{\mathbf{A/Best}}$. Wherever $\mathbf{O}^{\mathbf{A}}$ is vacant, pick an individual who possesses, at that world-time, the *best* configuration of good properties that any individual possesses at that world-time. (If there are ties, make it the pick of the best.) There are, of course, many world-times, perhaps most of them, that feature no truly *awesome* individuals at all, even if they feature some reasonably good ones – awesomeness is a property that is exemplified only rarely – and at all those world-times $\mathbf{O}^{\mathbf{A^*Best}}$ is going to be filled by some less than awesome individuals, some very much less so. Consider learning of an individual simply that she occupies $\mathbf{O}^{\mathbf{A^*Best}}$. Would it be appropriate to be in *awe* of her? No. At worlds at which no one at all is awesome, the occupant of $\mathbf{O}^{\mathbf{A^*Best}}$ fails to be awesome too. In many or most of those worlds, the occupant will turn out to be very far from awesome. In fact, at any world-time at which all individuals are both despicable and all equally bad, $\mathbf{O}^{\mathbf{A^*Best}}$ and $\mathbf{O}^{\mathbf{A^*Worst}}$ and $\mathbf{O}^{\mathbf{Worst}}$ will all be occupied *by the very same individual.*

$\mathbf{O}^{\mathbf{A^*Best}}$ is, I think, the most promising candidate on offer for a total extension of $\mathbf{O}^{\mathbf{A}}$ greater than $\mathbf{O}^{\mathbf{A}}$ itself, but $\mathbf{O}^{\mathbf{A^*Best}}$ clearly fails in that regard. To obtain a total extension of $\mathbf{O}^{\mathbf{A}}$ we have to relax its very stringent requisites, and in doing so we replace the highly demanding and valuable trio of requisites in **A** with something much less demanding and much less valuable, thereby tumbling down the ladder of greatness to a rung occupancy of which does not and should not command our awe. Since (G) is among the weakest of the intuitively plausible consequences of (A) that would still guarantee (B), prospects for an axiologically sound version of Anselm's argument are grim.

7 Upshot

Interpreted within a higher-order office ontology, Anselm's argument in *Proslogion III* is not only much clearer than its *Proslogion II* partner, and much richer than its Cartesian descendant, it appeals to a coherent account of existence. But Anselm was a better logician than he was an axiologist. It is Anselm's assumptions about the *value* of existence, rather than about its logic, that render the argument in *Proslogion III* unsound. And the basic flaw in Anselm's axiology is unfortunately essential to his strategy. The greatness of an office does not increase with the probability of its being embodied. Necessary existence is really nothing to write home about.

11 Conceivability and Possibility

Joshua Spencer*

Consider the following simple, modal ontological argument:

1. It is possible that God exists.
2. If it is possible that God exists, then God exists.
3. So, God exists.[1]

A lot of interesting work in modal logic has been marshalled in defence of line (2). Here's the basic idea. Suppose it's necessary that if God exists, then God necessarily exists. Then, under the assumption that it's possible that God exists, it follows it's possible that God necessarily exists. But – here's where the modal logic comes in handy – if it's possible that God necessarily exists, then God necessarily exists; and if God necessarily exists, then God just flat out exists. So, from our assumption that it's possible God exists, it follows that God exists. Hence, line (2).

What about line (1)? Why should anyone believe it's possible that God exists? Here's one answer: we should believe it's possible that God exists because we can conceive that God exists. In this chapter, I will be exploring the connection between conceivability and possibility, and support from conceivability for the argument presented above. Here's how the chapter will be structured. First, I will characterize the notion of conceivability by comparing it to perceivability. Then, I will consider analyses of conceivability in terms of imagination. Next, I will consider analyses in terms of conceptual coherence. Finally, I will look at the prospects of supporting the modal ontological argument through conceivability.

* Thanks to the members of my fall 2015 seminar on conceivability and possibility for many helpful discussions and for reading an early draft of this paper. Thanks to Stan Husi and Kris McDaniel for reading and commenting on early drafts of this paper. And special thanks to Fabrizio Mandadori who extensively discussed these issues with me throughout the 2015/16 academic year. Fabrizio's insights on this topic are extensive and I am afraid that I cannot do this topic the kind of justice it deserves in a short essay.

[1] A more complex variant of the modal ontological argument is developed by Hartshorne (1965), Malcolm (1960) and Plantinga (1974). The argument is further discussed by Oppy (1995, 2016) and by van Inwagen (1977, 2015).

1 Conceivability and Perceivability

Some people take the fact that one conceives a proposition as a premise in a little argument for the conclusion that that proposition is possible. Others take the fact that one conceives a proposition to constitute prima facie evidence for the possibility of that proposition. In this paper, I will be interested in the latter of these approaches. I find it fruitful, on the latter approach, to investigate another evidence-constituting mental state. Specifically, I find it fruitful to investigate perceivability in order to learn what an adequate theory of conceivability (as an evidence-constituting mental state) must look like.

The claim that something is perceivable may be taken in one of two ways. First, it may be taken as the claim that someone, either a particular someone or someone in general, is able to perceive it. On this way of taking the claim, our attention should properly be focused on *subjects* (i.e., perceivers) and their mental states of perceiving. We should be seeking to characterize and analyse the mental state of perceiving and asking what it is about various perceivers that makes them able to grasp objects by way of that mental state. Alternatively, it might be taken as the claim that something is apt to be perceived. On this way of taking the claim, our attention should properly be focused on the *objects* of perception (which, for simplicity, we will take to be states of affairs). We should be asking what it is about various objects that makes them apt to be grasped by way of that mental state.[2]

Focus on the subject side of perception for a moment. Note that perceptions can go awry. There's a difference between perceiving and *mis*perceiving. Presumably a misperceiving occurs when someone has nearly everything that it takes to be perceiving, but somehow or other gets things wrong. Let's say that when someone, S, is in a mental state as if S were perceiving O being F, then S perceives O being F only if it is actually the case that O is F. On the other hand, when S is in a sensory state as if S were

[2] A similar distinction appears in Aquinas, clearly stated in *Expositio Super Librum Boethii De Trinitate*, q. 4, a. 3, ad 1; Aquinas (1959: 151). The distinction also appears in Scotus (1298/9), where it is most clearly stated in *Lectura II*, Dist. 3, pars 1, Q 5–6, n. 180. In *Lectura II*, Scotus says: '. . .the fact that [the singular] is not understood *per se* by our intellect is not due to the singular itself but to the imperfection of our intellect; in the same way the fact that the owl does not see the sun is not due to the sun itself, but to the owl'. Thanks to Fabrizio Mondadori for translating this passage.

perceiving O being F, if it's not actually the case that O is F, then S misperceives O being F.[3]

Focus, now, on the object side of perception. Some states of affairs are apt to be perceived and others are not. The state of affairs of three being prime just isn't apt to be perceived. It involves an abstract object rather than a concrete object and it involves a feature that cannot be detected via sensory perception. But what about states of affairs that *do* involve concrete things and that *do* involve features that can be detected by sensory perception? Are all of those states of affairs apt to be perceived? Probably not. The state of affairs of Wesley (my cat) being orange is apt to be perceived. It's apt to be perceived partly because Wesley is in fact orange. The state of affairs of Wesley being grey, if it exists, is not apt to be perceived. That's because Wesley just isn't grey. Of course, if Wesley had been grey, then the state of affairs of Wesley being grey would have been apt to be perceived. But that isn't enough to make it actually apt to be perceived.

Now let's turn to conceivability. Just as with perceivability, the claim that something is conceivable may be taken in one of two ways. First, it may be taken as the claim that someone, either a particular someone or someone in general, is able to conceive it. On this way of taking the claim, our attention should properly be focused on *subjects* (i.e., conceivers) and their mental states of conceiving. We should be seeking to characterize and analyse the mental state of conceiving and asking what it is about various conceivers that makes them able to grasp objects by way of that mental state. Alternatively, it might be taken as the claim that something is apt to be conceived. On this way of taking the claim, our attention should properly be focused on the *objects* of conceiving (i.e., propositions). We should be asking what it is about various objects that makes them apt to be grasped by way of that mental state.

Focus on the subject side for a moment. Note that conceiving can go awry. There's a difference between conceiving and *mis*conceiving. Presumably a misconceiving occurs when someone has nearly everything that it takes to be conceiving, but somehow or other gets things wrong. Let's say that when someone, S, is in a mental state as if S were conceiving that O is F then S conceives that O is F only if it's possible that O is F. On the other hand, when S is in a mental state as if S were conceiving that O is F, if it impossible for O to be F, then S misconceives that O is F. But if all of that is true, then someone is able to conceive a proposition only if it is possible.

[3] It isn't obvious to me what the difference is between a misperception and a hallucination. For the remainder of this paper, I will be ignoring this distinction.

Focus, now, on the object side of conceiving. Are all propositions apt to be conceived? Probably not. Although some impossible propositions would be apt to be conceived if they were possible, it seems plausible that a proposition is apt to be conceived only if it is in fact possible. We again have, then, that a proposition is conceivable only if it is possible.

So, from the subject side of things, we have that someone conceives (rather than misconceives) a proposition only if it is possible. And from the object side of things, we have that a proposition is apt to be conceived by someone only if it is possible. So, we will take this as our first constraint on an adequate account of conceivability.

The Representation Constraint: If S conceives that P, then P is possible.[4]

Now, let's briefly return to perceiving. When someone, S, perceives O being F, then S is prima facie reasonable in believing that O is F. After all, there is an explanatory connection between an actual state of affairs and S's perceiving; the state of affairs causes S's perceiving. Moreover, this causal connection is underwritten by a law-like pattern between actual states of affairs of a particular type and perceivings of a particular type. The causal connection which is underwritten by a law-like pattern partly grounds that S is prima facie reasonable in believing that O is F when S perceives O being F.

Similarly, if conceivability generates reasonable belief in possibility, then when S conceives that P, S is prima facie reasonable in believing that P. We'll take this to be the second constraint on an adequate theory of conceivability.

The Epistemic Constraint: If S conceives that P, then S is prima facie reasonable in believing that P is possible.[5]

And, on an adequate theory of conceivability, there should be an explanatory connection between the possible truth of a proposition and one's conceiving that proposition; an explanatory connection that partly grounds that S is prima facie reasonable in believing that P is possible when S conceives that P. We'll take this to be the third constraint on an adequate theory of conceivability.

[4] Yablo (1993) considers a similar constraint. But since he assumes that conceivings can be fallible, he suggests that the veracity condition for conceiving includes the possibility of what is conceived. So, according to Yablo, if I conceive that P, then my conceiving that P is veridical only if P is in fact possible. Most of what I say below could be said if the constraint were stated as a veracity condition rather than a necessary condition on conceiving itself.

[5] One might also hold that if S is in a mental state as if S were conceiving that P, then S is prima facie reasonable in believing that P is possible. This would allow one to be reasonable in believing that P is possible even when one has misconceived that P.

The Explanatory Constraint: If S conceives that P, then there is an explanatory connection between the fact that P is possible and the fact that S conceives that P.

This third constraint is probably the most difficult to accommodate. It is highly implausible that facts about what is possible cause facts about what various people conceive. What seems more likely is that whatever grounds that P is possible also grounds that S is able to conceive that P.

Let's keep each of these constraints in mind as we consider two of the most plausible and best-defended approaches of conceivability. We'll say that any notion of conceivability that satisfies these three constraints is a notion of *philosophical conceivability*.

2 Conceivability as Imaginability

Some people try to assimilate conceivability and imaginability. Stephen Yablo (1993) for example, defends the following account of conceiving:[6]

The First Imagination Account: S conceives that P iff S imagines a world, w, such that S takes w to verify that P.[7]

So, on this view, if I imagine a world such that I take it to verify that some lions have stripes, I thereby conceive that some lions have stripes. I imagine such a world, presumably, by 'seeing with my mind's eye' or 'hearing with my mind's ear' or by any other kind of what we might call 'sensory imaginings'. However, Yablo is clear that one need not imagine oneself, or anyone else, having an experience in the imagined world. So, I imagine a world such that

[6] Others who defend views on which conceiving is a type of imagining include Gregory (2010), Ichikawa and Jarvis (2012) and Kung (2010, 2016), though Ichikawa and Jarvis should perhaps more properly be thought of as conceptual coherence theorists. Critics of conceiving as imagining include Roca-Royes (2011), Tidman (1994) and van Inwagen (1998).

[7] Three minor comments are in order about Yablo's thesis. First, it is unclear why it must be a *world* that is imagined rather than just an object. After all, Yablo explicitly says that one need not imagine a whole world in order to imagine a world. For example, one could imagine a world in which a lion has stripes simply by imagining a lion with stripes. But, then, it isn't clear why it's important to imagine the *world* rather than just the lion. Second, whether or not someone *takes* something to verify a proposition seems to me epistemically irrelevant. A religious fanatic might irrationally take geopolitical events to verify that the end is nigh, but that doesn't make the fanatic rational in believing that the end is nigh. And, third, it seems that 'verify' is too strong of a word. After all, 'verify' is a success term. If something verifies that P, then it is in fact the case that P. But the presence of a particular object in one's experience might give one evidence that P without verifying that P (and without one taking the presence in experience to verify that P). Similarly, the presence of an object in one's conceiving or imagining might give one evidence that P is true in one's conceiving without verifying that P (and without one taking the presence in the conceiving or imagining to verify that P is true in the conceiving/imagining).

I take it to verify, from the outside so to speak, that some lions have stripes; I need not imagine a world *in which* I or anyone else has an experience of striped lions or of anything. Yablo is also clear that one need not imagine a world in complete detail or in its entirety. So, when I imagine a world such that I take it to verify that some lions have stripes, I need not imagine the particular numbers of stripes that various lions have. That's just more detail than is necessary. I just need to imagine lions with some number of stripes or other. Moreover, I need not imagine either the presence or non-presence of a kangaroo in the Woodland Park Zoo. That's a portion of the world that I can just safely ignore.

2.1 The Imagination Account and the Representation Constraint

One standard objection to The First Imagination Account is that we can imagine worlds that we take to verify propositions that are impossible. For example, we can imagine a world in which mathematicians announce that they have discovered and verified a proof of Goldbach's Conjecture. We would take this world to verify that Goldbach's Conjecture is true. Likewise we can imagine a world in which those same mathematicians announce in the same circumstances that they have discovered and verified that there is a counterexample to Goldbach's Conjecture. We would take this world to verify that Goldbach's Conjecture is false. Since Goldbach's Conjecture is necessarily true if true at all and necessarily false if false, we have conceived in one of these situations of something that happens to be impossible.

Most straightforwardly, this objection is meant to show that The Imagination Account fails to capture philosophical conceivability because it fails to meet The Representation Constraint. But since The Representation Constraint is generated from both the objective side of conceivability and from the subjective side of conceivability, there are actually two problems here. What this means is that The Imagination Account both fails to distinguish between those propositions that are apt to be conceived and those that are not, but also fails to distinguish between someone who is conceiving and someone who is misconceiving.

One thing to note about The First Imagination Account is that the object of imagination is a *world* rather than a *possible world*. One might think, then, that the following simple modification will help to align the account with The Representation Constraint:

> *The Second Imagination Account*: S conceives that P iff S imagines a possible world, w, such that S takes w to verify that P.

But this modification seems to put the view in tension with The Epistemic Constraint. For, arguably, one cannot imagine an F without first having enough knowledge of Fs to guide one's imaginative activity; without knowing enough to imagine an F rather than something else. For example, one cannot imagine a television news report such that one takes it to verify that the end is nigh without first having enough knowledge of television news reports to guide one's imaginative activity. If I imagine such a news report, then I must know enough to imagine a television news report verifying that the end is nigh rather than a television production of *War of the Worlds*. It is partly because I already know what a television news report looks like that I *can* imagine one verifying that the end is nigh.

Similarly, if I imagine a possible world, w, such that I take w to verify that the end is nigh, I must first have enough knowledge of possibility to guide my imaginative activity. I must know enough to imagine a *possible world* rather than an impossible world. But if I know enough to imagine a possible world such that I take it to verify that the end is nigh, then I must already know it's possible for the end to be nigh. Hence, the imaginative experience cannot make me prima facie reasonable in believing it's possible that the end is nigh. Hence, The Second Imagination Account violates The Epistemic Constraint.[8]

What we need, clearly, is not a restriction on the object of imagination, but rather a separate condition on conceivability.

> *The Third Imagination Account*: S conceives that P iff (i) S imagines a world, w, such that S takes w to verify that P and (ii) P is possible.

As I mentioned above, there are two problems for imagination accounts associated with The Representation Constraint. One problem has to do with the fact that any adequate account of conceiving must distinguish propositions that are apt to be conceived from those that are not. The Third

[8] One might respond to my objection by claiming that imagination is not constrained in the way I am suggesting. Perhaps, the responder says, one can imagine one's television as a toaster or one's cat as a dog. Hence, perhaps one can imagine a possible world as any number of ways without knowing that those ways of imagining that world are possible. Unfortunately, if we are so unconstrained, then we can imagine all sorts of possible worlds in impossible ways. I can imagine a possible world as a world in which water is composed of XYZ rather than H_2O. Hence, I can imagine a possible world such that I take it to verify that water is composed of XYZ. Of course, I wouldn't be imagining a possible world as any possible world is, but neither am I imagining a cat as any cat is when I imagine a cat as a dog. If imagination is not constrained, then according to The Second Imagination Account, I can conceive that water is composed of XYZ. Hence I can conceive of an impossibility and The Second Imagination Account is, again, in violation of The Representation Constraint.

Imagination Account avoids this problem by making it explicit that a proposition can be conceived only if it is possible. What makes a proposition apt to be conceived, then, is that it is possible (or that it has whatever grounds its possibility). But the second problem associated with The Representation Constraint is that any adequate account of conceiving must distinguish those who are conceiving from those who are misconceiving. The Third Imagination Account falls to this second problem.

Intuitively, one misconceives that P when one has nearly everything that it takes to be conceiving, but somehow or other gets things wrong. But if that's right, then given The Third Imagination Account, one misconceives that P when one imagines that P and yet P is impossible. But it seems like we can imagine impossible things without thereby misconceiving. For example, when I am watching *Game of Thrones*, I am imagining a world and I take that imaginative world to verify that there are dragons. If, as many contemporary philosophers believe, dragons are impossible, then I am imagining an impossibility. But I have not thereby misconceived. After all, I am not engaged in any epistemic endeavour at all. Hence, I have not done anything epistemically awry and, in particular, I have not mistakenly conceived or misconceived. If I have not misconceived when I imagine an impossibility, then The Third Imagination Account is mistaken.[9]

Here is a simple modification that will avoid this problem:

> *The Fourth Imagination Account*: S conceives that P iff (i) S aims to discover what is possible by way of imagination, (ii) S imagines a world, w, such that S takes w to verify that P, and (iii) P is possible.

When one's aim is to discover what is possible by way of imagination, then (arguably) one makes a mistake when one imagines something that is impossible. Hence, The Fourth Imagination Account avoids violating The Representation Constraint even when the constraint is considered from the subject side.

[9] Here is a related objection. The conditions under which one has made a mistake in conceiving are very different from the conditions under which one has made a mistake in imagining. Mistakes in conceiving are grounded in different norms than mistakes in imagining. When I watch the *Star Trek* episode 'A Piece of the Action', I make a mistake in imagining if I imagine that Captain Kirk and company are gangsters in Chicago during the 1920s rather than space explorers from the future. But the imagining is a mistake because one ought to imagine that P when viewing a television programme that depicts that P. When it comes to conceiving, on the other hand, we are following a different norm: one ought to conceive only what is possible. Hence, a mistake in conceiving and a mistake in imagining are violations of different norms and, so, The Third Imagination Account is mistaken.

2.2 The Imagination Account, The Explanatory Constraint and The Epistemic Constraint

The Imagination Account must also satisfy The Explanatory Constraint and The Epistemic Constraint in order to be a viable account of philosophical conceivability. It doesn't seem like an implausible hypothesis that given any sensory imagining one can have, there is something *in* it that's possible. Specifically, given any sensory imagining one can have, the distribution of sensory qualities that are imagined is possible.[10] In this way, one might argue, The Imagination Account does in fact satisfy The Explanatory Constraint. After all, the necessary connection between sensory imaginings and possible distributions of sensory qualities might partly ground that one is prima facie reasonable in believing something is possible when one is conceiving.

Let's suppose that there is something possible *in* each sensory imagining. Then it seems plausible that one who is imagining is thereby prima facie reasonable in believing in the possibility of something in that imagining. But what, exactly, is one prima facie reasonable in believing? Some might claim that one is *prima facie* reasonable in believing only what, *in general*, is possible in imaginings. Since the distributions of sensory qualities are what, in general, is possible in imaginings, it would follow that one is only reasonable in believing in the possibility of propositions about those distributions.[11] Of course, this requires a further modification of The Imagination Account:

> *The Fifth Imagination Account*: S conceives that P iff (i) S aims to discover what is possible by way of imagination, (ii) S imagines a world, w, such that S takes w to verify P, where (iii) P is about the distribution of sensory qualities imagined in w, and (iv) P is possible.

[10] One might object that I can see with my mind's eye Escher's Waterfall, but that that does not correspond to any possible distribution of sensory qualities. However, Shigeo Fukuda is a Japanese artist who has made three-dimensional models of some of Escher's drawings, including *Waterfall.* When viewed from a certain angle, one has a visual experience that matches the visual experience one has when looking at Escher's drawing. So, arguably, there is a possible distribution of sensory qualities corresponding to each sensory imagining. For a more elaborate defence of this general claim see Sorensen (2006).

[11] Or, perhaps a bit less narrowly, one might prima facie reasonably believe in the possibility of certain more substantive propositions as long as such a proposition is supported by a proposition about the distribution of sensory qualities in an imagining. Gregory (2010) and Kung (2010) both defend something like this variant of The Imagination Account, though their variants are more sophisticated along a number of dimensions.

So, on this variant, one can conceive only of propositions about distributions of sensory qualities (or propositions that are supported by propositions about such distributions). Since those propositions are guaranteed to be possible, given the explanatory connection noted above, The Fifth Imagination Account arguably satisfies The Epistemic Constraint.

Recall the example of Goldbach's Conjecture. I can aim to discover what is possible by way of imagination while imagining a world, w, in which mathematicians announce that they have discovered and verified a proof of Goldbach's Conjecture. I can also aim to discover what is possible by way of imagination while imagining a world, w, in which mathematicians announce that they have discovered and verified the existence of a counterexample of Goldbach's Conjecture. Ordinarily, I might take the first imagined world to verify that Goldbach's Conjecture is true and the second to verify that Goldbach's Conjecture is false. So, on The Fourth Imagination Account, I have nearly all it takes to conceive that Goldbach's Conjecture is true and nearly all it takes to conceive that Goldbach's Conjecture is false. But, given The Fifth Imagination Account, I can conceive by way of these imaginings only that it *appears* as if mathematicians are making certain announcements, i.e., that there are distributions of sensory qualities as if there were mathematicians making certain announcements.

The suggestion above has its advantages. But a defender of The Imagination Account might resist any further modification. After all, since a necessary condition on conceiving a proposition, given The Fourth Imagination Account, is that the proposition in question is possible, then even though one can imagine both a world such that one takes it to verify Goldbach's Conjecture and another world such that one takes it to verify the negation of Goldbach's Conjecture, only one of these imaginings can constitute a genuine conceiving.

Moreover, if one were in fact looking at some mathematicians announcing a proof of Goldbach's Conjecture, then one would thereby be reasonable in believing that Goldbach's Conjecture is true. Similarly, if one were to imagine some mathematicians making such an announcement, then one might thereby be reasonable in believing that Goldbach's Conjecture is possibly true. So, one might think, even The Fourth Imagination Account satisfies The Epistemic Constraint.

However, I think there's a difference between perceiving Goldbach's Conjecture being true on the one hand and having a perceiving which provides evidence of Goldbach's Conjecture. One cannot plausibly perceive Goldbach's Conjecture being true since one cannot perceive mathematical states of affairs. So, in the case above, one has not perceived Goldbach's Conjecture being true but merely had a perceiving that, in the right circumstances, provides evidence in favour of Goldbach's Conjecture. Moreover, it provides evidence merely because of contingent facts connecting perceptions of mathematicians making announcements about mathematical results and the truth of those results.

Similarly, there's a difference between conceiving that Goldbach's Conjecture is true on the one hand and having a conceiving which, in the right circumstances, provides evidence in favour of the possibility of Goldbach's Conjecture. Arguably, in the case above, no one has conceived of Goldbach's Conjecture being true. Perhaps one has had a conceiving that provides evidence for the possibility of Goldbach's Conjecture. But *if* it does provide evidence, then it does so because of contingent facts connecting one's conceiving of mathematicians making announcements about mathematical results and the possible truth of those results. The Fifth Imagination Account can make sense of this distinction and The Fourth cannot.[12]

3 Conceivability and Conceptual Consistency

The explanatory connection between possibility and conceivability on The Fifth Imagination Account is very weak. Some might think that the mere necessary connection between sensory imaginings and possible distributions of sensory qualities is insufficient for generating prima facie reasonable belief in possibilities. The Conceptual Account of conceivability might provide a stronger explanatory connection if conceptual consistency is a partial grounds for possibility.

[12] Another reason some might favour The Fifth Account over The Fourth Account is that on The Fifth Account it may be transparent to the imaginer that that which is imagined is thereby conceived. For, suppose that I am aiming to discover what's possible by way of imagination while imagining a world in which mathematicians announce that they have discovered and verified a proof of Goldbach's Conjecture. On The Fifth Imagination Account, I can thereby conceive only that it appears as if mathematicians are announcing the proof of Goldbach's Conjecture and, as long as I know what it takes to conceive, I can recognize that I am conceiving rather than misconceiving. However, if The Fourth Imagination Account were true, then I could be in a mental state as if I were conceiving that Goldbach's Conjecture is true and, if it happens to be possibly true, then I would have thereby conceived it. But in some sense, I won't be able to recognize that I have conceived rather than misconceived. After all, on The Fourth Account, whether I have conceived rather than misconceived has everything to do with whether or not Goldbach's Conjecture is in fact possibly true.

Here's an initial idea. Let 'Modal Conceptualism' be the thesis that P is necessary iff and because P is a conceptual truth.[13] Then P is possible iff and because P is consistent with all conceptual truths. We may then give the following account:

> *The Initial Conceptual Account*: S conceives that P iff S knows that P is consistent with all conceptual truths.[14]

Given Modal Conceptualism and The Initial Conceptual Account, the fact that a proposition is consistent with all conceptual truths is a partial grounds for the fact that it is possible and for the fact that it is conceivable. Hence, there is a tight explanatory connection between conceivability and possibility and The Explanatory Constraint is met. Since something is possible because it is consistent with all conceptual truths, if someone knows that it is consistent with all conceptual truths, then she is in a position to know that it is possible. Hence, The Epistemic Constraint is met. And, finally, since knowledge entails truth, if someone knows that a proposition is consistent with all conceptual truths, it is in fact consistent with all conceptual truths and hence, given Modal Conceptualism, is possible. So, the view satisfies the Representational Constraint.

3.1 Sophisticated Modal Conceptualism

Unfortunately, Modal Conceptualism is false. In the latter half of the twentieth century, metaphysicians became more comfortable with certain necessities that seem to be non-conceptual. For example, it is often accepted that water is necessarily composed solely of the chemical elements hydrogen and oxygen. But, of course, it's not conceptually true that water is composed

[13] I assume, here and throughout the rest of the essay, that any truth that follows from solely conceptual truths is itself a conceptual truth.

Traditional Conventionalism is the conjunction of three theses: (i) For any p, p is necessary iff and because p is analytic, (ii) for any p, p is *a priori* knowable iff and because p is analytic, and (iii) for any p, p is analytic iff and because there is a sentence, S, that expresses p and S is true solely in virtue of the conventions of our language. See Ayer (1936) for a succinct statement. See Sider (2003) for a detailed critical discussion. The view I am considering in the text is slightly different from Traditional Conventionalism. First, although all analytic truths are conceptual truths, it is not the case that all conceptual truths are analytic. Second, I take no stand on whether or not either analytic truths or conceptual truths are true because of the conventions of our language. It is perfectly consistent with the view expressed in the text, for example, that conceptual truths are brute facts.

[14] Gendler and Hawthorne (2002) consider an account of conceivability similar to the one above which assumes that all necessary truths are *a priori* knowable.

solely of those chemical elements. Hence, some necessary truths are not conceptual truths.[15]

A variant of Modal Conceptualism can accommodate these necessary truths that are non-conceptual. Although it's not conceptually true that water is composed solely of chemical elements hydrogen and oxygen, it might be conceptually true that if water is in fact solely composed of certain chemical elements, then water is necessarily solely composed of those chemical elements. This conceptual truth, when combined with the non-conceptual truth that water is in fact solely composed of hydrogen and oxygen, entails that water is necessarily solely composed of hydrogen and oxygen. This suggests a variant of Modal Conceptualism on which all necessary truths can be traced back to conceptual truths. Let 'Sophisticated Modal Conceptualism' be the view that if something is a necessary truth, then either (i) it is necessary because it is conceptual or (ii) it is a necessary truth that follows ampliatively from a conceptual truth in conjunction with some non-conceptual truths. So, for example, the proposition that all blue things are extended is necessary because it is conceptual. But the proposition that water is necessarily composed of hydrogen and oxygen follows ampliatively from a conceptual truth and a non-conceptual truth; in particular, it follows from the conceptual truth that if water is in fact solely composed of certain chemical elements, then water is necessarily solely composed of those chemical elements, along with the proposition that water is in fact composed of hydrogen and oxygen. On this view, all necessary truths trace their necessity back to conceptual truths in one of these two ways.[16]

Now we can distinguish between two types of possibility. Let's say a proposition is conceptually possible iff it is consistent with all conceptual truths. And a proposition is metaphysically possible iff it is consistent with all conceptual truths together with those truths which, when combined with

[15] Early discussions of these necessities include Kripke (1971, 1980) and Putnam (1975). They, however, were not focused on whether or not these propositions are conceptual truths. Other examples of necessary truths that are not conceptual might include the propositions that Sasha Obama's parents are Barack and Michelle Obama, that gold has atomic number 79 and that pain is intrinsically bad.

Putnam (1975) briefly argues that conceivability is not a guide to possibility on the grounds that one might conceive of these necessities being false. Putnam, though, seems to be assuming something like the first imagination account of conceivability. As we have already seen, plausible imagination accounts are more sophisticated.

[16] This view is very similar to the view advocated by Alan Sidelle (1989). However, again, Sidelle focused on analytic truths instead of conceptual truths. Moreover, I take no stand on what grounds conceptual truths if anything. In particular, I take no stand on whether conceptual truths are grounded in either linguistic conventions, *a priori* conditions of cognition, or anything else thinker-centric. For example, it is consistent with the view as I have presented it that for each conceptual truth, it's a brute fact that it is a conceptual truth.

conceptual truths, ampliatively generate necessities. So, since it is consistent with all conceptual truths that water is solely composed of chemical elements other than hydrogen and oxygen, it is conceptually possible that water is solely composed of chemical elements other than hydrogen and oxygen. But, since it ampliatively follows from a conceptual and non-conceptual truth together that water is necessarily solely composed of hydrogen and oxygen, it isn't metaphysically possible for water to be composed solely of chemical elements other than hydrogen and oxygen.

Is there, one might ask, any connection between conceptual possibility and metaphysical possibility? Maybe. But I have to admit we're about to enter a rather dubious philosophical realm. Some people think that every conceptually possible proposition characterizes a genuine metaphysical possibility. So, consider the proposition that water is solely composed of chemical elements other than hydrogen and oxygen. Although this proposition isn't metaphysically possible, it is conceptually possible and hence might characterize a metaphysical possibility even though it isn't a metaphysical possibility. It might characterize the possibility in which the liquid that fills our lakes and oceans is solely composed of chemical elements other than hydrogen and oxygen. For, there's some sense in which, prior to our investigations into its chemical composition, water 'could have turned out' to be solely composed of elements other than hydrogen and oxygen.

Here's one way to make sense of all of this. Suppose the proposition that water is solely composed of chemical elements hydrogen and oxygen is identical to a certain descriptive proposition. For the sake of brevity, we'll say that it is identical to the proposition that the *actual* watery substance is solely composed of chemical elements hydrogen and oxygen. But the concept of being actual has two dimensions to it. Consider the proposition that if Obama had lost the 2012 election, then we would have actually had a Republican president in 2013. That proposition has two dimensions of evaluation. Let's look at this given a nearest-worlds account of counterfactuals. First, the counterfactual might be evaluated as true since in the nearest world at which Obama loses the 2012 election, Romney is elected president and so *in that world* there is a Republican president in 2013. For, along this dimension, that alternative world is taken as *actual.* However, the counterfactual might be evaluated as false since even though there is a nearby world at which Obama loses the 2012 election, still *in this world* Obama won and we do not have a Republican president. Along this dimension, our world is taken as *actual.* Each proposition containing the concepts of being actual, then, must be evaluated at a pair of worlds, one of which is the world taken as actual and the other of which is the world taken as counterfactual.

Let's go back to our watery example and let's suppose our world is taken as actual. The water substance in our world happens to be composed of hydrogen and oxygen. Moreover, that very substance will be composed of hydrogen and oxygen in any world in which it is found. So, the proposition that water is composed of hydrogen and oxygen (i.e., the proposition that the actual watery substance is composed of hydrogen and oxygen) is necessary. This can be represented in the two-dimensional chart below where, let's just stipulate, the watery substance in W1 is H_2O and the watery substance in W2 is H_2O, but the watery substance in W3 has some other chemical composition, XYZ. In the first row, W1 is taken as actual and the watery substance in W1 happens to be composed solely of hydrogen and oxygen. So, no matter which world we consider as counterfactual in that row, since the watery substance *in W1* is solely composed of hydrogen and oxygen, it will be true in those worlds that any substance that is an actual watery substance is composed solely of hydrogen and oxygen.

*		**World taken as Counterfactual**		
World taken as actual		W1	W2	W3
	W1	T	T	T
	W2			
	W3			

* Partial chart for the proposition that the actual watery substance is composed solely of chemical elements hydrogen and oxygen (i.e., water is composed solely of chemical elements hydrogen and oxygen).

Similarly, if W2 were taken as actual, then no matter which world is taken as counterfactual, the actual water substance, i.e., the substance that is the watery substance in W2, is composed solely of hydrogen and oxygen. However, if W3 is taken as actual, then no matter which world is taken as counterfactual, the actual water substance, i.e., the substance that is the watery substance in W3, is composed solely of XYZ and *not* hydrogen and oxygen. So, we can complete the chart as follows:

**		**World taken as Counterfactual**		
World taken as actual		W1	W2	W3
	W1	T	T	T
	W2	T	T	T
	W3	F	F	F

** Complete chart for the proposition that water is composed solely of chemical elements hydrogen and oxygen (i.e., water is composed solely of chemical elements hydrogen and oxygen).

But if each counterfactual world is itself taken as actual, then the proposition is contingent since there are some worlds such that the substance that is the watery substance *in those worlds* is solely composed of chemical elements other than hydrogen and oxygen. This is represented below by the truth values along the diagonal.

***		World taken as Counterfactual		
World taken as actual		W1	W2	W3
	W1	**T**	T	T
	W2	T	**T**	T
	W3	F	F	**F**

*** Complete chart for the proposition that the actual watery substance is composed solely of chemical elements hydrogen and oxygen (with diagonal bolded).

This diagonal represents how things could have turned out to be prior to our chemical investigations. It represents the space of conceptual possibility. The proposition that water is composed solely of hydrogen and oxygen, although necessarily true when our world is taken as actual, is only contingently true when each counterfactual world is taken as actual. It is metaphysically necessary, but conceptually contingent. Similarly, the proposition that water is composed solely of some chemical elements other than hydrogen and oxygen is necessarily false when our world is taken as actual, but only contingently false when each counterfactual world is taken as actual. It is metaphysically impossible, but conceptually contingent. Below is the two-dimensional chart for the proposition that water is composed of some chemical elements other than H_2O, namely XYZ.

#		World taken as Counterfactual		
World taken as actual		W1	W2	W3
	W1	F	F	F
	W2	F	F	F
	W3	T	T	T

Complete chart for the proposition that the actual watery substance is composed solely of chemical elements other than hydrogen and oxygen (i.e., water is composed solely of chemical elements other than hydrogen and oxygen).

Notice that it is conceptually possible that water is composed solely of chemical elements other than hydrogen and oxygen. That's represented by the fact that it is true in at least one position on the diagonal. But that conceptual possibility *just is* a metaphysical possibility characterized in a different way. The conceptual possibility of water being composed of something other than hydrogen and oxygen *just is* the metaphysical possibility of the watery stuff being composed of something other than hydrogen and oxygen. Although in Section 5, we will see some reason to reject this link between conceptual possibility and metaphysical possibility, for now let's just accept the link and see whether it will help us to develop a notion of philosophical conceivability.

3.2 Two Conceptual Accounts of Conceivability

Corresponding to the two kinds of possibility, there are two kinds of conceivability.[17] Let's start with The Secondary Conceptual Account since that account corresponds directly, rather than indirectly, with metaphysical possibility:

> *The Secondary Conceptual Account*: S secondarily conceives that P iff S knows that P is consistent with all conceptual truths together with all truths which, when combined with conceptual truths, ampliatively entail necessary truths.

Let's call a truth which, when combined with conceptual truths, ampliatively entails necessary truths an 'ampliative truth'. Given Sophisticated Modal Conceptualism and The Secondary Conceptual Account, the fact that a proposition is consistent with all conceptual and ampliative truths is a partial grounds for the fact that it is possible and for the fact that it is secondarily conceivable. Hence, there is a tight explanatory connection between secondary conceivability and possibility and The Explanatory Constraint is met. Since something is possible because it is consistent with all conceptual and ampliative truths, if someone knows that it is consistent with all such truths, then she is in a position to know that it is possible. Hence, The Epistemic Constraint is met. And, finally, since knowledge entails truth, if someone knows that a proposition is consistent with all conceptual and ampliative

[17] The notions of conceivability expressed in this section are a simplified version of the notions developed and defended by Chalmers (2002). The names I have given to these accounts and to the corresponding notions of conceivability match the names used by Chalmers. Moreover, since Ichikawa and Jarvis (2012) focus primarily on conceptual coherence as a constraint on imagination, I tend to consider them defenders of a variety of the conceptual account. Finally, Menzies (1998) might also be considered a sort of conceptualist more broadly construed. Critics of the conceptual approach include Mizrahi and Morrow (2015), Roca-Royes (2011) and Yablo (2002)

truths, then it is in fact consistent with all such truths and hence, given Sophisticated Modal Conceptualism, is possible. So, the view satisfies The Representational Constraint.[18]

The Primary Conceptual Account is less straightforward. It corresponds directly with conceptual possibility and indirectly with metaphysical possibility:

> *The Primary Conceptual Account*: S primarily conceives that P iff and because S knows that P is consistent with all conceptual truths.

Let's start with The Representational Constraint. Recall that something is conceptually possible if it is consistent with all conceptual truths. So, since knowledge is factive, if someone primarily conceives that P, then P is conceptually possible. But, since conceptual possibilities *just are* metaphysical possibilities differently characterized, it follows that P, under a slightly different characterization, is metaphysically possible. So, The Primary Conceptual Account satisfies The Representational Constraint.[19] Moreover, the fact that a proposition is conceptually consistent partially grounds that it is conceptually possible. But, again, conceptual possibility just is metaphysical possibility differently characterized and, so, the fact that a proposition is conceptually consistent also partially grounds that it is metaphysically possible, at least under some characterization. But, on the account above, conceptual consistency also partially grounds primary conceivability. Hence, there is a tight explanatory connection between primary conceivability and possibility and The Explanatory Constraint is met. Since something is possible, under one characterization, partly because it is consistent with all conceptual truths, if someone knows that it is consistent with all such truths, then she is in a position to know that it is possible. Hence, The Epistemic Constraint is met.

4 Conceivability and the Modal Ontological Argument

Recall the modal ontological argument from the introduction:

1. It is possible that God exists.
2. If it is possible that God exists, then God exists.
3. So, God exists.

[18] Moreover, we can say that S secondarily misconceives that P iff S reasonably believes that P is consistent with all conceptual truths together with all truths which, when combined with conceptual truths, ampliatively entail necessary truths even though P is not consistent with all such truths.

[19] We can say that S primarily misconceives that P iff S reasonably believes that P is consistent with all conceptual truths even though P is not consistent with all such truths.

One might reasonably believe the second premise given certain plausible modal principles and the assumption that, necessarily, if God exists, then God necessarily exists. One might reasonably believe the first premise if one *philosophically* conceives that God exists, that is, conceives that God exists in whatever sense, if any, generates reasonable belief in the possibility of what's conceived. Or if one philosophically conceives of something that otherwise supports the first premise.

We have three candidate notions of conceiving, The Fifth Imagination Account and The Primary and Secondary Conceptual Accounts, each one of which, arguably, satisfies at least the three constraints we have laid out for philosophical conceivability. Setting aside whether or not any of these three notions really is *philosophical* conceiving, can anyone conceive, in any of these four senses, that God exists or conceive of something that otherwise supports the first premise? I'm not sure. But I'll consider each of them in turn and see whether or not *I* can conceive that God exists or conceive of something that otherwise supports the first premise.

4.1 Conceiving as Imagining and Premise (1)

First, according to The Fifth Imagination Account:

> S conceives that P iff (i) S aims to discover what is possible by way of imagination, (ii) S imagines a world, w, such that S takes w to verify P, where (iii) P is about the distribution of sensory qualities imagined in w, and (iv) P is possible.

Certainly, I can aim to discover what is possible by way of imagination while imagining a world such that I take it to verify that there is a certain distribution of sensory qualities, a distribution as if there were authorities announcing the discovery of God in circumstances very similar to the actual circumstances. Since such a distribution of sensory qualities is possible, I would thereby be conceiving of such a distribution. And, finally, if The Fifth Imagination Account correctly characterizes philosophical conceivability, I would be reasonable in believing in the possibility of that distribution of sensory qualities. But how do I get from these facts to the possibility that God exists?

Here's one idea. Suppose I reasonably believe in the possibility of a distribution of sensory qualities as if there were authorities announcing the discovery of God in a circumstance very similar to the actual circumstance. Since the circumstance is very similar to the actual circumstance, then arguably I am reasonable in believing of that possible circumstance whatever I would be reasonable in believing if that possible circumstance had been actual. And, since I would be reasonable in believing that various authorities are announcing the discovery of God if that possible circumstance had been actual, I would be reasonable in believing that it's possible for authorities to announce the discovery of God. Finally, since I would be reasonable in believing that God exists if that possible circumstance had been actual, then I am reasonable in believing that possibly, God exists.

The problem is that I can also conceive of possible circumstances that similarly support, as reasonable, belief in the possibility that God does not exist. Since we are assuming that, necessarily, if God exists, then God necessarily exists, one of these beliefs is mistaken. Moreover, I can easily recognize that fact. When I recognize that I seem to reasonably believe both of two incompatible propositions and I have no reason to favour one of those beliefs over the other, then I ought to amend my attitude and instead suspend judgment. I am at a stand-off with myself and, if The Fifth Imagination Account correctly characterizes philosophical conceivability, I see no way to break the stand-off.[20]

4.2 The Conceptual Accounts and Premise (1)

Perhaps, though, there's better support for the first premise if we accept one of the conceptual accounts of conceivability. Consider The Secondary Conceptual Account:

> S secondarily conceives that P iff and because S knows that P is consistent with all conceptual truths together with all truths which, when combined with conceptual truths, ampliatively entail necessary truths.

Recall that secondary conceivability entails metaphysical possibility on the assumption that Sophisticated Modal Conceptualism is correct. So, can I secondarily conceive that God exists?

[20] Tidman (1994) presents a general problem for conceivability accounts of modal knowledge that he calls 'the standoff problem'. Tidman claims that anytime one can conceive that P, one can also conceive that P is impossible and since one can easily recognize that the possibility of P and the possibility of the impossibility of P are incompatible, one cannot gain reasonable belief in the possibility of a proposition by conceiving it. I think Tidman is mistaken when he claims that anytime one can conceive that P, one can also conceive that P is impossible. Remember that, given The Representation Constraint, a proposition cannot be conceivable unless it is genuinely possible. However, I do think that the particular stand-off indicated above prevents one from supporting the second premise of the modal argument on the basis of imagination. But the stand-off above occurs because of the gap that must be filled between what is conceived (a proposition about the distribution of sensory qualities) and the putative possibility under investigation (God's existence).

Well, let me run though some of the things I think I know (or will assume I know) to see whether or not I know that God's existence is consistent with all conceptual truths together with all ampliative truths. First, I'll assume I know that Sophisticated Modal Conceptualism is correct. I'll also assume I know it neither follows from conceptual truths alone that God exists nor that God doesn't exist, i.e., it's neither a conceptual truth that God exists nor a conceptual truth that God does not exist. But, I also know that either it's necessary that God exists or it's necessary that God doesn't exist. So, one of those necessities, given Sophisticated Modal Conceptualism, must follow from some conceptual truth combined with an ampliative truth.

To make things simple, I'll assume it's a conceptual truth that if God exists, then God necessarily exists and, similarly, that it's a conceptual truth that if God doesn't exist, then, necessarily, God doesn't exist.[21] So, if God exists, then that is an ampliative truth which, when combined with a conceptual truth just noted, entails that God necessarily exists. And if God does not exist, then that is an ampliative truth that, when combined with a conceptual truth just noted, entails that necessarily God does not exist. But the claim that God exists is clearly inconsistent with the claim that God does not exist. So, whether or not the proposition that God exists is consistent with all conceptual truths together with all ampliative truths depends on whether or not the proposition that God does not exist is an ampliative truth, and, moreover, I *know* that fact. So, since I (let's suppose) have no idea whether or not God exists prior to considering the ontological argument, I have no idea whether or not God's existence is consistent with all conceptual truths together with all ampliative truths. Hence, I cannot secondarily conceive that God exists. Moreover, even if I could

[21] Things can get very complicated. Presumably if Sophisticated Modal Conceptualism is true, then it is a conceptual truth. But it seems like a conceptual truth, also, that if Sophisticated Modal Conceptualism is true, then it is necessary that if God exists, then there is some truth, T, such that if T, then God necessarily exists. It follows that it is a conceptual truth that it's necessary that if God exists then there is some truth, T, such that if T, then God necessarily exists. But the embedded necessary conditional must either be a conceptual truth itself or follow from some conceptual truth together with an ampliative truth. Honestly, I can't say for certain that the latter option isn't correct, but the former option just seems far more plausible. So, let's suppose it is a conceptual truth that if God exists, then there is some truth, T, such that if T, then God necessarily exists. It follows by simple conceptual truths of logic that if God exists, then God necessarily exists. So, it is a conceptual truth that if God exists, then God necessarily exists. A similar argument can show that it is a conceptual truth that if God doesn't exist, then it's necessary that God doesn't exist.

come to know that God exists and, hence, come to know that God's existence is consistent with all conceptual truths together with all ampliative truths, thereby secondarily conceiving that God exists, no such conceiving could unobjectionably be used as partial support for the modal ontological argument.

So what about the primary conceptual account?

> S primarily conceives that P iff and because S knows that P is consistent with all conceptual truths.

I am assuming I know that it is neither a conceptual truth that God exists nor a conceptual truth that God doesn't exist. So, I can know that the proposition that God exists is consistent with all conceptual truths and, hence, I can primarily conceive that God exists. But remember that the route from primary conceivability to metaphysical possibility is not straightforward. What I can reasonably believe on the basis of my conceiving is that the proposition that God exists is conceptually possible. Given the assumption that conceptual possibilities just are metaphysical possibilities characterized in a different way, the proposition that God exists is metaphysically possible when differently characterized. However, I will argue against that assumption and, hence, block any support for the first premise by way of primary conceivability; primary conceivability, if I am right, cannot be philosophical conceivability.

As I noted above, if I know that it is neither a conceptual truth that God exists nor a conceptual truth that God doesn't exist, I can primarily conceive that God exists. But I can also, then, primarily conceive that God doesn't exist. What is it that I am conceiving and how, if at all, are such conceivings linked to metaphysical possibility? Well, let's follow our watery example and assume the proposition that God exists just is the descriptive proposition that the actual essentially unsurpassable necessary being exists and the proposition that God doesn't exist just is the descriptive proposition that the actual essentially unsurpassable necessary being doesn't exist. Using the apparatus of possible worlds and assuming, for *reductio*, that conceptual possibilities are metaphysical possibilities differently characterized, it follows that there is a world taken as actual at which there is an essentially unsurpassable necessary being. But, then, the being which at that world is an essentially unsurpassable necessary being must, being a *necessary* being, exist at each other world and must, being an *essentially* unsurpassable being, be unsurpassable at each other world as well. But that means that no matter what world is taken as actual, there will be an essentially unsurpassable necessary being there. Things seem to be looking good for premise (1)! But, recall, the proposition that the actual essentially unsurpassable necessary being doesn't exist is also conceptually possible. So, there must be some world taken as actual at which there is no such being. But it cannot be both that no matter what world is taken as actual, there will be an essentially unsurpassable necessary being there and there is some world taken as actual at which there is no such being. Hence, contrary to our assumption, some conceptual possibilities do not characterize metaphysical possibilities.[22]

I see three options available to the defender of primary conceivability as philosophical conceivability, none of which will help the defender of the modal ontological argument. First, one can say that it is neither primarily conceivable that God exists nor that God doesn't exist. On this option, since it is either necessary that God exists or necessary that God doesn't exist, given Sophisticated Modal Conceptualism, one of those two facts must follow from an ampliative truth and, hence, we must fall back on secondary conceivability. But we've already seen that secondary conceivability doesn't seem to help us support premise (1).

Second, one can say that it is either primarily conceivable that God exists or primarily conceivable that God doesn't exist, but that it is not both. If one of those propositions is not primarily conceivable, then that proposition is inconsistent with some conceptual truths. And if one of those propositions is inconsistent with some conceptual truths, then its negation follows from conceptual truths alone and, hence, is itself a conceptual truth. So, either it is a conceptual truth that God exists or it is a conceptual truth that God doesn't exist. So, whether or not God exists will have to be determined by conceptual analysis before any primary conceiving can occur and, hence, no such conceiving could unobjectionably be used as partial support for the modal ontological argument.

Finally, one might claim that the concept of being unsurpassable is itself descriptive and whereas one thing might be essentially unsurpassable when one possibility is taken as actual it is not unsurpassable at all, much less essentially unsurpassable, when another world is taken as actual. In that case, although we might be able to conceive of an essentially unsurpassable necessary being, we have no reason to believe that, when our

[22] This problem did not arise in our watery case because the descriptive content associated with water did not contain the concept of necessity or essentiality.

world is taken as actual, it is an unsurpassable being. In other words, what we conceive when we conceive of an essentially unsurpassable necessary being characterizes a metaphysical possibility, but not the possibility of an essentially unsurpassable necessary being. Hence, our primary conceiving does not support premise (1).[23]

[23] Similarly, we might think that what is necessary and what is essential depends on which world is taken as actual. In that case, although we might be able to conceive of an essentially unsurpassable necessary being, when our world is taken as actual, it might be neither a necessary nor essentially unsurpassable being. This option has the same problems as the one just discussed.

12 Begging the Question

Peter van Inwagen

Immanuel Kant coined the term *der ontologische Beweis* as a name for an argument that had been invented by Descartes and had later been refined by Leibniz and the members of the Wolff–Baumgarten school. At some point in the nineteenth century, the term began also to be applied to a rather different argument that had been devised by St Anselm over five hundred years before Descartes wrote his *Meditations on First Philosophy*. Apparently the word *Beweis* was not regarded by Kant (and has not been regarded by later philosophers writing in German) as an 'achievement term'; for Kant, there could be a *Beweis* that was incorrect or a failure, the Cartesio-Leibnizian argument of course being a case in point. But, although the usual English translation of *Beweis* is 'proof', Anglophone philosophers (none of whom, perhaps, believes that the Anselmian or the Cartesian arguments demonstrate their conclusions) are very strongly inclined to hear 'proof' as an achievement term, and, for that reason, generally prefer 'ontological argument' to 'ontological proof'. The term 'ontological argument' has, for the last half-century or so, also been applied to various arguments that are significantly different from both those arguments, certain modal arguments that are due largely to the work of Charles Hartshorne[1] and Alvin Plantinga.[2] There is, therefore, no one argument that can be called *the* ontological argument, and it has become common to speak of 'ontological arguments'. Even this term, however, is suspect, for it is not obvious that the arguments that are generally collectively referred to as 'ontological arguments' have enough in common to justify a taxonomy of argument that includes just them and excludes all other arguments for the existence of God.

For the purposes of this chapter, however, it will not be necessary to decide whether all the arguments that have been called 'ontological arguments'

[1] See Hartshorne (1962); especially §6 ('The Irreducibly Modal Structure of the Argument') in ch. 2 ('Ten Ontological or Modal Proofs for God's Existence') at pp. 49–57.

[2] See Plantinga (1974: ch. 10).

should or should not be grouped together under one name. It will be assumed in this chapter that all 'ontological arguments' other than the modal arguments of Hartshorne and Plantinga are irremediably flawed[3] and that there is therefore no reason to determine whether they beg the question: if they beg the question, that is, so to speak, the least of their worries. The topic of this chapter is therefore the question whether any of or all the modal arguments beg the question.

But this description of our topic *raises*[4] the question: What is it to beg the question? I must confess that I am unable to give a satisfactory account of what it is for an argument to beg the question. (Some of my own philosophical arguments have been accused of something very like 'begging the question' – I concede the phrase was not used – simply because they were formally valid arguments for a conclusion the accusers thought was false. Their reasoning seems to have been something like this: if the conclusion of an argument can be formally deduced from its premises, then that conclusion is, as one might put it, logically contained in the premises – and thus one who affirms those premises is assuming that the conclusion is true. As R. M. Chisholm once remarked when confronted with a similar criticism, 'I stand accused of the fallacy of affirming the antecedent.') I will, however, propose a *sufficient* condition for begging the question – that is, a condition such that if an argument satisfies that condition it can reasonably be said to beg the question.

> If it would be impossible to know whether one or more of the premises of a logically valid argument was true without first (or at least simultaneously) knowing whether its conclusion was true, then that argument begs the question.

The main conclusion of this chapter will be that all modal ontological arguments have this feature.[5]

I turn now to the various modal ontological arguments.

1 Formulation

In the sequel, I will take for granted the concepts of a possible world, and various allied concepts, such as the actuality and non-actuality (of worlds), the

[3] My arguments for this contention can be found in part 1 ('The Meinongian Argument') and part 2 ('The Conceptual Argument') of van Inwagen (2012).

[4] Most readers of this chapter will be excruciatingly aware of the deplorable recent tendency among non-philosophers to use 'beg the question' to mean 'raise the question'.

[5] But see note 9.

existence of an object in a world, the truth of a proposition in a world, and one world's being 'accessible from' or 'possible in relation to' another world.

As there are versions of the ontological argument, there are versions of versions of the ontological argument. At any rate, there is more than one version of the modal argument. Here is a version I think is as clear and elegant as any.

A perfect being, let us say, is a being that possesses all perfections essentially. (That is to say, a being is perfect in a possible world w if and only if it possesses all perfections in every world accessible from w.) Necessary existence, moreover, is a perfection. (A being possesses necessary existence in a world w if and only if it exists in every world accessible from w.) Suppose that a perfect being (so defined) is possible. Suppose, that is, that there is a perfect being in some world w accessible from the actual world (α). But then some being x that exists in α is a perfect being in w – since there is a perfect being (and hence a necessarily existent being) in w, w is accessible from α, and the accessibility relation is symmetrical. Might x exist only contingently in α? No, for in that case there is some world w' accessible from α in which x does not exist; and w' is accessible from w, since the accessibility relation is transitive.

But is x a perfect being in α? Yes, for consider any given perfection – say, wisdom. The being x is essentially wise in w, and hence is wise in α, since α is accessible from w. But might x be only accidentally wise in α? No, for in that case there is a world w'', accessible from α, in which x exists but is not wise. But, owing to the transitivity of the accessibility relation, w'' is accessible from w. And the point is perfectly general: given the symmetry and transitivity of the accessibility relation, x will have a property essentially in α if it has it essentially in any world accessible from α. There therefore actually exists a being that has all perfections essentially – that is to say, there actually exists a perfect being. (Might someone protest that we have shown that the being x possesses necessary existence in α but have not shown that x possesses necessary existence *essentially* in α? Well, if the accessibility relation is transitive, then anything that is necessarily existent is essentially necessarily existent. But it is not necessary to include a demonstration of that thesis in our argument, for we know that x possesses all perfections essentially in w, and hence is essentially necessarily existent in w; it therefore follows from what we have shown that x is essentially necessarily existent in α.)

This argument has only two premises: that necessary existence is a perfection (or that contingent existence is incompatible with perfection), and that a perfect being is possible. One might say that it also had the premise that the accessibility relation was an equivalence relation, but if that is a premise of the argument, it can be eliminated by reformulating the argument in terms not of quantification over possible worlds but as what one might call an explicitly modal argument, that is an argument containing modal sentential operators:

$\Box\, \forall x\, (x \text{ is a perfect being} \rightarrow \Box\, (\exists y\; y = x))$[6]

$\Diamond\, \exists x\; x$ is a perfect being,
hence, $\exists x\; x$ is a perfect being.

But, although this argument does not require the premise that the accessibility relation is an equivalence relation (for it does not mention possible worlds at all), it is not (as was the above argument) valid in ordinary quantifier logic. It is valid only in S5, the strongest system of *modal* logic.

There are 'explicitly modal' versions of the ontological argument that are valid in weaker modal systems than S5, but those arguments require additional premises. Consider, for example, the first of Hartshorne's modal arguments.[7] Let 'G' represent the conclusion of the argument – 'A perfect being exists,' 'God exists,' however you want to state Hartshorne's conclusion. This argument had two premises:

$G \prec \Box\, G$

$\Diamond\, G$

(Here '$\prec$' represents strict implication: $p \prec q =_{df} \Box\, (p \rightarrow q)$.) Hartshorne appealed to S5 in his deduction of G from these two premises, but it was soon pointed out that the deduction was valid in the weaker system B. (The validity of B is, loosely speaking, equivalent to the statement that the accessibility relation is symmetrical; it does not require that it be transitive.) Hartshorne,

[6] This formula contains a sub-formula that consists of the necessity sign followed by a sentence containing a free variable. We understand, e.g., '$\Box\, x$ is wise' as follows: an object satisfies this sentence in a world w just in the case that that object exists in all worlds accessible from w and is wise in all those worlds. That is to say, an object satisfies this sentence if and only if it is *necessarily* wise; an object that was *essentially* wise – wise in every world in which it existed – would not satisfy this sentence if there were worlds in which it did not exist. Thus, '$\Box\, \exists y\; y = x$' expresses necessary existence and not the trivial property of essential existence – a property that, of necessity, everything has. (Of *course* existence is an essential property of Socrates: he couldn't exist without having it.)

[7] See Hartshorne (1962: ch. 2.

moreover, later offered an explicitly modal ontological argument that required almost no 'modal logic' at all:

1	. $\Box G \vee \Box \sim G$	*premise*
2	. $\Diamond G$	*premise*
3	. $\sim \Box \sim G$	2
4	. $\Box G$	1, 3 *disjunctive syllogism*
5	. G	4

This argument requires the validity only of two trivial modal inference rules ('$\Diamond p \vdash \sim \Box \sim p$' and '$\Box p \vdash p$' – 'trivial' in the sense that they must be valid in every modal system in which the sentential operators represent possibility and necessity in any intuitive sense).[8] One could regard the first premise of each of Hartshorne's arguments as substitutes for an appeal to the strong modal system S5. At any rate, both premises follow from the assumption that the accessibility relation is both symmetrical and transitive (if we read 'G' as 'There is a necessarily existent being that has all perfections essentially').

2 Epistemic Neutrality

The modal ontological argument – in any of its versions, for they all have a 'possibility' premise, a premise of the same sort as 'It it possible for there to be a necessarily existent being that has all perfections essentially'[9] – suffers from only one defect: there seems to be no *a priori* reason, or none accessible to the human intellect (perhaps none accessible to any finite intellect) to think that it is possible for there to be a necessarily existent being that has all perfections essentially. I myself think that this premise of the argument is true – but only because I think that there in fact *is* a necessarily existent being who has all perfections essentially. And my reasons for thinking that are by no means *a priori*; they depend (so *I* suppose) on what that being has revealed about

[8] A qualification: if we think of deontic logic as a kind of modal logic, and if we think of the box as representing 'moral necessity', that is, being 'non-negotiably' demanded by morality, then it is sad but true that the second principle fails. But obviously the necessity involved in modal ontological arguments is not moral necessity.

[9] Lowe (2012) presents an argument that can, without misuse of either term, be called a 'modal ontological' argument, and this argument does not have a 'possibility premise'. Lowe's argument, however, in no way resembles the arguments of Hartshorne and Plantinga, and it is therefore not an argument of the sort that the phrase 'modal ontological argument' would suggest to most philosophers. For that reason, I will not include a discussion of Lowe's argument in this chapter.

himself to humanity. And I do not mean simply that no *conclusive* reason for thinking that such a being is possible can be supplied by *a priori* human reasoning. I mean that human reason is impotent to discover by *a priori* reasoning any consideration whatever that should cause a human reasoner to raise whatever prior probability he or she may assign to the possibility of such a being.

And I would go further. I would say that, divine revelation apart, a human being should either assign a prior probability of 0.5 to the proposition that it is possible for there to be a necessarily existent being who possesses all perfections essentially, or else refuse to assign it any probability at all. (Which of these would be the right thing to do depends on the resolution of some thorny questions in the philosophy of probability.)

My conviction that this is so rests in part on my conviction that no one has presented any cogent argument *a priori* for the conclusion that we ought to assign some probability lower than 0.5 to that proposition, a conviction that I will not defend here – since a defence could only take the form of successive examinations of each of the many arguments that have been offered for that conclusion. And, of course, it rests on my conviction that the arguments that have been offered (by Leibniz and Gödel, among others) for the conclusion that a perfect being is possible lend no support whatever to their conclusions. I will not defend this conviction either, since an adequate examination of these arguments is not possible within the scope of this paper (and since I have done so elsewhere).[10]

I conclude that whatever value the modal ontological argument may have, whatever philosophical rewards may attend a careful study of the argument, this value and these rewards are not epistemological: they will not provide the student of the argument with any sort of *reason for believing* that a perfect being exists. If a philosopher's sole interest in the modal ontological argument is in that sense epistemological, he or she will find it of no more interest than the following argument (formally identical with Hartshorne's second argument) for the truth of Goldbach's Conjecture (that every even number greater than 2 is equal to the sum of two primes – abbreviate this statement as 'G'):

1	. $\Box G \vee \Box \sim G$	*premise*
2	. $\Diamond G$	*premise*
3	. $\sim \Box \sim G$	2
4	. $\Box G$	1, 3
5	. G	4

[10] See Van Inwagen (2007).

This argument is indisputably valid and its first premise is indisputably true. It is equally indisputable, however, that this argument is not only not a proof of Goldbach's Conjecture but provides no reason whatever for thinking that Goldbach's Conjecture is true. And the reason for this can be simply stated: one could have no reason for thinking that Goldbach's Conjecture was possibly true (true in some possible world accessible from the actual world) unless that reason were a reason for thinking that Goldbach's Conjecture was true simpliciter (true in the actual world).[11] The point that this example illustrates may be generalized.

Let us say that a proposition is *epistemically neutral* (for a certain person or a certain population at a certain time) if the epistemic status of that proposition and the epistemic status of its denial (with respect to that person or population at that time) are identical. If an example of an epistemically neutral proposition (epistemically neutral for us, now) is wanted, I offer the following: the proposition that at the present moment the number of stars in the Milky Way galaxy with a mass greater than that of our sun is even.

And let us say that a proposition is *non-contingent* if either that proposition or its denial is a necessary truth.

I contend that the 'Goldbach' example is a special case of and illustrates the following general principle:

> If a proposition *p* is non-contingent, and is known to be non-contingent by a certain person or certain population at a certain time, and if *p* is epistemically neutral for that person or population at that time, then the proposition that *p* is possibly true is also epistemically neutral for that person or population at that time.

(This principle would obviously not be true if its application were not restricted to non-contingent propositions: consider the proposition that I offered as an example of a proposition that is epistemically neutral for us; I take it to be obvious that we are warranted or perfectly justified – insert your favourite term of epistemic commendation here – in believing that it is metaphysically possible that at the present moment the number of stars in the Milky Way galaxy with a mass greater than that of our sun is even.)

[11] Suppose it could be shown (perhaps by brute-force computation) that *if* there is a counterexample to Goldbach's Conjecture, it is greater than 10^{100}. That, to my mind, would be a reason, albeit not a decisive reason, for thinking that Goldbach's conjecture was true. And it would of course be a (non-decisive) reason for thinking that Goldbach's Conjecture was possibly true.

Any instance of this principle I can think of is obviously true. Here is an example that is, if anything, even more obviously true than the 'Goldbach's Conjecture' instance. Consider some 'vast' or 'enormous' natural number – say Skewes' Number, at one time said to have been the largest finite number that had figured essentially in any important mathematical result. Or, rather, take the following powers-of-10 approximation of that number: 10 exp (10 exp (10^{34})).[12] And consider the proposition that the number of primes smaller than that number is even. It is evident that this proposition is non-contingent, and I believe it to be epistemically neutral for us. (It is certain that its truth-value could not be established by an enumeration of the primes smaller than 10 exp (10 exp (10^{34})) in any reasonable amount of time. A computer the size of the Hubble universe and capable of executing a trillion operations per second that had been engaged in the task of counting the primes smaller than 10 exp (10 exp (10^{34})) for a trillion years would have counted only a minuscule portion of them. This would be true even if information could be transferred from one site in the computer to any other instantaneously.) But it is certainly evident that there could not be a reason for thinking that this proposition was possibly true that was not a reason for thinking it true.

If the principle I have proposed is true, then – since the conclusion of any version of the modal ontological must be a non-contingent proposition, and since one of the premises of that argument must be the proposition that its conclusion is possibly true – no version of the modal ontological argument can serve as a vehicle from which one can pass from epistemic neutrality as regards its conclusion to justification or warrant. Nor can it serve even as a vehicle that can transport its passengers from epistemic neutrality to some status that lies between epistemic neutrality and warrant.

I do not claim to have shown that the principle is correct. But I would propose that proponents of the thesis that the modal ontological argument might have some epistemic value do at least this much: provide an example (an example that is at least somewhat plausible; I do not demand that it be indisputable) of a non-contingent proposition that is epistemically neutral for some population and is such that the proposition that it, the chosen proposition, is possibly true is not epistemically neutral for that population.

[12] For the mathematically sensitive: in using the word 'approximation' I am speaking very loosely. Skewes' Number is *e* exp (*e* exp (e^{79})), where *e* is an irrational number in the vicinity of 2.71828. The powers-of-10 number given in the text is the number closest to Skewes' Number that can be expressed in powers-of-10 notation using only integral exponents. It is greater than Skewes' Number; no doubt its ratio to Skewes' Number is a very large number indeed.

In my view, the discovery of a proposition with those properties would be an important contribution to the study of the modal ontological argument.

3 Rational Permissibility

Alvin Plantinga has contended that the modal ontological argument does have epistemic value.[13] He concedes that it cannot, as I have put it, 'serve as a vehicle from which one can pass from epistemic neutrality as regards its conclusion to warrant'. He ascribes, rather, a different sort of epistemic value to it: that it can be used to show that it is not irrational to accept its conclusion. His argument is essentially this: one can rationally believe, one can believe without violating any canon of reason, that a perfect being possibly exists or that the concept 'perfect being' is not an impossible concept. The modal ontological argument shows that if it is possible for a perfect being to exist, then a perfect being does exist. A theist (a person who believes in the existence of a perfect being) may therefore defend the rationality of his or her allegiance to theism by the following reasoning: 'It is not irrational for me to believe that it is possible for a perfect being to exist; I am aware that it follows logically from the proposition that it is possible for a perfect being to exist that a perfect being does exist; my belief that a perfect being exists is therefore not irrational.'

The plausibility of this hypothetical theist's reasoning obviously depends on the following principle, or something very like it: If it can be rational to believe that *p*, and if it is demonstrable that *q* follows logically from *p*, then it can be rational to believe that *q*. Let us call this the Rationality Principle (RP). We shall presently examine RP carefully, but let us first ask why Plantinga holds that it can be rational to believe that a perfect being is possible.

Plantinga points out that there are lots of respectable, widely held philosophical positions for which there is no argument that is accepted by all (or even by most) competent philosophers. (One might cite Meinong's thesis that properties can be truly ascribed to objects that have no sort of being whatever, the thesis that there cannot be a private language, and the thesis that the rightness or wrongness of an act is solely a function of its consequences.) That a perfect being is possible is, Plantinga contends, one of these respectable, widely held philosophical positions. Many philosophers accept it, and various important philosophers have attempted to show that it is false – Sartre, for example ('Such a being would be an impossible amalgam

[13] See Plantinga (1974: 220–1).

of *être-pour-soi* and *être-en-soi* ') and J. N. Findlay ('A perfect being must be necessarily existent, and if there is a necessarily existent being, there are necessarily true existential propositions, which is impossible'). And, Plantinga further contends, any respectable, widely held philosophical position is one that it can be rational for a philosopher to hold, even if there is no argument for that position that is accepted by all or most competent philosophers. His argument is, in the final analysis, *ad homines*: philosophers had *better* believe this; philosophers who do not – and who do not wish to affirm theses that they themselves say cannot be rationally affirmed – will find themselves 'with a pretty slim and pretty dull philosophy' (Plantinga (1974: 221).

Let us not dispute this conclusion; let us stipulate that it can be rational to believe that a perfect being is possible.[14] Does it follow that (given the validity of the modal argument) it can be rational to believe that there is a perfect being? The right answer to this question obviously depends on whether RP is true. And it would seem that it is not – not if it is true that any respectable philosophical position is a position that it can be rational to hold. A simple example shows this.

That there are universals is obviously a respectable, widely held philosophical position. Therefore, if Plantinga is right, it can be rational to believe that there are universals. Let us suppose that this possibility is realized: a certain philosopher, Alice, does believe that there are universals and this belief of hers is rational. Now suppose that someone presents Alice with an indisputably sound demonstration of both these propositions: every universal occupies some region of space; no universal occupies any region of space (note that these two propositions are not logical contradictories, and that there is therefore no logical barrier to there being a demonstration of each). Would it then be reasonable for Alice to believe that something both occupies some region of space and does not occupy any region of space? Obviously not: no one can rationally believe an obvious and straightforward contradiction. It is obvious that what Alice ought to do, in the situation in which she finds herself, is to withdraw her assent to 'There are universals' – and in fact to assent to 'There are no universals.' And we therefore have a counterexample to RP: it is true that it can be rational to believe that there are universals (this is shown by example: Alice rationally believed that there were universals

[14] The thesis, however, is certainly highly disputable. Why is it rational to believe that it is true in some possible world that there is a perfect being, but not (as presumably it is not) rational to believe that it is true in some possible world that the number of primes smaller than Skewes' Number is even?

before she was aware of the demonstration that their existence implied a contradiction); it is demonstrable that the existence of universals implies a certain contradiction; it cannot be rational to believe that contradiction. If someone is unhappy with this example on the pedantic ground that it is not in fact possible to demonstrate both the proposition that each universal occupies some region of space and the proposition that no universal occupies any region of space, I offer a second example. Joaquima, who lives in the Ibizan village of Santa Eulàlia, believes that in her village there lives an adult male barber who shaves all and only the adult males living in Santa Eulàlia who do not shave themselves. It is rational for her to believe this, because it was told to her by her uncle Filip, renowned for his knowledge of all matters pertaining to Ibiza. It is then demonstrated to her that her belief logically implies that some adult male who lives in Santa Eulàlia both shaves himself and does not shave himself. It does not follow that this demonstration renders it rational for her to believe that some adult male who lives in Santa Eulàlia both shaves himself and does not shave himself.

The general lesson of these counterexamples to RP is this: It may (a) be true that someone can rationally believe that *p*, and (b) demonstrable that *p* entails *q*, and (c) *false* that anyone can rationally believe that *q* – because no one can rationally believe that *q* and one can rationally believe that *p* only if one is unaware that it is demonstrable that *p* entails *q*. For all Plantinga has said therefore, it may be that, although it can be rational to believe that a perfect being is possible and demonstrable that the possibility of a perfect being entails the existence of a perfect being, it cannot be rational to believe in the existence of a perfect being – since it cannot be rational to believe in the existence of a perfect being and it can be rational for one to believe that a perfect being is possible only if one is unaware that the possibility of a perfect being entails the existence of a perfect being.

Plantinga's argument is therefore unconvincing. But even if the argument were convincing, even if it were wholly unobjectionable, it is not easy to see why it would be *necessary*.[15] If one believes, as Plantinga does, that any respectable, widely held philosophical position is one that it can be rational to hold, why should one not apply this thesis 'directly' to 'A perfect being exists'? Why need one bother with an argument that appeals to 'A perfect

[15] The point that follows would apply to any elaboration of Plantinga's argument that was not subject to my criticism of the original argument. An example of such an elaboration: Replace RP with 'If it can be rational to believe that *p*, and if it is demonstrable that *q* follows logically from *p*, and if there is no known demonstration that it is irrational to believe that *q*, then it can be rational to believe that *q*. '

being is possible' and the modal argument and RP? 'A perfect being exists,' after all, is a thesis that has been affirmed by many respectable philosophers. If, moreover, one does for some reason think that an argument for the conclusion that it can be reasonable to believe that a perfect being exists that appeals to RP is preferable to one that does not, one will find it easy to construct 'RP' arguments that appeal to entailments that can be demonstrated by reasoning much simpler than the reasoning contained in the modal argument. For example: 'It can be rational to believe that some material thing has been created by a perfect being; "Some material thing has been created by a perfect being" demonstrably entails "There is a perfect being"; therefore, it can be rational to believe that there is a perfect being.'

13 Characterisation, Existence and Necessity

Graham Priest

Ontological arguments feature prominently in the history of Christian philosophy. An ontological argument is, roughly, one that tries to establish the existence of God from their[1] nature, or definition which captures that nature. The aim of this paper is not to present a survey of such arguments.[2] Rather, the point is to home in on what I take to be the central nerve of such arguments: the Characterization Principle – essentially, a principle to the effect that an object has those properties it is characterized as having. The Principle interacts in important ways with two other notions: existence and necessity. They will also, therefore, fall within the ambit of our discussion.

1 The Ontological Argument in Early Modern Philosophy

We will analyse matters by looking at ontological arguments as presented at various historical times. The earliest ontological argument for a Christian god was given by Anselm of Canterbury. I will come to him in due course. I want to start with early modern philosophy, where the nerve of the argument is at its most exposed. We will then turn back to Anselm. After that, we will move on to later modern philosophy.

1.1 Descartes

In his *Meditations on First Philosophy V*, Descartes gives a very straightforward version of the ontological argument, which goes as follows:[3]

[1] Traditionally, of course, the male pronoun is used. I prefer a gender-neutral pronoun. *It*, however, is far too depersonalizing for what is supposed to be, after all, a personal god. So I intend to use third-person plural. If you want, you can think of this as the 'royal they'.

[2] For a general overview, see Oppy (2016). [3] Hick (1964: 35).

> [W]henever it happens that I think of a first and sovereign Being, and, so to speak, derive the idea of Him from the storehouse of my mind, it is necessary that I should attribute to Him every sort of perfection, although I do not get so far as to enumerate them all, or to apply my mind to each one in particular. And this necessarily suffices to make me conclude (after having recognized that existence is a perfection) that this first and sovereign Being really exists; just as though it is not necessary for me to imagine any triangle, yet, whenever I consider a rectilinear figure composed of three angles it is absolutely essential that I should attribute to it all those properties that serve to bring about the conclusion that its three angles are no greater than two right angles, even though I may not be considering this point in particular.

The thought is that existence is part of God's essence, or definition, which is to possess all the perfections. Since existence is a perfection, God exists.

God is characterized in a certain way. A characterization is a description, so to examine the logic of the argument, we need a description operator, εx (an x such that) or ιx (the x such that). One may, in fact define the definite in terms of the indefinite, simply by invoking an appropriate uniqueness clause. Thus, $\iota xA(x)$ may be defined as $\varepsilon x(A(x) \wedge \forall y(A(y) \rightarrow y = x))$. Since uniqueness plays no real role in the arguments we will be looking at, I will use the indefinite description operator, which keeps matters simpler, whilst sacrificing nothing relevant.

Descartes characterizes God as an object with all perfections. So let monadic predicates expressing the perfections be: P_0x, P_1x, . . . , P_nx ('x is omnipotent', 'x is omniscient', etc.). Descartes takes the existence predicate, Ex, to be one of these. One might worry about the thought that existence is a perfection, but this is not very important here. Even if it is not, we can just add it to the list of the predicates. So let us take P_0x to be Ex. Let g (God) be the description: $\varepsilon x(Ex \wedge P_1x \wedge \ldots \wedge P_nx)$. Descartes then infers that $Eg \wedge P_1g \wedge \ldots \wedge P_ng$. It follows that Eg.[4]

The crucial principle of inference employed here is the Characterization Principle (CP): $A(\varepsilon xA(x))$: if a thing is characterized as being so and so, it is so and so. Now, plausible as this principle might seem, no one can endorse it in full generality. The reason is simple. Leave existence aside for the moment.

[4] I assume that the perfections are finite in number, but nothing hangs on this. If they are not, we simply define g as $\varepsilon x\forall P(\Gamma(P) \rightarrow Px)$. Here, Γ is a second-level predicate applying to the perfections (and E, if necessary).

Using it, one can prove everything. Let B be any sentence. Let b be the description $\varepsilon x(x = x \wedge B)$. The CP gives us, $b = b \wedge B$; from which, B follows.[5]

So what is an appropriate restriction for the principle? An answer is provided by standard theories of descriptions: $A(\varepsilon xA(x))$ iff something satisfies A(x). Thus, in Hilbert's ε-calculus, $\exists xA(x) \leftrightarrow A(\varepsilon xA(x))$, and for definite descriptions, we have $\exists x!A(x) \leftrightarrow A(\iota xA(x))$ (where ! expresses uniqueness). Indeed, in Russell's theory, this is true because of the contextual definition of ι-terms.[6] Given this restriction on the CP for ε, one can apply it as required in the argument only if $\exists x(Ex \wedge P_1x \wedge \ldots \wedge P_nx)$, and this is essentially what the argument sets out to prove. So its application would beg the question.

Given that the CP is not, and obviously not, in general, true, why is it so tempting? I suspect that it is so because one can express it by saying: 'a thing that is P is P'. But this is ambiguous; it can indeed express an instance of the CP; it can also express the thought that anything that is P is P (that is, $\forall x(Px \rightarrow Px)$) and this is, indeed, analytically true. Descartes suggests that he is considering the CP in this way, when, in the quotation, he likens matters to the analytically true: for all x, if x is a triangle, x has three sides.

1.2 Leibniz

Let us turn to Leibniz. Commenting on Descartes's argument, he says:[7]

> I call every simple quality which is positive and absolute, or expresses whatever it expresses without limits, a *perfection*.
>
> But a quality of this sort, because it is simple, is therefore irresolvable or indefinable, for otherwise, it will not be a simple quality but an aggregate of many, or, if it is one, it will be circumscribed by limits and so be known through negations of further progress contrary to the hypothesis, for a purely positive quality was assumed.
>
> For let the proposition be of this kind:
>
> A and B are incompatible
>
> (for understanding by A and B two simple forms of this kind of perfections, and it is the same if more are assumed like them), it is evident that it cannot be demonstrated without the resolution of the terms A and B, of each or both; for otherwise their nature would not enter into the ratiocination and

5 See Priest (2005: §4.2).

6 For Hilbert's theory, see Leisenring (1969). Russell's theory first appeared in Russell (1905).

7 Hick (1964: 37f.).

> the incompatibility could be demonstrated as well from any others as from themselves. But now (by hypothesis) they are irresolvable. Therefore this proposition cannot be demonstrated from these forms.
>
> But it certainly might be demonstrated by these if it were true, because it is not true *per se*, for all propositions necessarily true are either demonstrable or known *per se*. Therefore, this proposition is not necessarily true. Or if it is not necessary that A and B exist in the same subject, they cannot therefore exist in the same subject, and since the reasoning is the same as regards any other assumed qualities of this kind, therefore all perfections are compatible.
>
> It is granted, therefore, that either a subject of all perfections or the most perfect being can be known.
>
> Whence it is evident that it also exists, since existence is contained in the number of perfections.

Leibniz – being a better logician than Descartes – realizes that the CP cannot hold in full generality. For it to hold, he claims, the properties in the enumeration of the characterization must be compatible. Otherwise, for example, we could show the existence of a round square, by applying the CP to the description $\varepsilon x(Ex \wedge x \text{ is round} \wedge x \text{ is square})$.

Leibniz offers an argument that the perfections are mutually compatible, but we can set this aside for the moment. (We will come back to the matter later in the essay.) The reason is that this version of the CP is still too strong. Let Q_1x be 'x is a horse-like creature', and Q_2x be 'x has a horn on the middle of its forehead'. Then Ex, Q_1x and Q_2x are mutually compatible. There *could*, after all, have been unicorns. But using the CP in this form we can show that there actually are, since if u is the description $\varepsilon x(Ex \wedge Q_1x \wedge Q_2x)$, it gives us: $Eu \wedge Q_1u \wedge Q_2u$. And quite generally, if P is any property such that it is possible that something instantiates it, we can prove that there exists something that actually does so, by considering the characterization $\varepsilon x(Ex \wedge Px)$. This is clearly unacceptable. (I note, in case this is not entirely obvious, that considerations of non-existent objects – 'Meinongianism' – are completely irrelevant here. We are not proving that something is P; we are proving that something is existent and P.)

1.3 Kant

So let us move on to Kant. Unlike Descartes and Leibniz, he (famously) thought that the ontological argument does not work. His discussion of the matter is in the *Critique of Pure Reason*, A592=B620 to A603=B631. He starts this by saying (in his own inimitable way) that of course you can think about God, characterized as a necessarily existent being, but the mere fact of this does not guarantee that there is such a thing (A593=B621):[8]

> In all ages men have spoken of an *absolutely necessary* being, and in doing so have endeavoured, not so much to understand whether and how a thing of this kind allows even of being thought, but rather to prove its existence. There is, of course, no difficulty in giving a verbal definition of the concept, namely that it is something the non-existence of which is impossible. But this gives no insight into the conditions which make it necessary to regard the non-existence of a thing as absolutely unthinkable. It is precisely those conditions that we desire to know, in order that we may determine whether or not, in resorting to this concept, we are thinking of anything at all.

What might such conditions be?

Kant considers an obvious suggestion. The claim that ‘a thing that necessarily exists, necessarily exists’ (an instance of the CP) might appear to be necessarily true, so that its negation is a contradiction. But this, Kant denies. If ‘a thing that necessarily exists’ refers to something, it *is* a contradiction. But if it refers to nothing, it is not. Quite generally (A595=B623):

> If, in an identical proposition, I reject the predicate while retaining the subject, a contradiction results; and I therefore say that the former belongs necessarily to the latter. But if we reject subject and predicate alike, there is no contradiction; for nothing is left that can be contradicted.

In other words, if $\varepsilon xA(x)$ denotes something (existent), then $A(\varepsilon xA(x))$ is true; but if it does not, it may be false.

He continues:

> We have seen that if the predicate of a judgment is rejected together with its subject, no internal contradiction can result, and that this holds no matter what the predicate is. The only way of evading this conclusion is to argue that there are subjects that cannot be removed, and must always remain. That, however, would only be another way of saying that there are absolutely necessary subjects; and that is the very assumption I have called into question, and the possibility of which the above argument is meant to establish.

[8] Translations from the *Critique* are taken from Kemp-Smith (1933).

In other words, simply to assume in an application of the CP that the subject $\varepsilon x A(x)$ must denote something is just to beg the question. Indeed it does, since it is entails $\exists x A(x)$.

Kant's demolition of the CP, and so of the ontological argument, is essentially over; but he goes on to consider a possible objection. This is to the effect that when A(x) contains the existence predicate, matters are different. The objection has clearly failed to grasp the point, and Kant shows his frustration at the ineptitude of such an objector (A598=B626, italics original):

> I should have hoped to put an end to these idle and fruitless disputations in a direct manner, by an accurate determination of the concept of existence, had I not found that the illusion which is caused by the confusion of a logical with a real predicate (that is, a predicate, which determines a thing) is almost beyond correction. Anything we please can be made to serve as a logical predicate; the subject can even be predicated of itself; for logic abstracts from all content. But a *determining* predicate is a predicate which is added to the concept of the subject which enlarges it. Consequently, it must not already be contained in the concept. '*Being*' is not a real predicate; that is, it is not a concept of something which could be added to the concept of a thing. It is merely the positing of a thing, or of certain determinations, as existing in themselves.

In other words, there is no difference between a P and an existing P. So throwing the existence predicate into the characterization makes absolutely no difference. He goes on (A599=B627) to illustrate the point: there is no difference between 100 thalers and 100 existing thalers. These concepts come to the same thing.

Now, it is not at all clear that a P and an existing P are always the same thing. An existing P is certainly a P; and for some Ps, a P is an existing P. A thaler is a concrete banknote. It is in space/time, and so exists. So a thaler is an existent thaler. But this is not true for all Ps. A fictional character is one which appears in a work of fiction. Some fictional characters exist (like Napoleon in *War and Peace* and Gladstone in the Holmes stories) and some do not (like Holmes himself and Gandalf in *Lord of the Rings*). So a fictional character is not necessarily an existing fictional character.

This is beside the point, though. For Kant had already demolished the ontological argument before this. If there are no Ps then 'a thing which is P is P' is not true. And this is so for any P, whether it contains the existence predicate or not.

2 Anselm of Canterbury

Having dealt with the ontological argument in early modern philosophy, let us now backtrack and deal with the mother of all ontological arguments – Anselm's.

2.1 Anselm

In chapter 2 of his Proslogion, Anselm states the argument (addressed to God!), as follows:[9]

> Is there, then, no such nature as You, for the Fool has said in his heart that God does not exist? But surely when this very Fool hears the words 'something nothing greater than which can be thought', he understands what he hears. And what he understands is in his understanding, even if he does not understand [judge] it to exist ... But surely that than which a greater cannot be thought cannot be only in the understanding. For if it were only in the understanding, it could be thought to exist in reality–which is greater [than existing only in the understanding]. Therefore, if that than which a greater cannot be thought existed only in the understanding, then that than which a greater *cannot* be thought would be that than which a greater *can* be thought! But surely this conclusion is impossible. Hence, without doubt, something than which a greater cannot be thought exists both in the understanding and in reality.

How to understand Anselm's argument is not at all obvious. It is clearly a *reductio* argument, but beyond that, the logical details are somewhat murky.[10] Fairly obviously, God is characterized in a certain way, as a being no greater than which can be thought. So if τx is 'x is thought of', let g be the description $\varepsilon x \sim \exists z(\tau z \wedge z > x)$. I note that quantifiers here must be understood as not existentially loaded: they range over things that may or may not exist.[11] Harder to understand is what exactly it is which is supposed to be greater than g. It is something which is exactly the same, except that it exists. So let us take g^* to be the description $\varepsilon x(Ex \wedge \forall P(P \neq E \rightarrow (Px \leftrightarrow Pg))$. Now suppose, for *reductio*, that g does not exist, $\sim Eg$. Then $g^* > g$. (More on this in a second.) But, as is clear, τg^*. (You are thinking about it now.)

9 Hopkins and Richardson (1974).

10 What follows draws on Priest (1995: §4.1), though it is slightly simpler.

11 In this essay, I use $\exists$ as an existentially loaded quantifier unless otherwise noted.

Hence $\tau g^* \wedge g^* > g$. So $\exists z(\tau z \wedge z > g)$. Applying the CP to g gives us: $\sim\exists z(\tau z \wedge z > g)$, which is the contradiction required for *reductio.*[12]

Why is $g^* > g$? It is because g and g^* are alike in all respects, except that g does not exist and g^* does. One might wonder why this makes g^* greater, but let us pass this over. $\sim Eg$ by assumption; to get Eg^*, one needs to apply the CP to g^* to get: $Eg^* \wedge \forall P(P \neq E \rightarrow (Pg^* \leftrightarrow Pg))$.

How, exactly, to reconstruct the argument might certainly be contested. But what is clear is that the CP is required to establish that nothing thought of is greater than g. And probably it is also required to establish that Eg^*. The CP is therefore crucial to the argument, as are the problems I have already discussed in virtue of this.[13]

2.2 Gaunilo

Anselm's argument drew immediate criticism from Gaunilo. In 'On Behalf of the Fool', Gaunilo presented a *reductio* of Anselm's *reductio*. This went as follows:[14]

> Consider this example: Certain people say that somewhere in the ocean is an island, which they call the 'Lost Island' because of the difficulty or, rather, impossibility of finding what does not exist. They say that it is more abundantly filled with inestimable riches and delights then the Isles of the Blessed, and that although it has no owner or inhabitant, it excels all the lands that men inhabit taken together in the unceasing abundance of its fertility.
>
> When someone tells me that there is such an island, I easily understand what is being said, for there is nothing difficult here. Suppose, however, as a consequence of this, that he goes on to say: 'You cannot doubt that this island, more excellent than all lands, actually exists somewhere in reality, because it undoubtedly stands in relation to your understanding. Since it is more excellent, not simply to stand in relation to the understanding, but to be in reality as well, therefore this island must necessarily be in reality. Otherwise, any other island would be more excellent than this island, and

[12] I note that in Anselm's description for God, he uses a modal operator, 'can'. It is not clear where to insert this in the description for g: $\varepsilon x{\sim}\Diamond\exists z(\tau z \wedge z > x)$, $\varepsilon x{\sim}\exists z\Diamond(\tau z \wedge z > x)$, $\varepsilon x{\sim}\exists z(\Diamond\tau z \wedge z > x)$, $\varepsilon x{\sim}\exists z(\tau z \wedge \Diamond z > x)$. In fact, it makes very little difference. For what would need to be established as possible in each case is established as actual (and so possible). So the modal operator is doing no real work. I therefore omitted it to simplify things.

[13] A somewhat different reconstruction of the argument is given by Oppenheimer and Zalta (1991). But as they point out at 514, a version of the CP, in the form of Description Theorem 2, is central to it.

[14] Hick and McGill (1967: 22f.).

> this island, which you understand to be the most excellent of lands, would not then be the most excellent.' If, I repeat, someone should wish by this argument to demonstrate to me that this island truly exists and is no longer to be doubted, I would think he were joking; or, if I accepted the argument, I do not know whom I would regard as the greater fool, me for accepting it, or him for supposing that he had proved the existence of this island with any kind of certainty.

Gaunilo does not attempt to show where Anselm's argument goes wrong. He merely argues that it cannot be sound, since an exactly parallel argument establishes the existence of an island no greater ('more excellent') than which can be conceived. The island is merely an example, and the argument clearly generalizes to any kind of entity. And Gaunilo is quite right. Let A(x) be any condition whatsoever. Define g, this time, as $\varepsilon x{\sim}\exists z(\tau z \wedge z > x \wedge A(x))$. Then the argument runs in exactly the same way, and its conclusion is that Eg, i.e., that something satisfying the condition A(x) exists. This is too much, as I pointed out with respect to Leibniz's formulation of the argument.

Anselm was aware of Gaunilo's criticism, and noted a reply, as follows:[15]

> I can confidently say that if someone discovers for me something existing either in fact or at least in thought, other than that than which 'a greater cannot be conceived', and apply the logic of my argument to it, I shall find the 'Lost Island' for him and shall give it to him as something he will never lose again.

The reply is opaque. Is Anselm saying that the argument does not apply to arbitrary As? In that case he is wrong. Or is he simply accepting the conclusion of the supposed *reductio*, so that there exists a novel no greater than which can be conceived, a person no greater than which can be conceived, a political state no greater than which can be conceived? That way, it would seem, lies madness.[16]

3 To Exist

After dealing with this bit of history, let us return to modern philosophy, and specifically its later parts. Clearly, the ontological argument involves the notion of existence, and given modern developments in logic concerning

[15] Hick and McGill (1967: 23).

[16] Hick (1971), p. 78, suggests that Anselm thinks that the argument works only for necessarily existent beings, not contingently existing beings, such as islands. But that g (or g*) is a necessary being is nowhere appealed to in the argument. Indeed, using the argument, one can show that the island and its like are necessary beings. Just redefine g as $\varepsilon x\neg\exists z(\tau z \wedge z > x \wedge A(x) \wedge \Box E(x))$

quantification and existence, one might well suppose that this has some bearing on the argument. Let us see.

3.1 Frege

Start with Frege.[17] In a very well-known passage, Frege says that existence is a property of a concept. That is, it is expressed by the particular quantifier ('particular', as opposed to 'universal'). He says:[18]

> I have called existence a property of a concept. How I mean this to be taken is best made clear by an example. In the sentence 'there is at least one square root of 4', we have an assertion not about (say) the definite number 2, nor about −2, but about a concept *square root of* 4; viz. that it is not empty.

And in §53 of *Foundations of Arithmetic*, Frege writes casually, 'Because existence is a property of concepts, the ontological argument for the existence of God breaks down.'[19] No further explanation is given. So why does it break down?

In a much less well-known passage of Frege, commenting on Peano, he says:[20]

> Existential sentences, beginning 'there is' ('*es gibt*'), are closely related to particular ones: compare the sentence 'there are numbers which are prime' with 'some numbers are prime'. This existence is still too often confused with reality and objectivity.

His point is this. By all means use the phrase *there exists* as meaning *some* if you wish. That is a very standard way for mathematicians to talk. But don't confuse this with a heavy-duty notion of existence. It's just a manner of speaking.

So what has this to do with the ontological argument? In the academic year 1910/11, Frege lectured on the ontological argument. The lectures were attended by Carnap, whose notes have recently been published.[21] In these, Frege explains that *existence* may mean either a first-order property of an object or a second-order property of a concept, to the effect that something satisfies it. One can take the first-order concept to be a part of the definition of 'God'. However, 'we always want to ask ourselves whether there really is such a thing', i.e., whether *something* satisfies the concept. Frege's objection to the ontological argument is, then, essentially the same as Kant's. $Ex \wedge P_1x \wedge \ldots \wedge$

[17] What follows draws on the second edition of Priest (2005: §18.3.2).

[18] Geach and Black (1970: 48f.). [19] Austin, J. L. (1968). [20] McGuinness (1984: 239).

[21] Reck and Awodey (2004: 80f.).

$P_n x$ is a perfectly good concept, but the mere fact that Ex is part of it does nothing to show that something satisfies it.

3.2 Russell

In 'On Denoting', Russell also makes a brief comment on the ontological argument. He phrases the argument as: The most perfect Being has all perfections; existence is a perfection; therefore that one exists. Using his theory of descriptions, he expands this as:[22]

> There is one and only one entity x that is most perfect; that one has all perfections; existence is a perfection; therefore that one exists.

He then notes the consequent failure of the argument:[23]

> As a proof, this fails for want of a proof of the premise 'there is one and only one entity x which is most perfect'.

His point, then, is exactly the same as Frege's. Given a concept, you need an argument that something satisfies it, even if the concept has existence as a part.

Note that though, in the argument, 'the most perfect Being' is analysed in terms of the theory of definite descriptions, there is no attempt to parse away the monadic existence predicate.

Things change markedly by the time Russell comes to give his lectures on logical atomism (1918). Here he argues that a monadic existence predicate is meaningless. Existence is a second-order concept, expressible by the particular quantifier. Russell's arguments are dismal. Here I note only one of them.[24] This goes as follows:[25]

> If you say 'Men exist, and Socrates is a man, therefore Socrates exists', this is the same sort of fallacy as it would be if you said 'Men are numerous, Socrates is a man, therefore Socrates is numerous', because existence is a predicate of a propositional function, or derivatively of a class. When you say of a propositional function that it is numerous, you will mean that there are several values of x that will satisfy it, that there are more than one; or, if you like to take 'numerous' in a larger sense, more than ten, more than twenty, or

[22] Russell (1905: 117 reprint). [23] Russell (1905: 117 reprint).

[24] For an analysis of the whole set of arguments, see the second edition of Priest (2005: §18.3.4).

[25] Pears (1972: 67, second edition).

> whatever number you think fitting. If x, y, and z all satisfy a propositional function, you may say that that proposition is numerous, but x, y, and z severally are not. Exactly the same applies to existence, that is to say that the actual things there are in the world do not exist, or, at least, that is putting it too strongly, because that is utter nonsense. To say that they do not exist is strictly nonsense, but to say that they exist is also strictly nonsense.

Russell asks us to compare two inferences:

Men exist	Men are numerous
Socrates is a man	Socrates is a man
Socrates exists	Socrates is numerous

and claims that the same sort of fallacy is involved in both. We are supposed to conclude that the conclusion of the first is ungrammatical, as is that of the second. But the analogy is lame. To say that men are numerous is indeed to say that many things are men. In the right context, this is true, as is the other premise. The conclusion, however, is *clearly* nonsense. The inference is therefore fallacious. The first argument, too, is fallacious. But that is simply because it is of the form:

Some things which are men are existent
Socrates is a man
―――――――――――――
Socrates exists

Note that the corresponding inference with a universal major premise seems perfectly valid:

All things which are men are existent
Socrates is a man
―――――――――――――
Socrates exists

in *Towards Non-Being* I tell a story about the late Richard Sylvan.[26] It happens to be the case that all the people in the story are real people. So it is perfectly correct to argue thus: All the people in the story exist. Nick Griffin is in the story. So Nick Griffin exists (unlike, say, the purely fictional Anna Karenina). And the conclusion of Russell's argument, that Socrates exists, is prima facie perfectly grammatical. Compare: 'Nick Griffin exists, but Anna Karenina does not.'

[26] See Priest (2005: §6.6).

There is no mention of the ontological argument in Russell's lectures. But a few years later, in a short lecture on logical atomism, Russell spells out the consequence of his view for the ontological argument:[27]

> An important consequence of the theory of descriptions is that it is meaningless to say 'A exists' unless 'A' is (or stands for) a phrase of the form 'the so-and-so'. If the so-and-so exists, and x is the so-and-so, to say 'x exists' is nonsense. Existence, in the sense in which it is ascribed to single entities, is thus removed altogether from the list of fundamentals. The ontological argument and most of its refutations are found to depend upon bad grammar.

The thought would seem to be this. Since there is no such thing as a meaningful monadic existence predicate, the characterization $Ex \wedge P_1x \wedge \ldots \wedge P_nx$, where the Ps are the perfections, is also meaningless, as, therefore, is any argument employing it.

However, not only does Russell not have any good arguments against a monadic existence predicate, and not only are statements such as 'God exists' clearly meaningful[28] – indeed its truth is the subject of much contention – the view is false even by Russell's own lights. Given that existence is expressed by the particular quantifier, and given that we have an identity predicate, a monadic existence predicate, Ex, can be defined simply as $\exists y\ y = x$. It may be a universal predicate, in that it applies to everything, but meaningless it is not. Neither is there anything in the universality of the predicate which, of itself, invalidates the ontological argument.

3.3 Meinong

Let me finish this section of the discussion with a few comments on Meinong and the CP. In his early writings, it does appear that Meinong endorses the naive CP. He certainly endorses instances of it, such as that the golden mountain is golden and a mountain, and that the round square is round and square.

27 Russell (1924).

28 Russell does have a possible way out here, as reference to the theory of descriptions indicates. He might suggest that the proper name 'God' is a covert definite description (e.g., 'a being with all the perfections'). However, names are not covert descriptions. For example, they have different logical properties. Descriptions show differences of scope in modal contexts; proper names do not. As is generally accepted, the view that names are covert descriptions was demolished by Kripke (1972).

The naive CP was attacked by Russell in his post-'On Denoting' critique of Meinong.[29] Russell's objections were essentially two. The first is that the round square violates the principle of non-contradiction. If it is round, it is not square, so it is square and not square. Meinong accepted this, saying that of course impossible objects can violate the principle, though he later clarified that the negation in question was predicate negation, not sentential negation. He took the law of non-contradiction to hold for sentential negation. If so, the CP cannot hold completely generally, though what an appropriate restriction might be, Meinong never said.

Russell's second objection – and the one germane to present matters – is essentially Gaunilo's. According to the naive CP, the existent King of France exists (and is King of France). Meinong replied that it is indeed existent, but does not exist. Russell, replied that he could see no difference, and it is hard to demur. Maybe, by analogy with the case for negation, Meinong was thinking of 'existent' as a predicate modifier. But again, there must be a restriction on the CP using an existence predicate: Meinong did not accept the Ontological Argument.[30] But again, what such restrictions might be, he does not say.

Meinong, then, left the CP in a very unsatisfactory state. Neo-Meinongians have cleaned matters up. There are currently three ways in which this has been attempted. The first[31] is to distinguish between two sorts of predicates, nuclear and non-nuclear. For the CP, $A(\varepsilon x A(x))$, to hold, all the predicates in $A(x)$ have to be nuclear. Being golden and being a mountain are nuclear; but the existence predicate (or a predicate containing sentential negation) is not. The second way[32] is to distinguish between two modes of predication, instantiation and encoding. $\varepsilon x A(x)$ will always encode $A(x)$ (strictly speaking, as long as $A(x)$ does not itself contain the encoding symbol), but it will instantiate it only if something (or some existing thing, depending on how one interprets the particular quantifier) satisfies $A(x)$. A third way[33] is to hold that $A(\varepsilon x A(x))$ always holds, but it may not hold at this world; it may hold only at other (possible or impossible) worlds. It holds at this world if something (not necessarily something existent) actually satisfies $A(x)$.

This is not the place to go into these variations further,[34] since in none of them is $\varepsilon x(Ex \wedge P_1x \wedge \ldots \wedge P_nx)$ guaranteed to satisfy $Ex \wedge P_1x \wedge \ldots \wedge P_nx$. So none of them does anything to help the ontological argument.

[29] For a full discussion and the references to the Russell/Meinong exchange, see Marek (2008: §4.4).

[30] See Marek (2008: §4.4.2). [31] To be found, for example, in Parsons (1980).

[32] To be found, for example, in Zalta (1983). [33] To be found, for example, in Priest (2005).

[34] Matters are discussed further in Reicher (2014), Berto (2012) and the preface to the second edition of Priest (2005).

4 Later Versions of the Argument

In the final section of this essay, I want to take up two more contemporary forms of the argument.

4.1 Hartshorne

The first was given by Hartshorne, and is an essentially modal argument.[35] He claims to find this in Anselm's *Proslogion III* (that is, the chapter after the one I discussed above), and it goes essentially as follows.

Let Px be 'x is a perfect being', and let H be ∃xPx. The argument has two premises:

1. $\Box(H \rightarrow \Box H)$
2. $\Diamond H$

Here, □ expresses analyticity,[36] though the argument might also – and perhaps more profitably – be run for metaphysical necessity. The modal logic employed is S5. The argument then goes essentially as follows.[37] In S5, $\Box(A \rightarrow B) \vdash \Diamond A \rightarrow \Diamond B$. Applying this to 1 gives $\Diamond H \rightarrow \Diamond\Box H$. But, in S5, $\Diamond\Box A \rightarrow A$. Hence $\Diamond H \rightarrow H$. By premise 2, H follows.

One may have some worries about whether the modal logic for the requisite notion of necessity is S5, but the view is plausible enough. This leaves the two premises.

For premise 1: Let us define Px as $\Box(Ex \wedge P_0x \wedge \ldots \wedge P_nx)$, where the P_is enumerate the (other) perfections. (The existence predicate is unnecessary if quantifiers are existentially loaded.) Let g be the description $\varepsilon x\Box(Ex \wedge P_0x \wedge \ldots \wedge P_nx)$. Then by an uncontentious version of the CP, $\exists xPx \rightarrow Pg$. Moreover, $Pg \rightarrow \Box Pg$ (by S5). Further, $\Box(Pg \rightarrow \exists xPx)$, and so $\Box Pg \rightarrow \Box\exists xPx$. Chaining these three things together gives us: $\exists xPx \rightarrow \Box\exists xPx$. Finally, this has all been established by *a priori* reasoning, and so is necessary. That is, $\Box(\exists xPx \rightarrow \Box\exists xPx)$.

Matters are less plausible with respect to premise 2. Necessity has many meanings. One is epistemic. And it certainly seems to be right that the existence of God is epistemically possible. But that is not the notion of necessity in play here. It is worth noting that the fact that ◊H is an explicit

[35] Hartshorne (1962: 49–57); reprinted as Hick and McGill (1967: 334–40). Similar arguments were given by Malcolm (1960) and Plantinga (1974).

[36] Hartshorne (1962: 337 in reprint).

[37] Hartshorne's argument is more cumbersome than necessary. Here I streamline it.

premise of the argument allows a reply to the objection that the argument could be run for any H. Suppose that P characterizes a necessarily existent island or unicorn. Unicorns, islands and their like are contingent existences. So a necessarily existent one is a contradiction in terms: the statement that it is possible for one to exist is false.

Be that as it may, it is not clear that the premise is true for the required notion of necessity. Things may be impossible in the required way without one realizing it. Thus, the claim that there is a greatest prime number is impossible, but someone uneducated in number theory might not realize this. And even for someone who is so educated, there will be statements, A, which are theorems of, say, Peano Arithmetic, which are not known to be so. Hence $\sim A$ is impossible, but not realized to be such.

The worry is enhanced by the fact that, as we saw, $\Diamond H \rightarrow H$. So $\sim H \rightarrow \sim\Diamond H$, that is, $\sim H \rightarrow \Box\sim H$. So if H is false it is necessarily false. In other words H is either a necessary truth or a necessary falsity; and both seem equally plausible. One might try to invoke the fact that we can at least conceive H to be true, and since what is conceivable is possible, H is possible. But this is a bad move. Conceivability is not a good test of possibility.[38] But even if it were, $\sim H$ seems equally conceivable. So we are no better off.

I note, moreover, that $H \rightarrow \Diamond H$ in S5; given that $\Diamond H \rightarrow H$, H is equivalent to $\Diamond H$. So to assume premise 2 is to assume H, and so beg the question.

Finally, there are real worries concerning whether the perfections are consistent, and so about premise 2. Thus, God is omnipotent and so can do anything. But God is morally perfect, and so cannot do anything wrong. One may even worry that single perfections are not consistent. God is omnipotent, and so can create a stone that is so great that it cannot be lifted. So God can limit God's own power. But an omnipotent being cannot have their power limited. There is a substantial literature on these matters, and this is not the place to go into it.[39] It does take us, however, into the final argument we will consider.

4.2 Gödel

At some point in the 1940s and 50s (and so before Hartshorne's proof), Gödel developed an ontological argument, a version of which was published

[38] See Priest (2005: ch. 9, second edition).

[39] To give just a few examples: Cowan (2003), Hoffman and Rosenkrantz (2006), Blumenfeld (2003), Kretzmann (1966). A much longer list of references can be found in McCormick (2016).

posthumously.[40] The note is terse (just over one printed page), and sometimes cryptic, but it is clear that the argument is inspired by Leibniz's argument.

The argument is couched in a higher-order modal logic (S5). Crucial to it is the notion of a positive property. No definition is given. Gödel glosses it, somewhat opaquely, as follows:[41]

> Positive means positive in the moral aesthetic sense (independently of the accidental structure of the world). Only then [are] the axioms true. It may also mean pure 'attribution' <Footnote: I.e., the disjunctive normal form in terms of elementary properties contains a member without negation.> as opposed to 'privation' (or *containing* privation). This interpretation [supports a] simpler proof.

The predicate Gx, 'x is God', is defined as 'x has all positive properties'. (In fact, Gödel's axioms then imply that x has exactly the positive properties.) For the argument to be an argument for the existence of *God*, it would have to be the case that all the perfections are positive properties. Whether this is so is unclear, due to the unclarity of what it is to be positive, but certainly some of the standard perfections don't look very positive. Thus, to be unchanging is *not* to change.

The argument then comes in two stages. For the first, there is a predicate Qx concerning essences, and an axiom to the effect that being Q is positive.[42] Given this, if x is God then Qx, and from this and the definition of Q, it follows that if x is God then x necessarily exists. Gödel's argument here (not spelled out in the note) concerns a certain notion of what an essence is (namely, the essence of an object is a property that entails all of its properties). This is certainly a contentious notion of essence, even for those who accept that there are essences.[43] And I must confess that this

[40] In Feferman (1995: 388–404). There is a substantial and helpful introduction by Robert Adams. Hazen (1998) is also a helpful commentary. For those with a taste for matters formal, Fitting (2002: ch. 11) contains an excellent presentation. There is no evidence to suggest that Gödel thought that the argument actually worked. In what follows, I modernize Gödel's notation. Many thanks go to Allen Hazen, for helpful discussions.

[41] Feferman (1995: 404). The material in square brackets is the editor's interpolations, and the italics are original.

[42] Gödel uses the letter E instead of Q. I change this to avoid confusion with an existence predicate.

[43] Moreover, there is a problem with it, as noted by Sobel (1987). Let A be any true statement, and consider the property expressed by $A \wedge x = x$. This is a property of God, so God's essence entails that God has it. But God's essence is necessary, so A is necessary. In other words, Gödel's axioms entail that $A \rightarrow \Box A$. One may rework the axioms to try to avoid this consequence. (See Fitting (2002: 163–71).) However, perhaps Leibniz himself would not have been too troubled by it. For him, every true statement can indeed by inferred *a priori* by an agent (such as God, whom, after all, we are dealing with here) capable of 'infinite analysis'. (See, e.g., Look (2013: §2).)

part of the argument strikes me as needlessly complex. Much simpler would have been to say that the property of necessary existence is positive. That is, if Nx is $\Box Ex$ – or, if you don't like that, $\Box\exists y\ y = x$ – then N is positive.[44] It seems to me that it is just as intuitive to suppose that N is positive as to suppose that Q is – maybe even more so. (Nor is there a problem about having a modal operator in a positive property, since the definition of Q has one.[45]) It then follows very simply that if something is God, God necessarily exists.

At any rate, we have the conditional $\exists xGx \rightarrow \Box\exists yGy$. The argument then proceeds as in Hartshorne:

$\Box(\exists xGx \rightarrow \Box\exists yGy)$
$\Diamond\exists xGx \rightarrow \Diamond\Box\exists yGy$
$\Diamond\exists Gx \rightarrow \exists yGy$

Each step follows in S5.

Hartshorne takes it to be evident that $\Diamond\exists xGx$; Gödel does not. He gives an argument for this. This is the second part of his ontological argument, and it is a variant of Leibniz's argument that the perfections are compossible. This goes as follows. Being God is essentially having the property $\bigwedge_{i\in I}P_i$, where $\{P_i: i \in I\}$ is the set of all positive properties. Gödel now lists three axioms. Axiom 1 tells us that if Q_1 and Q_2 are positive so is their conjunction. (A footnote adds 'And for any number of summands'.) So $\bigwedge_{i\in I}P_i$ is positive.

Axiom 5 tells us that if Q_1 is positive, and being Q_1 strictly implies being Q_2, then Q_2 is positive. It follows that the property expressed by $x = x$ is positive. Axiom 2 tells us that if Q is positive, its negation is not. So the property expressed by $x \neq x$ is not positive.

Gödel then argues:[46]

> [I]f a system S of positive properties were incompatible, it would mean that the sum property, s (which is positive) would be $x \neq x$.

Thus, if $\bigwedge_{i\in I}P_i$ were inconsistent, it would entail the property expressed by $x \neq x$. So this would have to be positive, which it is not.

[44] In constant-domain modal logic, it is a logical truth that $\forall x\Box\exists y\ y = x$; but in variable-domain modal logic it is not.

[45] Gödel's apparatus does avoid the use of first-order *de re* machinery (that is, quantification into the scope of a modal operator), though not second-order. Perhaps one might take this to be an advantage.

[46] Feferman (1995: 404).

How plausible these three axioms are is somewhat moot, because, again, of the unclarity of the notion of being positive. But, together, they are problematic. Being red seems to be a positive property if anything is; but so does being green. (There certainly seems to be no negation sign in their disjunctive normal forms!) Being red and green is not a satisfiable property.[47] If it is not positive, we have a counterexample to Axiom 1. So suppose it is. x is red and x is green strictly implies $x \neq x$. (There is no possible world in which something is red and green.) Then either we have a counterexample to Axiom 5 (strict implication does not preserve positivity) or Axiom 2 ($x \neq x$ is positive).

Of course, $\Box$((x is red $\wedge$ x is green) $\rightarrow x \neq x$) is not a theorem of S5. But to restrict the meaning of Axiom 5 to things that are formally provable seems entirely arbitrary. Moreover, the point obviously generalizes to any family of exclusive predicates. So consider arithmetic. The predicates $x = 0$, $x = 1$, $x = 2$, . . ., form such a family. $x = 0 \wedge x = 1$ is not satisfiable, and $\Box((x = 0 \wedge x = 1) \rightarrow x \neq x)$ is a theorem of, say, Peano Arithmetic (extended with a standard modal operator). Finally, it must be remembered that what is really at issue here are the perfections (being omniscient, being unchangeable, etc.). Nothing about these is formally provable in S5 either. So Gödel's machinery must extend beyond what is formally provable in that system.

And of course, if the perfections are, indeed, positive, to suppose that they are not like red and green is exactly to assume what needs to be proved, viz., the consistency of the perfections – and so begs the question.

The role of the CP in Gödel's version of the Ontological Argument is not evident; but it is there, just covered up by the fact that the argument does not use descriptions. Essentially, God is defined as the object with all positive properties. One of these is Q. A legitimate version of the CP tells us that if God exists, they have the property Q. Q is not quite necessary existence (despite Gödel's gloss on its definition). Rather, it is a property such that having it ensures that God necessarily exists (though this has to be untangled from Gödel's definitions involving essences) – which is Hartshorne's premise 1.

5 Conclusion

Much more has been said about the ontological argument than I have commented on here. But we have looked at some of the most significant things

[47] It is worth remembering that it was consideration of colour predicates which caused Wittgenstein to start to dismantle the *Tractatus*, since they show that atomic states of affairs can be incompatible. See Wittgenstein (1929).

that have been said about the argument in the history of Western philosophy. What we have seen is that at the core of the argument is the Characterization Principle, a naive version of which cannot be held. Existence not being a predicate has nothing whatsoever to do with the matter (even for Kant). What has everything to do with the matter is whether some restricted version of the CP can be established – a restricted version that applies when the characterization is that of God. No way of doing this without begging the question seems possible.

Bibliography

Abaci, U. (2008) 'Kant's Theses on Existence', *British Journal for the History of Philosophy* 16: 559–93

Adams, R. (1994) *Leibniz: Determinist, Theist, Idealist*. Oxford: Oxford University Press

Adams, R. (1997) 'The Logical Structure of Anselm's Arguments' in *The Virtue of Faith*. Oxford: Oxford University Press, 221–42

Adams, R. (2007) 'The Priority of the Perfect in the Philosophical Theology of the Continental Rationalists' in M. Ayers (ed.) *Rationalism, Platonism and God*. Oxford: Oxford University Press, 91–116

Allison, H. (2004) *Kant's Transcendental Idealism*, second edition. New Haven, CT: Yale University Press

Anderson, C. (1990) 'Some Emendations on Gödel's Ontological Proof', *Faith and Philosophy* 7: 291–303

Anderson, R. (2015) *The Poverty of Conceptual Truth: Kant's Analytic/Synthetic Distinction and the Limits of Metaphysics*. Oxford: Oxford University Press

Anscombe, G. (1993) 'Russell or Anselm?' *Philosophical Quarterly* 43: 500–4

Anselm (1077–8) *Monologion* (translated by S. Harrison), *Proslogion* and *Reply to Gaunilo* (translated by M. J. Charlesworth) in *Anselm of Canterbury: The Major Works*, ed. B. Davies and G. R. Evans (Oxford: Oxford University Press, 1998), pp. 5–81, 82–104 and 111–22 respectively

Anselm (1078/2001) *Proslogion: With the Replies of Gaunilo and Anselm*, edited and translated by T. Williams. Indianapolis, IN: Hackett

Antognazza, M. (2007) 'Comments on Adams "The Priority of the Perfect"' in M. Ayers (ed.) *Rationalism, Platonism and God*. Oxford: Oxford University Press, 117–31

Antognazza, M. (2015) 'The Hypercategorematic Infinite', *The Leibniz Review* 25: 5–30

Austin, J. L. (tr.) (1968) *The Foundations of Arithmetic*, Oxford: Basil Blackwell

Aquinas, T. (1077/1856) *Scriptum Super Sententiis*, available at www.corpusthomisticum.org/snp1003.html (Cited as 'SSS')

Aquinas, T. (1930) *Summa Contra Gentiles*, edited by P. Ucelli. Rome. (Also cited as 'SCG')

Aquinas, T. (1941) *Summa Theologiae*. Ottawa: Studium Generalis. (Also cited as 'ST')

Aquinas, T. (1944) 'Summa Theologiae Part I' in *Basic Writings*, translated by A. C. Pegis. New York: Kopf

Aquinas, T. (1947) *Summa Theologica*, translated by the Fathers of the English Dominic Province. New York: Benziger Brothers (Also cited as 'ST')

Aquinas, T. (1952) *Quaestiones Disputatae de Potentia Dei*, translated by J. Kenny. Westminster, MD: Newman Press. (Cited as 'QDPD')

Aquinas, T. (1959) *Expositio Super Librum Boethii De Trinitate*, edited by B. Decker. Leiden: Brill. (Also cited as 'ESLBDT')

Aquinas, T. (1975) *Summa Contra Gentiles, Book One: God*, translated by A. Pegis. Notre Dame, IN: University of Notre Dame Press

Ayer, A. (1936/46) *Language, Truth and Logic*. London: Victor Gollancz Ltd

Baker, L. and Matthews, G. (2010) 'Anselm's Argument Reconsidered', *Review of Metaphysics* 64: 31–54

Barnes, J. (1972) *The Ontological Argument*. London: Macmillan

Bell, D. (1984) *Spinoza in Germany from 1670 to the Age of Goethe*. London: Institute of Germanic Studies, University of London

Berto, F. (2012) *Existence as a Real Property*. Dordrecht: Springer

Blumenfeld, D. (1995) 'Leibniz's Ontological and Cosmological Arguments' in N. Jolley (ed.) *The Cambridge Companion to Leibniz*. Cambridge: Cambridge University Press, 353–81

Blumenfeld, D. (2003) 'On the Compossibility of the Divine Attributes' in M. Martin and R. Monnier (eds.) *The Impossibility of God*. Amherst, NY: Prometheus Press, 91–103

Bonaventure, G. (1979) *Disputed Questions on the Mystery of the Trinity*, translated by Z. Hayes. New York: Franciscan Institute

Bosley, R. and Tweedale, M. (2006) *Basic Issues in Medieval Philosophy*, second edition. Peterborough: Broadview Press

Cameron, R. (2009) 'God Exists at Every (Modal Realist) World: A Reply to Sheehy', *Religious Studies* 45: 95–100

Campbell, R. (1976) *From Belief to Understanding*. Canberra: Australian National University Press

Chalmers, D. (2002) 'Does Conceivability Entail Possibility?' in T. Gendler and J. Hawthorne (eds.) *Conceivability and Possibility*. Oxford: Oxford University Press, 145–200

Charlesworth, M. (1965) *St Anselm's Proslogion*. Oxford: Clarendon Press

Church, A. (1940) 'A Formulation of the Simple Theory of Types', *Journal of Symbolic Logic* 5: 56–68

Cowan, J. (2003) 'The Paradox of Omnipotence' in M. Martin and R. Monnier (eds.) *The Impossibility of God*. Amherst, NY: Prometheus Press

Curley, E. (1978) *Descartes against the Skeptics*. Cambridge, MA: Harvard University Press

Curley, E. (2005) 'Back to the Ontological Argument' in C. Mercer and E. O'Neill (eds.) *Early Modern Philosophy: Mind, Matter, and Metaphysics*. Oxford: Oxford University Press, 46–64

Descartes, R. (1641) 'Meditations on First Philosophy', translated by J. Cottingham in (1984) *The Philosophical Writings of Descartes, Volume II*, edited by J. Cottingham, R. Stoothoff and D. Murdoch. Cambridge: Cambridge University Press, 3–62

Descartes, R. (1897–1909) *Oeuvres de Descartes*, 11 volumes, edited by C. Adam and P. Tannery. Paris: Leopold Cerf. (Cited as 'AT')

Descartes, R. (1911) *Meditations*, translated by E. Haldane and G. Ross, in *Philosophical Works of Descartes, Volume 1*. Cambridge: Cambridge University Press

Descartes, R. (1964–76) *Oeuvres de Descartes*, 12 volumes, revised edition, edited by C. Adam and P. Tannery. Paris: J. Vrin/CNRS. (Cited as 'AT')

Descartes, R. (1984–91) *The Philosophical Writings of Descartes*, translated by J. Cottingham, R. Stoothoff, D. Murdoch and (for volume 3) A. Kenny. New York: Cambridge University Press. (Cited as 'CSM(K)')

Doney, W. (1978) 'The Geometrical Presentation of Descartes's A Priori Proof' in M. Hooker (ed.) *Descartes: Critical and Interpretive Essays*. Baltimore, MD: Johns Hopkins University Press, 1–25

Doney, W. (1993) 'Did Caterus Misunderstand Descartes' Ontological Proof?' in S. Voss (ed.) *Essays on the Philosophy and Science of René Descartes*. Oxford: Oxford University Press, 75–84

Ellis, F. (2010) 'God and Other Minds', *Religious Studies* 46: 331–51

Feferman, S. (ed.) (1995) *Kurt Gödel, Collected Works, Volume III: Unpublished Essay and Lectures*. New York: Oxford University Press

Fitting, M. (2002) *Types, Tableaus and Gödel's God*. Dordrecht: Kluwer

Forgie, J. (2008) 'How is the Question "Is Existence a Predicate?" Relevant to the Ontological Argument?' *International Journal for Philosophy of Religion* 64: 117–33

Frege, G. (1981) *Posthumous Writings*, edited by Hans Hermes, Friedrich Kambartel and Friedrich Kaulbach, translated by Peter Ogon and Roger White. Oxford: Blackwell

Frege, G. (2000) 'Vorschläge für ein Wahlgesetz' in G. Gabriel and U. Dathe (eds.) *Gottlob Frege: Werk und Wirking*, edited and introduced by U. Dathe and W. Kienzler. Paderborn: Verlag Mentis, 283–313

Gardner, S. (1999) *Routledge Philosophy Guidebook to Kant and the Critique of Pure Reason*. London: Routledge

Geach, P. and Black, M. (eds.) (1970) *Translations from the Philosophical Writings of Gottlob Frege*. Oxford: Basil Blackwell

Geach, P. and Black, M. (eds. and trs.) (1970) *Translations from the Philosophical Writings of Gottlob Frege*, Oxford: Basil Blackwell

Gendler, T. and Hawthorne, J. (2002) 'Introduction: Conceivability and Possibility' in T. Gendler and J. Hawthorne (eds.) *Conceivability and Possibility*. Oxford: Oxford University Press, 1–70

Gregory, D. (2010) 'Conceivability and Apparent Possibility' in B. Hale and A. Hoffman (eds.) *Modality: Metaphysics, Logic, and Epistemology*. Oxford: Oxford University Press, 319–42

Grier, M. (2001) *Kant's Doctrine of Transcendental Illusion*. Cambridge: Cambridge University Press

Gueroult, M. (1984) *Descartes's Philosophy Interpreted According to the Order of Reasons*, volume 1, trans. Roger Ariew. Minneapolis: University of Minnesota Press

Guyer, P. and Wood, A. (1992–) *The Cambridge Edition of the Works of Immanuel Kant*. Cambridge: Cambridge University Press

Harrelson, K. (2009) *The Ontological Argument from Descartes to Hegel*. Amherst, NY: Humanity Books

Hartshorne, C. (1962) *The Logic of Perfection*. La Salle, IL: Open Court

Hartshorne, C. (1965) *Anselm's Discovery: A Re-Examination of the Ontological Proof for God's Existence.* La Salle, IL: Open Court

Hazen, A. (1998) 'On Gödel's Ontological Proof', *Australasian Journal of Philosophy* 76: 361–77

Hegel, G. (1832/95) *Lectures on the Philosophy of Religion*, translated by E. Speirs and J. Sanderson. London: Routledge and Kegan Paul

Hegel, G. (1952) *Philosophy of Right*, translated by T. M. Knox. Oxford: Clarendon

Hegel, G. (1966) *Vorlesungen über die Beweise vom Dasein Gottes*, edited by Georg Lasson. Hamburg: Meiner. (Cited as 'VBDG')

Hegel, G. (1970) *Philosophy of Nature*, translated by A. Miller. Oxford: Clarendon

Hegel, G. (1976) *Phenomenology of Spirit*, translated by A. Miller. Oxford: Oxford University Press

Hegel, G. (1985) *Lectures on the Philosophy of Religion*, volume III: *The Consummate Religion*, edited by P. Hodgson, translated by R. Brown, P. Hodgson and J. Stewart. Berkeley: University of California Press

Hegel, G. (1991) *The Encyclopaedia Logic*, translated by T. Geraets, W. Suchting and H. Harris. Indianapolis, IN: Hackett

Hegel, G. (2007) *Philosophy of Mind*, translated by W. Wallace and A. Miller, revised by M. Inwood. Oxford: Oxford University Press

Hegel, G. (2009) *Heidelberg Writings*, translated by B. Bowman and A. Speight. Cambridge: Cambridge University Press

Hegel, G. (2010) *The Science of Logic*, translated by G. di Giovanni. Cambridge: Cambridge University Press

Hick, J. (1964) *The Existence of God.* New York: The Macmillan Company

Hick, J. (1971) *Arguments for the Existence of God.* New York: Herder and Herder

Hick, J. and McGill, A. (eds.) (1967) *The Many Faced Argument.* New York: The Macmillan Company

Hintikka, J. (1959) 'Existential Presuppositions and Existential Commitments', *Journal of Philosophy* 56: 125–37

Hoffman, J. and Rosenkrantz, G. (2006) 'Omnipotence' in E. Zalta (ed.) *The Stanford Encyclopedia of Philosophy*, http://plato.stanford.edu/entries/omnipotence/

Hong, W. (2012) 'An Almost Neglected Aspect of Kant's Theology', *Bijdragen: International Journal for Philosophy and Theology* 73: 28–54

Hopkins, J. and Richardson, H. (eds.) (1974) *Anselm of Canterbury, Volume 1.* New York: Edwin Mellen Press

Hume, D. (1748/2007) *Enquiry Concerning Human Understanding*, edited by P. Millican. Oxford: Oxford University Press

Ichikawa, J. and Jarvis, B. (2012) 'Rational Imagination and Modal Knowledge', *Noûs* 46: 127–58

Inwood, J. (2002) *Hegel.* Abingdon: Routledge

Jacquette, D. (1994) 'Meinongian Logic and Anselm's Ontological Proof for the Existence of God', *The Philosophical Forum* 25: 231–40

Janke, W. (1963) 'Das Ontologische Argument in der Frühzeit des Leibnizschen Denkens (1676–78)', *Kant-Studien* 54: 259–87

Johnston, M. (1992) 'Explanation, Response-Dependence, and Judgement-Dependence' in P. Menzies (ed.) *Response-Dependent Concepts*. Canberra: RSSS ANU Working Papers in Philosophy, 123–83

Kant, I. (1781/1787/1929) *Critique of Pure Reason*, translated by N. Smith. London: Macmillan (corrected edition 1933)

Kant, I. (1781/1787/1998) *Critique of Pure Reason*, translated by P. Guyer and A. Wood. Cambridge: Cambridge University Press

Kant, I. (1781/1900–) *Kritik der reinen Vernunft*, first edition; Volume 3 of *Kant's gesammelte Schriften*, edited by Königlichen Preußischen Akademie der Wissenschaften. Berlin: Georg Riemer

Kant, I. (1787/1900–) *Kritik der reinen Vernunft*, second edition; Volume 4 of *Kant's gesammelte Schriften*, edited by Königlichen Preußischen Akademie der Wissenschaften. Berlin: Georg Riemer

Keller, J. (2016) 'Philosophical Individualism' in J. Keller (ed.) *Being, Freedom, and Method: Themes from Van Inwagen*. Oxford: Oxford University Press, 299–323

Kemp-Smith, N. (tr.) (1933) *Immanuel Kant's Critique of Pure Reason*, second edition. London: Macmillan & Co.

Kenny, A. (1968) *Descartes: A Study of His Philosophy*. New York: Random House

Kretzmann, N. (1966) 'Omniscience and Immutability', *Journal of Philosophy* 63: 409–21

Kripke, S. (1971) 'Identity and Necessity' in M. Munitz (ed.) *Identity and Individuation*. New York: New York University Press, 135–64

Kripke, S. (1972) 'Naming and Necessity' in D. Davidson and G. Harman (eds.) *Semantics of Natural Language*. Dordrecht: Reidel, 253–355; reprinted as *Naming and Necessity*. Oxford: Basil Blackwell, 1980

Kung, P. (2010) 'Imagining as a Guide to Possibility', *Philosophy and Phenomenological Research* 81: 620–63.

Kung, P. (2016) 'You Really Do Imagine It: Against Error Theories of Imagination', *Noûs* 50: 90–120.

Lambert, K. (1960) 'The Definition of E! in Free Logic'. In *Abstracts: The International Congress for Logic, Methodology and Philosophy of Science*. Stanford, CA: Stanford University Press

Leftow, B. (in press) *Anselm's Proofs*. Oxford: Oxford University Press

Leibniz, G. (1875–90) *Die Philosophischen Schriften*, edited by C. Gerhardt, 7 volumes. Berlin: Weidmannsche Buchhandlung. (Cited as 'GP')

Leibniz, G. (1923–) *Sämtliche Schriften und Briefe*, edited by Deutsche Akademie der Wissenschaften zu Berlin, Series 1-VIII. Darmstadt, 1923–, Leipzig, 1938–, Berlin, 1950–. (Cited as 'A')

Leibniz, G. (1948) *Textes inédits d'après les manuscrits de la Bibliothèque Provinciale de Hanovre*, 2 volumes, edited by G. Grua. Paris: PUF. (Cited as 'Grua')

Leibniz, G. (1960–1) *Die Philosophischen Schriften*, edited by C. Gerhardt, 7 volumes. Hildesheim: Olms

Leibniz, G. (1965) 'Two Notations for Discussions with Spinoza' in Plantinga (1965), 55–65

Leibniz, G. (1981) *New Essays on Human Understanding*, edited and translated by P. Remnant and J. Bennett. Cambridge: Cambridge University Press. (Cited as 'NE')

Leibniz, G. (1989) *Philosophical Essays*, edited and translated by R. Ariew and D. Garber. Indianapolis, IN: Hackett. (Cited as 'AG')

Leibniz, G. (1992) *De Summa Rerum: Metaphysical Papers, 1675–1676*, translated with an introduction and notes by G. Parkinson. New Haven, CT: Yale University Press. (Cited as 'Parkinson')

Leibniz, G. and Des Bosses, B. (2007) *The Leibniz–Des Bosses Correspondence*, translated, edited and with an introduction by B. Look and D. Rutherford. New Haven, CT: Yale University Press. (Cited as 'LDB')

Leisenring, A. (1969) *Mathematical Logic and Hilbert's ε-Symbol*. London: Macdonald Technical and Scientific

Lenzen, W. (2017) 'Leibniz's Ontological Proof of the Existence of God and the Problem of "Impossible Objects"', *Logica Universalis* 11: 85–104 (Special Issue on 'Logic and Religion' edited by R. Silvestre)

Lewis, D. (1970) 'Anselm and Actuality', *Noûs* 4: 175–88

Lewis, D. (1983a) 'Postscripts to "Anselm and Actuality"' in *Philosophical Papers Volume I*. Oxford: Oxford University Press, 21–5

Lewis, D. (1983b) 'Postscript to "Counterpart Theory and Quantified Modal Logic"' in *Philosophical Papers Volume I*. Oxford: Oxford University Press, 39–46

Lewis, D. (1990) 'Noneism or Allism?' *Mind* 99: 23–31

Lewis, D. (1999) 'New Work for a Theory of Universals' in *Papers in Metaphysics and Epistemology*. Cambridge: Cambridge University Press, 8–55

Logan, I. (2009) *Reading Anselm's Proslogion*. Farnham: Ashgate

Longuenesse, B. (1998) *Kant and the Capacity to Judge: Sensibility and Discursivity in the Transcendental Analytic of the Critique of Pure Reason*. Princeton, NJ: Princeton University Press

Look, B. (2013) 'Leibniz's Modal Metaphysics' in E. Zalta (ed.) *The Stanford Encyclopedia of Philosophy*, http://plato.stanford.edu/entries/leibniz-modal/

Look, B. (2018) 'Leibniz's Arguments for the Existence of God' in M. R. Antognazza (ed.) *The Oxford Handbook of Leibniz*. Oxford: Oxford University Press, 701–716. Online version DOI:10.1093/oxfordhb/9780199744725.013.010

Lowe, E. (2012) 'A New Modal Version of the Ontological Argument' in M. Szatkowski (ed.) *Ontological Proofs Today*. Heusenstamm: Ontos Verlag, 179–91

Mackie, J. (1982) *The Miracle of Theism*. Oxford: Clarendon Press

Malcolm, N. (1960) 'Anselm's Ontological Arguments', *Philosophical Review* 69: 41–62; reprinted as pp. 301–20 of Hick and McGill (1967)

Mann, W. (2012) 'Locating the Lost Island', *Review of Metaphysics* 66: 295–316

Marek, J. (2008) 'Alexius Meinong', in E. Zalta (ed.) *The Stanford Encyclopedia of Philosophy*, http://plato.stanford.edu/entries/meinong/. (Accessed May 2016)

Matthews, G. (1963) 'Aquinas on Saying that God Doesn't Exist', *Monist* 47, 472–7

Maydole, R. (2003) 'The Modal Perfection Argument for the Existence of a Supreme Being', *Philo* 6: 299–313

McCormick, M. (2016) 'Atheism' in J. Feiser and B. Dowdan (eds.) *Internet Encyclopedia of Philosophy*, www.iep.utm.edu/atheism/

McDaniel, K. (2004) 'Modal Realism with Overlap', *Australasian Journal of Philosophy* 82: 137–52

McGuinness, B. (ed.) (1984) 'On Mr. Peano's Conceptual Notation and My Own', in *Collected Papers on Mathematics, Logic, and Philosophy*. Oxford: Basil Blackwell, 234–48

Meinong, A. (1960) 'The Theory of Objects' in R. Chisholm (ed.) Realism and the Background of Phenomenology. Glencoe: Free Press, 76–117

Menzel, C. (2015) 'Actualism' in E. Zalta (ed.) *The Stanford Encyclopedia of Philosophy*, http://plato.stanford.edu/archives/spr2015/entries/actualism/

Menzies, P. (1998) 'Possibility and Conceivability: A Response-Dependent Account of Their Connections' in R. Casati (ed.) *European Review of Philosophy, Volume 3: Response-Dependence*. Stanford, CA: CSLI Publications, 255–77

Millican, P. (2004) 'The One Fatal Flaw in Anselm's Argument', *Mind* 113: 437–76. (Cited as 'M2004')

Millican, P. (2007) 'Ontological Arguments and the Superiority of Existence: Reply to Nagasawa', *Mind* 116: 1041–53

Millican, P. (2017) 'Hume's Fork, and His Theory of Relations', *Philosophy and Phenomenological Research* 95: 3–65

Mizrahi, M. and Morrow, D. (2015) 'Does Conceivability Entail Metaphysical Possibility?' *Ratio* 28: 1–13

Murdoch, D. (1993) 'Exclusion and Abstraction in Descartes', *Metaphysics: Philosophical Quarterly* 43: 38–57

Nagasawa, Y. (2007) 'Millican on the Ontological Argument', *Mind* 116: 1027–40

Newman, L. and Nelson, A. (1999) 'Circumventing Cartesian Circles', *Noûs*, 33: 370–404

Nolan, L. (1997) 'The Ontological Status of Cartesian Natures', *Pacific Philosophical Quarterly* 78: 169–94

Nolan, L. (1998) 'Descartes' Theory of Universals', *Philosophical Studies* 89: 161–80

Nolan, L. (2001) (revised 2015) 'Descartes' Ontological Argument' in E. Zalta (ed.) *The Stanford Encyclopedia of Philosophy*, http://plato.stanford.edu/entries/descartes-ontological/

Nolan, L. (2005) 'The Ontological Argument as an Exercise in Cartesian Therapy', *Canadian Journal of Philosophy* 35: 521–62

Nolan, L. and Nelson, A. (2006) 'Proofs for the Existence of God' in S. Gaukroger (ed.) *The Blackwell Guide to Descartes' Meditations*. Oxford: Blackwell Publishing, 104–21

Oddie, G. (2001) 'Scrumptious Functions', *Grazer Philosophische Studien* 62: 137–56

Oddie, G. (forthcoming) 'The Statue and the Lump: Beyond Monism and Dualism'

Oppenheimer, P. and Zalta, E. (1991) 'On the Logic of the Ontological Argument', *Philosophy of Religion* 5: 509–29

Oppy, G. (1995) *Ontological Arguments and Belief in God*. Cambridge: Cambridge University Press

Oppy, G. (2009) 'Pruss's Ontological Arguments', *Religious Studies* 45: 355–63

Oppy, G. (2016) 'Ontological Arguments' in E. Zalta (ed.) *The Stanford Encyclopedia of Philosophy*, http://plato.stanford.edu/entries/ontological-arguments/

Parsons, T. (1980) *Non-Existent Objects*. New Haven, CT: Yale University Press

Pasternack, L. (2001) 'The Ens Realissimum and Necessary Being in *The Critique of Pure Reason*', *Religious Studies* 37: 467–74

Pearce, K. and Pruss, A. (2012) 'Understanding Omnipotence', *Religious Studies* 48: 403–14

Pears, D. (ed.) (1972) *Russell's Logical Atomism*. London: Fontana; second edition, Abingdon: Taylor and Francis, 2010

Plantinga, A. (ed.) (1965) *The Ontological Argument*. New York: Anchor Books

Plantinga, A. (1966) 'Kant's Objection to the Ontological Argument', *The Journal of Philosophy* 63: 537–46

Plantinga, A. (1974) *The Nature of Necessity*. Oxford: Oxford University Press

Priest, G. (1995) *Beyond the Limits of Thought*. Oxford: Oxford University Press; second (extended) edition, 2002

Priest, G. (2005) *Towards Non-Being*. Oxford: Oxford University Press; second (extended) edition, 2016

Proops, I. (2015) 'Kant on the Ontological Argument', *Noûs* 49: 1–27

Pruss, A. (2009) 'A Gödelian Ontological Argument Improved', *Religious Studies* 45: 347–53

Pruss, A. (2012) 'A Gödelian Ontological Argument Improved Even More' in M. Szatkowski (ed.) *Ontological Proofs Today*. Frankfurt: Ontos Verlag, 203–11

Putnam, H. (1975) 'The Meaning of "Meaning"', *Minnesota Studies in the Philosophy of Science* 7: 131–93

Rasmussen, J. (2014) 'Continuity as a Guide to Possibility', *Australasian Journal of Philosophy* 92: 525–38

Reck, E. and Awodey, S. (eds.) (2004) *Frege's Lectures on Logic: Carnap's Student Notes, 1910–1914*. Chicago: Open Court

Reicher, M. (2014) 'Non-Existent Objects' in E. Zalta (ed.) *The Stanford Encyclopedia of Philosophy*, http://plato.stanford.edu/entries/nonexistent-objects/

Roca-Royes, S. (2011) 'Conceivability and De Re Modal Knowledge', *Noûs* 45: 22–49

Russell, B. (1903) *Principles of Mathematics*. Cambridge: Cambridge University Press

Russell, B. (1905) 'On Denoting', *Mind* 14: 479–93; reprinted as chapter 5 of D. Lackey (ed.) *Essays in Analysis*. London: Allen & Unwin, 1973

Russell, B. (1924) 'Logical Atomism' in J. H. Muirhead (ed.) *Contemporary British Philosophy*. Abingdon: Routledge; reprinted in the second edition of Pears (2010)

Schopenhauer, A. (1813) *On the Fourfold Root of the Principle of Sufficient Reason*. Doctoral dissertation, University of Jena

Scotus, D. (1298/9) *Lectura II*, www.logicmuseum.com/wiki/Authors/Duns_Scotus/Lectura/Lectura_II

Sidelle, A. (1989) *Necessity, Essence, and Individuation*. Ithaca, NY: Cornell University Press

Sider, T. (2003) 'Reductive Theories of Modality' in M. Loux and D. Zimmerman (eds.) *The Oxford Handbook of Metaphysics*. Oxford: Oxford University Press, 180–208

Smith, A. (2014) *Anselm's Other Argument*. Cambridge, MA: Harvard University Press

Sobel, J. (1987) 'Gödel's Ontological Proof' in J. J. Thompson (ed.) *On Being and Saying: Essays for Richard Cartwright*. Cambridge, MA: MIT Press, 241–61

Sobel, J. (2004) *Logic and Theism: Arguments for and against Beliefs in God*. Cambridge: Cambridge University Press

Sorensen, R. (2006) 'Meta-conceivability and Thought Experiments' in S. Nichols (ed.) *The Architecture of the Imagination: New Essays on Pretence, Possibility and Fiction*. Oxford: Oxford University Press, 257–72

Spinoza, B. (1925) *Spinoza Opera*, 4 volumes, edited by C. Gebhardt. Heidelberg: Carl Winter

Spinoza, B. (1951) *Chief Works*, translated by R. Elwes. New York: Dover

Stang, N. (2015) 'Kant's Argument that Existence is not a Determination', *Philosophy and Phenomenological Research* 91: 583–626

Szatkowski, M. (ed.) (2012) *Ontological Proofs Today*. Heusenstamm: Ontos Verlag

Tichý, P. (1971) 'An Approach to Intensional Analysis', *Noûs* 5: 273–97

Tichý, P. (1978a) '*De Dicto* and *De Re*', *Philosophia* 8: 1–16

Tichý, P. (1978b) 'Two Kinds of Intensional Logic', *Epistemologia* 1: 143–64

Tichý, P. (1979) 'Existence and God', *Journal of Philosophy* 76: 403–20

Tichý, P. (1982) 'The Foundations of Partial Type Theory', *Reports on Mathematical Logic* 14: 57–72

Tichý, P. (1986) 'Indiscernibility of Identicals', *Studia Logica* 45: 257–73

Tichý, P. (1987) 'Individuals and their Roles' in V. Svoboda et al. (eds.) *Pavel Tichý's Collected Papers in Logic and Philosophy*. Prague and Dunedin: Filosofia and University of Otago Press, 749–63

Tichý, P. (1988) *The Foundations of Frege's Logic*. Berlin–New York: Walter de Gruyter

Tidman, P. (1994) 'Conceivability as a Test for Possibility', *American Philosophical Quarterly* 31: 297–309

Van Cleve, J. (1999) *Problems from Kant*. Oxford: Oxford University Press.

Van Inwagen, P. (1977) 'Ontological Arguments', *Noûs* 11: 375–95

Van Inwagen, P. (1998) 'Modal Epistemology', *Philosophical Studies* 92: 67–84

Van Inwagen, P. (2007) 'Some Remarks on the Modal Ontological Argument' in M. Lutz-Bachmann and T. Schmidt (eds.) *Metaphysik heute – Probleme und Perspektiven der Ontologie*. Freiburg and Munich: Verlag Karl Alber, 132–45

Van Inwagen, P. (2012) 'Three Versions of the Ontological Argument' in M. Szatkowski (ed.) *Ontological Proofs Today*. Heusenstamm: Ontos Verlag, 143–62, available at http://andrewmbailey.com/pvi/ThreeVersions.pdf

Van Inwagen, P. (2015) *Metaphysics*. Boulder, CO: Westview Press

Wasserman, R. (2015) 'Material Constitution', in E. Zalta (ed.),*The Stanford Encyclopedia of Philosophy* (Spring 2015 Edition), http://plato.stanford.edu/archives/spr2015/entries/material-constitution/

Williamson, T. (2002) 'Necessary Existents', *Royal Institute of Philosophy Supplement* 51: 233–51

Wilson, M. (1978) *Descartes*. New York: Routledge and Kegan Paul

Wippel, J. (1982) 'Essence and Existence' in N. Kretzmann, A. Kenny and J. Pinborg (eds.) *The Cambridge History of Later Medieval Philosophy*. New York: Cambridge University Press, 385–410

Wittgenstein, L. (1929) 'Some Remarks on Logical Form', *Proceedings of the Aristotelian Society* Supplementary Volume 9: 162–71

Wood, A. (1978) *Kant's Rational Theology*. Ithaca, NY: Cornell University Press

Yablo, S. (1993) 'Is Conceivability a Guide to Possibility?' *Philosophy and Phenomenological Research* 53: 1–42

Yablo, S. (2002) 'Coulda, Woulda, Shoulda' in T. Gendler and J. Hawthorne (eds.) *Conceivability and Possibility*. Oxford: Oxford University Press, 441–92

Zalta, E. (1983) *Abstract Objects: An Introduction to Axiomatic Metaphysics*. Dordrecht: Reidel

Index